GCC 6.1 Manual 1/2

A catalogue record for this book is available from the Hong Kong Public Libraries.

Published in Hong Kong by Samurai Media Limited.

Email: info@samuraimedia.org

ISBN 978-988-8406-41-8

Background Cover Image by https://www.flickr.com/people/webtreatsetc/

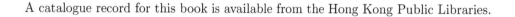

Short Contents

Introduction 1
1 Programming Languages Supported by GCC 3
2 Language Standards Supported by GCC 5
3 GCC Command Options 9
4 C Implementation-Defined Behavior 373
5 C++ Implementation-Defined Behavior 381
6 Extensions to the C Language Family 383
7 Extensions to the C++ Language 681
8 GNU Objective-C Features 697
9 Binary Compatibility 713
10 `gcov`—a Test Coverage Program 717
11 `gcov-tool`—an Offline Gcda Profile Processing Tool 727
12 Known Causes of Trouble with GCC 731
13 Reporting Bugs 747
14 How To Get Help with GCC 749
15 Contributing to GCC Development 751
Funding Free Software 753
The GNU Project and GNU/Linux 755
GNU General Public License 757
GNU Free Documentation License 769
Contributors to GCC 777
Option Index 795
Keyword Index 819

Table of Contents

Introduction 1

1 Programming Languages Supported by GCC 3

2 Language Standards Supported by GCC 5

2.1 C Language 5
2.2 C++ Language 6
2.3 Objective-C and Objective-C++ Languages 7
2.4 Go Language 8
2.5 References for Other Languages 8

3 GCC Command Options 9

3.1 Option Summary 9
3.2 Options Controlling the Kind of Output 27
3.3 Compiling C++ Programs 32
3.4 Options Controlling C Dialect 33
3.5 Options Controlling C++ Dialect 39
3.6 Options Controlling Objective-C and Objective-C++ Dialects.. 51
3.7 Options to Control Diagnostic Messages Formatting 55
3.8 Options to Request or Suppress Warnings 56
3.9 Options for Debugging Your Program 88
3.10 Options That Control Optimization 93
3.11 Program Instrumentation Options 148
3.12 Options Controlling the Preprocessor 159
3.13 Passing Options to the Assembler 170
3.14 Options for Linking 171
3.15 Options for Directory Search 175
3.16 Options for Code Generation Conventions 177
3.17 GCC Developer Options 186
3.18 Machine-Dependent Options 202
3.18.1 AArch64 Options 203
3.18.1.1 '-march' and '-mcpu' Feature Modifiers 205
3.18.2 Adapteva Epiphany Options 206
3.18.3 ARC Options 208
3.18.4 ARM Options 216
3.18.5 AVR Options 222
3.18.5.1 EIND and Devices with More Than 128 Ki Bytes of Flash 226
3.18.5.2 Handling of the RAMPD, RAMPX, RAMPY and RAMPZ Special Function Registers 228
3.18.5.3 AVR Built-in Macros 228

3.18.6 Blackfin Options 230
3.18.7 C6X Options 233
3.18.8 CRIS Options 234
3.18.9 CR16 Options 235
3.18.10 Darwin Options 236
3.18.11 DEC Alpha Options 239
3.18.12 FR30 Options 244
3.18.13 FT32 Options 244
3.18.14 FRV Options 244
3.18.15 GNU/Linux Options 248
3.18.16 H8/300 Options 249
3.18.17 HPPA Options 249
3.18.18 IA-64 Options 252
3.18.19 LM32 Options 256
3.18.20 M32C Options 256
3.18.21 M32R/D Options 257
3.18.22 M680x0 Options 258
3.18.23 MCore Options 263
3.18.24 MeP Options 264
3.18.25 MicroBlaze Options 266
3.18.26 MIPS Options 267
3.18.27 MMIX Options 281
3.18.28 MN10300 Options 282
3.18.29 Moxie Options 283
3.18.30 MSP430 Options 284
3.18.31 NDS32 Options 285
3.18.32 Nios II Options 286
3.18.33 Nvidia PTX Options 291
3.18.34 PDP-11 Options 291
3.18.35 picoChip Options 292
3.18.36 PowerPC Options 293
3.18.37 RL78 Options 293
3.18.38 IBM RS/6000 and PowerPC Options 294
3.18.39 RX Options 311
3.18.40 S/390 and zSeries Options 314
3.18.41 Score Options 317
3.18.42 SH Options 318
3.18.43 Solaris 2 Options 324
3.18.44 SPARC Options 325
3.18.45 SPU Options 330
3.18.46 Options for System V 332
3.18.47 TILE-Gx Options 332
3.18.48 TILEPro Options 332
3.18.49 V850 Options 333
3.18.50 VAX Options 335
3.18.51 Visium Options 335
3.18.52 VMS Options 336
3.18.53 VxWorks Options 337

3.18.54 x86 Options 337
3.18.55 x86 Windows Options 357
3.18.56 Xstormy16 Options 358
3.18.57 Xtensa Options 358
3.18.58 zSeries Options 360
3.19 Specifying Subprocesses and the Switches to Pass to Them .. 360
3.20 Environment Variables Affecting GCC 367
3.21 Using Precompiled Headers 370

4 C Implementation-Defined Behavior 373

4.1 Translation 373
4.2 Environment 373
4.3 Identifiers 373
4.4 Characters 374
4.5 Integers 375
4.6 Floating Point 375
4.7 Arrays and Pointers 376
4.8 Hints 377
4.9 Structures, Unions, Enumerations, and Bit-Fields 377
4.10 Qualifiers 378
4.11 Declarators 379
4.12 Statements 379
4.13 Preprocessing Directives 379
4.14 Library Functions 380
4.15 Architecture 380
4.16 Locale-Specific Behavior 380

5 C++ Implementation-Defined Behavior ... 381

5.1 Conditionally-Supported Behavior 381
5.2 Exception Handling 381

6 Extensions to the C Language Family 383

6.1 Statements and Declarations in Expressions 383
6.2 Locally Declared Labels 384
6.3 Labels as Values 385
6.4 Nested Functions 386
6.5 Constructing Function Calls 388
6.6 Referring to a Type with `typeof` 390
6.7 Conditionals with Omitted Operands 391
6.8 128-bit Integers 392
6.9 Double-Word Integers 392
6.10 Complex Numbers 392
6.11 Additional Floating Types 393
6.12 Half-Precision Floating Point 394
6.13 Decimal Floating Types 394
6.14 Hex Floats 395
6.15 Fixed-Point Types 395

6.16 Named Address Spaces 396
6.16.1 AVR Named Address Spaces 397
6.16.2 M32C Named Address Spaces 398
6.16.3 RL78 Named Address Spaces 398
6.16.4 SPU Named Address Spaces 399
6.16.5 x86 Named Address Spaces 399
6.17 Arrays of Length Zero 399
6.18 Structures with No Members 400
6.19 Arrays of Variable Length 400
6.20 Macros with a Variable Number of Arguments 401
6.21 Slightly Looser Rules for Escaped Newlines 402
6.22 Non-Lvalue Arrays May Have Subscripts 402
6.23 Arithmetic on `void`- and Function-Pointers 403
6.24 Pointers to Arrays with Qualifiers Work as Expected 403
6.25 Non-Constant Initializers 403
6.26 Compound Literals 403
6.27 Designated Initializers 404
6.28 Case Ranges 406
6.29 Cast to a Union Type 406
6.30 Mixed Declarations and Code 407
6.31 Declaring Attributes of Functions 407
6.31.1 Common Function Attributes 407
6.31.2 AArch64 Function Attributes 423
6.31.2.1 Inlining rules 424
6.31.3 ARC Function Attributes 425
6.31.4 ARM Function Attributes 425
6.31.5 AVR Function Attributes 427
6.31.6 Blackfin Function Attributes 428
6.31.7 CR16 Function Attributes 429
6.31.8 Epiphany Function Attributes 429
6.31.9 H8/300 Function Attributes 430
6.31.10 IA-64 Function Attributes 430
6.31.11 M32C Function Attributes 430
6.31.12 M32R/D Function Attributes 431
6.31.13 m68k Function Attributes 432
6.31.14 MCORE Function Attributes 432
6.31.15 MeP Function Attributes 432
6.31.16 MicroBlaze Function Attributes 433
6.31.17 Microsoft Windows Function Attributes 433
6.31.18 MIPS Function Attributes 435
6.31.19 MSP430 Function Attributes 436
6.31.20 NDS32 Function Attributes 438
6.31.21 Nios II Function Attributes 439
6.31.22 Nvidia PTX Function Attributes 439
6.31.23 PowerPC Function Attributes 439
6.31.24 RL78 Function Attributes 442
6.31.25 RX Function Attributes 443
6.31.26 S/390 Function Attributes 444

6.31.27 SH Function Attributes ... 445
6.31.28 SPU Function Attributes ... 446
6.31.29 Symbian OS Function Attributes ... 446
6.31.30 V850 Function Attributes ... 446
6.31.31 Visium Function Attributes ... 446
6.31.32 x86 Function Attributes ... 446
6.31.33 Xstormy16 Function Attributes ... 450
6.32 Specifying Attributes of Variables ... 450
6.32.1 Common Variable Attributes ... 451
6.32.2 AVR Variable Attributes ... 454
6.32.3 Blackfin Variable Attributes ... 455
6.32.4 H8/300 Variable Attributes ... 456
6.32.5 IA-64 Variable Attributes ... 456
6.32.6 M32R/D Variable Attributes ... 456
6.32.7 MeP Variable Attributes ... 456
6.32.8 Microsoft Windows Variable Attributes ... 457
6.32.9 MSP430 Variable Attributes ... 458
6.32.10 PowerPC Variable Attributes ... 458
6.32.11 RL78 Variable Attributes ... 458
6.32.12 SPU Variable Attributes ... 459
6.32.13 V850 Variable Attributes ... 459
6.32.14 x86 Variable Attributes ... 459
6.32.15 Xstormy16 Variable Attributes ... 459
6.33 Specifying Attributes of Types ... 459
6.33.1 Common Type Attributes ... 460
6.33.2 ARM Type Attributes ... 465
6.33.3 MeP Type Attributes ... 465
6.33.4 PowerPC Type Attributes ... 465
6.33.5 SPU Type Attributes ... 466
6.33.6 x86 Type Attributes ... 466
6.34 Label Attributes ... 466
6.35 Enumerator Attributes ... 467
6.36 Attribute Syntax ... 468
6.37 Prototypes and Old-Style Function Definitions ... 471
6.38 C++ Style Comments ... 472
6.39 Dollar Signs in Identifier Names ... 472
6.40 The Character ESC in Constants ... 472
6.41 Inquiring on Alignment of Types or Variables ... 472
6.42 An Inline Function is As Fast As a Macro ... 472
6.43 When is a Volatile Object Accessed? ... 474
6.44 How to Use Inline Assembly Language in C Code ... 475
6.44.1 Basic Asm — Assembler Instructions Without Operands ... 475
6.44.2 Extended Asm - Assembler Instructions with C Expression Operands ... 477
6.44.2.1 Volatile ... 478
6.44.2.2 Assembler Template ... 480
6.44.2.3 Output Operands ... 482

6.44.2.4 Flag Output Operands 484
6.44.2.5 Input Operands 486
6.44.2.6 Clobbers 487
6.44.2.7 Goto Labels 488
6.44.2.8 x86 Operand Modifiers 489
6.44.2.9 x86 Floating-Point `asm` Operands 490
6.44.3 Constraints for `asm` Operands 491
6.44.3.1 Simple Constraints 491
6.44.3.2 Multiple Alternative Constraints 494
6.44.3.3 Constraint Modifier Characters 494
6.44.3.4 Constraints for Particular Machines 495
6.44.4 Controlling Names Used in Assembler Code 523
6.44.5 Variables in Specified Registers 524
6.44.5.1 Defining Global Register Variables 524
6.44.5.2 Specifying Registers for Local Variables 525
6.44.6 Size of an `asm` 526
6.45 Alternate Keywords 527
6.46 Incomplete `enum` Types 527
6.47 Function Names as Strings 527
6.48 Getting the Return or Frame Address of a Function 528
6.49 Using Vector Instructions through Built-in Functions 529
6.50 Support for `offsetof` 532
6.51 Legacy `__sync` Built-in Functions for Atomic Memory Access 532
6.52 Built-in Functions for Memory Model Aware Atomic Operations 534
6.53 Built-in Functions to Perform Arithmetic with Overflow Checking 538
6.54 x86-Specific Memory Model Extensions for Transactional Memory 540
6.55 Object Size Checking Built-in Functions 540
6.56 Pointer Bounds Checker Built-in Functions 542
6.57 Cilk Plus C/C++ Language Extension Built-in Functions 544
6.58 Other Built-in Functions Provided by GCC 545
6.59 Built-in Functions Specific to Particular Target Machines 556
6.59.1 AArch64 Built-in Functions 556
6.59.2 Alpha Built-in Functions 556
6.59.3 Altera Nios II Built-in Functions 557
6.59.4 ARC Built-in Functions 559
6.59.5 ARC SIMD Built-in Functions 561
6.59.6 ARM iWMMXt Built-in Functions 565
6.59.7 ARM C Language Extensions (ACLE) 567
6.59.8 ARM Floating Point Status and Control Intrinsics 568
6.59.9 AVR Built-in Functions 568
6.59.10 Blackfin Built-in Functions 569
6.59.11 FR-V Built-in Functions 569
6.59.11.1 Argument Types 569
6.59.11.2 Directly-Mapped Integer Functions 570

6.59.11.3 Directly-Mapped Media Functions 570
6.59.11.4 Raw Read/Write Functions 572
6.59.11.5 Other Built-in Functions 572
6.59.12 MIPS DSP Built-in Functions 573
6.59.13 MIPS Paired-Single Support 577
6.59.14 MIPS Loongson Built-in Functions 578
6.59.14.1 Paired-Single Arithmetic 580
6.59.14.2 Paired-Single Built-in Functions 580
6.59.14.3 MIPS-3D Built-in Functions 581
6.59.15 Other MIPS Built-in Functions 583
6.59.16 MSP430 Built-in Functions 584
6.59.17 NDS32 Built-in Functions 584
6.59.18 picoChip Built-in Functions 585
6.59.19 PowerPC Built-in Functions 585
6.59.20 PowerPC AltiVec Built-in Functions 589
6.59.21 PowerPC Hardware Transactional Memory Built-in Functions 633
6.59.21.1 PowerPC HTM Low Level Built-in Functions 633
6.59.21.2 PowerPC HTM High Level Inline Functions 635
6.59.22 RX Built-in Functions 636
6.59.23 S/390 System z Built-in Functions 638
6.59.24 SH Built-in Functions 639
6.59.25 SPARC VIS Built-in Functions 640
6.59.26 SPU Built-in Functions 642
6.59.27 TI C6X Built-in Functions 643
6.59.28 TILE-Gx Built-in Functions 643
6.59.29 TILEPro Built-in Functions 644
6.59.30 x86 Built-in Functions 644
6.59.31 x86 Transactional Memory Intrinsics 667
6.60 Format Checks Specific to Particular Target Machines 668
6.60.1 Solaris Format Checks 668
6.60.2 Darwin Format Checks 668
6.61 Pragmas Accepted by GCC 668
6.61.1 AArch64 Pragmas 669
6.61.2 ARM Pragmas 669
6.61.3 M32C Pragmas 669
6.61.4 MeP Pragmas 669
6.61.5 RS/6000 and PowerPC Pragmas 670
6.61.6 S/390 Pragmas 670
6.61.7 Darwin Pragmas 671
6.61.8 Solaris Pragmas 671
6.61.9 Symbol-Renaming Pragmas 671
6.61.10 Structure-Layout Pragmas 672
6.61.11 Weak Pragmas 673
6.61.12 Diagnostic Pragmas 673
6.61.13 Visibility Pragmas 674
6.61.14 Push/Pop Macro Pragmas 674
6.61.15 Function Specific Option Pragmas 675

6.61.16 Loop-Specific Pragmas 675
6.62 Unnamed Structure and Union Fields 676
6.63 Thread-Local Storage 677
6.63.1 ISO/IEC 9899:1999 Edits for Thread-Local Storage 677
6.63.2 ISO/IEC 14882:1998 Edits for Thread-Local Storage 678
6.64 Binary Constants using the '0b' Prefix 679

7 Extensions to the C++ Language 681

7.1 When is a Volatile C++ Object Accessed? 681
7.2 Restricting Pointer Aliasing 681
7.3 Vague Linkage 682
7.4 C++ Interface and Implementation Pragmas 683
7.5 Where's the Template? 684
7.6 Extracting the Function Pointer from a Bound Pointer to Member Function 687
7.7 C++-Specific Variable, Function, and Type Attributes 687
7.8 Function Multiversioning 688
7.9 Namespace Association 689
7.10 Type Traits 690
7.11 C++ Concepts 692
7.12 Java Exceptions 693
7.13 Deprecated Features 693
7.14 Backwards Compatibility 694

8 GNU Objective-C Features 697

8.1 GNU Objective-C Runtime API 697
8.1.1 Modern GNU Objective-C Runtime API 697
8.1.2 Traditional GNU Objective-C Runtime API 698
8.2 `+load`: Executing Code before `main` 698
8.2.1 What You Can and Cannot Do in `+load` 699
8.3 Type Encoding 700
8.3.1 Legacy Type Encoding 702
8.3.2 `@encode` 702
8.3.3 Method Signatures 703
8.4 Garbage Collection 703
8.5 Constant String Objects 704
8.6 `compatibility_alias` 705
8.7 Exceptions 705
8.8 Synchronization 707
8.9 Fast Enumeration 707
8.9.1 Using Fast Enumeration 707
8.9.2 C99-Like Fast Enumeration Syntax 707
8.9.3 Fast Enumeration Details 708
8.9.4 Fast Enumeration Protocol 709
8.10 Messaging with the GNU Objective-C Runtime 710
8.10.1 Dynamically Registering Methods 710
8.10.2 Forwarding Hook 710

9 Binary Compatibility **713**

10 gcov—a Test Coverage Program **717**

10.1 Introduction to gcov 717
10.2 Invoking gcov 717
10.3 Using gcov with GCC Optimization........................ 723
10.4 Brief Description of gcov Data Files........................ 724
10.5 Data File Relocation to Support Cross-Profiling 725

11 gcov-tool—an Offline Gcda Profile Processing Tool **727**

11.1 Introduction to gcov-tool................................ 727
11.2 Invoking gcov-tool 727

12 Known Causes of Trouble with GCC **731**

12.1 Actual Bugs We Haven't Fixed Yet 731
12.2 Interoperation 731
12.3 Incompatibilities of GCC.................................. 733
12.4 Fixed Header Files.. 736
12.5 Standard Libraries.. 736
12.6 Disappointments and Misunderstandings 737
12.7 Common Misunderstandings with GNU C++ 738
12.7.1 Declare *and* Define Static Members 738
12.7.2 Name Lookup, Templates, and Accessing Members of Base Classes 739
12.7.3 Temporaries May Vanish Before You Expect............ 740
12.7.4 Implicit Copy-Assignment for Virtual Bases 741
12.8 Certain Changes We Don't Want to Make.................. 742
12.9 Warning Messages and Error Messages 745

13 Reporting Bugs **747**

13.1 Have You Found a Bug?.................................... 747
13.2 How and Where to Report Bugs 747

14 How To Get Help with GCC **749**

15 Contributing to GCC Development **751**

Funding Free Software **753**

The GNU Project and GNU/Linux **755**

GNU General Public License **757**

GNU Free Documentation License **769**
ADDENDUM: How to use this License for your documents 776

Contributors to GCC **777**

Option Index **795**

Keyword Index **819**

Introduction

This manual documents how to use the GNU compilers, as well as their features and incompatibilities, and how to report bugs. It corresponds to the compilers (GCC) version 6.1.0. The internals of the GNU compilers, including how to port them to new targets and some information about how to write front ends for new languages, are documented in a separate manual. See Section "Introduction" in *GNU Compiler Collection (GCC) Internals*.

1 Programming Languages Supported by GCC

GCC stands for "GNU Compiler Collection". GCC is an integrated distribution of compilers for several major programming languages. These languages currently include C, C++, Objective-C, Objective-C++, Java, Fortran, Ada, and Go.

The abbreviation *GCC* has multiple meanings in common use. The current official meaning is "GNU Compiler Collection", which refers generically to the complete suite of tools. The name historically stood for "GNU C Compiler", and this usage is still common when the emphasis is on compiling C programs. Finally, the name is also used when speaking of the *language-independent* component of GCC: code shared among the compilers for all supported languages.

The language-independent component of GCC includes the majority of the optimizers, as well as the "back ends" that generate machine code for various processors.

The part of a compiler that is specific to a particular language is called the "front end". In addition to the front ends that are integrated components of GCC, there are several other front ends that are maintained separately. These support languages such as Pascal, Mercury, and COBOL. To use these, they must be built together with GCC proper.

Most of the compilers for languages other than C have their own names. The C++ compiler is G++, the Ada compiler is GNAT, and so on. When we talk about compiling one of those languages, we might refer to that compiler by its own name, or as GCC. Either is correct.

Historically, compilers for many languages, including C++ and Fortran, have been implemented as "preprocessors" which emit another high level language such as C. None of the compilers included in GCC are implemented this way; they all generate machine code directly. This sort of preprocessor should not be confused with the *C preprocessor*, which is an integral feature of the C, C++, Objective-C and Objective-C++ languages.

2 Language Standards Supported by GCC

For each language compiled by GCC for which there is a standard, GCC attempts to follow one or more versions of that standard, possibly with some exceptions, and possibly with some extensions.

2.1 C Language

The original ANSI C standard (X3.159-1989) was ratified in 1989 and published in 1990. This standard was ratified as an ISO standard (ISO/IEC 9899:1990) later in 1990. There were no technical differences between these publications, although the sections of the ANSI standard were renumbered and became clauses in the ISO standard. The ANSI standard, but not the ISO standard, also came with a Rationale document. This standard, in both its forms, is commonly known as *C89*, or occasionally as *C90*, from the dates of ratification. To select this standard in GCC, use one of the options '`-ansi`', '`-std=c90`' or '`-std=iso9899:1990`'; to obtain all the diagnostics required by the standard, you should also specify '`-pedantic`' (or '`-pedantic-errors`' if you want them to be errors rather than warnings). See Section 3.4 [Options Controlling C Dialect], page 33.

Errors in the 1990 ISO C standard were corrected in two Technical Corrigenda published in 1994 and 1996. GCC does not support the uncorrected version.

An amendment to the 1990 standard was published in 1995. This amendment added digraphs and `__STDC_VERSION__` to the language, but otherwise concerned the library. This amendment is commonly known as *AMD1*; the amended standard is sometimes known as *C94* or *C95*. To select this standard in GCC, use the option '`-std=iso9899:199409`' (with, as for other standard versions, '`-pedantic`' to receive all required diagnostics).

A new edition of the ISO C standard was published in 1999 as ISO/IEC 9899:1999, and is commonly known as *C99*. (While in development, drafts of this standard version were referred to as *C9X*.) GCC has substantially complete support for this standard version; see `http://gcc.gnu.org/c99status.html` for details. To select this standard, use '`-std=c99`' or '`-std=iso9899:1999`'.

Errors in the 1999 ISO C standard were corrected in three Technical Corrigenda published in 2001, 2004 and 2007. GCC does not support the uncorrected version.

A fourth version of the C standard, known as *C11*, was published in 2011 as ISO/IEC 9899:2011. (While in development, drafts of this standard version were referred to as *C1X*.) GCC has substantially complete support for this standard, enabled with '`-std=c11`' or '`-std=iso9899:2011`'.

By default, GCC provides some extensions to the C language that, on rare occasions conflict with the C standard. See Chapter 6 [Extensions to the C Language Family], page 383. Some features that are part of the C99 standard are accepted as extensions in C90 mode, and some features that are part of the C11 standard are accepted as extensions in C90 and C99 modes. Use of the '`-std`' options listed above disables these extensions where they conflict with the C standard version selected. You may also select an extended version of the C language explicitly with '`-std=gnu90`' (for C90 with GNU extensions), '`-std=gnu99`' (for C99 with GNU extensions) or '`-std=gnu11`' (for C11 with GNU extensions).

The default, if no C language dialect options are given, is '`-std=gnu11`'.

The ISO C standard defines (in clause 4) two classes of conforming implementation. A *conforming hosted implementation* supports the whole standard including all the library facilities; a *conforming freestanding implementation* is only required to provide certain library facilities: those in `<float.h>`, `<limits.h>`, `<stdarg.h>`, and `<stddef.h>`; since AMD1, also those in `<iso646.h>`; since C99, also those in `<stdbool.h>` and `<stdint.h>`; and since C11, also those in `<stdalign.h>` and `<stdnoreturn.h>`. In addition, complex types, added in C99, are not required for freestanding implementations.

The standard also defines two environments for programs, a *freestanding environment*, required of all implementations and which may not have library facilities beyond those required of freestanding implementations, where the handling of program startup and termination are implementation-defined; and a *hosted environment*, which is not required, in which all the library facilities are provided and startup is through a function `int main (void)` or `int main (int, char *[])`. An OS kernel is an example of a program running in a freestanding environment; a program using the facilities of an operating system is an example of a program running in a hosted environment.

GCC aims towards being usable as a conforming freestanding implementation, or as the compiler for a conforming hosted implementation. By default, it acts as the compiler for a hosted implementation, defining `__STDC_HOSTED__` as `1` and presuming that when the names of ISO C functions are used, they have the semantics defined in the standard. To make it act as a conforming freestanding implementation for a freestanding environment, use the option '`-ffreestanding`'; it then defines `__STDC_HOSTED__` to `0` and does not make assumptions about the meanings of function names from the standard library, with exceptions noted below. To build an OS kernel, you may well still need to make your own arrangements for linking and startup. See Section 3.4 [Options Controlling C Dialect], page 33.

GCC does not provide the library facilities required only of hosted implementations, nor yet all the facilities required by C99 of freestanding implementations on all platforms. To use the facilities of a hosted environment, you need to find them elsewhere (for example, in the GNU C library). See Section 12.5 [Standard Libraries], page 736.

Most of the compiler support routines used by GCC are present in '`libgcc`', but there are a few exceptions. GCC requires the freestanding environment provide `memcpy`, `memmove`, `memset` and `memcmp`. Finally, if `__builtin_trap` is used, and the target does not implement the `trap` pattern, then GCC emits a call to `abort`.

For references to Technical Corrigenda, Rationale documents and information concerning the history of C that is available online, see `http://gcc.gnu.org/readings.html`

2.2 C++ Language

GCC supports the original ISO C++ standard published in 1998, and the 2011 and 2014 revisions.

The original ISO C++ standard was published as the ISO standard (ISO/IEC 14882:1998) and amended by a Technical Corrigenda published in 2003 (ISO/IEC 14882:2003). These standards are referred to as C++98 and C++03, respectively. GCC implements the majority of C++98 (`export` is a notable exception) and most of the changes in C++03. To select this standard in GCC, use one of the options '`-ansi`', '`-std=c++98`', or '`-std=c++03`'; to obtain all the diagnostics required by the standard, you should also specify '`-pedantic`' (or '`-pedantic-errors`' if you want them to be errors rather than warnings).

A revised ISO C++ standard was published in 2011 as ISO/IEC 14882:2011, and is referred to as C++11; before its publication it was commonly referred to as C++0x. C++11 contains several changes to the C++ language, all of which have been implemented in GCC. For details see `https://gcc.gnu.org/projects/cxx0x.html`. To select this standard in GCC, use the option '`-std=c++11`'.

Another revised ISO C++ standard was published in 2014 as ISO/IEC 14882:2014, and is referred to as C++14; before its publication it was sometimes referred to as C++1y. C++14 contains several further changes to the C++ language, all of which have been implemented in GCC. For details see `https://gcc.gnu.org/projects/cxx1y.html`. To select this standard in GCC, use the option '`-std=c++14`'.

GCC also supports the C++ Concepts Technical Specification, ISO/IEC TS 19217:2015, which allows constraints to be defined for templates, allowing template arguments to be checked and for templates to be overloaded or specialized based on the constraints. Support for C++ Concepts is included in an experimental C++1z mode that corresponds to the next revision of the ISO C++ standard, expected to be published in 2017. To enable C++1z support in GCC, use the option '`-std=c++17`' or '`-std=c++1z`'.

More information about the C++ standards is available on the ISO C++ committee's web site at `http://www.open-std.org/jtc1/sc22/wg21/`.

To obtain all the diagnostics required by any of the standard versions described above you should specify '`-pedantic`' or '`-pedantic-errors`', otherwise GCC will allow some non-ISO C++ features as extensions. See Section 3.8 [Warning Options], page 56.

By default, GCC also provides some additional extensions to the C++ language that on rare occasions conflict with the C++ standard. See Section 3.5 [C++ Dialect Options], page 39. Use of the '`-std`' options listed above disables these extensions where they they conflict with the C++ standard version selected. You may also select an extended version of the C++ language explicitly with '`-std=gnu++98`' (for C++98 with GNU extensions), or '`-std=gnu++11`' (for C++11 with GNU extensions), or '`-std=gnu++14`' (for C++14 with GNU extensions), or '`-std=gnu++1z`' (for C++1z with GNU extensions).

The default, if no C++ language dialect options are given, is '`-std=gnu++14`'.

2.3 Objective-C and Objective-C++ Languages

GCC supports "traditional" Objective-C (also known as "Objective-C 1.0") and contains support for the Objective-C exception and synchronization syntax. It has also support for a number of "Objective-C 2.0" language extensions, including properties, fast enumeration (only for Objective-C), method attributes and the @optional and @required keywords in protocols. GCC supports Objective-C++ and features available in Objective-C are also available in Objective-C++.

GCC by default uses the GNU Objective-C runtime library, which is part of GCC and is not the same as the Apple/NeXT Objective-C runtime library used on Apple systems. There are a number of differences documented in this manual. The options '`-fgnu-runtime`' and '`-fnext-runtime`' allow you to switch between producing output that works with the GNU Objective-C runtime library and output that works with the Apple/NeXT Objective-C runtime library.

There is no formal written standard for Objective-C or Objective-C++. The authoritative manual on traditional Objective-C (1.0) is "Object-Oriented Programming and the Objective-C Language":

- `http://www.gnustep.org/resources/documentation/ObjectivCBook.pdf` is the original NeXTstep document;
- `http://objc.toodarkpark.net` is the same document in another format.

The Objective-C exception and synchronization syntax (that is, the keywords `@try`, `@throw`, `@catch`, `@finally` and `@synchronized`) is supported by GCC and is enabled with the option '`-fobjc-exceptions`'. The syntax is briefly documented in this manual and in the Objective-C 2.0 manuals from Apple.

The Objective-C 2.0 language extensions and features are automatically enabled; they include properties (via the `@property`, `@synthesize` and `@dynamic keywords`), fast enumeration (not available in Objective-C++), attributes for methods (such as `deprecated`, `noreturn`, `sentinel`, `format`), the `unused` attribute for method arguments, the `@package` keyword for instance variables and the `@optional` and `@required` keywords in protocols. You can disable all these Objective-C 2.0 language extensions with the option '`-fobjc-std=objc1`', which causes the compiler to recognize the same Objective-C language syntax recognized by GCC 4.0, and to produce an error if one of the new features is used.

GCC has currently no support for non-fragile instance variables.

The authoritative manual on Objective-C 2.0 is available from Apple:

- `https://developer.apple.com/library/mac/documentation/Cocoa/Conceptual/ProgrammingWithObjectiveC/Introduction/Introduction.html`

For more information concerning the history of Objective-C that is available online, see `http://gcc.gnu.org/readings.html`

2.4 Go Language

As of the GCC 4.7.1 release, GCC supports the Go 1 language standard, described at `http://golang.org/doc/go1.html`.

2.5 References for Other Languages

See Section "About This Guide" in *GNAT Reference Manual*, for information on standard conformance and compatibility of the Ada compiler.

See Section "Standards" in *The GNU Fortran Compiler*, for details of standards supported by GNU Fortran.

See Section "Compatibility with the Java Platform" in *GNU gcj*, for details of compatibility between `gcj` and the Java Platform.

3 GCC Command Options

When you invoke GCC, it normally does preprocessing, compilation, assembly and linking. The "overall options" allow you to stop this process at an intermediate stage. For example, the '`-c`' option says not to run the linker. Then the output consists of object files output by the assembler. See Section 3.2 [Options Controlling the Kind of Output], page 27.

Other options are passed on to one or more stages of processing. Some options control the preprocessor and others the compiler itself. Yet other options control the assembler and linker; most of these are not documented here, since you rarely need to use any of them.

Most of the command-line options that you can use with GCC are useful for C programs; when an option is only useful with another language (usually C++), the explanation says so explicitly. If the description for a particular option does not mention a source language, you can use that option with all supported languages.

The usual way to run GCC is to run the executable called `gcc`, or `machine-gcc` when cross-compiling, or `machine-gcc-version` to run a specific version of GCC. When you compile C++ programs, you should invoke GCC as `g++` instead. See Section 3.3 [Compiling C++ Programs], page 32, for information about the differences in behavior between `gcc` and `g++` when compiling C++ programs.

The `gcc` program accepts options and file names as operands. Many options have multi-letter names; therefore multiple single-letter options may *not* be grouped: '`-dv`' is very different from '`-d -v`'.

You can mix options and other arguments. For the most part, the order you use doesn't matter. Order does matter when you use several options of the same kind; for example, if you specify '`-L`' more than once, the directories are searched in the order specified. Also, the placement of the '`-l`' option is significant.

Many options have long names starting with '`-f`' or with '`-W`'—for example, '`-fmove-loop-invariants`', '`-Wformat`' and so on. Most of these have both positive and negative forms; the negative form of '`-ffoo`' is '`-fno-foo`'. This manual documents only one of these two forms, whichever one is not the default.

See [Option Index], page 795, for an index to GCC's options.

3.1 Option Summary

Here is a summary of all the options, grouped by type. Explanations are in the following sections.

Overall Options

See Section 3.2 [Options Controlling the Kind of Output], page 27.

```
-c -S -E -o file -x language
-v -### --help[=class[,...]] --target-help --version
-pass-exit-codes -pipe -specs=file -wrapper
@file -fplugin=file -fplugin-arg-name=arg
-fdump-ada-spec[-slim] -fada-spec-parent=unit -fdump-go-spec=file
```

C Language Options

See Section 3.4 [Options Controlling C Dialect], page 33.

-ansi -std=*standard* -fgnu89-inline
-aux-info *filename* -fallow-parameterless-variadic-functions
-fno-asm -fno-builtin -fno-builtin-*function*
-fhosted -ffreestanding -fopenacc -fopenmp -fopenmp-simd
-fms-extensions -fplan9-extensions -fsso-struct=*endianness* -fallow-single-precision -fcond-mismatch -flax-vector-conversions
-fsigned-bitfields -fsigned-char
-funsigned-bitfields -funsigned-char
-trigraphs -traditional -traditional-cpp

C++ Language Options

See Section 3.5 [Options Controlling C++ Dialect], page 39.

-fabi-version=*n* -fno-access-control -fcheck-new
-fconstexpr-depth=*n* -ffriend-injection
-fno-elide-constructors
-fno-enforce-eh-specs
-ffor-scope -fno-for-scope -fno-gnu-keywords
-fno-implicit-templates
-fno-implicit-inline-templates
-fno-implement-inlines -fms-extensions
-fno-nonansi-builtins -fnothrow-opt -fno-operator-names
-fno-optional-diags -fpermissive
-fno-pretty-templates
-frepo -fno-rtti -fsized-deallocation
-ftemplate-backtrace-limit=*n*
-ftemplate-depth=*n*
-fno-threadsafe-statics -fuse-cxa-atexit
-fno-weak -nostdinc++
-fvisibility-inlines-hidden
-fvisibility-ms-compat
-fext-numeric-literals
-Wabi=*n* -Wabi-tag -Wconversion-null -Wctor-dtor-privacy
-Wdelete-non-virtual-dtor -Wliteral-suffix -Wmultiple-inheritance
-Wnamespaces -Wnarrowing
-Wnoexcept -Wnon-virtual-dtor -Wreorder
-Weffc++ -Wstrict-null-sentinel -Wtemplates
-Wno-non-template-friend -Wold-style-cast
-Woverloaded-virtual -Wno-pmf-conversions
-Wsign-promo -Wvirtual-inheritance

Objective-C and Objective-C++ Language Options

See Section 3.6 [Options Controlling Objective-C and Objective-C++ Dialects], page 51.

-fconstant-string-class=*class-name*
-fgnu-runtime -fnext-runtime
-fno-nil-receivers
-fobjc-abi-version=*n*
-fobjc-call-cxx-cdtors
-fobjc-direct-dispatch
-fobjc-exceptions
-fobjc-gc
-fobjc-nilcheck
-fobjc-std=objc1
-fno-local-ivars
-fivar-visibility=[public|protected|private|package]
-freplace-objc-classes
-fzero-link
-gen-decls

```
-Wassign-intercept
-Wno-protocol -Wselector
-Wstrict-selector-match
-Wundeclared-selector
```

Diagnostic Message Formatting Options

See Section 3.7 [Options to Control Diagnostic Messages Formatting], page 55.

```
-fmessage-length=n
-fdiagnostics-show-location=[once|every-line]
-fdiagnostics-color=[auto|never|always]
-fno-diagnostics-show-option -fno-diagnostics-show-caret
```

Warning Options

See Section 3.8 [Options to Request or Suppress Warnings], page 56.

```
-fsyntax-only -fmax-errors=n -Wpedantic
-pedantic-errors
-w -Wextra -Wall -Waddress -Waggregate-return
-Wno-aggressive-loop-optimizations -Warray-bounds -Warray-bounds=n
-Wno-attributes -Wbool-compare -Wno-builtin-macro-redefined
-Wc90-c99-compat -Wc99-c11-compat
-Wc++-compat -Wc++11-compat -Wc++14-compat -Wcast-align -Wcast-qual
-Wchar-subscripts -Wclobbered -Wcomment -Wconditionally-supported
-Wconversion -Wcoverage-mismatch -Wno-cpp -Wdate-time -Wdelete-incomplete
-Wno-deprecated -Wno-deprecated-declarations -Wno-designated-init
-Wdisabled-optimization
-Wno-discarded-qualifiers -Wno-discarded-array-qualifiers
-Wno-div-by-zero -Wdouble-promotion -Wduplicated-cond
-Wempty-body -Wenum-compare -Wno-endif-labels
-Werror -Werror=* -Wfatal-errors -Wfloat-equal -Wformat -Wformat=2
-Wno-format-contains-nul -Wno-format-extra-args -Wformat-nonliteral
-Wformat-security -Wformat-signedness -Wformat-y2k -Wframe-address
-Wframe-larger-than=len -Wno-free-nonheap-object -Wjump-misses-init
-Wignored-qualifiers -Wignored-attributes -Wincompatible-pointer-types
-Wimplicit -Wimplicit-function-declaration -Wimplicit-int
-Winit-self -Winline -Wno-int-conversion
-Wno-int-to-pointer-cast -Winvalid-memory-model -Wno-invalid-offsetof
-Winvalid-pch -Wlarger-than=len
-Wlogical-op -Wlogical-not-parentheses -Wlong-long
-Wmain -Wmaybe-uninitialized -Wmemset-transposed-args
-Wmisleading-indentation -Wmissing-braces
-Wmissing-field-initializers -Wmissing-include-dirs
-Wno-multichar -Wnonnull -Wnonnull-compare
-Wnormalized=[none|id|nfc|nfkc]
-Wnull-dereference -Wodr -Wno-overflow -Wopenmp-simd
-Woverride-init-side-effects -Woverlength-strings
-Wpacked -Wpacked-bitfield-compat -Wpadded
-Wparentheses -Wno-pedantic-ms-format
-Wplacement-new -Wplacement-new=n
-Wpointer-arith -Wno-pointer-to-int-cast
-Wno-pragmas -Wredundant-decls -Wno-return-local-addr
-Wreturn-type -Wsequence-point -Wshadow -Wno-shadow-ivar
-Wshift-overflow -Wshift-overflow=n
-Wshift-count-negative -Wshift-count-overflow -Wshift-negative-value
-Wsign-compare -Wsign-conversion -Wfloat-conversion
-Wno-scalar-storage-order
-Wsizeof-pointer-memaccess -Wsizeof-array-argument
-Wstack-protector -Wstack-usage=len -Wstrict-aliasing
-Wstrict-aliasing=n -Wstrict-overflow -Wstrict-overflow=n
```

-Wsuggest-attribute=[pure|const|noreturn|format]
-Wsuggest-final-types
-Wsuggest-final-methods -Wsuggest-override
-Wmissing-format-attribute -Wsubobject-linkage
-Wswitch -Wswitch-default -Wswitch-enum -Wswitch-bool -Wsync-nand
-Wsystem-headers -Wtautological-compare -Wtrampolines -Wtrigraphs
-Wtype-limits -Wundef
-Wuninitialized -Wunknown-pragmas -Wunsafe-loop-optimizations
-Wunsuffixed-float-constants -Wunused -Wunused-function
-Wunused-label -Wunused-local-typedefs -Wunused-parameter
-Wno-unused-result -Wunused-value
-Wunused-variable
-Wunused-const-variable -Wunused-const-variable=*n*
-Wunused-but-set-parameter -Wunused-but-set-variable
-Wuseless-cast -Wvariadic-macros -Wvector-operation-performance
-Wvla -Wvolatile-register-var -Wwrite-strings
-Wzero-as-null-pointer-constant -Whsa

C and Objective-C-only Warning Options

-Wbad-function-cast -Wmissing-declarations
-Wmissing-parameter-type -Wmissing-prototypes -Wnested-externs
-Wold-style-declaration -Wold-style-definition
-Wstrict-prototypes -Wtraditional -Wtraditional-conversion
-Wdeclaration-after-statement -Wpointer-sign

Debugging Options

See Section 3.9 [Options for Debugging Your Program], page 88.

-g -g*level* -gcoff -gdwarf -gdwarf-*version*
-ggdb -grecord-gcc-switches -gno-record-gcc-switches
-gstabs -gstabs+ -gstrict-dwarf -gno-strict-dwarf
-gvms -gxcoff -gxcoff+ -gz[=*type*]
-fdebug-prefix-map=*old*=*new* -fdebug-types-section
-feliminate-dwarf2-dups -fno-eliminate-unused-debug-types
-femit-struct-debug-baseonly -femit-struct-debug-reduced
-femit-struct-debug-detailed[=*spec-list*]
-feliminate-unused-debug-symbols -femit-class-debug-always
-fno-merge-debug-strings -fno-dwarf2-cfi-asm
-fvar-tracking -fvar-tracking-assignments

Optimization Options

See Section 3.10 [Options that Control Optimization], page 93.

-faggressive-loop-optimizations -falign-functions[=*n*]
-falign-jumps[=*n*]
-falign-labels[=*n*] -falign-loops[=*n*]
-fassociative-math -fauto-profile -fauto-profile[=*path*]
-fauto-inc-dec -fbranch-probabilities
-fbranch-target-load-optimize -fbranch-target-load-optimize2
-fbtr-bb-exclusive -fcaller-saves
-fcombine-stack-adjustments -fconserve-stack
-fcompare-elim -fcprop-registers -fcrossjumping
-fcse-follow-jumps -fcse-skip-blocks -fcx-fortran-rules
-fcx-limited-range
-fdata-sections -fdce -fdelayed-branch
-fdelete-null-pointer-checks -fdevirtualize -fdevirtualize-speculatively
-fdevirtualize-at-ltrans -fdse
-fearly-inlining -fipa-sra -fexpensive-optimizations -ffat-lto-objects
-ffast-math -ffinite-math-only -ffloat-store -fexcess-precision=*style*
-fforward-propagate -ffp-contract=*style* -ffunction-sections

```
-fgcse -fgcse-after-reload -fgcse-las -fgcse-lm -fgraphite-identity
-fgcse-sm -fhoist-adjacent-loads -fif-conversion
-fif-conversion2 -findirect-inlining
-finline-functions -finline-functions-called-once -finline-limit=n
-finline-small-functions -fipa-cp -fipa-cp-clone -fipa-cp-alignment
-fipa-pta -fipa-profile -fipa-pure-const -fipa-reference -fipa-icf
-fira-algorithm=algorithm
-fira-region=region -fira-hoist-pressure
-fira-loop-pressure -fno-ira-share-save-slots
-fno-ira-share-spill-slots
-fisolate-erroneous-paths-dereference -fisolate-erroneous-paths-attribute
-fivopts -fkeep-inline-functions -fkeep-static-functions
-fkeep-static-consts -flive-range-shrinkage
-floop-block -floop-interchange -floop-strip-mine
-floop-unroll-and-jam -floop-nest-optimize
-floop-parallelize-all -flra-remat -flto -flto-compression-level
-flto-partition=alg -fmerge-all-constants
-fmerge-constants -fmodulo-sched -fmodulo-sched-allow-regmoves
-fmove-loop-invariants -fno-branch-count-reg
-fno-defer-pop -fno-function-cse -fno-guess-branch-probability
-fno-inline -fno-math-errno -fno-peephole -fno-peephole2
-fno-sched-interblock -fno-sched-spec -fno-signed-zeros
-fno-toplevel-reorder -fno-trapping-math -fno-zero-initialized-in-bss
-fomit-frame-pointer -foptimize-sibling-calls
-fpartial-inlining -fpeel-loops -fpredictive-commoning
-fprefetch-loop-arrays
-fprofile-correction
-fprofile-use -fprofile-use=path -fprofile-values
-fprofile-reorder-functions
-freciprocal-math -free -frename-registers -freorder-blocks
-freorder-blocks-algorithm=algorithm
-freorder-blocks-and-partition -freorder-functions
-frerun-cse-after-loop -freschedule-modulo-scheduled-loops
-frounding-math -fsched2-use-superblocks -fsched-pressure
-fsched-spec-load -fsched-spec-load-dangerous
-fsched-stalled-insns-dep[=n] -fsched-stalled-insns[=n]
-fsched-group-heuristic -fsched-critical-path-heuristic
-fsched-spec-insn-heuristic -fsched-rank-heuristic
-fsched-last-insn-heuristic -fsched-dep-count-heuristic
-fschedule-fusion
-fschedule-insns -fschedule-insns2 -fsection-anchors
-fselective-scheduling -fselective-scheduling2
-fsel-sched-pipelining -fsel-sched-pipelining-outer-loops
-fsemantic-interposition -fshrink-wrap -fsignaling-nans
-fsingle-precision-constant -fsplit-ivs-in-unroller
-fsplit-paths
-fsplit-wide-types -fssa-backprop -fssa-phiopt
-fstdarg-opt -fstrict-aliasing
-fstrict-overflow -fthread-jumps -ftracer -ftree-bit-ccp
-ftree-builtin-call-dce -ftree-ccp -ftree-ch
-ftree-coalesce-vars -ftree-copy-prop -ftree-dce -ftree-dominator-opts
-ftree-dse -ftree-forwprop -ftree-fre -ftree-loop-if-convert
-ftree-loop-if-convert-stores -ftree-loop-im
-ftree-phiprop -ftree-loop-distribution -ftree-loop-distribute-patterns
-ftree-loop-ivcanon -ftree-loop-linear -ftree-loop-optimize
-ftree-loop-vectorize
-ftree-parallelize-loops=n -ftree-pre -ftree-partial-pre -ftree-pta
-ftree-reassoc -ftree-sink -ftree-slsr -ftree-sra
```

```
-ftree-switch-conversion -ftree-tail-merge -ftree-ter
-ftree-vectorize -ftree-vrp -funconstrained-commons
-funit-at-a-time -funroll-all-loops -funroll-loops
-funsafe-loop-optimizations -funsafe-math-optimizations -funswitch-loops
-fipa-ra -fvariable-expansion-in-unroller -fvect-cost-model -fvpt
-fweb -fwhole-program -fwpa -fuse-linker-plugin
--param name=value -O -O0 -O1 -O2 -O3 -Os -Ofast -Og
```

Program Instrumentation Options

See Section 3.11 [Program Instrumentation Options], page 148.

```
-p -pg -fprofile-arcs --coverage -ftest-coverage
-fprofile-dir=path -fprofile-generate -fprofile-generate=path
-fsanitize=style -fsanitize-recover -fsanitize-recover=style
-fasan-shadow-offset=number -fsanitize-sections=s1,s2,...
-fsanitize-undefined-trap-on-error -fbounds-check
-fcheck-pointer-bounds -fchkp-check-incomplete-type
-fchkp-first-field-has-own-bounds -fchkp-narrow-bounds
-fchkp-narrow-to-innermost-array -fchkp-optimize
-fchkp-use-fast-string-functions -fchkp-use-nochk-string-functions
-fchkp-use-static-bounds -fchkp-use-static-const-bounds
-fchkp-treat-zero-dynamic-size-as-infinite -fchkp-check-read
-fchkp-check-read -fchkp-check-write -fchkp-store-bounds
-fchkp-instrument-calls -fchkp-instrument-marked-only
-fchkp-use-wrappers
-fstack-protector -fstack-protector-all -fstack-protector-strong
-fstack-protector-explicit -fstack-check
-fstack-limit-register=reg -fstack-limit-symbol=sym
-fno-stack-limit -fsplit-stack
-fvtable-verify=[std|preinit|none]
-fvtv-counts -fvtv-debug
-finstrument-functions
-finstrument-functions-exclude-function-list=sym,sym,...
-finstrument-functions-exclude-file-list=file,file,...
```

Preprocessor Options

See Section 3.12 [Options Controlling the Preprocessor], page 159.

```
-Aquestion=answer
-A-question[=answer]
-C -dD -dI -dM -dN
-Dmacro[=defn] -E -H
-idirafter dir
-include file -imacros file
-iprefix file -iwithprefix dir
-iwithprefixbefore dir -isystem dir
-imultilib dir -isysroot dir
-M -MM -MF -MG -MP -MQ -MT -nostdinc
-P -fdebug-cpp -ftrack-macro-expansion -fworking-directory
-remap -trigraphs -undef -Umacro
-Wp,option -Xpreprocessor option -no-integrated-cpp
```

Assembler Option

See Section 3.13 [Passing Options to the Assembler], page 170.

```
-Wa,option -Xassembler option
```

Linker Options

See Section 3.14 [Options for Linking], page 171.

```
object-file-name -fuse-ld=linker -llibrary
-nostartfiles -nodefaultlibs -nostdlib -pie -rdynamic
```

```
-s -static -static-libgcc -static-libstdc++
-static-libasan -static-libtsan -static-liblsan -static-libubsan
-static-libmpx -static-libmpxwrappers
-shared -shared-libgcc -symbolic
-T script -Wl,option -Xlinker option
-u symbol -z keyword
```

Directory Options

See Section 3.15 [Options for Directory Search], page 175.

```
-Bprefix -Idir -iplugindir=dir
-iquotedir -Ldir -no-canonical-prefixes -I-
--sysroot=dir --no-sysroot-suffix
```

Code Generation Options

See Section 3.16 [Options for Code Generation Conventions], page 177.

```
-fcall-saved-reg -fcall-used-reg
-ffixed-reg -fexceptions
-fnon-call-exceptions -fdelete-dead-exceptions -funwind-tables
-fasynchronous-unwind-tables
-fno-gnu-unique
-finhibit-size-directive -fno-common -fno-ident
-fpcc-struct-return -fpic -fPIC -fpie -fPIE -fno-plt
-fno-jump-tables
-frecord-gcc-switches
-freg-struct-return -fshort-enums -fshort-wchar
-fverbose-asm -fpack-struct[=n]
-fleading-underscore -ftls-model=model
-fstack-reuse=reuse_level
-ftrapv -fwrapv
-fvisibility=[default|internal|hidden|protected]
-fstrict-volatile-bitfields -fsync-libcalls
```

Developer Options

See Section 3.17 [GCC Developer Options], page 186.

```
-dletters -dumpspecs -dumpmachine -dumpversion
-fchecking -fdbg-cnt-list -fdbg-cnt=counter-value-list
-fdisable-ipa-pass_name
-fdisable-rtl-pass_name
-fdisable-rtl-pass-name=range-list
-fdisable-tree-pass_name
-fdisable-tree-pass-name=range-list
-fdump-noaddr -fdump-unnumbered -fdump-unnumbered-links
-fdump-translation-unit[-n]
-fdump-class-hierarchy[-n]
-fdump-ipa-all -fdump-ipa-cgraph -fdump-ipa-inline
-fdump-passes
-fdump-rtl-pass -fdump-rtl-pass=filename
-fdump-statistics
-fdump-tree-all
-fdump-tree-original[-n]
-fdump-tree-optimized[-n]
-fdump-tree-cfg -fdump-tree-alias
-fdump-tree-ch
-fdump-tree-ssa[-n] -fdump-tree-pre[-n]
-fdump-tree-ccp[-n] -fdump-tree-dce[-n]
-fdump-tree-gimple[-raw]
-fdump-tree-dom[-n]
-fdump-tree-dse[-n]
```

```
-fdump-tree-phiprop[-n]
-fdump-tree-phiopt[-n]
-fdump-tree-backprop[-n]
-fdump-tree-forwprop[-n]
-fdump-tree-nrv -fdump-tree-vect
-fdump-tree-sink
-fdump-tree-sra[-n]
-fdump-tree-forwprop[-n]
-fdump-tree-fre[-n]
-fdump-tree-vtable-verify
-fdump-tree-vrp[-n]
-fdump-tree-split-paths[-n]
-fdump-tree-storeccp[-n]
-fdump-final-insns=file
-fcompare-debug[=opts] -fcompare-debug-second
-fenable-kind-pass
-fenable-kind-pass=range-list
-fira-verbose=n
-flto-report -flto-report-wpa -fmem-report-wpa
-fmem-report -fpre-ipa-mem-report -fpost-ipa-mem-report
-fopt-info -fopt-info-options[=file]
-fprofile-report
-frandom-seed=string -fsched-verbose=n
-fsel-sched-verbose -fsel-sched-dump-cfg -fsel-sched-pipelining-verbose
-fstats -fstack-usage -ftime-report
-fvar-tracking-assignments-toggle -gtoggle
-print-file-name=library -print-libgcc-file-name
-print-multi-directory -print-multi-lib -print-multi-os-directory
-print-prog-name=program -print-search-dirs -Q
-print-sysroot -print-sysroot-headers-suffix
-save-temps -save-temps=cwd -save-temps=obj -time[=file]
```

Machine-Dependent Options

See Section 3.18 [Machine-Dependent Options], page 202.

AArch64 Options

```
-mabi=name -mbig-endian -mlittle-endian
-mgeneral-regs-only
-mcmodel=tiny -mcmodel=small -mcmodel=large
-mstrict-align
-momit-leaf-frame-pointer -mno-omit-leaf-frame-pointer
-mtls-dialect=desc -mtls-dialect=traditional
-mtls-size=size
-mfix-cortex-a53-835769 -mno-fix-cortex-a53-835769
-mfix-cortex-a53-843419 -mno-fix-cortex-a53-843419
-mlow-precision-recip-sqrt -mno-low-precision-recip-sqrt
-march=name -mcpu=name -mtune=name
```

Adapteva Epiphany Options

```
-mhalf-reg-file -mprefer-short-insn-regs
-mbranch-cost=num -mcmove -mnops=num -msoft-cmpsf
-msplit-lohi -mpost-inc -mpost-modify -mstack-offset=num
-mround-nearest -mlong-calls -mshort-calls -msmall16
-mfp-mode=mode -mvect-double -max-vect-align=num
-msplit-vecmove-early -m1reg-reg
```

ARC Options

```
-mbarrel-shifter
-mcpu=cpu -mA6 -mARC600 -mA7 -mARC700
```

-mdpfp -mdpfp-compact -mdpfp-fast -mno-dpfp-lrsr
-mea -mno-mpy -mmul32x16 -mmul64 -matomic
-mnorm -mspfp -mspfp-compact -mspfp-fast -msimd -msoft-float -mswap
-mcrc -mdsp-packa -mdvbf -mlock -mmac-d16 -mmac-24 -mrtsc -mswape
-mtelephony -mxy -misize -mannotate-align -marclinux -marclinux_prof
-mlong-calls -mmedium-calls -msdata
-mucb-mcount -mvolatile-cache
-malign-call -mauto-modify-reg -mbbit-peephole -mno-brcc
-mcase-vector-pcrel -mcompact-casesi -mno-cond-exec -mearly-cbranchsi
-mexpand-adddi -mindexed-loads -mlra -mlra-priority-none
-mlra-priority-compact mlra-priority-noncompact -mno-millicode
-mmixed-code -mq-class -mRcq -mRcw -msize-level=*level*
-mtune=*cpu* -mmultcost=*num*
-munalign-prob-threshold=*probability* -mmpy-option=*multo*
-mdiv-rem -mcode-density -mll64 -mfpu=*fpu*

ARM Options

-mapcs-frame -mno-apcs-frame
-mabi=*name*
-mapcs-stack-check -mno-apcs-stack-check
-mapcs-float -mno-apcs-float
-mapcs-reentrant -mno-apcs-reentrant
-msched-prolog -mno-sched-prolog
-mlittle-endian -mbig-endian
-mfloat-abi=*name*
-mfp16-format=*name* -mthumb-interwork -mno-thumb-interwork
-mcpu=*name* -march=*name* -mfpu=*name*
-mtune=*name* -mprint-tune-info
-mstructure-size-boundary=*n*
-mabort-on-noreturn
-mlong-calls -mno-long-calls
-msingle-pic-base -mno-single-pic-base
-mpic-register=*reg*
-mnop-fun-dllimport
-mpoke-function-name
-mthumb -marm
-mtpcs-frame -mtpcs-leaf-frame
-mcaller-super-interworking -mcallee-super-interworking
-mtp=*name* -mtls-dialect=*dialect*
-mword-relocations
-mfix-cortex-m3-ldrd
-munaligned-access
-mneon-for-64bits
-mslow-flash-data
-masm-syntax-unified
-mrestrict-it

AVR Options

-mmcu=*mcu* -maccumulate-args -mbranch-cost=*cost*
-mcall-prologues -mint8 -mn_flash=*size* -mno-interrupts
-mrelax -mrmw -mstrict-X -mtiny-stack -nodevicelib -Waddr-space-convert

Blackfin Options

-mcpu=*cpu*[-*sirevision*]
-msim -momit-leaf-frame-pointer -mno-omit-leaf-frame-pointer
-mspecld-anomaly -mno-specld-anomaly -mcsync-anomaly -mno-csync-anomaly
-mlow-64k -mno-low64k -mstack-check-l1 -mid-shared-library
-mno-id-shared-library -mshared-library-id=*n*
-mleaf-id-shared-library -mno-leaf-id-shared-library

-msep-data -mno-sep-data -mlong-calls -mno-long-calls
-mfast-fp -minline-plt -mmulticore -mcorea -mcoreb -msdram
-micplb

C6X Options

-mbig-endian -mlittle-endian -march=*cpu*
-msim -msdata=*sdata-type*

CRIS Options

-mcpu=*cpu* -march=*cpu* -mtune=*cpu*
-mmax-stack-frame=*n* -melinux-stacksize=*n*
-metrax4 -metrax100 -mpdebug -mcc-init -mno-side-effects
-mstack-align -mdata-align -mconst-align
-m32-bit -m16-bit -m8-bit -mno-prologue-epilogue -mno-gotplt
-melf -maout -melinux -mlinux -sim -sim2
-mmul-bug-workaround -mno-mul-bug-workaround

CR16 Options

-mmac
-mcr16cplus -mcr16c
-msim -mint32 -mbit-ops -mdata-model=*model*

Darwin Options

-all_load -allowable_client -arch -arch_errors_fatal
-arch_only -bind_at_load -bundle -bundle_loader
-client_name -compatibility_version -current_version
-dead_strip
-dependency-file -dylib_file -dylinker_install_name
-dynamic -dynamiclib -exported_symbols_list
-filelist -flat_namespace -force_cpusubtype_ALL
-force_flat_namespace -headerpad_max_install_names
-iframework
-image_base -init -install_name -keep_private_externs
-multi_module -multiply_defined -multiply_defined_unused
-noall_load -no_dead_strip_inits_and_terms
-nofixprebinding -nomultidefs -noprebind -noseglinkedit
-pagezero_size -prebind -prebind_all_twolevel_modules
-private_bundle -read_only_relocs -sectalign
-sectobjectsymbols -whyload -seg1addr
-sectcreate -sectobjectsymbols -sectorder
-segaddr -segs_read_only_addr -segs_read_write_addr
-seg_addr_table -seg_addr_table_filename -seglinkedit
-segprot -segs_read_only_addr -segs_read_write_addr
-single_module -static -sub_library -sub_umbrella
-twolevel_namespace -umbrella -undefined
-unexported_symbols_list -weak_reference_mismatches
-whatsloaded -F -gused -gfull -mmacosx-version-min=*version*
-mkernel -mone-byte-bool

DEC Alpha Options

-mno-fp-regs -msoft-float
-mieee -mieee-with-inexact -mieee-conformant
-mfp-trap-mode=*mode* -mfp-rounding-mode=*mode*
-mtrap-precision=*mode* -mbuild-constants
-mcpu=*cpu-type* -mtune=*cpu-type*
-mbwx -mmax -mfix -mcix
-mfloat-vax -mfloat-ieee
-mexplicit-relocs -msmall-data -mlarge-data
-msmall-text -mlarge-text
-mmemory-latency=*time*

FR30 Options

-msmall-model -mno-lsim

FT32 Options

-msim -mlra -mnodiv

FRV Options

-mgpr-32 -mgpr-64 -mfpr-32 -mfpr-64
-mhard-float -msoft-float
-malloc-cc -mfixed-cc -mdword -mno-dword
-mdouble -mno-double
-mmedia -mno-media -mmuladd -mno-muladd
-mfdpic -minline-plt -mgprel-ro -multilib-library-pic
-mlinked-fp -mlong-calls -malign-labels
-mlibrary-pic -macc-4 -macc-8
-mpack -mno-pack -mno-eflags -mcond-move -mno-cond-move
-moptimize-membar -mno-optimize-membar
-mscc -mno-scc -mcond-exec -mno-cond-exec
-mvliw-branch -mno-vliw-branch
-mmulti-cond-exec -mno-multi-cond-exec -mnested-cond-exec
-mno-nested-cond-exec -mtomcat-stats
-mTLS -mtls
-mcpu=*cpu*

GNU/Linux Options

-mglibc -muclibc -mmusl -mbionic -mandroid
-tno-android-cc -tno-android-ld

H8/300 Options

-mrelax -mh -ms -mn -mexr -mno-exr -mint32 -malign-300

HPPA Options

-march=*architecture-type*
-mdisable-fpregs -mdisable-indexing
-mfast-indirect-calls -mgas -mgnu-ld -mhp-ld
-mfixed-range=*register-range*
-mjump-in-delay -mlinker-opt -mlong-calls
-mlong-load-store -mno-disable-fpregs
-mno-disable-indexing -mno-fast-indirect-calls -mno-gas
-mno-jump-in-delay -mno-long-load-store
-mno-portable-runtime -mno-soft-float
-mno-space-regs -msoft-float -mpa-risc-1-0
-mpa-risc-1-1 -mpa-risc-2-0 -mportable-runtime
-mschedule=*cpu-type* -mspace-regs -msio -mwsio
-munix=*unix-std* -nolibdld -static -threads

IA-64 Options

-mbig-endian -mlittle-endian -mgnu-as -mgnu-ld -mno-pic
-mvolatile-asm-stop -mregister-names -msdata -mno-sdata
-mconstant-gp -mauto-pic -mfused-madd
-minline-float-divide-min-latency
-minline-float-divide-max-throughput
-mno-inline-float-divide
-minline-int-divide-min-latency
-minline-int-divide-max-throughput
-mno-inline-int-divide
-minline-sqrt-min-latency -minline-sqrt-max-throughput
-mno-inline-sqrt
-mdwarf2-asm -mearly-stop-bits
-mfixed-range=*register-range* -mtls-size=*tls-size*

-mtune=*cpu-type* -milp32 -mlp64
-msched-br-data-spec -msched-ar-data-spec -msched-control-spec
-msched-br-in-data-spec -msched-ar-in-data-spec -msched-in-control-spec
-msched-spec-ldc -msched-spec-control-ldc
-msched-prefer-non-data-spec-insns -msched-prefer-non-control-spec-insns
-msched-stop-bits-after-every-cycle -msched-count-spec-in-critical-path
-msel-sched-dont-check-control-spec -msched-fp-mem-deps-zero-cost
-msched-max-memory-insns-hard-limit -msched-max-memory-insns=*max-insns*

LM32 Options

-mbarrel-shift-enabled -mdivide-enabled -mmultiply-enabled
-msign-extend-enabled -muser-enabled

M32R/D Options

-m32r2 -m32rx -m32r
-mdebug
-malign-loops -mno-align-loops
-missue-rate=*number*
-mbranch-cost=*number*
-mmodel=*code-size-model-type*
-msdata=*sdata-type*
-mno-flush-func -mflush-func=*name*
-mno-flush-trap -mflush-trap=*number*
-G *num*

M32C Options

-mcpu=*cpu* -msim -memregs=*number*

M680x0 Options

-march=*arch* -mcpu=*cpu* -mtune=*tune*
-m68000 -m68020 -m68020-40 -m68020-60 -m68030 -m68040
-m68060 -mcpu32 -m5200 -m5206e -m528x -m5307 -m5407
-mcfv4e -mbitfield -mno-bitfield -mc68000 -mc68020
-mnobitfield -mrtd -mno-rtd -mdiv -mno-div -mshort
-mno-short -mhard-float -m68881 -msoft-float -mpcrel
-malign-int -mstrict-align -msep-data -mno-sep-data
-mshared-library-id=n -mid-shared-library -mno-id-shared-library
-mxgot -mno-xgot

MCore Options

-mhardlit -mno-hardlit -mdiv -mno-div -mrelax-immediates
-mno-relax-immediates -mwide-bitfields -mno-wide-bitfields
-m4byte-functions -mno-4byte-functions -mcallgraph-data
-mno-callgraph-data -mslow-bytes -mno-slow-bytes -mno-lsim
-mlittle-endian -mbig-endian -m210 -m340 -mstack-increment

MeP Options

-mabsdiff -mall-opts -maverage -mbased=*n* -mbitops
-mc=*n* -mclip -mconfig=*name* -mcop -mcop32 -mcop64 -mivc2
-mdc -mdiv -meb -mel -mio-volatile -ml -mleadz -mm -mminmax
-mmult -mno-opts -mrepeat -ms -msatur -msdram -msim -msimnovec -mtf
-mtiny=*n*

MicroBlaze Options

-msoft-float -mhard-float -msmall-divides -mcpu=*cpu*
-mmemcpy -mxl-soft-mul -mxl-soft-div -mxl-barrel-shift
-mxl-pattern-compare -mxl-stack-check -mxl-gp-opt -mno-clearbss
-mxl-multiply-high -mxl-float-convert -mxl-float-sqrt
-mbig-endian -mlittle-endian -mxl-reorder -mxl-mode-*app-model*

MIPS Options

-EL -EB -march=*arch* -mtune=*arch*
-mips1 -mips2 -mips3 -mips4 -mips32 -mips32r2 -mips32r3 -mips32r5
-mips32r6 -mips64 -mips64r2 -mips64r3 -mips64r5 -mips64r6
-mips16 -mno-mips16 -mflip-mips16
-minterlink-compressed -mno-interlink-compressed
-minterlink-mips16 -mno-interlink-mips16
-mabi=*abi* -mabicalls -mno-abicalls
-mshared -mno-shared -mplt -mno-plt -mxgot -mno-xgot
-mgp32 -mgp64 -mfp32 -mfpxx -mfp64 -mhard-float -msoft-float
-mno-float -msingle-float -mdouble-float
-modd-spreg -mno-odd-spreg
-mabs=*mode* -mnan=*encoding*
-mdsp -mno-dsp -mdspr2 -mno-dspr2
-mmcu -mmno-mcu
-meva -mno-eva
-mvirt -mno-virt
-mxpa -mno-xpa
-mmicromips -mno-micromips
-mfpu=*fpu-type*
-msmartmips -mno-smartmips
-mpaired-single -mno-paired-single -mdmx -mno-mdmx
-mips3d -mno-mips3d -mmt -mno-mt -mllsc -mno-llsc
-mlong64 -mlong32 -msym32 -mno-sym32
-G*num* -mlocal-sdata -mno-local-sdata
-mextern-sdata -mno-extern-sdata -mgpopt -mno-gopt
-membedded-data -mno-embedded-data
-muninit-const-in-rodata -mno-uninit-const-in-rodata
-mcode-readable=*setting*
-msplit-addresses -mno-split-addresses
-mexplicit-relocs -mno-explicit-relocs
-mcheck-zero-division -mno-check-zero-division
-mdivide-traps -mdivide-breaks
-mmemcpy -mno-memcpy -mlong-calls -mno-long-calls
-mmad -mno-mad -mimadd -mno-imadd -mfused-madd -mno-fused-madd -nocpp
-mfix-24k -mno-fix-24k
-mfix-r4000 -mno-fix-r4000 -mfix-r4400 -mno-fix-r4400
-mfix-r10000 -mno-fix-r10000 -mfix-rm7000 -mno-fix-rm7000
-mfix-vr4120 -mno-fix-vr4120
-mfix-vr4130 -mno-fix-vr4130 -mfix-sb1 -mno-fix-sb1
-mflush-func=*func* -mno-flush-func
-mbranch-cost=*num* -mbranch-likely -mno-branch-likely
-mcompact-branches=*policy*
-mfp-exceptions -mno-fp-exceptions
-mvr4130-align -mno-vr4130-align -msynci -mno-synci
-mrelax-pic-calls -mno-relax-pic-calls -mmcount-ra-address
-mframe-header-opt -mno-frame-header-opt

MMIX Options

-mlibfuncs -mno-libfuncs -mepsilon -mno-epsilon -mabi=gnu
-mabi=mmixware -mzero-extend -mknuthdiv -mtoplevel-symbols
-melf -mbranch-predict -mno-branch-predict -mbase-addresses
-mno-base-addresses -msingle-exit -mno-single-exit

MN10300 Options

-mmult-bug -mno-mult-bug
-mno-am33 -mam33 -mam33-2 -mam34
-mtune=*cpu-type*
-mreturn-pointer-on-d0
-mno-crt0 -mrelax -mliw -msetlb

Moxie Options

`-meb -mel -mmul.x -mno-crt0`

MSP430 Options

```
-msim -masm-hex -mmcu= -mcpu= -mlarge -msmall -mrelax
-mwarn-mcu
-mcode-region= -mdata-region=
-msilicon-errata= -msilicon-errata-warn=
-mhwmult= -minrt
```

NDS32 Options

```
-mbig-endian -mlittle-endian
-mreduced-regs -mfull-regs
-mcmov -mno-cmov
-mperf-ext -mno-perf-ext
-mv3push -mno-v3push
-m16bit -mno-16bit
-misr-vector-size=num
-mcache-block-size=num
-march=arch
-mcmodel=code-model
-mctor-dtor -mrelax
```

Nios II Options

```
-G num -mgpopt=option -mgpopt -mno-gpopt
-mel -meb
-mno-bypass-cache -mbypass-cache
-mno-cache-volatile -mcache-volatile
-mno-fast-sw-div -mfast-sw-div
-mhw-mul -mno-hw-mul -mhw-mulx -mno-hw-mulx -mno-hw-div -mhw-div
-mcustom-insn=N -mno-custom-insn
-mcustom-fpu-cfg=name
-mhal -msmallc -msys-crt0=name -msys-lib=name
-march=arch -mbmx -mno-bmx -mcdx -mno-cdx
```

Nvidia PTX Options

`-m32 -m64 -mmainkernel -moptimize`

PDP-11 Options

```
-mfpu -msoft-float -mac0 -mno-ac0 -m40 -m45 -m10
-mbcopy -mbcopy-builtin -mint32 -mno-int16
-mint16 -mno-int32 -mfloat32 -mno-float64
-mfloat64 -mno-float32 -mabshi -mno-abshi
-mbranch-expensive -mbranch-cheap
-munix-asm -mdec-asm
```

picoChip Options

```
-mae=ae_type -mvliw-lookahead=N
-msymbol-as-address -mno-inefficient-warnings
```

PowerPC Options See RS/6000 and PowerPC Options.

RL78 Options

```
-msim -mmul=none -mmul=g13 -mmul=g14 -mallregs
-mcpu=g10 -mcpu=g13 -mcpu=g14 -mg10 -mg13 -mg14
-m64bit-doubles -m32bit-doubles
```

RS/6000 and PowerPC Options

```
-mcpu=cpu-type
-mtune=cpu-type
```

-mcmodel=*code-model*
-mpowerpc64
-maltivec -mno-altivec
-mpowerpc-gpopt -mno-powerpc-gpopt
-mpowerpc-gfxopt -mno-powerpc-gfxopt
-mmfcrf -mno-mfcrf -mpopcntb -mno-popcntb -mpopcntd -mno-popcntd
-mfprnd -mno-fprnd
-mcmpb -mno-cmpb -mmfpgpr -mno-mfpgpr -mhard-dfp -mno-hard-dfp
-mfull-toc -mminimal-toc -mno-fp-in-toc -mno-sum-in-toc
-m64 -m32 -mxl-compat -mno-xl-compat -mpe
-malign-power -malign-natural
-msoft-float -mhard-float -mmultiple -mno-multiple
-msingle-float -mdouble-float -msimple-fpu
-mstring -mno-string -mupdate -mno-update
-mavoid-indexed-addresses -mno-avoid-indexed-addresses
-mfused-madd -mno-fused-madd -mbit-align -mno-bit-align
-mstrict-align -mno-strict-align -mrelocatable
-mno-relocatable -mrelocatable-lib -mno-relocatable-lib
-mtoc -mno-toc -mlittle -mlittle-endian -mbig -mbig-endian
-mdynamic-no-pic -maltivec -mswdiv -msingle-pic-base
-mprioritize-restricted-insns=*priority*
-msched-costly-dep=*dependence_type*
-minsert-sched-nops=*scheme*
-mcall-sysv -mcall-netbsd
-maix-struct-return -msvr4-struct-return
-mabi=*abi-type* -msecure-plt -mbss-plt
-mblock-move-inline-limit=*num*
-misel -mno-isel
-misel=yes -misel=no
-mspe -mno-spe
-mspe=yes -mspe=no
-mpaired
-mgen-cell-microcode -mwarn-cell-microcode
-mvrsave -mno-vrsave
-mmulhw -mno-mulhw
-mdlmzb -mno-dlmzb
-mfloat-gprs=yes -mfloat-gprs=no -mfloat-gprs=single -mfloat-gprs=double
-mprototype -mno-prototype
-msim -mmvme -mads -myellowknife -memb -msdata
-msdata=*opt* -mvxworks -G *num* -pthread
-mrecip -mrecip=*opt* -mno-recip -mrecip-precision
-mno-recip-precision
-mveclibabi=*type* -mfriz -mno-friz
-mpointers-to-nested-functions -mno-pointers-to-nested-functions
-msave-toc-indirect -mno-save-toc-indirect
-mpower8-fusion -mno-mpower8-fusion -mpower8-vector -mno-power8-vector
-mcrypto -mno-crypto -mdirect-move -mno-direct-move
-mquad-memory -mno-quad-memory
-mquad-memory-atomic -mno-quad-memory-atomic
-mcompat-align-parm -mno-compat-align-parm
-mupper-regs-df -mno-upper-regs-df -mupper-regs-sf -mno-upper-regs-sf
-mupper-regs -mno-upper-regs -mmodulo -mno-modulo
-mfloat128 -mno-float128 -mfloat128-hardware -mno-float128-hardware
-mpower9-fusion -mno-mpower9-fusion -mpower9-vector -mno-power9-vector

RX Options

-m64bit-doubles -m32bit-doubles -fpu -nofpu
-mcpu=
-mbig-endian-data -mlittle-endian-data

```
-msmall-data
-msim -mno-sim
-mas100-syntax -mno-as100-syntax
-mrelax
-mmax-constant-size=
-mint-register=
-mpid
-mallow-string-insns -mno-allow-string-insns
-mjsr
-mno-warn-multiple-fast-interrupts
-msave-acc-in-interrupts
```

S/390 and zSeries Options

```
-mtune=cpu-type -march=cpu-type
-mhard-float -msoft-float -mhard-dfp -mno-hard-dfp
-mlong-double-64 -mlong-double-128
-mbackchain -mno-backchain -mpacked-stack -mno-packed-stack
-msmall-exec -mno-small-exec -mmvcle -mno-mvcle
-m64 -m31 -mdebug -mno-debug -mesa -mzarch
-mhtm -mvx -mzvector
-mtpf-trace -mno-tpf-trace -mfused-madd -mno-fused-madd
-mwarn-framesize -mwarn-dynamicstack -mstack-size -mstack-guard
-mhotpatch=halfwords,halfwords
```

Score Options

```
-meb -mel
-mnhwloop
-muls
-mmac
-mscore5 -mscore5u -mscore7 -mscore7d
```

SH Options

```
-m1 -m2 -m2e
-m2a-nofpu -m2a-single-only -m2a-single -m2a
-m3 -m3e
-m4-nofpu -m4-single-only -m4-single -m4
-m4a-nofpu -m4a-single-only -m4a-single -m4a -m4al
-mb -ml -mdalign -mrelax
-mbigtable -mfmovd -mrenesas -mno-renesas -mnomacsave
-mieee -mno-ieee -mbitops -misize -minline-ic_invalidate -mpadstruct
-mspace -mprefergot -musermode -multcost=number -mdiv=strategy
-mdivsi3_libfunc=name -mfixed-range=register-range
-maccumulate-outgoing-args
-matomic-model=atomic-model
-mbranch-cost=num -mzdcbranch -mno-zdcbranch
-mcbranch-force-delay-slot
-mfused-madd -mno-fused-madd -mfsca -mno-fsca -mfsrra -mno-fsrra
-mpretend-cmove -mtas
```

Solaris 2 Options

```
-mclear-hwcap -mno-clear-hwcap -mimpure-text -mno-impure-text
-pthreads -pthread
```

SPARC Options

```
-mcpu=cpu-type
-mtune=cpu-type
-mcmodel=code-model
-mmemory-model=mem-model
-m32 -m64 -mapp-regs -mno-app-regs
-mfaster-structs -mno-faster-structs -mflat -mno-flat
```

-mfpu -mno-fpu -mhard-float -msoft-float
-mhard-quad-float -msoft-quad-float
-mstack-bias -mno-stack-bias
-mstd-struct-return -mno-std-struct-return
-munaligned-doubles -mno-unaligned-doubles
-muser-mode -mno-user-mode
-mv8plus -mno-v8plus -mvis -mno-vis
-mvis2 -mno-vis2 -mvis3 -mno-vis3
-mcbcond -mno-cbcond
-mfmaf -mno-fmaf -mpopc -mno-popc
-mfix-at697f -mfix-ut699

SPU Options

-mwarn-reloc -merror-reloc
-msafe-dma -munsafe-dma
-mbranch-hints
-msmall-mem -mlarge-mem -mstdmain
-mfixed-range=*register-range*
-mea32 -mea64
-maddress-space-conversion -mno-address-space-conversion
-mcache-size=*cache-size*
-matomic-updates -mno-atomic-updates

System V Options

-Qy -Qn -YP,*paths* -Ym,*dir*

TILE-Gx Options

-mcpu=CPU -m32 -m64 -mbig-endian -mlittle-endian
-mcmodel=*code-model*

TILEPro Options

-mcpu=*cpu* -m32

V850 Options

-mlong-calls -mno-long-calls -mep -mno-ep
-mprolog-function -mno-prolog-function -mspace
-mtda=*n* -msda=*n* -mzda=*n*
-mapp-regs -mno-app-regs
-mdisable-callt -mno-disable-callt
-mv850e2v3 -mv850e2 -mv850e1 -mv850es
-mv850e -mv850 -mv850e3v5
-mloop
-mrelax
-mlong-jumps
-msoft-float
-mhard-float
-mgcc-abi
-mrh850-abi
-mbig-switch

VAX Options

-mg -mgnu -munix

Visium Options

-mdebug -msim -mfpu -mno-fpu -mhard-float -msoft-float
-mcpu=*cpu-type* -mtune=*cpu-type* -msv-mode -muser-mode

VMS Options

-mvms-return-codes -mdebug-main=*prefix* -mmalloc64
-mpointer-size=*size*

VxWorks Options

-mrtp -non-static -Bstatic -Bdynamic
-Xbind-lazy -Xbind-now

x86 Options

-mtune=*cpu-type* -march=*cpu-type*
-mtune-ctrl=*feature-list* -mdump-tune-features -mno-default
-mfpmath=*unit*
-masm=*dialect* -mno-fancy-math-387
-mno-fp-ret-in-387 -msoft-float
-mno-wide-multiply -mrtd -malign-double
-mpreferred-stack-boundary=*num*
-mincoming-stack-boundary=*num*
-mcld -mcx16 -msahf -mmovbe -mcrc32
-mrecip -mrecip=*opt*
-mvzeroupper -mprefer-avx128
-mmmx -msse -msse2 -msse3 -mssse3 -msse4.1 -msse4.2 -msse4 -mavx
-mavx2 -mavx512f -mavx512pf -mavx512er -mavx512cd -mavx512vl
-mavx512bw -mavx512dq -mavx512ifma -mavx512vbmi -msha -maes
-mpclmul -mfsgsbase -mrdrnd -mf16c -mfma
-mprefetchwt1 -mclflushopt -mxsavec -mxsaves
-msse4a -m3dnow -mpopcnt -mabm -mbmi -mtbm -mfma4 -mxop -mlzcnt
-mbmi2 -mfxsr -mxsave -mxsaveopt -mrtm -mlwp -mmpx -mmwaitx -mclzero -mpku -
mthreads
-mms-bitfields -mno-align-stringops -minline-all-stringops
-minline-stringops-dynamically -mstringop-strategy=*alg*
-mmemcpy-strategy=*strategy* -mmemset-strategy=*strategy*
-mpush-args -maccumulate-outgoing-args -m128bit-long-double
-m96bit-long-double -mlong-double-64 -mlong-double-80 -mlong-double-128
-mregparm=*num* -msseregparm
-mveclibabi=*type* -mvect8-ret-in-mem
-mpc32 -mpc64 -mpc80 -mstackrealign
-momit-leaf-frame-pointer -mno-red-zone -mno-tls-direct-seg-refs
-mcmodel=*code-model* -mabi=*name* -maddress-mode=*mode*
-m32 -m64 -mx32 -m16 -miamcu -mlarge-data-threshold=*num*
-msse2avx -mfentry -mrecord-mcount -mnop-mcount -m8bit-idiv
-mavx256-split-unaligned-load -mavx256-split-unaligned-store
-malign-data=*type* -mstack-protector-guard=*guard*
-mmitigate-rop

x86 Windows Options

-mconsole -mcygwin -mno-cygwin -mdll
-mnop-fun-dllimport -mthread
-municode -mwin32 -mwindows -fno-set-stack-executable

Xstormy16 Options

-msim

Xtensa Options

-mconst16 -mno-const16
-mfused-madd -mno-fused-madd
-mforce-no-pic
-mserialize-volatile -mno-serialize-volatile
-mtext-section-literals -mno-text-section-literals
-mauto-litpools -mno-auto-litpools
-mtarget-align -mno-target-align
-mlongcalls -mno-longcalls

zSeries Options See S/390 and zSeries Options.

3.2 Options Controlling the Kind of Output

Compilation can involve up to four stages: preprocessing, compilation proper, assembly and linking, always in that order. GCC is capable of preprocessing and compiling several files either into several assembler input files, or into one assembler input file; then each assembler input file produces an object file, and linking combines all the object files (those newly compiled, and those specified as input) into an executable file.

For any given input file, the file name suffix determines what kind of compilation is done:

file`.c` C source code that must be preprocessed.

file`.i` C source code that should not be preprocessed.

file`.ii` C++ source code that should not be preprocessed.

file`.m` Objective-C source code. Note that you must link with the '`libobjc`' library to make an Objective-C program work.

file`.mi` Objective-C source code that should not be preprocessed.

file`.mm`
file`.M` Objective-C++ source code. Note that you must link with the '`libobjc`' library to make an Objective-C++ program work. Note that '`.M`' refers to a literal capital M.

file`.mii` Objective-C++ source code that should not be preprocessed.

file`.h` C, C++, Objective-C or Objective-C++ header file to be turned into a precompiled header (default), or C, C++ header file to be turned into an Ada spec (via the '`-fdump-ada-spec`' switch).

file`.cc`
file`.cp`
file`.cxx`
file`.cpp`
file`.CPP`
file`.c++`
file`.C` C++ source code that must be preprocessed. Note that in '`.cxx`', the last two letters must both be literally '`x`'. Likewise, '`.C`' refers to a literal capital C.

file`.mm`
file`.M` Objective-C++ source code that must be preprocessed.

file`.mii` Objective-C++ source code that should not be preprocessed.

file`.hh`
file`.H`
file`.hp`
file`.hxx`
file`.hpp`
file`.HPP`
file`.h++`
file`.tcc` C++ header file to be turned into a precompiled header or Ada spec.

file.f
file.for
file.ftn Fixed form Fortran source code that should not be preprocessed.

file.F
file.FOR
file.fpp
file.FPP
file.FTN Fixed form Fortran source code that must be preprocessed (with the traditional preprocessor).

file.f90
file.f95
file.f03
file.f08 Free form Fortran source code that should not be preprocessed.

file.F90
file.F95
file.F03
file.F08 Free form Fortran source code that must be preprocessed (with the traditional preprocessor).

file.go Go source code.

file.ads Ada source code file that contains a library unit declaration (a declaration of a package, subprogram, or generic, or a generic instantiation), or a library unit renaming declaration (a package, generic, or subprogram renaming declaration). Such files are also called *specs*.

file.adb Ada source code file containing a library unit body (a subprogram or package body). Such files are also called *bodies*.

file.s Assembler code.

file.S
file.sx Assembler code that must be preprocessed.

other An object file to be fed straight into linking. Any file name with no recognized suffix is treated this way.

You can specify the input language explicitly with the '-x' option:

-x *language*

Specify explicitly the *language* for the following input files (rather than letting the compiler choose a default based on the file name suffix). This option applies to all following input files until the next '-x' option. Possible values for *language* are:

```
c  c-header  cpp-output
c++  c++-header  c++-cpp-output
objective-c  objective-c-header  objective-c-cpp-output
objective-c++ objective-c++-header objective-c++-cpp-output
assembler  assembler-with-cpp
ada
f77  f77-cpp-input f95  f95-cpp-input
go
java
```

`-x none` Turn off any specification of a language, so that subsequent files are handled according to their file name suffixes (as they are if '`-x`' has not been used at all).

If you only want some of the stages of compilation, you can use '`-x`' (or filename suffixes) to tell `gcc` where to start, and one of the options '`-c`', '`-S`', or '`-E`' to say where `gcc` is to stop. Note that some combinations (for example, '`-x cpp-output -E`') instruct `gcc` to do nothing at all.

`-c` Compile or assemble the source files, but do not link. The linking stage simply is not done. The ultimate output is in the form of an object file for each source file.

By default, the object file name for a source file is made by replacing the suffix '`.c`', '`.i`', '`.s`', etc., with '`.o`'.

Unrecognized input files, not requiring compilation or assembly, are ignored.

`-S` Stop after the stage of compilation proper; do not assemble. The output is in the form of an assembler code file for each non-assembler input file specified.

By default, the assembler file name for a source file is made by replacing the suffix '`.c`', '`.i`', etc., with '`.s`'.

Input files that don't require compilation are ignored.

`-E` Stop after the preprocessing stage; do not run the compiler proper. The output is in the form of preprocessed source code, which is sent to the standard output.

Input files that don't require preprocessing are ignored.

`-o` *`file`* Place output in file *file*. This applies to whatever sort of output is being produced, whether it be an executable file, an object file, an assembler file or preprocessed C code.

If '`-o`' is not specified, the default is to put an executable file in '`a.out`', the object file for '*`source.suffix`*' in '*`source`*`.o`', its assembler file in '*`source`*`.s`', a precompiled header file in '*`source.suffix`*`.gch`', and all preprocessed C source on standard output.

`-v` Print (on standard error output) the commands executed to run the stages of compilation. Also print the version number of the compiler driver program and of the preprocessor and the compiler proper.

`-###` Like '`-v`' except the commands are not executed and arguments are quoted unless they contain only alphanumeric characters or `./-_`. This is useful for shell scripts to capture the driver-generated command lines.

`--help` Print (on the standard output) a description of the command-line options understood by `gcc`. If the '`-v`' option is also specified then '`--help`' is also passed on to the various processes invoked by `gcc`, so that they can display the command-line options they accept. If the '`-Wextra`' option has also been specified (prior to the '`--help`' option), then command-line options that have no documentation associated with them are also displayed.

`--target-help`

Print (on the standard output) a description of target-specific command-line options for each tool. For some targets extra target-specific information may also be printed.

`--help={class|[^]qualifier}[,...]`

Print (on the standard output) a description of the command-line options understood by the compiler that fit into all specified classes and qualifiers. These are the supported classes:

'`optimizers`'
: Display all of the optimization options supported by the compiler.

'`warnings`'
: Display all of the options controlling warning messages produced by the compiler.

'`target`'
: Display target-specific options. Unlike the '`--target-help`' option however, target-specific options of the linker and assembler are not displayed. This is because those tools do not currently support the extended '`--help=`' syntax.

'`params`'
: Display the values recognized by the '`--param`' option.

language
: Display the options supported for *language*, where *language* is the name of one of the languages supported in this version of GCC.

'`common`'
: Display the options that are common to all languages.

These are the supported qualifiers:

'`undocumented`'
: Display only those options that are undocumented.

'`joined`'
: Display options taking an argument that appears after an equal sign in the same continuous piece of text, such as: '`--help=target`'.

'`separate`'
: Display options taking an argument that appears as a separate word following the original option, such as: '`-o output-file`'.

Thus for example to display all the undocumented target-specific switches supported by the compiler, use:

```
--help=target,undocumented
```

The sense of a qualifier can be inverted by prefixing it with the '`^`' character, so for example to display all binary warning options (i.e., ones that are either on or off and that do not take an argument) that have a description, use:

```
--help=warnings,^joined,^undocumented
```

The argument to '`--help=`' should not consist solely of inverted qualifiers.

Combining several classes is possible, although this usually restricts the output so much that there is nothing to display. One case where it does work, however, is when one of the classes is *target*. For example, to display all the target-specific optimization options, use:

```
--help=target,optimizers
```

The '--help=' option can be repeated on the command line. Each successive use displays its requested class of options, skipping those that have already been displayed.

If the '-Q' option appears on the command line before the '--help=' option, then the descriptive text displayed by '--help=' is changed. Instead of describing the displayed options, an indication is given as to whether the option is enabled, disabled or set to a specific value (assuming that the compiler knows this at the point where the '--help=' option is used).

Here is a truncated example from the ARM port of gcc:

```
% gcc -Q -mabi=2 --help=target -c
The following options are target specific:
-mabi=                                2
-mabort-on-noreturn                   [disabled]
-mapcs                                [disabled]
```

The output is sensitive to the effects of previous command-line options, so for example it is possible to find out which optimizations are enabled at '-O2' by using:

```
-Q -O2 --help=optimizers
```

Alternatively you can discover which binary optimizations are enabled by '-O3' by using:

```
gcc -c -Q -O3 --help=optimizers > /tmp/O3-opts
gcc -c -Q -O2 --help=optimizers > /tmp/O2-opts
diff /tmp/O2-opts /tmp/O3-opts | grep enabled
```

`--version`
Display the version number and copyrights of the invoked GCC.

`-pass-exit-codes`
Normally the gcc program exits with the code of 1 if any phase of the compiler returns a non-success return code. If you specify '-pass-exit-codes', the gcc program instead returns with the numerically highest error produced by any phase returning an error indication. The C, C++, and Fortran front ends return 4 if an internal compiler error is encountered.

`-pipe` Use pipes rather than temporary files for communication between the various stages of compilation. This fails to work on some systems where the assembler is unable to read from a pipe; but the GNU assembler has no trouble.

`-specs=`*`file`*
Process *file* after the compiler reads in the standard 'specs' file, in order to override the defaults which the gcc driver program uses when determining what switches to pass to cc1, cc1plus, as, ld, etc. More than one '-specs=*file*' can be specified on the command line, and they are processed in order, from left to right. See Section 3.19 [Spec Files], page 360, for information about the format of the *file*.

`-wrapper` Invoke all subcommands under a wrapper program. The name of the wrapper program and its parameters are passed as a comma separated list.

```
gcc -c t.c -wrapper gdb,--args
```

This invokes all subprograms of `gcc` under '`gdb --args`', thus the invocation of `cc1` is '`gdb --args cc1 ...`'.

`-fplugin=`*name*`.so`
: Load the plugin code in file *name*.so, assumed to be a shared object to be dlopen'd by the compiler. The base name of the shared object file is used to identify the plugin for the purposes of argument parsing (See '`-fplugin-arg-`*name*`-`*key*`=`*value*' below). Each plugin should define the callback functions specified in the Plugins API.

`-fplugin-arg-`*name*`-`*key*`=`*value*
: Define an argument called *key* with a value of *value* for the plugin called *name*.

`-fdump-ada-spec[-slim]`
: For C and C++ source and include files, generate corresponding Ada specs. See Section "Generating Ada Bindings for C and C++ headers" in *GNAT User's Guide*, which provides detailed documentation on this feature.

`-fada-spec-parent=`*unit*
: In conjunction with '`-fdump-ada-spec[-slim]`' above, generate Ada specs as child units of parent *unit*.

`-fdump-go-spec=`*file*
: For input files in any language, generate corresponding Go declarations in *file*. This generates Go `const`, `type`, `var`, and `func` declarations which may be a useful way to start writing a Go interface to code written in some other language.

`@`*file*
: Read command-line options from *file*. The options read are inserted in place of the original @*file* option. If *file* does not exist, or cannot be read, then the option will be treated literally, and not removed.

Options in *file* are separated by whitespace. A whitespace character may be included in an option by surrounding the entire option in either single or double quotes. Any character (including a backslash) may be included by prefixing the character to be included with a backslash. The *file* may itself contain additional @*file* options; any such options will be processed recursively.

3.3 Compiling C++ Programs

C++ source files conventionally use one of the suffixes '`.C`', '`.cc`', '`.cpp`', '`.CPP`', '`.c++`', '`.cp`', or '`.cxx`'; C++ header files often use '`.hh`', '`.hpp`', '`.H`', or (for shared template code) '`.tcc`'; and preprocessed C++ files use the suffix '`.ii`'. GCC recognizes files with these names and compiles them as C++ programs even if you call the compiler the same way as for compiling C programs (usually with the name `gcc`).

However, the use of `gcc` does not add the C++ library. `g++` is a program that calls GCC and automatically specifies linking against the C++ library. It treats '`.c`', '`.h`' and '`.i`' files as C++ source files instead of C source files unless '`-x`' is used. This program is also useful when precompiling a C header file with a '`.h`' extension for use in C++ compilations. On many systems, `g++` is also installed with the name `c++`.

When you compile C++ programs, you may specify many of the same command-line options that you use for compiling programs in any language; or command-line options meaningful for C and related languages; or options that are meaningful only for C++ programs. See Section 3.4 [Options Controlling C Dialect], page 33, for explanations of options for languages related to C. See Section 3.5 [Options Controlling C++ Dialect], page 39, for explanations of options that are meaningful only for C++ programs.

3.4 Options Controlling C Dialect

The following options control the dialect of C (or languages derived from C, such as C++, Objective-C and Objective-C++) that the compiler accepts:

`-ansi`
: In C mode, this is equivalent to '`-std=c90`'. In C++ mode, it is equivalent to '`-std=c++98`'.

  This turns off certain features of GCC that are incompatible with ISO C90 (when compiling C code), or of standard C++ (when compiling C++ code), such as the `asm` and `typeof` keywords, and predefined macros such as `unix` and `vax` that identify the type of system you are using. It also enables the undesirable and rarely used ISO trigraph feature. For the C compiler, it disables recognition of C++ style '`//`' comments as well as the `inline` keyword.

  The alternate keywords `__asm__`, `__extension__`, `__inline__` and `__typeof__` continue to work despite '`-ansi`'. You would not want to use them in an ISO C program, of course, but it is useful to put them in header files that might be included in compilations done with '`-ansi`'. Alternate predefined macros such as `__unix__` and `__vax__` are also available, with or without '`-ansi`'.

  The '`-ansi`' option does not cause non-ISO programs to be rejected gratuitously. For that, '`-Wpedantic`' is required in addition to '`-ansi`'. See Section 3.8 [Warning Options], page 56.

  The macro `__STRICT_ANSI__` is predefined when the '`-ansi`' option is used. Some header files may notice this macro and refrain from declaring certain functions or defining certain macros that the ISO standard doesn't call for; this is to avoid interfering with any programs that might use these names for other things.

  Functions that are normally built in but do not have semantics defined by ISO C (such as `alloca` and `ffs`) are not built-in functions when '`-ansi`' is used. See Section 6.58 [Other built-in functions provided by GCC], page 545, for details of the functions affected.

`-std=`
: Determine the language standard. See Chapter 2 [Language Standards Supported by GCC], page 5, for details of these standard versions. This option is currently only supported when compiling C or C++.

  The compiler can accept several base standards, such as '`c90`' or '`c++98`', and GNU dialects of those standards, such as '`gnu90`' or '`gnu++98`'. When a base standard is specified, the compiler accepts all programs following that standard plus those using GNU extensions that do not contradict it. For example, '`-std=c90`' turns off certain features of GCC that are incompatible with ISO C90, such as the `asm` and `typeof` keywords, but not other GNU extensions that do not have a meaning in ISO C90, such as omitting the middle term of a `?:` expression. On the other hand, when a GNU dialect of a standard is specified, all features supported by the compiler are enabled, even when those features change the meaning of the base standard. As a result, some strict-conforming programs may be rejected. The particular standard is used by '**-Wpedantic**' to identify which features are GNU extensions given that version of the standard. For example '**-std=gnu90 -Wpedantic**' warns about C++ style '//' comments, while '**-std=gnu99 -Wpedantic**' does not.

A value for this option must be provided; possible values are

'c90'
'c89'
'iso9899:1990'
: Support all ISO C90 programs (certain GNU extensions that conflict with ISO C90 are disabled). Same as '**-ansi**' for C code.

'iso9899:199409'
: ISO C90 as modified in amendment 1.

'c99'
'c9x'
'iso9899:1999'
'iso9899:199x'
: ISO C99. This standard is substantially completely supported, modulo bugs and floating-point issues (mainly but not entirely relating to optional C99 features from Annexes F and G). See `http://gcc.gnu.org/c99status.html` for more information. The names '**c9x**' and '**iso9899:199x**' are deprecated.

'c11'
'c1x'
'iso9899:2011'
: ISO C11, the 2011 revision of the ISO C standard. This standard is substantially completely supported, modulo bugs, floating-point issues (mainly but not entirely relating to optional C11 features from Annexes F and G) and the optional Annexes K (Bounds-checking interfaces) and L (Analyzability). The name '**c1x**' is deprecated.

'gnu90'
'gnu89'
: GNU dialect of ISO C90 (including some C99 features).

'gnu99'
'gnu9x'
: GNU dialect of ISO C99. The name '**gnu9x**' is deprecated.

'gnu11'
'gnu1x'
: GNU dialect of ISO C11. This is the default for C code. The name '**gnu1x**' is deprecated.

'c++98'
'c++03'
: The 1998 ISO C++ standard plus the 2003 technical corrigendum and some additional defect reports. Same as '**-ansi**' for C++ code.

'gnu++98'
'gnu++03' GNU dialect of '-std=c++98'.

'c++11'
'c++0x' The 2011 ISO C++ standard plus amendments. The name 'c++0x' is deprecated.

'gnu++11'
'gnu++0x' GNU dialect of '-std=c++11'. The name 'gnu++0x' is deprecated.

'c++14'
'c++1y' The 2014 ISO C++ standard plus amendments. The name 'c++1y' is deprecated.

'gnu++14'
'gnu++1y' GNU dialect of '-std=c++14'. This is the default for C++ code. The name 'gnu++1y' is deprecated.

'c++1z' The next revision of the ISO C++ standard, tentatively planned for 2017. Support is highly experimental, and will almost certainly change in incompatible ways in future releases.

'gnu++1z' GNU dialect of '-std=c++1z'. Support is highly experimental, and will almost certainly change in incompatible ways in future releases.

`-fgnu89-inline`

The option '`-fgnu89-inline`' tells GCC to use the traditional GNU semantics for `inline` functions when in C99 mode. See Section 6.42 [An Inline Function is As Fast As a Macro], page 472. Using this option is roughly equivalent to adding the `gnu_inline` function attribute to all inline functions (see Section 6.31 [Function Attributes], page 407).

The option '`-fno-gnu89-inline`' explicitly tells GCC to use the C99 semantics for `inline` when in C99 or gnu99 mode (i.e., it specifies the default behavior). This option is not supported in '`-std=c90`' or '`-std=gnu90`' mode.

The preprocessor macros `__GNUC_GNU_INLINE__` and `__GNUC_STDC_INLINE__` may be used to check which semantics are in effect for `inline` functions. See Section "Common Predefined Macros" in *The C Preprocessor*.

`-aux-info` ***filename***

Output to the given filename prototyped declarations for all functions declared and/or defined in a translation unit, including those in header files. This option is silently ignored in any language other than C.

Besides declarations, the file indicates, in comments, the origin of each declaration (source file and line), whether the declaration was implicit, prototyped or unprototyped ('I', 'N' for new or 'O' for old, respectively, in the first character after the line number and the colon), and whether it came from a declaration or a definition ('C' or 'F', respectively, in the following character). In the case of function definitions, a K&R-style list of arguments followed by their declarations is also provided, inside comments, after the declaration.

`-fallow-parameterless-variadic-functions`

Accept variadic functions without named parameters.

Although it is possible to define such a function, this is not very useful as it is not possible to read the arguments. This is only supported for C as this construct is allowed by C++.

`-fno-asm` Do not recognize `asm`, `inline` or `typeof` as a keyword, so that code can use these words as identifiers. You can use the keywords `__asm__`, `__inline__` and `__typeof__` instead. '`-ansi`' implies '`-fno-asm`'.

In C++, this switch only affects the `typeof` keyword, since `asm` and `inline` are standard keywords. You may want to use the '`-fno-gnu-keywords`' flag instead, which has the same effect. In C99 mode ('`-std=c99`' or '`-std=gnu99`'), this switch only affects the `asm` and `typeof` keywords, since `inline` is a standard keyword in ISO C99.

`-fno-builtin`
`-fno-builtin-`*`function`*

Don't recognize built-in functions that do not begin with '`__builtin_`' as prefix. See Section 6.58 [Other built-in functions provided by GCC], page 545, for details of the functions affected, including those which are not built-in functions when '`-ansi`' or '`-std`' options for strict ISO C conformance are used because they do not have an ISO standard meaning.

GCC normally generates special code to handle certain built-in functions more efficiently; for instance, calls to `alloca` may become single instructions which adjust the stack directly, and calls to `memcpy` may become inline copy loops. The resulting code is often both smaller and faster, but since the function calls no longer appear as such, you cannot set a breakpoint on those calls, nor can you change the behavior of the functions by linking with a different library. In addition, when a function is recognized as a built-in function, GCC may use information about that function to warn about problems with calls to that function, or to generate more efficient code, even if the resulting code still contains calls to that function. For example, warnings are given with '`-Wformat`' for bad calls to `printf` when `printf` is built in and `strlen` is known not to modify global memory.

With the '`-fno-builtin-`*`function`*' option only the built-in function *function* is disabled. *function* must not begin with '`__builtin_`'. If a function is named that is not built-in in this version of GCC, this option is ignored. There is no corresponding '`-fbuiltin-`*`function`*' option; if you wish to enable built-in functions selectively when using '`-fno-builtin`' or '`-ffreestanding`', you may define macros such as:

```
#define abs(n)          __builtin_abs ((n))
#define strcpy(d, s)    __builtin_strcpy ((d), (s))
```

`-fhosted`

Assert that compilation targets a hosted environment. This implies '`-fbuiltin`'. A hosted environment is one in which the entire standard library is available, and in which `main` has a return type of `int`. Examples are nearly everything except a kernel. This is equivalent to '`-fno-freestanding`'.

`-ffreestanding`

Assert that compilation targets a freestanding environment. This implies '`-fno-builtin`'. A freestanding environment is one in which the standard library may not exist, and program startup may not necessarily be at `main`. The most obvious example is an OS kernel. This is equivalent to '`-fno-hosted`'.

See Chapter 2 [Language Standards Supported by GCC], page 5, for details of freestanding and hosted environments.

`-fopenacc`

Enable handling of OpenACC directives `#pragma acc` in C/C++ and `!$acc` in Fortran. When '`-fopenacc`' is specified, the compiler generates accelerated code according to the OpenACC Application Programming Interface v2.0 `http://www.openacc.org/`. This option implies '`-pthread`', and thus is only supported on targets that have support for '`-pthread`'.

`-fopenacc-dim=`*geom*

Specify default compute dimensions for parallel offload regions that do not explicitly specify. The *geom* value is a triple of ':'-separated sizes, in order 'gang', 'worker' and, 'vector'. A size can be omitted, to use a target-specific default value.

`-fopenmp`

Enable handling of OpenMP directives `#pragma omp` in C/C++ and `!$omp` in Fortran. When '`-fopenmp`' is specified, the compiler generates parallel code according to the OpenMP Application Program Interface v4.0 `http://www.openmp.org/`. This option implies '`-pthread`', and thus is only supported on targets that have support for '`-pthread`'. '`-fopenmp`' implies '`-fopenmp-simd`'.

`-fopenmp-simd`

Enable handling of OpenMP's SIMD directives with `#pragma omp` in C/C++ and `!$omp` in Fortran. Other OpenMP directives are ignored.

`-fcilkplus`

Enable the usage of Cilk Plus language extension features for C/C++. When the option '`-fcilkplus`' is specified, enable the usage of the Cilk Plus Language extension features for C/C++. The present implementation follows ABI version 1.2. This is an experimental feature that is only partially complete, and whose interface may change in future versions of GCC as the official specification changes. Currently, all features but `_Cilk_for` have been implemented.

`-fgnu-tm`

When the option '`-fgnu-tm`' is specified, the compiler generates code for the Linux variant of Intel's current Transactional Memory ABI specification document (Revision 1.1, May 6 2009). This is an experimental feature whose interface may change in future versions of GCC, as the official specification changes. Please note that not all architectures are supported for this feature.

For more information on GCC's support for transactional memory, See Section "The GNU Transactional Memory Library" in *GNU Transactional Memory Library*.

Note that the transactional memory feature is not supported with non-call exceptions ('-fnon-call-exceptions').

-fms-extensions
: Accept some non-standard constructs used in Microsoft header files.

In C++ code, this allows member names in structures to be similar to previous types declarations.

```
typedef int UOW;
struct ABC {
  UOW UOW;
};
```

Some cases of unnamed fields in structures and unions are only accepted with this option. See Section 6.62 [Unnamed struct/union fields within structs/unions], page 676, for details.

Note that this option is off for all targets but x86 targets using ms-abi.

-fplan9-extensions
: Accept some non-standard constructs used in Plan 9 code.

This enables '-fms-extensions', permits passing pointers to structures with anonymous fields to functions that expect pointers to elements of the type of the field, and permits referring to anonymous fields declared using a typedef. See Section 6.62 [Unnamed struct/union fields within structs/unions], page 676, for details. This is only supported for C, not C++.

-trigraphs
: Support ISO C trigraphs. The '-ansi' option (and '-std' options for strict ISO C conformance) implies '-trigraphs'.

-traditional
-traditional-cpp
: Formerly, these options caused GCC to attempt to emulate a pre-standard C compiler. They are now only supported with the '-E' switch. The preprocessor continues to support a pre-standard mode. See the GNU CPP manual for details.

-fcond-mismatch
: Allow conditional expressions with mismatched types in the second and third arguments. The value of such an expression is void. This option is not supported for C++.

-flax-vector-conversions
: Allow implicit conversions between vectors with differing numbers of elements and/or incompatible element types. This option should not be used for new code.

-funsigned-char
: Let the type char be unsigned, like unsigned char.

Each kind of machine has a default for what char should be. It is either like unsigned char by default or like signed char by default.

Ideally, a portable program should always use signed char or unsigned char when it depends on the signedness of an object. But many programs have been written to use plain `char` and expect it to be signed, or expect it to be unsigned, depending on the machines they were written for. This option, and its inverse, let you make such a program work with the opposite default.

The type `char` is always a distinct type from each of `signed char` or `unsigned char`, even though its behavior is always just like one of those two.

`-fsigned-char`

Let the type `char` be signed, like `signed char`.

Note that this is equivalent to '`-fno-unsigned-char`', which is the negative form of '`-funsigned-char`'. Likewise, the option '`-fno-signed-char`' is equivalent to '`-funsigned-char`'.

`-fsigned-bitfields`
`-funsigned-bitfields`
`-fno-signed-bitfields`
`-fno-unsigned-bitfields`

These options control whether a bit-field is signed or unsigned, when the declaration does not use either `signed` or `unsigned`. By default, such a bit-field is signed, because this is consistent: the basic integer types such as `int` are signed types.

`-fsso-struct=`*`endianness`*

Set the default scalar storage order of structures and unions to the specified endianness. The accepted values are '`big-endian`' and '`little-endian`'. If the option is not passed, the compiler uses the native endianness of the target. This option is not supported for C++.

Warning: the '`-fsso-struct`' switch causes GCC to generate code that is not binary compatible with code generated without it if the specified endianness is not the native endianness of the target.

3.5 Options Controlling C++ Dialect

This section describes the command-line options that are only meaningful for C++ programs. You can also use most of the GNU compiler options regardless of what language your program is in. For example, you might compile a file '`firstClass.C`' like this:

```
g++ -g -fstrict-enums -O -c firstClass.C
```

In this example, only '`-fstrict-enums`' is an option meant only for C++ programs; you can use the other options with any language supported by GCC.

Some options for compiling C programs, such as '`-std`', are also relevant for C++ programs. See Section 3.4 [Options Controlling C Dialect], page 33.

Here is a list of options that are *only* for compiling C++ programs:

`-fabi-version=`*`n`*

Use version *n* of the C++ ABI. The default is version 0.

Version 0 refers to the version conforming most closely to the C++ ABI specification. Therefore, the ABI obtained using version 0 will change in different versions of G++ as ABI bugs are fixed.

Version 1 is the version of the C++ ABI that first appeared in G++ 3.2.

Version 2 is the version of the C++ ABI that first appeared in G++ 3.4, and was the default through G++ 4.9.

Version 3 corrects an error in mangling a constant address as a template argument.

Version 4, which first appeared in G++ 4.5, implements a standard mangling for vector types.

Version 5, which first appeared in G++ 4.6, corrects the mangling of attribute const/volatile on function pointer types, decltype of a plain decl, and use of a function parameter in the declaration of another parameter.

Version 6, which first appeared in G++ 4.7, corrects the promotion behavior of C++11 scoped enums and the mangling of template argument packs, const/static_cast, prefix ++ and –, and a class scope function used as a template argument.

Version 7, which first appeared in G++ 4.8, that treats nullptr_t as a builtin type and corrects the mangling of lambdas in default argument scope.

Version 8, which first appeared in G++ 4.9, corrects the substitution behavior of function types with function-cv-qualifiers.

Version 9, which first appeared in G++ 5.2, corrects the alignment of `nullptr_t`.

Version 10, which first appeared in G++ 6.1, adds mangling of attributes that affect type identity, such as ia32 calling convention attributes (e.g. '`stdcall`').

See also '`-Wabi`'.

`-fabi-compat-version=`*n*

On targets that support strong aliases, G++ works around mangling changes by creating an alias with the correct mangled name when defining a symbol with an incorrect mangled name. This switch specifies which ABI version to use for the alias.

With '`-fabi-version=0`' (the default), this defaults to 8 (GCC 5 compatibility). If another ABI version is explicitly selected, this defaults to 0. For compatibility with GCC versions 3.2 through 4.9, use '`-fabi-compat-version=2`'.

If this option is not provided but '`-Wabi=`*n*' is, that version is used for compatibility aliases. If this option is provided along with '`-Wabi`' (without the version), the version from this option is used for the warning.

`-fno-access-control`

Turn off all access checking. This switch is mainly useful for working around bugs in the access control code.

`-fcheck-new`

Check that the pointer returned by `operator new` is non-null before attempting to modify the storage allocated. This check is normally unnecessary because the C++ standard specifies that `operator new` only returns `0` if it is declared `throw()`, in which case the compiler always checks the return value even without this option. In all other cases, when `operator new` has a non-empty exception specification, memory exhaustion is signalled by throwing `std::bad_alloc`. See also '`new (nothrow)`'.

`-fconcepts`
Enable support for the C++ Extensions for Concepts Technical Specification, ISO 19217 (2015), which allows code like

```
template <class T> concept bool Addable = requires (T t) { t + t; };
template <Addable T> T add (T a, T b) { return a + b; }
```

`-fconstexpr-depth=`*n*
Set the maximum nested evaluation depth for C++11 constexpr functions to *n*. A limit is needed to detect endless recursion during constant expression evaluation. The minimum specified by the standard is 512.

`-fdeduce-init-list`
Enable deduction of a template type parameter as `std::initializer_list` from a brace-enclosed initializer list, i.e.

```
template <class T> auto forward(T t) -> decltype (realfn (t))
{
  return realfn (t);
}

void f()
{
  forward({1,2}); // call forward<std::initializer_list<int>>
}
```

This deduction was implemented as a possible extension to the originally proposed semantics for the C++11 standard, but was not part of the final standard, so it is disabled by default. This option is deprecated, and may be removed in a future version of G++.

`-ffriend-injection`
Inject friend functions into the enclosing namespace, so that they are visible outside the scope of the class in which they are declared. Friend functions were documented to work this way in the old Annotated C++ Reference Manual. However, in ISO C++ a friend function that is not declared in an enclosing scope can only be found using argument dependent lookup. GCC defaults to the standard behavior.

This option is for compatibility, and may be removed in a future release of G++.

`-fno-elide-constructors`
The C++ standard allows an implementation to omit creating a temporary that is only used to initialize another object of the same type. Specifying this option disables that optimization, and forces G++ to call the copy constructor in all cases.

`-fno-enforce-eh-specs`
Don't generate code to check for violation of exception specifications at run time. This option violates the C++ standard, but may be useful for reducing code size in production builds, much like defining `NDEBUG`. This does not give user code permission to throw exceptions in violation of the exception specifications; the compiler still optimizes based on the specifications, so throwing an unexpected exception results in undefined behavior at run time.

`-fextern-tls-init`
`-fno-extern-tls-init`

The C++11 and OpenMP standards allow `thread_local` and `threadprivate` variables to have dynamic (runtime) initialization. To support this, any use of such a variable goes through a wrapper function that performs any necessary initialization. When the use and definition of the variable are in the same translation unit, this overhead can be optimized away, but when the use is in a different translation unit there is significant overhead even if the variable doesn't actually need dynamic initialization. If the programmer can be sure that no use of the variable in a non-defining TU needs to trigger dynamic initialization (either because the variable is statically initialized, or a use of the variable in the defining TU will be executed before any uses in another TU), they can avoid this overhead with the '`-fno-extern-tls-init`' option.

On targets that support symbol aliases, the default is '`-fextern-tls-init`'. On targets that do not support symbol aliases, the default is '`-fno-extern-tls-init`'.

`-ffor-scope`
`-fno-for-scope`

If '`-ffor-scope`' is specified, the scope of variables declared in a *for-init-statement* is limited to the `for` loop itself, as specified by the C++ standard. If '`-fno-for-scope`' is specified, the scope of variables declared in a *for-init-statement* extends to the end of the enclosing scope, as was the case in old versions of G++, and other (traditional) implementations of C++.

If neither flag is given, the default is to follow the standard, but to allow and give a warning for old-style code that would otherwise be invalid, or have different behavior.

`-fno-gnu-keywords`

Do not recognize `typeof` as a keyword, so that code can use this word as an identifier. You can use the keyword `__typeof__` instead. This option is implied by the strict ISO C++ dialects: '`-ansi`', '`-std=c++98`', '`-std=c++11`', etc.

`-fno-implicit-templates`

Never emit code for non-inline templates that are instantiated implicitly (i.e. by use); only emit code for explicit instantiations. See Section 7.5 [Template Instantiation], page 684, for more information.

`-fno-implicit-inline-templates`

Don't emit code for implicit instantiations of inline templates, either. The default is to handle inlines differently so that compiles with and without optimization need the same set of explicit instantiations.

`-fno-implement-inlines`

To save space, do not emit out-of-line copies of inline functions controlled by `#pragma implementation`. This causes linker errors if these functions are not inlined everywhere they are called.

`-fms-extensions`
: Disable Wpedantic warnings about constructs used in MFC, such as implicit int and getting a pointer to member function via non-standard syntax.

`-fno-nonansi-builtins`
: Disable built-in declarations of functions that are not mandated by ANSI/ISO C. These include `ffs`, `alloca`, `_exit`, `index`, `bzero`, `conjf`, and other related functions.

`-fnothrow-opt`
: Treat a `throw()` exception specification as if it were a `noexcept` specification to reduce or eliminate the text size overhead relative to a function with no exception specification. If the function has local variables of types with non-trivial destructors, the exception specification actually makes the function smaller because the EH cleanups for those variables can be optimized away. The semantic effect is that an exception thrown out of a function with such an exception specification results in a call to `terminate` rather than `unexpected`.

`-fno-operator-names`
: Do not treat the operator name keywords `and`, `bitand`, `bitor`, `compl`, `not`, `or` and `xor` as synonyms as keywords.

`-fno-optional-diags`
: Disable diagnostics that the standard says a compiler does not need to issue. Currently, the only such diagnostic issued by G++ is the one for a name having multiple meanings within a class.

`-fpermissive`
: Downgrade some diagnostics about nonconformant code from errors to warnings. Thus, using '`-fpermissive`' allows some nonconforming code to compile.

`-fno-pretty-templates`
: When an error message refers to a specialization of a function template, the compiler normally prints the signature of the template followed by the template arguments and any typedefs or typenames in the signature (e.g. `void f(T) [with T = int]` rather than `void f(int)`) so that it's clear which template is involved. When an error message refers to a specialization of a class template, the compiler omits any template arguments that match the default template arguments for that template. If either of these behaviors make it harder to understand the error message rather than easier, you can use '`-fno-pretty-templates`' to disable them.

`-frepo`
: Enable automatic template instantiation at link time. This option also implies '`-fno-implicit-templates`'. See Section 7.5 [Template Instantiation], page 684, for more information.

`-fno-rtti`
: Disable generation of information about every class with virtual functions for use by the C++ run-time type identification features (`dynamic_cast` and `typeid`). If you don't use those parts of the language, you can save some space by using this flag. Note that exception handling uses the same information,

but G++ generates it as needed. The `dynamic_cast` operator can still be used for casts that do not require run-time type information, i.e. casts to `void *` or to unambiguous base classes.

`-fsized-deallocation`
Enable the built-in global declarations

```
void operator delete (void *, std::size_t) noexcept;
void operator delete[] (void *, std::size_t) noexcept;
```

as introduced in C++14. This is useful for user-defined replacement deallocation functions that, for example, use the size of the object to make deallocation faster. Enabled by default under '`-std=c++14`' and above. The flag '`-Wsized-deallocation`' warns about places that might want to add a definition.

`-fstrict-enums`
Allow the compiler to optimize using the assumption that a value of enumerated type can only be one of the values of the enumeration (as defined in the C++ standard; basically, a value that can be represented in the minimum number of bits needed to represent all the enumerators). This assumption may not be valid if the program uses a cast to convert an arbitrary integer value to the enumerated type.

`-ftemplate-backtrace-limit=`*n*
Set the maximum number of template instantiation notes for a single warning or error to *n*. The default value is 10.

`-ftemplate-depth=`*n*
Set the maximum instantiation depth for template classes to *n*. A limit on the template instantiation depth is needed to detect endless recursions during template class instantiation. ANSI/ISO C++ conforming programs must not rely on a maximum depth greater than 17 (changed to 1024 in C++11). The default value is 900, as the compiler can run out of stack space before hitting 1024 in some situations.

`-fno-threadsafe-statics`
Do not emit the extra code to use the routines specified in the C++ ABI for thread-safe initialization of local statics. You can use this option to reduce code size slightly in code that doesn't need to be thread-safe.

`-fuse-cxa-atexit`
Register destructors for objects with static storage duration with the `__cxa_atexit` function rather than the `atexit` function. This option is required for fully standards-compliant handling of static destructors, but only works if your C library supports `__cxa_atexit`.

`-fno-use-cxa-get-exception-ptr`
Don't use the `__cxa_get_exception_ptr` runtime routine. This causes `std::uncaught_exception` to be incorrect, but is necessary if the runtime routine is not available.

`-fvisibility-inlines-hidden`

This switch declares that the user does not attempt to compare pointers to inline functions or methods where the addresses of the two functions are taken in different shared objects.

The effect of this is that GCC may, effectively, mark inline methods with `__attribute__ ((visibility ("hidden")))` so that they do not appear in the export table of a DSO and do not require a PLT indirection when used within the DSO. Enabling this option can have a dramatic effect on load and link times of a DSO as it massively reduces the size of the dynamic export table when the library makes heavy use of templates.

The behavior of this switch is not quite the same as marking the methods as hidden directly, because it does not affect static variables local to the function or cause the compiler to deduce that the function is defined in only one shared object.

You may mark a method as having a visibility explicitly to negate the effect of the switch for that method. For example, if you do want to compare pointers to a particular inline method, you might mark it as having default visibility. Marking the enclosing class with explicit visibility has no effect.

Explicitly instantiated inline methods are unaffected by this option as their linkage might otherwise cross a shared library boundary. See Section 7.5 [Template Instantiation], page 684.

`-fvisibility-ms-compat`

This flag attempts to use visibility settings to make GCC's C++ linkage model compatible with that of Microsoft Visual Studio.

The flag makes these changes to GCC's linkage model:

1. It sets the default visibility to `hidden`, like '`-fvisibility=hidden`'.
2. Types, but not their members, are not hidden by default.
3. The One Definition Rule is relaxed for types without explicit visibility specifications that are defined in more than one shared object: those declarations are permitted if they are permitted when this option is not used.

In new code it is better to use '`-fvisibility=hidden`' and export those classes that are intended to be externally visible. Unfortunately it is possible for code to rely, perhaps accidentally, on the Visual Studio behavior.

Among the consequences of these changes are that static data members of the same type with the same name but defined in different shared objects are different, so changing one does not change the other; and that pointers to function members defined in different shared objects may not compare equal. When this flag is given, it is a violation of the ODR to define types with the same name differently.

`-fno-weak`

Do not use weak symbol support, even if it is provided by the linker. By default, G++ uses weak symbols if they are available. This option exists only for testing, and should not be used by end-users; it results in inferior code and has no benefits. This option may be removed in a future release of G++.

`-nostdinc++`

Do not search for header files in the standard directories specific to C++, but do still search the other standard directories. (This option is used when building the C++ library.)

In addition, these optimization, warning, and code generation options have meanings only for C++ programs:

`-Wabi` (C, Objective-C, C++ and Objective-C++ only)

Warn when G++ it generates code that is probably not compatible with the vendor-neutral C++ ABI. Since G++ now defaults to updating the ABI with each major release, normally '`-Wabi`' will warn only if there is a check added later in a release series for an ABI issue discovered since the initial release. '`-Wabi`' will warn about more things if an older ABI version is selected (with '`-fabi-version=`*n*').

'`-Wabi`' can also be used with an explicit version number to warn about compatibility with a particular '`-fabi-version`' level, e.g. '`-Wabi=2`' to warn about changes relative to '`-fabi-version=2`'.

If an explicit version number is provided and '`-fabi-compat-version`' is not specified, the version number from this option is used for compatibility aliases. If no explicit version number is provided with this option, but '`-fabi-compat-version`' is specified, that version number is used for ABI warnings.

Although an effort has been made to warn about all such cases, there are probably some cases that are not warned about, even though G++ is generating incompatible code. There may also be cases where warnings are emitted even though the code that is generated is compatible.

You should rewrite your code to avoid these warnings if you are concerned about the fact that code generated by G++ may not be binary compatible with code generated by other compilers.

Known incompatibilities in '`-fabi-version=2`' (which was the default from GCC 3.4 to 4.9) include:

- A template with a non-type template parameter of reference type was mangled incorrectly:

  ```
  extern int N;
  template <int &> struct S {};
  void n (S<N>) {2}
  ```

  This was fixed in '`-fabi-version=3`'.

- SIMD vector types declared using `__attribute ((vector_size))` were mangled in a non-standard way that does not allow for overloading of functions taking vectors of different sizes.

  The mangling was changed in '`-fabi-version=4`'.

- `__attribute ((const))` and `noreturn` were mangled as type qualifiers, and `decltype` of a plain declaration was folded away.

  These mangling issues were fixed in '`-fabi-version=5`'.

- Scoped enumerators passed as arguments to a variadic function are promoted like unscoped enumerators, causing `va_arg` to complain. On most targets this does not actually affect the parameter passing ABI, as there is no way to pass an argument smaller than `int`.

  Also, the ABI changed the mangling of template argument packs, `const_cast`, `static_cast`, prefix increment/decrement, and a class scope function used as a template argument.

  These issues were corrected in '`-fabi-version=6`'.
- Lambdas in default argument scope were mangled incorrectly, and the ABI changed the mangling of `nullptr_t`.

  These issues were corrected in '`-fabi-version=7`'.
- When mangling a function type with function-cv-qualifiers, the un-qualified function type was incorrectly treated as a substitution candidate.

  This was fixed in '`-fabi-version=8`', the default for GCC 5.1.
- `decltype(nullptr)` incorrectly had an alignment of 1, leading to unaligned accesses. Note that this did not affect the ABI of a function with a `nullptr_t` parameter, as parameters have a minimum alignment.

  This was fixed in '`-fabi-version=9`', the default for GCC 5.2.
- Target-specific attributes that affect the identity of a type, such as ia32 calling conventions on a function type (stdcall, regparm, etc.), did not affect the mangled name, leading to name collisions when function pointers were used as template arguments.

  This was fixed in '`-fabi-version=10`', the default for GCC 6.1.

It also warns about psABI-related changes. The known psABI changes at this point include:

- For SysV/x86-64, unions with `long double` members are passed in memory as specified in psABI. For example:

```
union U {
  long double ld;
  int i;
};
```

  `union U` is always passed in memory.

`-Wabi-tag` (C++ and Objective-C++ only)
: Warn when a type with an ABI tag is used in a context that does not have that ABI tag. See Section 7.7 [C++ Attributes], page 687 for more information about ABI tags.

`-Wctor-dtor-privacy` (C++ and Objective-C++ only)
: Warn when a class seems unusable because all the constructors or destructors in that class are private, and it has neither friends nor public static member functions. Also warn if there are no non-private methods, and there's at least one private member function that isn't a constructor or destructor.

`-Wdelete-non-virtual-dtor` (C++ and Objective-C++ only)
: Warn when `delete` is used to destroy an instance of a class that has virtual functions and non-virtual destructor. It is unsafe to delete an instance of a

derived class through a pointer to a base class if the base class does not have a virtual destructor. This warning is enabled by '-Wall'.

`-Wliteral-suffix` (C++ and Objective-C++ only)

Warn when a string or character literal is followed by a ud-suffix which does not begin with an underscore. As a conforming extension, GCC treats such suffixes as separate preprocessing tokens in order to maintain backwards compatibility with code that uses formatting macros from `<inttypes.h>`. For example:

```
#define __STDC_FORMAT_MACROS
#include <inttypes.h>
#include <stdio.h>

int main() {
  int64_t i64 = 123;
  printf("My int64: %" PRId64"\n", i64);
}
```

In this case, `PRId64` is treated as a separate preprocessing token.

This warning is enabled by default.

`-Wlto-type-mismatch`

During the link-time optimization warn about type mismatches in global declarations from different compilation units. Requires '-flto' to be enabled. Enabled by default.

`-Wnarrowing` (C++ and Objective-C++ only)

With '-std=gnu++98' or '-std=c++98', warn when a narrowing conversion prohibited by C++11 occurs within '{ }', e.g.

```
int i = { 2.2 }; // error: narrowing from double to int
```

This flag is included in '-Wall' and '-Wc++11-compat'.

When a later standard is in effect, e.g. when using '-std=c++11', narrowing conversions are diagnosed by default, as required by the standard. A narrowing conversion from a constant produces an error, and a narrowing conversion from a non-constant produces a warning, but '-Wno-narrowing' suppresses the diagnostic. Note that this does not affect the meaning of well-formed code; narrowing conversions are still considered ill-formed in SFINAE contexts.

`-Wnoexcept` (C++ and Objective-C++ only)

Warn when a noexcept-expression evaluates to false because of a call to a function that does not have a non-throwing exception specification (i.e. `throw()` or `noexcept`) but is known by the compiler to never throw an exception.

`-Wnon-virtual-dtor` (C++ and Objective-C++ only)

Warn when a class has virtual functions and an accessible non-virtual destructor itself or in an accessible polymorphic base class, in which case it is possible but unsafe to delete an instance of a derived class through a pointer to the class itself or base class. This warning is automatically enabled if '-Weffc++' is specified.

`-Wreorder` (C++ and Objective-C++ only)

Warn when the order of member initializers given in the code does not match the order in which they must be executed. For instance:

```
struct A {
  int i;
  int j;
  A(): j (0), i (1) { }
};
```

The compiler rearranges the member initializers for `i` and `j` to match the declaration order of the members, emitting a warning to that effect. This warning is enabled by '`-Wall`'.

`-fext-numeric-literals` (C++ and Objective-C++ only)
: Accept imaginary, fixed-point, or machine-defined literal number suffixes as GNU extensions. When this option is turned off these suffixes are treated as C++11 user-defined literal numeric suffixes. This is on by default for all pre-C++11 dialects and all GNU dialects: '`-std=c++98`', '`-std=gnu++98`', '`-std=gnu++11`', '`-std=gnu++14`'. This option is off by default for ISO C++11 onwards ('`-std=c++11`', ...).

The following '`-W...`' options are not affected by '`-Wall`'.

`-Weffc++` (C++ and Objective-C++ only)
: Warn about violations of the following style guidelines from Scott Meyers' *Effective C++* series of books:

- Define a copy constructor and an assignment operator for classes with dynamically-allocated memory.
- Prefer initialization to assignment in constructors.
- Have `operator=` return a reference to `*this`.
- Don't try to return a reference when you must return an object.
- Distinguish between prefix and postfix forms of increment and decrement operators.
- Never overload `&&`, `||`, or `,`.

This option also enables '`-Wnon-virtual-dtor`', which is also one of the effective C++ recommendations. However, the check is extended to warn about the lack of virtual destructor in accessible non-polymorphic bases classes too.

When selecting this option, be aware that the standard library headers do not obey all of these guidelines; use '`grep -v`' to filter out those warnings.

`-Wstrict-null-sentinel` (C++ and Objective-C++ only)
: Warn about the use of an uncasted `NULL` as sentinel. When compiling only with GCC this is a valid sentinel, as `NULL` is defined to `__null`. Although it is a null pointer constant rather than a null pointer, it is guaranteed to be of the same size as a pointer. But this use is not portable across different compilers.

`-Wno-non-template-friend` (C++ and Objective-C++ only)
: Disable warnings when non-templatized friend functions are declared within a template. Since the advent of explicit template specification support in G++, if the name of the friend is an unqualified-id (i.e., '`friend foo(int)`'), the C++ language specification demands that the friend declare or define an ordinary, nontemplate function. (Section 14.5.3). Before G++ implemented explicit

specification, unqualified-ids could be interpreted as a particular specialization of a templatized function. Because this non-conforming behavior is no longer the default behavior for G++, '-Wnon-template-friend' allows the compiler to check existing code for potential trouble spots and is on by default. This new compiler behavior can be turned off with '-Wno-non-template-friend', which keeps the conformant compiler code but disables the helpful warning.

-Wold-style-cast (C++ and Objective-C++ only)
: Warn if an old-style (C-style) cast to a non-void type is used within a C++ program. The new-style casts (dynamic_cast, static_cast, reinterpret_cast, and const_cast) are less vulnerable to unintended effects and much easier to search for.

-Woverloaded-virtual (C++ and Objective-C++ only)
: Warn when a function declaration hides virtual functions from a base class. For example, in:

```
struct A {
  virtual void f();
};

struct B: public A {
  void f(int);
};
```

the A class version of f is hidden in B, and code like:

```
B* b;
b->f();
```

fails to compile.

-Wno-pmf-conversions (C++ and Objective-C++ only)
: Disable the diagnostic for converting a bound pointer to member function to a plain pointer.

-Wsign-promo (C++ and Objective-C++ only)
: Warn when overload resolution chooses a promotion from unsigned or enumerated type to a signed type, over a conversion to an unsigned type of the same size. Previous versions of G++ tried to preserve unsignedness, but the standard mandates the current behavior.

-Wtemplates (C++ and Objective-C++ only)
: Warn when a primary template declaration is encountered. Some coding rules disallow templates, and this may be used to enforce that rule. The warning is inactive inside a system header file, such as the STL, so one can still use the STL. One may also instantiate or specialize templates.

-Wmultiple-inheritance (C++ and Objective-C++ only)
: Warn when a class is defined with multiple direct base classes. Some coding rules disallow multiple inheritance, and this may be used to enforce that rule. The warning is inactive inside a system header file, such as the STL, so one can still use the STL. One may also define classes that indirectly use multiple inheritance.

`-Wvirtual-inheritance`
: Warn when a class is defined with a virtual direct base classe. Some coding rules disallow multiple inheritance, and this may be used to enforce that rule. The warning is inactive inside a system header file, such as the STL, so one can still use the STL. One may also define classes that indirectly use virtual inheritance.

`-Wnamespaces`
: Warn when a namespace definition is opened. Some coding rules disallow namespaces, and this may be used to enforce that rule. The warning is inactive inside a system header file, such as the STL, so one can still use the STL. One may also use using directives and qualified names.

`-Wno-terminate` (C++ and Objective-C++ only)
: Disable the warning about a throw-expression that will immediately result in a call to `terminate`.

3.6 Options Controlling Objective-C and Objective-C++ Dialects

(NOTE: This manual does not describe the Objective-C and Objective-C++ languages themselves. See Chapter 2 [Language Standards Supported by GCC], page 5, for references.)

This section describes the command-line options that are only meaningful for Objective-C and Objective-C++ programs. You can also use most of the language-independent GNU compiler options. For example, you might compile a file '`some_class.m`' like this:

```
gcc -g -fgnu-runtime -O -c some_class.m
```

In this example, '`-fgnu-runtime`' is an option meant only for Objective-C and Objective-C++ programs; you can use the other options with any language supported by GCC.

Note that since Objective-C is an extension of the C language, Objective-C compilations may also use options specific to the C front-end (e.g., '`-Wtraditional`'). Similarly, Objective-C++ compilations may use C++-specific options (e.g., '`-Wabi`').

Here is a list of options that are *only* for compiling Objective-C and Objective-C++ programs:

`-fconstant-string-class=`*`class-name`*
: Use *class-name* as the name of the class to instantiate for each literal string specified with the syntax `@"..."`. The default class name is `NXConstantString` if the GNU runtime is being used, and `NSConstantString` if the NeXT runtime is being used (see below). The '`-fconstant-cfstrings`' option, if also present, overrides the '`-fconstant-string-class`' setting and cause `@"..."` literals to be laid out as constant CoreFoundation strings.

`-fgnu-runtime`
: Generate object code compatible with the standard GNU Objective-C runtime. This is the default for most types of systems.

`-fnext-runtime`
: Generate output compatible with the NeXT runtime. This is the default for NeXT-based systems, including Darwin and Mac OS X. The macro `__NEXT_RUNTIME__` is predefined if (and only if) this option is used.

`-fno-nil-receivers`

Assume that all Objective-C message dispatches (`[receiver message:arg]`) in this translation unit ensure that the receiver is not `nil`. This allows for more efficient entry points in the runtime to be used. This option is only available in conjunction with the NeXT runtime and ABI version 0 or 1.

`-fobjc-abi-version=`*n*

Use version *n* of the Objective-C ABI for the selected runtime. This option is currently supported only for the NeXT runtime. In that case, Version 0 is the traditional (32-bit) ABI without support for properties and other Objective-C 2.0 additions. Version 1 is the traditional (32-bit) ABI with support for properties and other Objective-C 2.0 additions. Version 2 is the modern (64-bit) ABI. If nothing is specified, the default is Version 0 on 32-bit target machines, and Version 2 on 64-bit target machines.

`-fobjc-call-cxx-cdtors`

For each Objective-C class, check if any of its instance variables is a C++ object with a non-trivial default constructor. If so, synthesize a special `- (id) .cxx_construct` instance method which runs non-trivial default constructors on any such instance variables, in order, and then return `self`. Similarly, check if any instance variable is a C++ object with a non-trivial destructor, and if so, synthesize a special `- (void) .cxx_destruct` method which runs all such default destructors, in reverse order.

The `- (id) .cxx_construct` and `- (void) .cxx_destruct` methods thusly generated only operate on instance variables declared in the current Objective-C class, and not those inherited from superclasses. It is the responsibility of the Objective-C runtime to invoke all such methods in an object's inheritance hierarchy. The `- (id) .cxx_construct` methods are invoked by the runtime immediately after a new object instance is allocated; the `- (void) .cxx_destruct` methods are invoked immediately before the runtime deallocates an object instance.

As of this writing, only the NeXT runtime on Mac OS X 10.4 and later has support for invoking the `- (id) .cxx_construct` and `- (void) .cxx_destruct` methods.

`-fobjc-direct-dispatch`

Allow fast jumps to the message dispatcher. On Darwin this is accomplished via the comm page.

`-fobjc-exceptions`

Enable syntactic support for structured exception handling in Objective-C, similar to what is offered by C++ and Java. This option is required to use the Objective-C keywords `@try`, `@throw`, `@catch`, `@finally` and `@synchronized`. This option is available with both the GNU runtime and the NeXT runtime (but not available in conjunction with the NeXT runtime on Mac OS X 10.2 and earlier).

`-fobjc-gc`

Enable garbage collection (GC) in Objective-C and Objective-C++ programs. This option is only available with the NeXT runtime; the GNU runtime has a different garbage collection implementation that does not require special compiler flags.

`-fobjc-nilcheck`
For the NeXT runtime with version 2 of the ABI, check for a nil receiver in method invocations before doing the actual method call. This is the default and can be disabled using '`-fno-objc-nilcheck`'. Class methods and super calls are never checked for nil in this way no matter what this flag is set to. Currently this flag does nothing when the GNU runtime, or an older version of the NeXT runtime ABI, is used.

`-fobjc-std=objc1`
Conform to the language syntax of Objective-C 1.0, the language recognized by GCC 4.0. This only affects the Objective-C additions to the C/C++ language; it does not affect conformance to C/C++ standards, which is controlled by the separate C/C++ dialect option flags. When this option is used with the Objective-C or Objective-C++ compiler, any Objective-C syntax that is not recognized by GCC 4.0 is rejected. This is useful if you need to make sure that your Objective-C code can be compiled with older versions of GCC.

`-freplace-objc-classes`
Emit a special marker instructing `ld(1)` not to statically link in the resulting object file, and allow `dyld(1)` to load it in at run time instead. This is used in conjunction with the Fix-and-Continue debugging mode, where the object file in question may be recompiled and dynamically reloaded in the course of program execution, without the need to restart the program itself. Currently, Fix-and-Continue functionality is only available in conjunction with the NeXT runtime on Mac OS X 10.3 and later.

`-fzero-link`
When compiling for the NeXT runtime, the compiler ordinarily replaces calls to `objc_getClass("...")` (when the name of the class is known at compile time) with static class references that get initialized at load time, which improves run-time performance. Specifying the '`-fzero-link`' flag suppresses this behavior and causes calls to `objc_getClass("...")` to be retained. This is useful in Zero-Link debugging mode, since it allows for individual class implementations to be modified during program execution. The GNU runtime currently always retains calls to `objc_get_class("...")` regardless of command-line options.

`-fno-local-ivars`
By default instance variables in Objective-C can be accessed as if they were local variables from within the methods of the class they're declared in. This can lead to shadowing between instance variables and other variables declared either locally inside a class method or globally with the same name. Specifying the '`-fno-local-ivars`' flag disables this behavior thus avoiding variable shadowing issues.

`-fivar-visibility=[public|protected|private|package]`
Set the default instance variable visibility to the specified option so that instance variables declared outside the scope of any access modifier directives default to the specified visibility.

`-gen-decls`
: Dump interface declarations for all classes seen in the source file to a file named '*sourcename*.decl'.

`-Wassign-intercept` (Objective-C and Objective-C++ only)
: Warn whenever an Objective-C assignment is being intercepted by the garbage collector.

`-Wno-protocol` (Objective-C and Objective-C++ only)
: If a class is declared to implement a protocol, a warning is issued for every method in the protocol that is not implemented by the class. The default behavior is to issue a warning for every method not explicitly implemented in the class, even if a method implementation is inherited from the superclass. If you use the '`-Wno-protocol`' option, then methods inherited from the superclass are considered to be implemented, and no warning is issued for them.

`-Wselector` (Objective-C and Objective-C++ only)
: Warn if multiple methods of different types for the same selector are found during compilation. The check is performed on the list of methods in the final stage of compilation. Additionally, a check is performed for each selector appearing in a `@selector(...)` expression, and a corresponding method for that selector has been found during compilation. Because these checks scan the method table only at the end of compilation, these warnings are not produced if the final stage of compilation is not reached, for example because an error is found during compilation, or because the '`-fsyntax-only`' option is being used.

`-Wstrict-selector-match` (Objective-C and Objective-C++ only)
: Warn if multiple methods with differing argument and/or return types are found for a given selector when attempting to send a message using this selector to a receiver of type `id` or `Class`. When this flag is off (which is the default behavior), the compiler omits such warnings if any differences found are confined to types that share the same size and alignment.

`-Wundeclared-selector` (Objective-C and Objective-C++ only)
: Warn if a `@selector(...)` expression referring to an undeclared selector is found. A selector is considered undeclared if no method with that name has been declared before the `@selector(...)` expression, either explicitly in an `@interface` or `@protocol` declaration, or implicitly in an `@implementation` section. This option always performs its checks as soon as a `@selector(...)` expression is found, while '`-Wselector`' only performs its checks in the final stage of compilation. This also enforces the coding style convention that methods and selectors must be declared before being used.

`-print-objc-runtime-info`
: Generate C header describing the largest structure that is passed by value, if any.

3.7 Options to Control Diagnostic Messages Formatting

Traditionally, diagnostic messages have been formatted irrespective of the output device's aspect (e.g. its width, ...). You can use the options described below to control the formatting algorithm for diagnostic messages, e.g. how many characters per line, how often source location information should be reported. Note that some language front ends may not honor these options.

`-fmessage-length=`*n*
: Try to format error messages so that they fit on lines of about *n* characters. If *n* is zero, then no line-wrapping is done; each error message appears on a single line. This is the default for all front ends.

`-fdiagnostics-show-location=once`
: Only meaningful in line-wrapping mode. Instructs the diagnostic messages reporter to emit source location information *once*; that is, in case the message is too long to fit on a single physical line and has to be wrapped, the source location won't be emitted (as prefix) again, over and over, in subsequent continuation lines. This is the default behavior.

`-fdiagnostics-show-location=every-line`
: Only meaningful in line-wrapping mode. Instructs the diagnostic messages reporter to emit the same source location information (as prefix) for physical lines that result from the process of breaking a message which is too long to fit on a single line.

`-fdiagnostics-color[=`*WHEN*`]`
`-fno-diagnostics-color`
: Use color in diagnostics. *WHEN* is '`never`', '`always`', or '`auto`'. The default depends on how the compiler has been configured, it can be any of the above *WHEN* options or also '`never`' if `GCC_COLORS` environment variable isn't present in the environment, and '`auto`' otherwise. '`auto`' means to use color only when the standard error is a terminal. The forms '`-fdiagnostics-color`' and '`-fno-diagnostics-color`' are aliases for '`-fdiagnostics-color=always`' and '`-fdiagnostics-color=never`', respectively.

The colors are defined by the environment variable `GCC_COLORS`. Its value is a colon-separated list of capabilities and Select Graphic Rendition (SGR) substrings. SGR commands are interpreted by the terminal or terminal emulator. (See the section in the documentation of your text terminal for permitted values and their meanings as character attributes.) These substring values are integers in decimal representation and can be concatenated with semicolons. Common values to concatenate include '`1`' for bold, '`4`' for underline, '`5`' for blink, '`7`' for inverse, '`39`' for default foreground color, '`30`' to '`37`' for foreground colors, '`90`' to '`97`' for 16-color mode foreground colors, '`38;5;0`' to '`38;5;255`' for 88-color and 256-color modes foreground colors, '`49`' for default background color, '`40`' to '`47`' for background colors, '`100`' to '`107`' for 16-color mode background colors, and '`48;5;0`' to '`48;5;255`' for 88-color and 256-color modes background colors.

The default `GCC_COLORS` is

```
error=01;31:warning=01;35:note=01;36:caret=01;32:locus=01:quote=01
```

where '`01;31`' is bold red, '`01;35`' is bold magenta, '`01;36`' is bold cyan, '`01;32`' is bold green and '`01`' is bold. Setting `GCC_COLORS` to the empty string disables colors. Supported capabilities are as follows.

`error=` SGR substring for error: markers.

`warning=` SGR substring for warning: markers.

`note=` SGR substring for note: markers.

`caret=` SGR substring for caret line.

`locus=` SGR substring for location information, '`file:line`' or '`file:line:column`' etc.

`quote=` SGR substring for information printed within quotes.

`-fno-diagnostics-show-option`

By default, each diagnostic emitted includes text indicating the command-line option that directly controls the diagnostic (if such an option is known to the diagnostic machinery). Specifying the '`-fno-diagnostics-show-option`' flag suppresses that behavior.

`-fno-diagnostics-show-caret`

By default, each diagnostic emitted includes the original source line and a caret '^' indicating the column. This option suppresses this information. The source line is truncated to *n* characters, if the '`-fmessage-length=n`' option is given. When the output is done to the terminal, the width is limited to the width given by the `COLUMNS` environment variable or, if not set, to the terminal width.

3.8 Options to Request or Suppress Warnings

Warnings are diagnostic messages that report constructions that are not inherently erroneous but that are risky or suggest there may have been an error.

The following language-independent options do not enable specific warnings but control the kinds of diagnostics produced by GCC.

`-fsyntax-only`

Check the code for syntax errors, but don't do anything beyond that.

`-fmax-errors=`*n*

Limits the maximum number of error messages to *n*, at which point GCC bails out rather than attempting to continue processing the source code. If *n* is 0 (the default), there is no limit on the number of error messages produced. If '`-Wfatal-errors`' is also specified, then '`-Wfatal-errors`' takes precedence over this option.

`-w` Inhibit all warning messages.

`-Werror` Make all warnings into errors.

`-Werror=` Make the specified warning into an error. The specifier for a warning is appended; for example '`-Werror=switch`' turns the warnings controlled by '`-Wswitch`' into errors. This switch takes a negative form, to be used to negate '`-Werror`' for specific warnings; for example '`-Wno-error=switch`' makes '`-Wswitch`' warnings not be errors, even when '`-Werror`' is in effect.

The warning message for each controllable warning includes the option that controls the warning. That option can then be used with '`-Werror=`' and '`-Wno-error=`' as described above. (Printing of the option in the warning message can be disabled using the '`-fno-diagnostics-show-option`' flag.)

Note that specifying '`-Werror=`'*foo* automatically implies '`-W`'*foo*. However, '`-Wno-error=`'*foo* does not imply anything.

`-Wfatal-errors`

This option causes the compiler to abort compilation on the first error occurred rather than trying to keep going and printing further error messages.

You can request many specific warnings with options beginning with '`-W`', for example '`-Wimplicit`' to request warnings on implicit declarations. Each of these specific warning options also has a negative form beginning '`-Wno-`' to turn off warnings; for example, '`-Wno-implicit`'. This manual lists only one of the two forms, whichever is not the default. For further language-specific options also refer to Section 3.5 [C++ Dialect Options], page 39 and Section 3.6 [Objective-C and Objective-C++ Dialect Options], page 51.

Some options, such as '`-Wall`' and '`-Wextra`', turn on other options, such as '`-Wunused`', which may turn on further options, such as '`-Wunused-value`'. The combined effect of positive and negative forms is that more specific options have priority over less specific ones, independently of their position in the command-line. For options of the same specificity, the last one takes effect. Options enabled or disabled via pragmas (see Section 6.61.12 [Diagnostic Pragmas], page 673) take effect as if they appeared at the end of the command-line.

When an unrecognized warning option is requested (e.g., '`-Wunknown-warning`'), GCC emits a diagnostic stating that the option is not recognized. However, if the '`-Wno-`' form is used, the behavior is slightly different: no diagnostic is produced for '`-Wno-unknown-warning`' unless other diagnostics are being produced. This allows the use of new '`-Wno-`' options with old compilers, but if something goes wrong, the compiler warns that an unrecognized option is present.

`-Wpedantic`
`-pedantic`

Issue all the warnings demanded by strict ISO C and ISO C++; reject all programs that use forbidden extensions, and some other programs that do not follow ISO C and ISO C++. For ISO C, follows the version of the ISO C standard specified by any '`-std`' option used.

Valid ISO C and ISO C++ programs should compile properly with or without this option (though a rare few require '`-ansi`' or a '`-std`' option specifying the required version of ISO C). However, without this option, certain GNU extensions and traditional C and C++ features are supported as well. With this option, they are rejected.

'-Wpedantic' does not cause warning messages for use of the alternate keywords whose names begin and end with '__'. Pedantic warnings are also disabled in the expression that follows `__extension__`. However, only system header files should use these escape routes; application programs should avoid them. See Section 6.45 [Alternate Keywords], page 527.

Some users try to use '-Wpedantic' to check programs for strict ISO C conformance. They soon find that it does not do quite what they want: it finds some non-ISO practices, but not all—only those for which ISO C *requires* a diagnostic, and some others for which diagnostics have been added.

A feature to report any failure to conform to ISO C might be useful in some instances, but would require considerable additional work and would be quite different from '-Wpedantic'. We don't have plans to support such a feature in the near future.

Where the standard specified with '-std' represents a GNU extended dialect of C, such as 'gnu90' or 'gnu99', there is a corresponding *base standard*, the version of ISO C on which the GNU extended dialect is based. Warnings from '-Wpedantic' are given where they are required by the base standard. (It does not make sense for such warnings to be given only for features not in the specified GNU C dialect, since by definition the GNU dialects of C include all features the compiler supports with the given option, and there would be nothing to warn about.)

`-pedantic-errors`

Give an error whenever the *base standard* (see '-Wpedantic') requires a diagnostic, in some cases where there is undefined behavior at compile-time and in some other cases that do not prevent compilation of programs that are valid according to the standard. This is not equivalent to '-Werror=pedantic', since there are errors enabled by this option and not enabled by the latter and vice versa.

`-Wall` This enables all the warnings about constructions that some users consider questionable, and that are easy to avoid (or modify to prevent the warning), even in conjunction with macros. This also enables some language-specific warnings described in Section 3.5 [C++ Dialect Options], page 39 and Section 3.6 [Objective-C and Objective-C++ Dialect Options], page 51.

'-Wall' turns on the following warning flags:

-Waddress
-Warray-bounds=1 (only with '-O2')
-Wbool-compare
-Wc++11-compat -Wc++14-compat
-Wchar-subscripts
-Wcomment
-Wenum-compare (in C/ObjC; this is on by default in C++)
-Wformat
-Wimplicit (C and Objective-C only)
-Wimplicit-int (C and Objective-C only)
-Wimplicit-function-declaration (C and Objective-C only)
-Winit-self (only for C++)
-Wlogical-not-parentheses -Wmain (only for C/ObjC and unless '-ffreestanding')
-Wmaybe-uninitialized

```
-Wmemset-transposed-args
-Wmisleading-indentation (only for C/C++)
-Wmissing-braces (only for C/ObjC)
-Wnarrowing (only for C++)
-Wnonnull
-Wnonnull-compare
-Wopenmp-simd
-Wparentheses
-Wpointer-sign
-Wreorder
-Wreturn-type
-Wsequence-point
-Wsign-compare (only in C++)
-Wsizeof-pointer-memaccess
-Wstrict-aliasing
-Wstrict-overflow=1
-Wswitch
-Wtautological-compare
-Wtrigraphs
-Wuninitialized
-Wunknown-pragmas
-Wunused-function
-Wunused-label
-Wunused-value
-Wunused-variable
-Wvolatile-register-var
```

Note that some warning flags are not implied by '-Wall'. Some of them warn about constructions that users generally do not consider questionable, but which occasionally you might wish to check for; others warn about constructions that are necessary or hard to avoid in some cases, and there is no simple way to modify the code to suppress the warning. Some of them are enabled by '-Wextra' but many of them must be enabled individually.

`-Wextra` This enables some extra warning flags that are not enabled by '-Wall'. (This option used to be called '-W'. The older name is still supported, but the newer name is more descriptive.)

```
-Wclobbered
-Wempty-body
-Wignored-qualifiers
-Wmissing-field-initializers
-Wmissing-parameter-type (C only)
-Wold-style-declaration (C only)
-Woverride-init
-Wsign-compare (C only)
-Wtype-limits
-Wuninitialized
-Wshift-negative-value (in C++03 and in C99 and newer)
-Wunused-parameter (only with '-Wunused' or '-Wall')
-Wunused-but-set-parameter (only with '-Wunused' or '-Wall')
```

The option '-Wextra' also prints warning messages for the following cases:

- A pointer is compared against integer zero with `<`, `<=`, `>`, or `>=`.
- (C++ only) An enumerator and a non-enumerator both appear in a conditional expression.

- (C++ only) Ambiguous virtual bases.
- (C++ only) Subscripting an array that has been declared `register`.
- (C++ only) Taking the address of a variable that has been declared `register`.
- (C++ only) A base class is not initialized in a derived class's copy constructor.

`-Wchar-subscripts`
: Warn if an array subscript has type `char`. This is a common cause of error, as programmers often forget that this type is signed on some machines. This warning is enabled by '`-Wall`'.

`-Wcomment`
: Warn whenever a comment-start sequence '`/*`' appears in a '`/*`' comment, or whenever a Backslash-Newline appears in a '`//`' comment. This warning is enabled by '`-Wall`'.

`-Wno-coverage-mismatch`
: Warn if feedback profiles do not match when using the '`-fprofile-use`' option. If a source file is changed between compiling with '`-fprofile-gen`' and with '`-fprofile-use`', the files with the profile feedback can fail to match the source file and GCC cannot use the profile feedback information. By default, this warning is enabled and is treated as an error. '`-Wno-coverage-mismatch`' can be used to disable the warning or '`-Wno-error=coverage-mismatch`' can be used to disable the error. Disabling the error for this warning can result in poorly optimized code and is useful only in the case of very minor changes such as bug fixes to an existing code-base. Completely disabling the warning is not recommended.

`-Wno-cpp` (C, Objective-C, C++, Objective-C++ and Fortran only)
: Suppress warning messages emitted by `#warning` directives.

`-Wdouble-promotion` (C, C++, Objective-C and Objective-C++ only)
: Give a warning when a value of type `float` is implicitly promoted to `double`. CPUs with a 32-bit "single-precision" floating-point unit implement `float` in hardware, but emulate `double` in software. On such a machine, doing computations using `double` values is much more expensive because of the overhead required for software emulation.

It is easy to accidentally do computations with `double` because floating-point literals are implicitly of type `double`. For example, in:

```
float area(float radius)
{
   return 3.14159 * radius * radius;
}
```

the compiler performs the entire computation with `double` because the floating-point literal is a `double`.

`-Wformat`
`-Wformat=n`

Check calls to `printf` and `scanf`, etc., to make sure that the arguments supplied have types appropriate to the format string specified, and that the conversions specified in the format string make sense. This includes standard functions, and others specified by format attributes (see Section 6.31 [Function Attributes], page 407), in the `printf`, `scanf`, `strftime` and `strfmon` (an X/Open extension, not in the C standard) families (or other target-specific families). Which functions are checked without format attributes having been specified depends on the standard version selected, and such checks of functions without the attribute specified are disabled by '`-ffreestanding`' or '`-fno-builtin`'.

The formats are checked against the format features supported by GNU libc version 2.2. These include all ISO C90 and C99 features, as well as features from the Single Unix Specification and some BSD and GNU extensions. Other library implementations may not support all these features; GCC does not support warning about features that go beyond a particular library's limitations. However, if '`-Wpedantic`' is used with '`-Wformat`', warnings are given about format features not in the selected standard version (but not for `strfmon` formats, since those are not in any version of the C standard). See Section 3.4 [Options Controlling C Dialect], page 33.

`-Wformat=1`
`-Wformat`

Option '`-Wformat`' is equivalent to '`-Wformat=1`', and '`-Wno-format`' is equivalent to '`-Wformat=0`'. Since '`-Wformat`' also checks for null format arguments for several functions, '`-Wformat`' also implies '`-Wnonnull`'. Some aspects of this level of format checking can be disabled by the options: '`-Wno-format-contains-nul`', '`-Wno-format-extra-args`', and '`-Wno-format-zero-length`'. '`-Wformat`' is enabled by '`-Wall`'.

`-Wno-format-contains-nul`

If '`-Wformat`' is specified, do not warn about format strings that contain NUL bytes.

`-Wno-format-extra-args`

If '`-Wformat`' is specified, do not warn about excess arguments to a `printf` or `scanf` format function. The C standard specifies that such arguments are ignored.

Where the unused arguments lie between used arguments that are specified with '`$`' operand number specifications, normally warnings are still given, since the implementation could not know what type to pass to `va_arg` to skip the unused arguments. However, in the case of `scanf` formats, this option suppresses the warning if the unused arguments are all pointers, since the Single Unix Specification says that such unused arguments are allowed.

`-Wno-format-zero-length`

If '`-Wformat`' is specified, do not warn about zero-length formats. The C standard specifies that zero-length formats are allowed.

`-Wformat=2`
: Enable '`-Wformat`' plus additional format checks. Currently equivalent to '`-Wformat -Wformat-nonliteral -Wformat-security -Wformat-y2k`'.

`-Wformat-nonliteral`
: If '`-Wformat`' is specified, also warn if the format string is not a string literal and so cannot be checked, unless the format function takes its format arguments as a `va_list`.

`-Wformat-security`
: If '`-Wformat`' is specified, also warn about uses of format functions that represent possible security problems. At present, this warns about calls to `printf` and `scanf` functions where the format string is not a string literal and there are no format arguments, as in `printf (foo);`. This may be a security hole if the format string came from untrusted input and contains '`%n`'. (This is currently a subset of what '`-Wformat-nonliteral`' warns about, but in future warnings may be added to '`-Wformat-security`' that are not included in '`-Wformat-nonliteral`'.)

`-Wformat-signedness`
: If '`-Wformat`' is specified, also warn if the format string requires an unsigned argument and the argument is signed and vice versa.

`-Wformat-y2k`
: If '`-Wformat`' is specified, also warn about `strftime` formats that may yield only a two-digit year.

`-Wnonnull`

Warn about passing a null pointer for arguments marked as requiring a non-null value by the `nonnull` function attribute.

'`-Wnonnull`' is included in '`-Wall`' and '`-Wformat`'. It can be disabled with the '`-Wno-nonnull`' option.

`-Wnonnull-compare`

Warn when comparing an argument marked with the `nonnull` function attribute against null inside the function.

'`-Wnonnull-compare`' is included in '`-Wall`'. It can be disabled with the '`-Wno-nonnull-compare`' option.

`-Wnull-dereference`

Warn if the compiler detects paths that trigger erroneous or undefined behavior due to dereferencing a null pointer. This option is only active when '`-fdelete-null-pointer-checks`' is active, which is enabled by optimizations in most targets. The precision of the warnings depends on the optimization options used.

`-Winit-self` (C, C++, Objective-C and Objective-C++ only)

Warn about uninitialized variables that are initialized with themselves. Note this option can only be used with the '`-Wuninitialized`' option.

For example, GCC warns about `i` being uninitialized in the following snippet only when '`-Winit-self`' has been specified:

```
int f()
{
  int i = i;
  return i;
}
```

This warning is enabled by '`-Wall`' in C++.

`-Wimplicit-int` (C and Objective-C only)
: Warn when a declaration does not specify a type. This warning is enabled by '`-Wall`'.

`-Wimplicit-function-declaration` (C and Objective-C only)
: Give a warning whenever a function is used before being declared. In C99 mode ('`-std=c99`' or '`-std=gnu99`'), this warning is enabled by default and it is made into an error by '`-pedantic-errors`'. This warning is also enabled by '`-Wall`'.

`-Wimplicit` (C and Objective-C only)
: Same as '`-Wimplicit-int`' and '`-Wimplicit-function-declaration`'. This warning is enabled by '`-Wall`'.

`-Wignored-qualifiers` (C and C++ only)
: Warn if the return type of a function has a type qualifier such as `const`. For ISO C such a type qualifier has no effect, since the value returned by a function is not an lvalue. For C++, the warning is only emitted for scalar types or `void`. ISO C prohibits qualified `void` return types on function definitions, so such return types always receive a warning even without this option.

This warning is also enabled by '`-Wextra`'.

`-Wignored-attributes` (C and C++ only)
: Warn when an attribute is ignored. This is different from the '`-Wattributes`' option in that it warns whenever the compiler decides to drop an attribute, not that the attribute is either unknown, used in a wrong place, etc. This warning is enabled by default.

`-Wmain`
: Warn if the type of `main` is suspicious. `main` should be a function with external linkage, returning int, taking either zero arguments, two, or three arguments of appropriate types. This warning is enabled by default in C++ and is enabled by either '`-Wall`' or '`-Wpedantic`'.

`-Wmisleading-indentation` (C and C++ only)
: Warn when the indentation of the code does not reflect the block structure. Specifically, a warning is issued for `if`, `else`, `while`, and `for` clauses with a guarded statement that does not use braces, followed by an unguarded statement with the same indentation.

In the following example, the call to "bar" is misleadingly indented as if it were guarded by the "if" conditional.

```
if (some_condition ())
  foo ();
  bar ();  /* Gotcha: this is not guarded by the "if".  */
```

In the case of mixed tabs and spaces, the warning uses the '-ftabstop=' option to determine if the statements line up (defaulting to 8).

The warning is not issued for code involving multiline preprocessor logic such as the following example.

```
    if (flagA)
      foo (0);
#if SOME_CONDITION_THAT_DOES_NOT_HOLD
    if (flagB)
#endif
      foo (1);
```

The warning is not issued after a #line directive, since this typically indicates autogenerated code, and no assumptions can be made about the layout of the file that the directive references.

This warning is enabled by '-Wall' in C and C++.

-Wmissing-braces

Warn if an aggregate or union initializer is not fully bracketed. In the following example, the initializer for a is not fully bracketed, but that for b is fully bracketed. This warning is enabled by '-Wall' in C.

```
int a[2][2] = { 0, 1, 2, 3 };
int b[2][2] = { { 0, 1 }, { 2, 3 } };
```

This warning is enabled by '-Wall'.

-Wmissing-include-dirs (C, C++, Objective-C and Objective-C++ only)

Warn if a user-supplied include directory does not exist.

-Wparentheses

Warn if parentheses are omitted in certain contexts, such as when there is an assignment in a context where a truth value is expected, or when operators are nested whose precedence people often get confused about.

Also warn if a comparison like x<=y<=z appears; this is equivalent to (x<=y ? 1 : 0) <= z, which is a different interpretation from that of ordinary mathematical notation.

Also warn about constructions where there may be confusion to which if statement an else branch belongs. Here is an example of such a case:

```
{
  if (a)
    if (b)
      foo ();
  else
    bar ();
}
```

In C/C++, every else branch belongs to the innermost possible if statement, which in this example is if (b). This is often not what the programmer expected, as illustrated in the above example by indentation the programmer chose. When there is the potential for this confusion, GCC issues a warning when this flag is specified. To eliminate the warning, add explicit braces around the innermost if statement so there is no way the else can belong to the enclosing if. The resulting code looks like this:

```
{
  if (a)
    {
      if (b)
        foo ();
      else
        bar ();
    }
}
```

Also warn for dangerous uses of the GNU extension to `?:` with omitted middle operand. When the condition in the `?:` operator is a boolean expression, the omitted value is always 1. Often programmers expect it to be a value computed inside the conditional expression instead.

This warning is enabled by '`-Wall`'.

`-Wsequence-point`

Warn about code that may have undefined semantics because of violations of sequence point rules in the C and C++ standards.

The C and C++ standards define the order in which expressions in a C/C++ program are evaluated in terms of *sequence points*, which represent a partial ordering between the execution of parts of the program: those executed before the sequence point, and those executed after it. These occur after the evaluation of a full expression (one which is not part of a larger expression), after the evaluation of the first operand of a `&&`, `||`, `? :` or `,` (comma) operator, before a function is called (but after the evaluation of its arguments and the expression denoting the called function), and in certain other places. Other than as expressed by the sequence point rules, the order of evaluation of subexpressions of an expression is not specified. All these rules describe only a partial order rather than a total order, since, for example, if two functions are called within one expression with no sequence point between them, the order in which the functions are called is not specified. However, the standards committee have ruled that function calls do not overlap.

It is not specified when between sequence points modifications to the values of objects take effect. Programs whose behavior depends on this have undefined behavior; the C and C++ standards specify that "Between the previous and next sequence point an object shall have its stored value modified at most once by the evaluation of an expression. Furthermore, the prior value shall be read only to determine the value to be stored.". If a program breaks these rules, the results on any particular implementation are entirely unpredictable.

Examples of code with undefined behavior are `a = a++;`, `a[n] = b[n++]` and `a[i++] = i;`. Some more complicated cases are not diagnosed by this option, and it may give an occasional false positive result, but in general it has been found fairly effective at detecting this sort of problem in programs.

The standard is worded confusingly, therefore there is some debate over the precise meaning of the sequence point rules in subtle cases. Links to discussions of the problem, including proposed formal definitions, may be found on the GCC readings page, at `http://gcc.gnu.org/readings.html`.

This warning is enabled by '`-Wall`' for C and C++.

`-Wno-return-local-addr`
: Do not warn about returning a pointer (or in C++, a reference) to a variable that goes out of scope after the function returns.

`-Wreturn-type`
: Warn whenever a function is defined with a return type that defaults to `int`. Also warn about any `return` statement with no return value in a function whose return type is not `void` (falling off the end of the function body is considered returning without a value), and about a `return` statement with an expression in a function whose return type is `void`.

For C++, a function without return type always produces a diagnostic message, even when '`-Wno-return-type`' is specified. The only exceptions are `main` and functions defined in system headers.

This warning is enabled by '`-Wall`'.

`-Wshift-count-negative`
: Warn if shift count is negative. This warning is enabled by default.

`-Wshift-count-overflow`
: Warn if shift count >= width of type. This warning is enabled by default.

`-Wshift-negative-value`
: Warn if left shifting a negative value. This warning is enabled by '`-Wextra`' in C99 and C++11 modes (and newer).

`-Wshift-overflow`
`-Wshift-overflow=`*n*
: Warn about left shift overflows. This warning is enabled by default in C99 and C++11 modes (and newer).

`-Wshift-overflow=1`
: This is the warning level of '`-Wshift-overflow`' and is enabled by default in C99 and C++11 modes (and newer). This warning level does not warn about left-shifting 1 into the sign bit. (However, in C, such an overflow is still rejected in contexts where an integer constant expression is required.)

`-Wshift-overflow=2`
: This warning level also warns about left-shifting 1 into the sign bit, unless C++14 mode is active.

`-Wswitch`
: Warn whenever a `switch` statement has an index of enumerated type and lacks a `case` for one or more of the named codes of that enumeration. (The presence of a `default` label prevents this warning.) `case` labels outside the enumeration range also provoke warnings when this option is used (even if there is a `default` label). This warning is enabled by '`-Wall`'.

`-Wswitch-default`
: Warn whenever a `switch` statement does not have a `default` case.

`-Wswitch-enum`
: Warn whenever a `switch` statement has an index of enumerated type and lacks a `case` for one or more of the named codes of that enumeration. `case` labels

outside the enumeration range also provoke warnings when this option is used. The only difference between '-Wswitch' and this option is that this option gives a warning about an omitted enumeration code even if there is a default label.

-Wswitch-bool
: Warn whenever a switch statement has an index of boolean type and the case values are outside the range of a boolean type. It is possible to suppress this warning by casting the controlling expression to a type other than bool. For example:

```
switch ((int) (a == 4))
  {
  ...
  }
```

This warning is enabled by default for C and C++ programs.

-Wsync-nand (C and C++ only)
: Warn when __sync_fetch_and_nand and __sync_nand_and_fetch built-in functions are used. These functions changed semantics in GCC 4.4.

-Wtrigraphs
: Warn if any trigraphs are encountered that might change the meaning of the program (trigraphs within comments are not warned about). This warning is enabled by '-Wall'.

-Wunused-but-set-parameter
: Warn whenever a function parameter is assigned to, but otherwise unused (aside from its declaration).

To suppress this warning use the unused attribute (see Section 6.32 [Variable Attributes], page 450).

This warning is also enabled by '-Wunused' together with '-Wextra'.

-Wunused-but-set-variable
: Warn whenever a local variable is assigned to, but otherwise unused (aside from its declaration). This warning is enabled by '-Wall'.

To suppress this warning use the unused attribute (see Section 6.32 [Variable Attributes], page 450).

This warning is also enabled by '-Wunused', which is enabled by '-Wall'.

-Wunused-function
: Warn whenever a static function is declared but not defined or a non-inline static function is unused. This warning is enabled by '-Wall'.

-Wunused-label
: Warn whenever a label is declared but not used. This warning is enabled by '-Wall'.

To suppress this warning use the unused attribute (see Section 6.32 [Variable Attributes], page 450).

-Wunused-local-typedefs (C, Objective-C, C++ and Objective-C++ only)
: Warn when a typedef locally defined in a function is not used. This warning is enabled by '-Wall'.

-Wunused-parameter
: Warn whenever a function parameter is unused aside from its declaration.

  To suppress this warning use the unused attribute (see Section 6.32 [Variable Attributes], page 450).

-Wno-unused-result
: Do not warn if a caller of a function marked with attribute warn_unused_result (see Section 6.31 [Function Attributes], page 407) does not use its return value. The default is '-Wunused-result'.

-Wunused-variable
: Warn whenever a local or static variable is unused aside from its declaration. This option implies '-Wunused-const-variable=1' for C, but not for C++. This warning is enabled by '-Wall'.

  To suppress this warning use the unused attribute (see Section 6.32 [Variable Attributes], page 450).

-Wunused-const-variable
-Wunused-const-variable=*n*
: Warn whenever a constant static variable is unused aside from its declaration. '-Wunused-const-variable=1' is enabled by '-Wunused-variable' for C, but not for C++. In C this declares variable storage, but in C++ this is not an error since const variables take the place of #defines.

  To suppress this warning use the unused attribute (see Section 6.32 [Variable Attributes], page 450).

  -Wunused-const-variable=1
  : This is the warning level that is enabled by '-Wunused-variable' for C. It warns only about unused static const variables defined in the main compilation unit, but not about static const variables declared in any header included.

  -Wunused-const-variable=2
  : This warning level also warns for unused constant static variables in headers (excluding system headers). This is the warning level of '-Wunused-const-variable' and must be explicitly requested since in C++ this isn't an error and in C it might be harder to clean up all headers included.

-Wunused-value
: Warn whenever a statement computes a result that is explicitly not used. To suppress this warning cast the unused expression to void. This includes an expression-statement or the left-hand side of a comma expression that contains no side effects. For example, an expression such as x[i,j] causes a warning, while x[(void)i,j] does not.

  This warning is enabled by '-Wall'.

-Wunused
: All the above '-Wunused' options combined.

  In order to get a warning about an unused function parameter, you must either specify '-Wextra -Wunused' (note that '-Wall' implies '-Wunused'), or separately specify '-Wunused-parameter'.

-Wuninitialized

Warn if an automatic variable is used without first being initialized or if a variable may be clobbered by a setjmp call. In C++, warn if a non-static reference or non-static const member appears in a class without constructors.

If you want to warn about code that uses the uninitialized value of the variable in its own initializer, use the '-Winit-self' option.

These warnings occur for individual uninitialized or clobbered elements of structure, union or array variables as well as for variables that are uninitialized or clobbered as a whole. They do not occur for variables or elements declared volatile. Because these warnings depend on optimization, the exact variables or elements for which there are warnings depends on the precise optimization options and version of GCC used.

Note that there may be no warning about a variable that is used only to compute a value that itself is never used, because such computations may be deleted by data flow analysis before the warnings are printed.

-Winvalid-memory-model

Warn for invocations of Section 6.52 [__atomic Builtins], page 534, Section 6.51 [__sync Builtins], page 532, and the C11 atomic generic functions with a memory consistency argument that is either invalid for the operation or outside the range of values of the memory_order enumeration. For example, since the __atomic_store and __atomic_store_n built-ins are only defined for the relaxed, release, and sequentially consistent memory orders the following code is diagnosed:

```
void store (int *i)
{
  __atomic_store_n (i, 0, memory_order_consume);
}
```

'-Winvalid-memory-model' is enabled by default.

-Wmaybe-uninitialized

For an automatic variable, if there exists a path from the function entry to a use of the variable that is initialized, but there exist some other paths for which the variable is not initialized, the compiler emits a warning if it cannot prove the uninitialized paths are not executed at run time. These warnings are made optional because GCC is not smart enough to see all the reasons why the code might be correct in spite of appearing to have an error. Here is one example of how this can happen:

```
{
  int x;
  switch (y)
    {
    case 1: x = 1;
      break;
    case 2: x = 4;
      break;
    case 3: x = 5;
    }
  foo (x);
}
```

If the value of `y` is always 1, 2 or 3, then `x` is always initialized, but GCC doesn't know this. To suppress the warning, you need to provide a default case with assert(0) or similar code.

This option also warns when a non-volatile automatic variable might be changed by a call to `longjmp`. These warnings as well are possible only in optimizing compilation.

The compiler sees only the calls to `setjmp`. It cannot know where `longjmp` will be called; in fact, a signal handler could call it at any point in the code. As a result, you may get a warning even when there is in fact no problem because `longjmp` cannot in fact be called at the place that would cause a problem.

Some spurious warnings can be avoided if you declare all the functions you use that never return as `noreturn`. See Section 6.31 [Function Attributes], page 407.

This warning is enabled by '`-Wall`' or '`-Wextra`'.

`-Wunknown-pragmas`
: Warn when a `#pragma` directive is encountered that is not understood by GCC. If this command-line option is used, warnings are even issued for unknown pragmas in system header files. This is not the case if the warnings are only enabled by the '`-Wall`' command-line option.

`-Wno-pragmas`
: Do not warn about misuses of pragmas, such as incorrect parameters, invalid syntax, or conflicts between pragmas. See also '`-Wunknown-pragmas`'.

`-Wstrict-aliasing`
: This option is only active when '`-fstrict-aliasing`' is active. It warns about code that might break the strict aliasing rules that the compiler is using for optimization. The warning does not catch all cases, but does attempt to catch the more common pitfalls. It is included in '`-Wall`'. It is equivalent to '`-Wstrict-aliasing=3`'

`-Wstrict-aliasing=n`
: This option is only active when '`-fstrict-aliasing`' is active. It warns about code that might break the strict aliasing rules that the compiler is using for optimization. Higher levels correspond to higher accuracy (fewer false positives). Higher levels also correspond to more effort, similar to the way '`-O`' works. '`-Wstrict-aliasing`' is equivalent to '`-Wstrict-aliasing=3`'.

Level 1: Most aggressive, quick, least accurate. Possibly useful when higher levels do not warn but '`-fstrict-aliasing`' still breaks the code, as it has very few false negatives. However, it has many false positives. Warns for all pointer conversions between possibly incompatible types, even if never dereferenced. Runs in the front end only.

Level 2: Aggressive, quick, not too precise. May still have many false positives (not as many as level 1 though), and few false negatives (but possibly more than level 1). Unlike level 1, it only warns when an address is taken. Warns about incomplete types. Runs in the front end only.

Level 3 (default for '-Wstrict-aliasing'): Should have very few false positives and few false negatives. Slightly slower than levels 1 or 2 when optimization is enabled. Takes care of the common pun+dereference pattern in the front end: `*(int*)&some_float`. If optimization is enabled, it also runs in the back end, where it deals with multiple statement cases using flow-sensitive points-to information. Only warns when the converted pointer is dereferenced. Does not warn about incomplete types.

`-Wstrict-overflow`
`-Wstrict-overflow=n`

This option is only active when '-fstrict-overflow' is active. It warns about cases where the compiler optimizes based on the assumption that signed overflow does not occur. Note that it does not warn about all cases where the code might overflow: it only warns about cases where the compiler implements some optimization. Thus this warning depends on the optimization level.

An optimization that assumes that signed overflow does not occur is perfectly safe if the values of the variables involved are such that overflow never does, in fact, occur. Therefore this warning can easily give a false positive: a warning about code that is not actually a problem. To help focus on important issues, several warning levels are defined. No warnings are issued for the use of undefined signed overflow when estimating how many iterations a loop requires, in particular when determining whether a loop will be executed at all.

`-Wstrict-overflow=1`

Warn about cases that are both questionable and easy to avoid. For example, with '-fstrict-overflow', the compiler simplifies `x + 1 > x` to `1`. This level of '-Wstrict-overflow' is enabled by '-Wall'; higher levels are not, and must be explicitly requested.

`-Wstrict-overflow=2`

Also warn about other cases where a comparison is simplified to a constant. For example: `abs (x) >= 0`. This can only be simplified when '-fstrict-overflow' is in effect, because `abs (INT_MIN)` overflows to `INT_MIN`, which is less than zero. '-Wstrict-overflow' (with no level) is the same as '-Wstrict-overflow=2'.

`-Wstrict-overflow=3`

Also warn about other cases where a comparison is simplified. For example: `x + 1 > 1` is simplified to `x > 0`.

`-Wstrict-overflow=4`

Also warn about other simplifications not covered by the above cases. For example: `(x * 10) / 5` is simplified to `x * 2`.

`-Wstrict-overflow=5`

Also warn about cases where the compiler reduces the magnitude of a constant involved in a comparison. For example: `x + 2 > y` is simplified to `x + 1 >= y`. This is reported only at the highest warning level because this simplification applies to many comparisons, so this warning level gives a very large number of false positives.

`-Wsuggest-attribute=[pure|const|noreturn|format]`
Warn for cases where adding an attribute may be beneficial. The attributes currently supported are listed below.

`-Wsuggest-attribute=pure`
`-Wsuggest-attribute=const`
`-Wsuggest-attribute=noreturn`
Warn about functions that might be candidates for attributes `pure`, `const` or `noreturn`. The compiler only warns for functions visible in other compilation units or (in the case of `pure` and `const`) if it cannot prove that the function returns normally. A function returns normally if it doesn't contain an infinite loop or return abnormally by throwing, calling `abort` or trapping. This analysis requires option '`-fipa-pure-const`', which is enabled by default at '`-O`' and higher. Higher optimization levels improve the accuracy of the analysis.

`-Wsuggest-attribute=format`
`-Wmissing-format-attribute`
Warn about function pointers that might be candidates for `format` attributes. Note these are only possible candidates, not absolute ones. GCC guesses that function pointers with `format` attributes that are used in assignment, initialization, parameter passing or return statements should have a corresponding `format` attribute in the resulting type. I.e. the left-hand side of the assignment or initialization, the type of the parameter variable, or the return type of the containing function respectively should also have a `format` attribute to avoid the warning.

GCC also warns about function definitions that might be candidates for `format` attributes. Again, these are only possible candidates. GCC guesses that `format` attributes might be appropriate for any function that calls a function like `vprintf` or `vscanf`, but this might not always be the case, and some functions for which `format` attributes are appropriate may not be detected.

`-Wsuggest-final-types`
Warn about types with virtual methods where code quality would be improved if the type were declared with the C++11 `final` specifier, or, if possible, declared in an anonymous namespace. This allows GCC to more aggressively devirtualize the polymorphic calls. This warning is more effective with link time optimization, where the information about the class hierarchy graph is more complete.

`-Wsuggest-final-methods`
Warn about virtual methods where code quality would be improved if the method were declared with the C++11 `final` specifier, or, if possible, its type were declared in an anonymous namespace or with the `final` specifier. This warning is more effective with link time optimization, where the information about the class hierarchy graph is more complete. It is recommended to first

consider suggestions of '-Wsuggest-final-types' and then rebuild with new annotations.

-Wsuggest-override
: Warn about overriding virtual functions that are not marked with the override keyword.

-Warray-bounds
-Warray-bounds=*n*
: This option is only active when '-ftree-vrp' is active (default for '-O2' and above). It warns about subscripts to arrays that are always out of bounds. This warning is enabled by '-Wall'.

  -Warray-bounds=1
  : This is the warning level of '-Warray-bounds' and is enabled by '-Wall'; higher levels are not, and must be explicitly requested.

  -Warray-bounds=2
  : This warning level also warns about out of bounds access for arrays at the end of a struct and for arrays accessed through pointers. This warning level may give a larger number of false positives and is deactivated by default.

-Wbool-compare
: Warn about boolean expression compared with an integer value different from true/false. For instance, the following comparison is always false:

```
int n = 5;
...
if ((n > 1) == 2) { ... }
```

This warning is enabled by '-Wall'.

-Wduplicated-cond
: Warn about duplicated conditions in an if-else-if chain. For instance, warn for the following code:

```
if (p->q != NULL) { ... }
else if (p->q != NULL) { ... }
```

-Wframe-address
: Warn when the '__builtin_frame_address' or '__builtin_return_address' is called with an argument greater than 0. Such calls may return indeterminate values or crash the program. The warning is included in '-Wall'.

-Wno-discarded-qualifiers (C and Objective-C only)
: Do not warn if type qualifiers on pointers are being discarded. Typically, the compiler warns if a const char * variable is passed to a function that takes a char * parameter. This option can be used to suppress such a warning.

-Wno-discarded-array-qualifiers (C and Objective-C only)
: Do not warn if type qualifiers on arrays which are pointer targets are being discarded. Typically, the compiler warns if a const int (*)[] variable is passed to a function that takes a int (*)[] parameter. This option can be used to suppress such a warning.

`-Wno-incompatible-pointer-types` (C and Objective-C only)
Do not warn when there is a conversion between pointers that have incompatible types. This warning is for cases not covered by '`-Wno-pointer-sign`', which warns for pointer argument passing or assignment with different signedness.

`-Wno-int-conversion` (C and Objective-C only)
Do not warn about incompatible integer to pointer and pointer to integer conversions. This warning is about implicit conversions; for explicit conversions the warnings '`-Wno-int-to-pointer-cast`' and '`-Wno-pointer-to-int-cast`' may be used.

`-Wno-div-by-zero`
Do not warn about compile-time integer division by zero. Floating-point division by zero is not warned about, as it can be a legitimate way of obtaining infinities and NaNs.

`-Wsystem-headers`
Print warning messages for constructs found in system header files. Warnings from system headers are normally suppressed, on the assumption that they usually do not indicate real problems and would only make the compiler output harder to read. Using this command-line option tells GCC to emit warnings from system headers as if they occurred in user code. However, note that using '`-Wall`' in conjunction with this option does *not* warn about unknown pragmas in system headers—for that, '`-Wunknown-pragmas`' must also be used.

`-Wtautological-compare`
Warn if a self-comparison always evaluates to true or false. This warning detects various mistakes such as:

```
int i = 1;
...
if (i > i) { ... }
```

This warning is enabled by '`-Wall`'.

`-Wtrampolines`
Warn about trampolines generated for pointers to nested functions. A trampoline is a small piece of data or code that is created at run time on the stack when the address of a nested function is taken, and is used to call the nested function indirectly. For some targets, it is made up of data only and thus requires no special treatment. But, for most targets, it is made up of code and thus requires the stack to be made executable in order for the program to work properly.

`-Wfloat-equal`
Warn if floating-point values are used in equality comparisons.

The idea behind this is that sometimes it is convenient (for the programmer) to consider floating-point values as approximations to infinitely precise real numbers. If you are doing this, then you need to compute (by analyzing the code, or in some other way) the maximum or likely maximum error that the computation introduces, and allow for it when performing comparisons (and when producing output, but that's a different problem). In particular, instead of testing for equality, you should check to see whether the two values have ranges that overlap; and this is done with the relational operators, so equality comparisons are probably mistaken.

`-Wtraditional` (C and Objective-C only)
: Warn about certain constructs that behave differently in traditional and ISO C. Also warn about ISO C constructs that have no traditional C equivalent, and/or problematic constructs that should be avoided.

- Macro parameters that appear within string literals in the macro body. In traditional C macro replacement takes place within string literals, but in ISO C it does not.
- In traditional C, some preprocessor directives did not exist. Traditional preprocessors only considered a line to be a directive if the '`#`' appeared in column 1 on the line. Therefore '`-Wtraditional`' warns about directives that traditional C understands but ignores because the '`#`' does not appear as the first character on the line. It also suggests you hide directives like `#pragma` not understood by traditional C by indenting them. Some traditional implementations do not recognize `#elif`, so this option suggests avoiding it altogether.
- A function-like macro that appears without arguments.
- The unary plus operator.
- The '`U`' integer constant suffix, or the '`F`' or '`L`' floating-point constant suffixes. (Traditional C does support the '`L`' suffix on integer constants.) Note, these suffixes appear in macros defined in the system headers of most modern systems, e.g. the '`_MIN`'/'`_MAX`' macros in `<limits.h>`. Use of these macros in user code might normally lead to spurious warnings, however GCC's integrated preprocessor has enough context to avoid warning in these cases.
- A function declared external in one block and then used after the end of the block.
- A `switch` statement has an operand of type `long`.
- A non-`static` function declaration follows a `static` one. This construct is not accepted by some traditional C compilers.
- The ISO type of an integer constant has a different width or signedness from its traditional type. This warning is only issued if the base of the constant is ten. I.e. hexadecimal or octal values, which typically represent bit patterns, are not warned about.
- Usage of ISO string concatenation is detected.
- Initialization of automatic aggregates.
- Identifier conflicts with labels. Traditional C lacks a separate namespace for labels.
- Initialization of unions. If the initializer is zero, the warning is omitted. This is done under the assumption that the zero initializer in user code appears conditioned on e.g. `__STDC__` to avoid missing initializer warnings and relies on default initialization to zero in the traditional C case.

- Conversions by prototypes between fixed/floating-point values and vice versa. The absence of these prototypes when compiling with traditional C causes serious problems. This is a subset of the possible conversion warnings; for the full set use '`-Wtraditional-conversion`'.
- Use of ISO C style function definitions. This warning intentionally is *not* issued for prototype declarations or variadic functions because these ISO C features appear in your code when using libiberty's traditional C compatibility macros, `PARAMS` and `VPARAMS`. This warning is also bypassed for nested functions because that feature is already a GCC extension and thus not relevant to traditional C compatibility.

`-Wtraditional-conversion` (C and Objective-C only)
: Warn if a prototype causes a type conversion that is different from what would happen to the same argument in the absence of a prototype. This includes conversions of fixed point to floating and vice versa, and conversions changing the width or signedness of a fixed-point argument except when the same as the default promotion.

`-Wdeclaration-after-statement` (C and Objective-C only)
: Warn when a declaration is found after a statement in a block. This construct, known from C++, was introduced with ISO C99 and is by default allowed in GCC. It is not supported by ISO C90. See Section 6.30 [Mixed Declarations], page 407.

`-Wundef`
: Warn if an undefined identifier is evaluated in an `#if` directive.

`-Wno-endif-labels`
: Do not warn whenever an `#else` or an `#endif` are followed by text.

`-Wshadow`
: Warn whenever a local variable or type declaration shadows another variable, parameter, type, class member (in C++), or instance variable (in Objective-C) or whenever a built-in function is shadowed. Note that in C++, the compiler warns if a local variable shadows an explicit typedef, but not if it shadows a struct/class/enum.

`-Wno-shadow-ivar` (Objective-C only)
: Do not warn whenever a local variable shadows an instance variable in an Objective-C method.

`-Wlarger-than=`*`len`*
: Warn whenever an object of larger than *len* bytes is defined.

`-Wframe-larger-than=`*`len`*
: Warn if the size of a function frame is larger than *len* bytes. The computation done to determine the stack frame size is approximate and not conservative. The actual requirements may be somewhat greater than *len* even if you do not get a warning. In addition, any space allocated via `alloca`, variable-length arrays, or related constructs is not included by the compiler when determining whether or not to issue a warning.

`-Wno-free-nonheap-object`
: Do not warn when attempting to free an object that was not allocated on the heap.

-Wstack-usage=*len*
Warn if the stack usage of a function might be larger than *len* bytes. The computation done to determine the stack usage is conservative. Any space allocated via `alloca`, variable-length arrays, or related constructs is included by the compiler when determining whether or not to issue a warning.

The message is in keeping with the output of '-fstack-usage'.

- If the stack usage is fully static but exceeds the specified amount, it's:
```
warning: stack usage is 1120 bytes
```
- If the stack usage is (partly) dynamic but bounded, it's:
```
warning: stack usage might be 1648 bytes
```
- If the stack usage is (partly) dynamic and not bounded, it's:
```
warning: stack usage might be unbounded
```

-Wunsafe-loop-optimizations
Warn if the loop cannot be optimized because the compiler cannot assume anything on the bounds of the loop indices. With '-funsafe-loop-optimizations' warn if the compiler makes such assumptions.

-Wno-pedantic-ms-format (MinGW targets only)
When used in combination with '-Wformat' and '-pedantic' without GNU extensions, this option disables the warnings about non-ISO `printf` / `scanf` format width specifiers `I32`, `I64`, and `I` used on Windows targets, which depend on the MS runtime.

-Wplacement-new
-Wplacement-new=*n*
Warn about placement new expressions with undefined behavior, such as constructing an object in a buffer that is smaller than the type of the object. For example, the placement new expression below is diagnosed because it attempts to construct an array of 64 integers in a buffer only 64 bytes large.
```
char buf [64];
new (buf) int[64];
```
This warning is enabled by default.

-Wplacement-new=1
This is the default warning level of '-Wplacement-new'. At this level the warning is not issued for some strictly undefined constructs that GCC allows as extensions for compatibility with legacy code. For example, the following `new` expression is not diagnosed at this level even though it has undefined behavior according to the C++ standard because it writes past the end of the one-element array.
```
struct S { int n, a[1]; };
S *s = (S *)malloc (sizeof *s + 31 * sizeof s->a[0]);
new (s->a)int [32]();
```

-Wplacement-new=2
At this level, in addition to diagnosing all the same constructs as at level 1, a diagnostic is also issued for placement new expressions that construct an object in the last member of structure whose type

is an array of a single element and whose size is less than the size of the object being constructed. While the previous example would be diagnosed, the following construct makes use of the flexible member array extension to avoid the warning at level 2.

```
struct S { int n, a[]; };
S *s = (S *)malloc (sizeof *s + 32 * sizeof s->a[0]);
new (s->a)int [32]();
```

-Wpointer-arith
: Warn about anything that depends on the "size of" a function type or of void. GNU C assigns these types a size of 1, for convenience in calculations with void * pointers and pointers to functions. In C++, warn also when an arithmetic operation involves NULL. This warning is also enabled by '-Wpedantic'.

-Wtype-limits
: Warn if a comparison is always true or always false due to the limited range of the data type, but do not warn for constant expressions. For example, warn if an unsigned variable is compared against zero with < or >=. This warning is also enabled by '-Wextra'.

-Wbad-function-cast (C and Objective-C only)
: Warn when a function call is cast to a non-matching type. For example, warn if a call to a function returning an integer type is cast to a pointer type.

-Wc90-c99-compat (C and Objective-C only)
: Warn about features not present in ISO C90, but present in ISO C99. For instance, warn about use of variable length arrays, long long type, bool type, compound literals, designated initializers, and so on. This option is independent of the standards mode. Warnings are disabled in the expression that follows __extension__.

-Wc99-c11-compat (C and Objective-C only)
: Warn about features not present in ISO C99, but present in ISO C11. For instance, warn about use of anonymous structures and unions, _Atomic type qualifier, _Thread_local storage-class specifier, _Alignas specifier, Alignof operator, _Generic keyword, and so on. This option is independent of the standards mode. Warnings are disabled in the expression that follows __extension__.

-Wc++-compat (C and Objective-C only)
: Warn about ISO C constructs that are outside of the common subset of ISO C and ISO C++, e.g. request for implicit conversion from void * to a pointer to non-void type.

-Wc++11-compat (C++ and Objective-C++ only)
: Warn about C++ constructs whose meaning differs between ISO C++ 1998 and ISO C++ 2011, e.g., identifiers in ISO C++ 1998 that are keywords in ISO C++ 2011. This warning turns on '-Wnarrowing' and is enabled by '-Wall'.

-Wc++14-compat (C++ and Objective-C++ only)
: Warn about C++ constructs whose meaning differs between ISO C++ 2011 and ISO C++ 2014. This warning is enabled by '-Wall'.

`-Wcast-qual`

Warn whenever a pointer is cast so as to remove a type qualifier from the target type. For example, warn if a `const char *` is cast to an ordinary `char *`.

Also warn when making a cast that introduces a type qualifier in an unsafe way. For example, casting `char **` to `const char **` is unsafe, as in this example:

```
/* p is char ** value.  */
const char **q = (const char **) p;
/* Assignment of readonly string to const char * is OK.  */
*q = "string";
/* Now char** pointer points to read-only memory.  */
**p = 'b';
```

`-Wcast-align`

Warn whenever a pointer is cast such that the required alignment of the target is increased. For example, warn if a `char *` is cast to an `int *` on machines where integers can only be accessed at two- or four-byte boundaries.

`-Wwrite-strings`

When compiling C, give string constants the type `const char[`*`length`*`]` so that copying the address of one into a non-`const char *` pointer produces a warning. These warnings help you find at compile time code that can try to write into a string constant, but only if you have been very careful about using `const` in declarations and prototypes. Otherwise, it is just a nuisance. This is why we did not make '`-Wall`' request these warnings.

When compiling C++, warn about the deprecated conversion from string literals to `char *`. This warning is enabled by default for C++ programs.

`-Wclobbered`

Warn for variables that might be changed by `longjmp` or `vfork`. This warning is also enabled by '`-Wextra`'.

`-Wconditionally-supported` (C++ and Objective-C++ only)

Warn for conditionally-supported (C++11 [intro.defs]) constructs.

`-Wconversion`

Warn for implicit conversions that may alter a value. This includes conversions between real and integer, like `abs (x)` when `x` is `double`; conversions between signed and unsigned, like `unsigned ui = -1`; and conversions to smaller types, like `sqrtf (M_PI)`. Do not warn for explicit casts like `abs ((int) x)` and `ui = (unsigned) -1`, or if the value is not changed by the conversion like in `abs (2.0)`. Warnings about conversions between signed and unsigned integers can be disabled by using '`-Wno-sign-conversion`'.

For C++, also warn for confusing overload resolution for user-defined conversions; and conversions that never use a type conversion operator: conversions to `void`, the same type, a base class or a reference to them. Warnings about conversions between signed and unsigned integers are disabled by default in C++ unless '`-Wsign-conversion`' is explicitly enabled.

`-Wno-conversion-null` (C++ and Objective-C++ only)

Do not warn for conversions between `NULL` and non-pointer types. '`-Wconversion-null`' is enabled by default.

`-Wzero-as-null-pointer-constant` (C++ and Objective-C++ only)
: Warn when a literal '`0`' is used as null pointer constant. This can be useful to facilitate the conversion to `nullptr` in C++11.

`-Wsubobject-linkage` (C++ and Objective-C++ only)
: Warn if a class type has a base or a field whose type uses the anonymous namespace or depends on a type with no linkage. If a type A depends on a type B with no or internal linkage, defining it in multiple translation units would be an ODR violation because the meaning of B is different in each translation unit. If A only appears in a single translation unit, the best way to silence the warning is to give it internal linkage by putting it in an anonymous namespace as well. The compiler doesn't give this warning for types defined in the main .C file, as those are unlikely to have multiple definitions. '`-Wsubobject-linkage`' is enabled by default.

`-Wdate-time`
: Warn when macros `__TIME__`, `__DATE__` or `__TIMESTAMP__` are encountered as they might prevent bit-wise-identical reproducible compilations.

`-Wdelete-incomplete` (C++ and Objective-C++ only)
: Warn when deleting a pointer to incomplete type, which may cause undefined behavior at runtime. This warning is enabled by default.

`-Wuseless-cast` (C++ and Objective-C++ only)
: Warn when an expression is casted to its own type.

`-Wempty-body`
: Warn if an empty body occurs in an `if`, `else` or `do while` statement. This warning is also enabled by '`-Wextra`'.

`-Wenum-compare`
: Warn about a comparison between values of different enumerated types. In C++ enumeral mismatches in conditional expressions are also diagnosed and the warning is enabled by default. In C this warning is enabled by '`-Wall`'.

`-Wjump-misses-init` (C, Objective-C only)
: Warn if a `goto` statement or a `switch` statement jumps forward across the initialization of a variable, or jumps backward to a label after the variable has been initialized. This only warns about variables that are initialized when they are declared. This warning is only supported for C and Objective-C; in C++ this sort of branch is an error in any case.

: '`-Wjump-misses-init`' is included in '`-Wc++-compat`'. It can be disabled with the '`-Wno-jump-misses-init`' option.

`-Wsign-compare`
: Warn when a comparison between signed and unsigned values could produce an incorrect result when the signed value is converted to unsigned. In C++, this warning is also enabled by '`-Wall`'. In C, it is also enabled by '`-Wextra`'.

`-Wsign-conversion`
: Warn for implicit conversions that may change the sign of an integer value, like assigning a signed integer expression to an unsigned integer variable. An explicit cast silences the warning. In C, this option is enabled also by '`-Wconversion`'.

`-Wfloat-conversion`
: Warn for implicit conversions that reduce the precision of a real value. This includes conversions from real to integer, and from higher precision real to lower precision real values. This option is also enabled by '`-Wconversion`'.

`-Wno-scalar-storage-order`
: Do not warn on suspicious constructs involving reverse scalar storage order.

`-Wsized-deallocation` (C++ and Objective-C++ only)
: Warn about a definition of an unsized deallocation function

```
void operator delete (void *) noexcept;
void operator delete[] (void *) noexcept;
```

without a definition of the corresponding sized deallocation function

```
void operator delete (void *, std::size_t) noexcept;
void operator delete[] (void *, std::size_t) noexcept;
```

or vice versa. Enabled by '`-Wextra`' along with '`-fsized-deallocation`'.

`-Wsizeof-pointer-memaccess`
: Warn for suspicious length parameters to certain string and memory built-in functions if the argument uses `sizeof`. This warning warns e.g. about `memset (ptr, 0, sizeof (ptr));` if `ptr` is not an array, but a pointer, and suggests a possible fix, or about `memcpy (&foo, ptr, sizeof (&foo));`. This warning is enabled by '`-Wall`'.

`-Wsizeof-array-argument`
: Warn when the `sizeof` operator is applied to a parameter that is declared as an array in a function definition. This warning is enabled by default for C and C++ programs.

`-Wmemset-transposed-args`
: Warn for suspicious calls to the `memset` built-in function, if the second argument is not zero and the third argument is zero. This warns e.g. about `memset (buf, sizeof buf, 0)` where most probably `memset (buf, 0, sizeof buf)` was meant instead. The diagnostics is only emitted if the third argument is literal zero. If it is some expression that is folded to zero, a cast of zero to some type, etc., it is far less likely that the user has mistakenly exchanged the arguments and no warning is emitted. This warning is enabled by '`-Wall`'.

`-Waddress`
: Warn about suspicious uses of memory addresses. These include using the address of a function in a conditional expression, such as `void func(void); if (func)`, and comparisons against the memory address of a string literal, such as `if (x == "abc")`. Such uses typically indicate a programmer error: the address of a function always evaluates to true, so their use in a conditional usually indicate that the programmer forgot the parentheses in a function call; and comparisons against string literals result in unspecified behavior and are not portable in C, so they usually indicate that the programmer intended to use `strcmp`. This warning is enabled by '`-Wall`'.

`-Wlogical-op`

Warn about suspicious uses of logical operators in expressions. This includes using logical operators in contexts where a bit-wise operator is likely to be expected. Also warns when the operands of a logical operator are the same:

```
extern int a;
if (a < 0 && a < 0) { ... }
```

`-Wlogical-not-parentheses`

Warn about logical not used on the left hand side operand of a comparison. This option does not warn if the RHS operand is of a boolean type. Its purpose is to detect suspicious code like the following:

```
int a;
...
if (!a > 1) { ... }
```

It is possible to suppress the warning by wrapping the LHS into parentheses:

```
if ((!a) > 1) { ... }
```

This warning is enabled by '`-Wall`'.

`-Waggregate-return`

Warn if any functions that return structures or unions are defined or called. (In languages where you can return an array, this also elicits a warning.)

`-Wno-aggressive-loop-optimizations`

Warn if in a loop with constant number of iterations the compiler detects undefined behavior in some statement during one or more of the iterations.

`-Wno-attributes`

Do not warn if an unexpected `__attribute__` is used, such as unrecognized attributes, function attributes applied to variables, etc. This does not stop errors for incorrect use of supported attributes.

`-Wno-builtin-macro-redefined`

Do not warn if certain built-in macros are redefined. This suppresses warnings for redefinition of `__TIMESTAMP__`, `__TIME__`, `__DATE__`, `__FILE__`, and `__BASE_FILE__`.

`-Wstrict-prototypes` (C and Objective-C only)

Warn if a function is declared or defined without specifying the argument types. (An old-style function definition is permitted without a warning if preceded by a declaration that specifies the argument types.)

`-Wold-style-declaration` (C and Objective-C only)

Warn for obsolescent usages, according to the C Standard, in a declaration. For example, warn if storage-class specifiers like `static` are not the first things in a declaration. This warning is also enabled by '`-Wextra`'.

`-Wold-style-definition` (C and Objective-C only)

Warn if an old-style function definition is used. A warning is given even if there is a previous prototype.

`-Wmissing-parameter-type` (C and Objective-C only)

A function parameter is declared without a type specifier in K&R-style functions:

```
void foo(bar) { }
```

This warning is also enabled by '-Wextra'.

-Wmissing-prototypes (C and Objective-C only)
: Warn if a global function is defined without a previous prototype declaration. This warning is issued even if the definition itself provides a prototype. Use this option to detect global functions that do not have a matching prototype declaration in a header file. This option is not valid for C++ because all function declarations provide prototypes and a non-matching declaration declares an overload rather than conflict with an earlier declaration. Use '-Wmissing-declarations' to detect missing declarations in C++.

-Wmissing-declarations
: Warn if a global function is defined without a previous declaration. Do so even if the definition itself provides a prototype. Use this option to detect global functions that are not declared in header files. In C, no warnings are issued for functions with previous non-prototype declarations; use '-Wmissing-prototypes' to detect missing prototypes. In C++, no warnings are issued for function templates, or for inline functions, or for functions in anonymous namespaces.

-Wmissing-field-initializers
: Warn if a structure's initializer has some fields missing. For example, the following code causes such a warning, because x.h is implicitly zero:

```
struct s { int f, g, h; };
struct s x = { 3, 4 };
```

This option does not warn about designated initializers, so the following modification does not trigger a warning:

```
struct s { int f, g, h; };
struct s x = { .f = 3, .g = 4 };
```

In C++ this option does not warn either about the empty { } initializer, for example:

```
struct s { int f, g, h; };
s x = { };
```

This warning is included in '-Wextra'. To get other '-Wextra' warnings without this one, use '-Wextra -Wno-missing-field-initializers'.

-Wno-multichar
: Do not warn if a multicharacter constant (''FOOF'') is used. Usually they indicate a typo in the user's code, as they have implementation-defined values, and should not be used in portable code.

-Wnormalized[=<none|id|nfc|nfkc>]
: In ISO C and ISO C++, two identifiers are different if they are different sequences of characters. However, sometimes when characters outside the basic ASCII character set are used, you can have two different character sequences that look the same. To avoid confusion, the ISO 10646 standard sets out some *normalization rules* which when applied ensure that two sequences that look the same are turned into the same sequence. GCC can warn you if you are using identifiers that have not been normalized; this option controls that warning.

There are four levels of warning supported by GCC. The default is '-Wnormalized=nfc', which warns about any identifier that is not in the ISO 10646 "C" normalized form, *NFC*. NFC is the recommended form for most uses. It is equivalent to '-Wnormalized'.

Unfortunately, there are some characters allowed in identifiers by ISO C and ISO C++ that, when turned into NFC, are not allowed in identifiers. That is, there's no way to use these symbols in portable ISO C or C++ and have all your identifiers in NFC. '-Wnormalized=id' suppresses the warning for these characters. It is hoped that future versions of the standards involved will correct this, which is why this option is not the default.

You can switch the warning off for all characters by writing '-Wnormalized=none' or '-Wno-normalized'. You should only do this if you are using some other normalization scheme (like "D"), because otherwise you can easily create bugs that are literally impossible to see.

Some characters in ISO 10646 have distinct meanings but look identical in some fonts or display methodologies, especially once formatting has been applied. For instance `\u207F`, "SUPERSCRIPT LATIN SMALL LETTER N", displays just like a regular `n` that has been placed in a superscript. ISO 10646 defines the *NFKC* normalization scheme to convert all these into a standard form as well, and GCC warns if your code is not in NFKC if you use '-Wnormalized=nfkc'. This warning is comparable to warning about every identifier that contains the letter O because it might be confused with the digit 0, and so is not the default, but may be useful as a local coding convention if the programming environment cannot be fixed to display these characters distinctly.

`-Wno-deprecated`
: Do not warn about usage of deprecated features. See Section 7.13 [Deprecated Features], page 693.

`-Wno-deprecated-declarations`
: Do not warn about uses of functions (see Section 6.31 [Function Attributes], page 407), variables (see Section 6.32 [Variable Attributes], page 450), and types (see Section 6.33 [Type Attributes], page 459) marked as deprecated by using the `deprecated` attribute.

`-Wno-overflow`
: Do not warn about compile-time overflow in constant expressions.

`-Wno-odr`
: Warn about One Definition Rule violations during link-time optimization. Requires '-flto-odr-type-merging' to be enabled. Enabled by default.

`-Wopenmp-simd`
: Warn if the vectorizer cost model overrides the OpenMP or the Cilk Plus simd directive set by user. The '-fsimd-cost-model=unlimited' option can be used to relax the cost model.

`-Woverride-init` (C and Objective-C only)
: Warn if an initialized field without side effects is overridden when using designated initializers (see Section 6.27 [Designated Initializers], page 404).

This warning is included in '-Wextra'. To get other '-Wextra' warnings without this one, use '-Wextra -Wno-override-init'.

-Woverride-init-side-effects (C and Objective-C only)
: Warn if an initialized field with side effects is overridden when using designated initializers (see Section 6.27 [Designated Initializers], page 404). This warning is enabled by default.

-Wpacked
: Warn if a structure is given the packed attribute, but the packed attribute has no effect on the layout or size of the structure. Such structures may be mis-aligned for little benefit. For instance, in this code, the variable f.x in struct bar is misaligned even though struct bar does not itself have the packed attribute:

```
struct foo {
  int x;
  char a, b, c, d;
} __attribute__((packed));
struct bar {
  char z;
  struct foo f;
};
```

-Wpacked-bitfield-compat
: The 4.1, 4.2 and 4.3 series of GCC ignore the packed attribute on bit-fields of type char. This has been fixed in GCC 4.4 but the change can lead to differences in the structure layout. GCC informs you when the offset of such a field has changed in GCC 4.4. For example there is no longer a 4-bit padding between field a and b in this structure:

```
struct foo
{
  char a:4;
  char b:8;
} __attribute__ ((packed));
```

This warning is enabled by default. Use '-Wno-packed-bitfield-compat' to disable this warning.

-Wpadded
: Warn if padding is included in a structure, either to align an element of the structure or to align the whole structure. Sometimes when this happens it is possible to rearrange the fields of the structure to reduce the padding and so make the structure smaller.

-Wredundant-decls
: Warn if anything is declared more than once in the same scope, even in cases where multiple declaration is valid and changes nothing.

-Wnested-externs (C and Objective-C only)
: Warn if an extern declaration is encountered within a function.

-Wno-inherited-variadic-ctor
: Suppress warnings about use of C++11 inheriting constructors when the base class inherited from has a C variadic constructor; the warning is on by default because the ellipsis is not inherited.

-Winline Warn if a function that is declared as inline cannot be inlined. Even with this option, the compiler does not warn about failures to inline functions declared in system headers.

The compiler uses a variety of heuristics to determine whether or not to inline a function. For example, the compiler takes into account the size of the function being inlined and the amount of inlining that has already been done in the current function. Therefore, seemingly insignificant changes in the source program can cause the warnings produced by '-Winline' to appear or disappear.

-Wno-invalid-offsetof (C++ and Objective-C++ only)

Suppress warnings from applying the offsetof macro to a non-POD type. According to the 2014 ISO C++ standard, applying offsetof to a non-standard-layout type is undefined. In existing C++ implementations, however, offsetof typically gives meaningful results. This flag is for users who are aware that they are writing nonportable code and who have deliberately chosen to ignore the warning about it.

The restrictions on offsetof may be relaxed in a future version of the C++ standard.

-Wno-int-to-pointer-cast

Suppress warnings from casts to pointer type of an integer of a different size. In C++, casting to a pointer type of smaller size is an error. 'Wint-to-pointer-cast' is enabled by default.

-Wno-pointer-to-int-cast (C and Objective-C only)

Suppress warnings from casts from a pointer to an integer type of a different size.

-Winvalid-pch

Warn if a precompiled header (see Section 3.21 [Precompiled Headers], page 370) is found in the search path but can't be used.

-Wlong-long

Warn if long long type is used. This is enabled by either '-Wpedantic' or '-Wtraditional' in ISO C90 and C++98 modes. To inhibit the warning messages, use '-Wno-long-long'.

-Wvariadic-macros

Warn if variadic macros are used in ISO C90 mode, or if the GNU alternate syntax is used in ISO C99 mode. This is enabled by either '-Wpedantic' or '-Wtraditional'. To inhibit the warning messages, use '-Wno-variadic-macros'.

-Wvarargs

Warn upon questionable usage of the macros used to handle variable arguments like va_start. This is default. To inhibit the warning messages, use '-Wno-varargs'.

-Wvector-operation-performance

Warn if vector operation is not implemented via SIMD capabilities of the architecture. Mainly useful for the performance tuning. Vector operation can be implemented `piecewise`, which means that the scalar operation is performed on every vector element; `in parallel`, which means that the vector operation is implemented using scalars of wider type, which normally is more performance efficient; and `as a single scalar`, which means that vector fits into a scalar type.

`-Wno-virtual-move-assign`
: Suppress warnings about inheriting from a virtual base with a non-trivial C++11 move assignment operator. This is dangerous because if the virtual base is reachable along more than one path, it is moved multiple times, which can mean both objects end up in the moved-from state. If the move assignment operator is written to avoid moving from a moved-from object, this warning can be disabled.

`-Wvla`
: Warn if variable length array is used in the code. '`-Wno-vla`' prevents the '`-Wpedantic`' warning of the variable length array.

`-Wvolatile-register-var`
: Warn if a register variable is declared volatile. The volatile modifier does not inhibit all optimizations that may eliminate reads and/or writes to register variables. This warning is enabled by '`-Wall`'.

`-Wdisabled-optimization`
: Warn if a requested optimization pass is disabled. This warning does not generally indicate that there is anything wrong with your code; it merely indicates that GCC's optimizers are unable to handle the code effectively. Often, the problem is that your code is too big or too complex; GCC refuses to optimize programs when the optimization itself is likely to take inordinate amounts of time.

`-Wpointer-sign` (C and Objective-C only)
: Warn for pointer argument passing or assignment with different signedness. This option is only supported for C and Objective-C. It is implied by '`-Wall`' and by '`-Wpedantic`', which can be disabled with '`-Wno-pointer-sign`'.

`-Wstack-protector`
: This option is only active when '`-fstack-protector`' is active. It warns about functions that are not protected against stack smashing.

`-Woverlength-strings`
: Warn about string constants that are longer than the "minimum maximum" length specified in the C standard. Modern compilers generally allow string constants that are much longer than the standard's minimum limit, but very portable programs should avoid using longer strings.

  The limit applies *after* string constant concatenation, and does not count the trailing NUL. In C90, the limit was 509 characters; in C99, it was raised to 4095. C++98 does not specify a normative minimum maximum, so we do not diagnose overlength strings in C++.

  This option is implied by '`-Wpedantic`', and can be disabled with '`-Wno-overlength-strings`'.

`-Wunsuffixed-float-constants` (C and Objective-C only)
: Issue a warning for any floating constant that does not have a suffix. When used together with '`-Wsystem-headers`' it warns about such constants in system header files. This can be useful when preparing code to use with the `FLOAT_CONST_DECIMAL64` pragma from the decimal floating-point extension to C99.

`-Wno-designated-init` (C and Objective-C only)
: Suppress warnings when a positional initializer is used to initialize a structure that has been marked with the `designated_init` attribute.

`-Whsa`
: Issue a warning when HSAIL cannot be emitted for the compiled function or OpenMP construct.

3.9 Options for Debugging Your Program

To tell GCC to emit extra information for use by a debugger, in almost all cases you need only to add '`-g`' to your other options.

GCC allows you to use '`-g`' with '`-O`'. The shortcuts taken by optimized code may occasionally be surprising: some variables you declared may not exist at all; flow of control may briefly move where you did not expect it; some statements may not be executed because they compute constant results or their values are already at hand; some statements may execute in different places because they have been moved out of loops. Nevertheless it is possible to debug optimized output. This makes it reasonable to use the optimizer for programs that might have bugs.

If you are not using some other optimization option, consider using '`-Og`' (see Section 3.10 [Optimize Options], page 93) with '`-g`'. With no '`-O`' option at all, some compiler passes that collect information useful for debugging do not run at all, so that '`-Og`' may result in a better debugging experience.

`-g`
: Produce debugging information in the operating system's native format (stabs, COFF, XCOFF, or DWARF). GDB can work with this debugging information.

  On most systems that use stabs format, '`-g`' enables use of extra debugging information that only GDB can use; this extra information makes debugging work better in GDB but probably makes other debuggers crash or refuse to read the program. If you want to control for certain whether to generate the extra information, use '`-gstabs+`', '`-gstabs`', '`-gxcoff+`', '`-gxcoff`', or '`-gvms`' (see below).

`-ggdb`
: Produce debugging information for use by GDB. This means to use the most expressive format available (DWARF, stabs, or the native format if neither of those are supported), including GDB extensions if at all possible.

`-gdwarf`
`-gdwarf-`*`version`*
: Produce debugging information in DWARF format (if that is supported). The value of *version* may be either 2, 3, 4 or 5; the default version for most targets is 4. DWARF Version 5 is only experimental.

  Note that with DWARF Version 2, some ports require and always use some non-conflicting DWARF 3 extensions in the unwind tables.

Version 4 may require GDB 7.0 and '-fvar-tracking-assignments' for maximum benefit.

GCC no longer supports DWARF Version 1, which is substantially different than Version 2 and later. For historical reasons, some other DWARF-related options (including '-feliminate-dwarf2-dups' and '-fno-dwarf2-cfi-asm') retain a reference to DWARF Version 2 in their names, but apply to all currently-supported versions of DWARF.

`-gstabs`
: Produce debugging information in stabs format (if that is supported), without GDB extensions. This is the format used by DBX on most BSD systems. On MIPS, Alpha and System V Release 4 systems this option produces stabs debugging output that is not understood by DBX or SDB. On System V Release 4 systems this option requires the GNU assembler.

`-gstabs+`
: Produce debugging information in stabs format (if that is supported), using GNU extensions understood only by the GNU debugger (GDB). The use of these extensions is likely to make other debuggers crash or refuse to read the program.

`-gcoff`
: Produce debugging information in COFF format (if that is supported). This is the format used by SDB on most System V systems prior to System V Release 4.

`-gxcoff`
: Produce debugging information in XCOFF format (if that is supported). This is the format used by the DBX debugger on IBM RS/6000 systems.

`-gxcoff+`
: Produce debugging information in XCOFF format (if that is supported), using GNU extensions understood only by the GNU debugger (GDB). The use of these extensions is likely to make other debuggers crash or refuse to read the program, and may cause assemblers other than the GNU assembler (GAS) to fail with an error.

`-gvms`
: Produce debugging information in Alpha/VMS debug format (if that is supported). This is the format used by DEBUG on Alpha/VMS systems.

`-g`*level*
`-ggdb`*level*
`-gstabs`*level*
`-gcoff`*level*
`-gxcoff`*level*
`-gvms`*level*
: Request debugging information and also use *level* to specify how much information. The default level is 2.

Level 0 produces no debug information at all. Thus, '-g0' negates '-g'.

Level 1 produces minimal information, enough for making backtraces in parts of the program that you don't plan to debug. This includes descriptions of functions and external variables, and line number tables, but no information about local variables.

Level 3 includes extra information, such as all the macro definitions present in the program. Some debuggers support macro expansion when you use '-g3'.

'-gdwarf' does not accept a concatenated debug level, to avoid confusion with '-gdwarf-*level*'. Instead use an additional '-g*level*' option to change the debug level for DWARF.

`-feliminate-unused-debug-symbols`
: Produce debugging information in stabs format (if that is supported), for only symbols that are actually used.

`-femit-class-debug-always`
: Instead of emitting debugging information for a C++ class in only one object file, emit it in all object files using the class. This option should be used only with debuggers that are unable to handle the way GCC normally emits debugging information for classes because using this option increases the size of debugging information by as much as a factor of two.

`-fno-merge-debug-strings`
: Direct the linker to not merge together strings in the debugging information that are identical in different object files. Merging is not supported by all assemblers or linkers. Merging decreases the size of the debug information in the output file at the cost of increasing link processing time. Merging is enabled by default.

`-fdebug-prefix-map=old=new`
: When compiling files in directory '*old*', record debugging information describing them as in '*new*' instead.

`-fvar-tracking`
: Run variable tracking pass. It computes where variables are stored at each position in code. Better debugging information is then generated (if the debugging information format supports this information).

  It is enabled by default when compiling with optimization ('-Os', '-O', '-O2', ...), debugging information ('-g') and the debug info format supports it.

`-fvar-tracking-assignments`
: Annotate assignments to user variables early in the compilation and attempt to carry the annotations over throughout the compilation all the way to the end, in an attempt to improve debug information while optimizing. Use of '-gdwarf-4' is recommended along with it.

  It can be enabled even if var-tracking is disabled, in which case annotations are created and maintained, but discarded at the end. By default, this flag is enabled together with '-fvar-tracking', except when selective scheduling is enabled.

`-gsplit-dwarf`
: Separate as much DWARF debugging information as possible into a separate output file with the extension '.dwo'. This option allows the build system to avoid linking files with debug information. To be useful, this option requires a debugger capable of reading '.dwo' files.

`-gpubnames`
: Generate DWARF `.debug_pubnames` and `.debug_pubtypes` sections.

`-ggnu-pubnames`
: Generate `.debug_pubnames` and `.debug_pubtypes` sections in a format suitable for conversion into a GDB index. This option is only useful with a linker that can produce GDB index version 7.

`-fdebug-types-section`
: When using DWARF Version 4 or higher, type DIEs can be put into their own `.debug_types` section instead of making them part of the `.debug_info` section. It is more efficient to put them in a separate comdat sections since the linker can then remove duplicates. But not all DWARF consumers support `.debug_types` sections yet and on some objects `.debug_types` produces larger instead of smaller debugging information.

`-grecord-gcc-switches`
`-gno-record-gcc-switches`
: This switch causes the command-line options used to invoke the compiler that may affect code generation to be appended to the DW_AT_producer attribute in DWARF debugging information. The options are concatenated with spaces separating them from each other and from the compiler version. It is enabled by default. See also '`-frecord-gcc-switches`' for another way of storing compiler options into the object file.

`-gstrict-dwarf`
: Disallow using extensions of later DWARF standard version than selected with '`-gdwarf-`*version*'. On most targets using non-conflicting DWARF extensions from later standard versions is allowed.

`-gno-strict-dwarf`
: Allow using extensions of later DWARF standard version than selected with '`-gdwarf-`*version*'.

`-gz`[=*type*]
: Produce compressed debug sections in DWARF format, if that is supported. If *type* is not given, the default type depends on the capabilities of the assembler and linker used. *type* may be one of '`none`' (don't compress debug sections), '`zlib`' (use zlib compression in ELF gABI format), or '`zlib-gnu`' (use zlib compression in traditional GNU format). If the linker doesn't support writing compressed debug sections, the option is rejected. Otherwise, if the assembler does not support them, '`-gz`' is silently ignored when producing object files.

`-feliminate-dwarf2-dups`
: Compress DWARF debugging information by eliminating duplicated information about each symbol. This option only makes sense when generating DWARF debugging information.

`-femit-struct-debug-baseonly`
: Emit debug information for struct-like types only when the base name of the compilation source file matches the base name of file in which the struct is defined.

: This option substantially reduces the size of debugging information, but at significant potential loss in type information to the debugger.

See '-femit-struct-debug-reduced' for a less aggressive option. See '-femit-struct-debug-detailed' for more detailed control.

This option works only with DWARF debug output.

-femit-struct-debug-reduced

Emit debug information for struct-like types only when the base name of the compilation source file matches the base name of file in which the type is defined, unless the struct is a template or defined in a system header.

This option significantly reduces the size of debugging information, with some potential loss in type information to the debugger. See '-femit-struct-debug-baseonly' for a more aggressive option. See '-femit-struct-debug-detailed' for more detailed control.

This option works only with DWARF debug output.

-femit-struct-debug-detailed[=*spec-list*]

Specify the struct-like types for which the compiler generates debug information. The intent is to reduce duplicate struct debug information between different object files within the same program.

This option is a detailed version of '-femit-struct-debug-reduced' and '-femit-struct-debug-baseonly', which serves for most needs.

A specification has the syntax
['dir:'|'ind:']['ord:'|'gen:']('any'|'sys'|'base'|'none')

The optional first word limits the specification to structs that are used directly ('dir:') or used indirectly ('ind:'). A struct type is used directly when it is the type of a variable, member. Indirect uses arise through pointers to structs. That is, when use of an incomplete struct is valid, the use is indirect. An example is 'struct one direct; struct two * indirect;'.

The optional second word limits the specification to ordinary structs ('ord:') or generic structs ('gen:'). Generic structs are a bit complicated to explain. For C++, these are non-explicit specializations of template classes, or non-template classes within the above. Other programming languages have generics, but '-femit-struct-debug-detailed' does not yet implement them.

The third word specifies the source files for those structs for which the compiler should emit debug information. The values 'none' and 'any' have the normal meaning. The value 'base' means that the base of name of the file in which the type declaration appears must match the base of the name of the main compilation file. In practice, this means that when compiling 'foo.c', debug information is generated for types declared in that file and 'foo.h', but not other header files. The value 'sys' means those types satisfying 'base' or declared in system or compiler headers.

You may need to experiment to determine the best settings for your application.

The default is '-femit-struct-debug-detailed=all'.

This option works only with DWARF debug output.

-fno-dwarf2-cfi-asm

Emit DWARF unwind info as compiler generated .eh_frame section instead of using GAS .cfi_* directives.

`-fno-eliminate-unused-debug-types`
: Normally, when producing DWARF output, GCC avoids producing debug symbol output for types that are nowhere used in the source file being compiled. Sometimes it is useful to have GCC emit debugging information for all types declared in a compilation unit, regardless of whether or not they are actually used in that compilation unit, for example if, in the debugger, you want to cast a value to a type that is not actually used in your program (but is declared). More often, however, this results in a significant amount of wasted space.

3.10 Options That Control Optimization

These options control various sorts of optimizations.

Without any optimization option, the compiler's goal is to reduce the cost of compilation and to make debugging produce the expected results. Statements are independent: if you stop the program with a breakpoint between statements, you can then assign a new value to any variable or change the program counter to any other statement in the function and get exactly the results you expect from the source code.

Turning on optimization flags makes the compiler attempt to improve the performance and/or code size at the expense of compilation time and possibly the ability to debug the program.

The compiler performs optimization based on the knowledge it has of the program. Compiling multiple files at once to a single output file mode allows the compiler to use information gained from all of the files when compiling each of them.

Not all optimizations are controlled directly by a flag. Only optimizations that have a flag are listed in this section.

Most optimizations are only enabled if an '`-O`' level is set on the command line. Otherwise they are disabled, even if individual optimization flags are specified.

Depending on the target and how GCC was configured, a slightly different set of optimizations may be enabled at each '`-O`' level than those listed here. You can invoke GCC with '`-Q --help=optimizers`' to find out the exact set of optimizations that are enabled at each level. See Section 3.2 [Overall Options], page 27, for examples.

`-O`
`-O1`
: Optimize. Optimizing compilation takes somewhat more time, and a lot more memory for a large function.

  With '`-O`', the compiler tries to reduce code size and execution time, without performing any optimizations that take a great deal of compilation time.

  '`-O`' turns on the following optimization flags:

```
-fauto-inc-dec
-fbranch-count-reg
-fcombine-stack-adjustments
-fcompare-elim
-fcprop-registers
-fdce
-fdefer-pop
-fdelayed-branch
-fdse
-fforward-propagate
```

```
-fguess-branch-probability
-fif-conversion2
-fif-conversion
-finline-functions-called-once
-fipa-pure-const
-fipa-profile
-fipa-reference
-fmerge-constants
-fmove-loop-invariants
-freorder-blocks
-fshrink-wrap
-fsplit-wide-types
-fssa-backprop
-fssa-phiopt
-ftree-bit-ccp
-ftree-ccp
-ftree-ch
-ftree-coalesce-vars
-ftree-copy-prop
-ftree-dce
-ftree-dominator-opts
-ftree-dse
-ftree-forwprop
-ftree-fre
-ftree-phiprop
-ftree-sink
-ftree-slsr
-ftree-sra
-ftree-pta
-ftree-ter
-funit-at-a-time
```

'-O' also turns on '-fomit-frame-pointer' on machines where doing so does not interfere with debugging.

-O2 Optimize even more. GCC performs nearly all supported optimizations that do not involve a space-speed tradeoff. As compared to '-O', this option increases both compilation time and the performance of the generated code.

'-O2' turns on all optimization flags specified by '-O'. It also turns on the following optimization flags:

```
-fthread-jumps
-falign-functions -falign-jumps
-falign-loops -falign-labels
-fcaller-saves
-fcrossjumping
-fcse-follow-jumps -fcse-skip-blocks
-fdelete-null-pointer-checks
-fdevirtualize -fdevirtualize-speculatively
-fexpensive-optimizations
-fgcse -fgcse-lm
-fhoist-adjacent-loads
-finline-small-functions
-findirect-inlining
-fipa-cp
-fipa-cp-alignment
-fipa-sra
-fipa-icf
-fisolate-erroneous-paths-dereference
```

```
-flra-remat
-foptimize-sibling-calls
-foptimize-strlen
-fpartial-inlining
-fpeephole2
-freorder-blocks-algorithm=stc
-freorder-blocks-and-partition -freorder-functions
-frerun-cse-after-loop
-fsched-interblock -fsched-spec
-fschedule-insns -fschedule-insns2
-fstrict-aliasing -fstrict-overflow
-ftree-builtin-call-dce
-ftree-switch-conversion -ftree-tail-merge
-ftree-pre
-ftree-vrp
-fipa-ra
```

Please note the warning under '`-fgcse`' about invoking '`-O2`' on programs that use computed gotos.

`-O3` Optimize yet more. '`-O3`' turns on all optimizations specified by '`-O2`' and also turns on the '`-finline-functions`', '`-funswitch-loops`', '`-fpredictive-commoning`', '`-fgcse-after-reload`', '`-ftree-loop-vectorize`', '`-ftree-loop-distribute-patterns`', '`-fsplit-paths`' '`-ftree-slp-vectorize`', '`-fvect-cost-model`', '`-ftree-partial-pre`' and '`-fipa-cp-clone`' options.

`-O0` Reduce compilation time and make debugging produce the expected results. This is the default.

`-Os` Optimize for size. '`-Os`' enables all '`-O2`' optimizations that do not typically increase code size. It also performs further optimizations designed to reduce code size.

'`-Os`' disables the following optimization flags:

```
-falign-functions -falign-jumps -falign-loops
-falign-labels -freorder-blocks -freorder-blocks-algorithm=stc
-freorder-blocks-and-partition -fprefetch-loop-arrays
```

`-Ofast` Disregard strict standards compliance. '`-Ofast`' enables all '`-O3`' optimizations. It also enables optimizations that are not valid for all standard-compliant programs. It turns on '`-ffast-math`' and the Fortran-specific '`-fno-protect-parens`' and '`-fstack-arrays`'.

`-Og` Optimize debugging experience. '`-Og`' enables optimizations that do not interfere with debugging. It should be the optimization level of choice for the standard edit-compile-debug cycle, offering a reasonable level of optimization while maintaining fast compilation and a good debugging experience.

If you use multiple '`-O`' options, with or without level numbers, the last such option is the one that is effective.

Options of the form '`-fflag`' specify machine-independent flags. Most flags have both positive and negative forms; the negative form of '`-ffoo`' is '`-fno-foo`'. In the table below, only one of the forms is listed—the one you typically use. You can figure out the other form by either removing '`no-`' or adding it.

The following options control specific optimizations. They are either activated by '-O' options or are related to ones that are. You can use the following flags in the rare cases when "fine-tuning" of optimizations to be performed is desired.

`-fno-defer-pop`
: Always pop the arguments to each function call as soon as that function returns. For machines that must pop arguments after a function call, the compiler normally lets arguments accumulate on the stack for several function calls and pops them all at once.

  Disabled at levels '-O', '-O2', '-O3', '-Os'.

`-fforward-propagate`
: Perform a forward propagation pass on RTL. The pass tries to combine two instructions and checks if the result can be simplified. If loop unrolling is active, two passes are performed and the second is scheduled after loop unrolling.

  This option is enabled by default at optimization levels '-O', '-O2', '-O3', '-Os'.

`-ffp-contract=`*`style`*
: '-ffp-contract=off' disables floating-point expression contraction. '-ffp-contract=fast' enables floating-point expression contraction such as forming of fused multiply-add operations if the target has native support for them. '-ffp-contract=on' enables floating-point expression contraction if allowed by the language standard. This is currently not implemented and treated equal to '-ffp-contract=off'.

  The default is '-ffp-contract=fast'.

`-fomit-frame-pointer`
: Don't keep the frame pointer in a register for functions that don't need one. This avoids the instructions to save, set up and restore frame pointers; it also makes an extra register available in many functions. **It also makes debugging impossible on some machines.**

  On some machines, such as the VAX, this flag has no effect, because the standard calling sequence automatically handles the frame pointer and nothing is saved by pretending it doesn't exist. The machine-description macro `FRAME_POINTER_REQUIRED` controls whether a target machine supports this flag. See Section "Register Usage" in *GNU Compiler Collection (GCC) Internals*.

  The default setting (when not optimizing for size) for 32-bit GNU/Linux x86 and 32-bit Darwin x86 targets is '-fomit-frame-pointer'. You can configure GCC with the '--enable-frame-pointer' configure option to change the default.

  Enabled at levels '-O', '-O2', '-O3', '-Os'.

`-foptimize-sibling-calls`
: Optimize sibling and tail recursive calls.

  Enabled at levels '-O2', '-O3', '-Os'.

`-foptimize-strlen`
: Optimize various standard C string functions (e.g. `strlen`, `strchr` or `strcpy`) and their `_FORTIFY_SOURCE` counterparts into faster alternatives.

Enabled at levels '-O2', '-O3'.

`-fno-inline`
: Do not expand any functions inline apart from those marked with the `always_inline` attribute. This is the default when not optimizing.

  Single functions can be exempted from inlining by marking them with the `noinline` attribute.

`-finline-small-functions`
: Integrate functions into their callers when their body is smaller than expected function call code (so overall size of program gets smaller). The compiler heuristically decides which functions are simple enough to be worth integrating in this way. This inlining applies to all functions, even those not declared inline.

  Enabled at level '-O2'.

`-findirect-inlining`
: Inline also indirect calls that are discovered to be known at compile time thanks to previous inlining. This option has any effect only when inlining itself is turned on by the '`-finline-functions`' or '`-finline-small-functions`' options.

  Enabled at level '-O2'.

`-finline-functions`
: Consider all functions for inlining, even if they are not declared inline. The compiler heuristically decides which functions are worth integrating in this way.

  If all calls to a given function are integrated, and the function is declared `static`, then the function is normally not output as assembler code in its own right.

  Enabled at level '-O3'.

`-finline-functions-called-once`
: Consider all `static` functions called once for inlining into their caller even if they are not marked `inline`. If a call to a given function is integrated, then the function is not output as assembler code in its own right.

  Enabled at levels '-O1', '-O2', '-O3' and '-Os'.

`-fearly-inlining`
: Inline functions marked by `always_inline` and functions whose body seems smaller than the function call overhead early before doing '`-fprofile-generate`' instrumentation and real inlining pass. Doing so makes profiling significantly cheaper and usually inlining faster on programs having large chains of nested wrapper functions.

  Enabled by default.

`-fipa-sra`
: Perform interprocedural scalar replacement of aggregates, removal of unused parameters and replacement of parameters passed by reference by parameters passed by value.

  Enabled at levels '-O2', '-O3' and '-Os'.

`-finline-limit=n`
By default, GCC limits the size of functions that can be inlined. This flag allows coarse control of this limit. *n* is the size of functions that can be inlined in number of pseudo instructions.

Inlining is actually controlled by a number of parameters, which may be specified individually by using '`--param name=value`'. The '`-finline-limit=n`' option sets some of these parameters as follows:

`max-inline-insns-single`
is set to $n/2$.

`max-inline-insns-auto`
is set to $n/2$.

See below for a documentation of the individual parameters controlling inlining and for the defaults of these parameters.

Note: there may be no value to '`-finline-limit`' that results in default behavior.

Note: pseudo instruction represents, in this particular context, an abstract measurement of function's size. In no way does it represent a count of assembly instructions and as such its exact meaning might change from one release to an another.

`-fno-keep-inline-dllexport`
This is a more fine-grained version of '`-fkeep-inline-functions`', which applies only to functions that are declared using the `dllexport` attribute or declspec (See Section 6.31 [Declaring Attributes of Functions], page 407.)

`-fkeep-inline-functions`
In C, emit `static` functions that are declared `inline` into the object file, even if the function has been inlined into all of its callers. This switch does not affect functions using the `extern inline` extension in GNU C90. In C++, emit any and all inline functions into the object file.

`-fkeep-static-functions`
Emit `static` functions into the object file, even if the function is never used.

`-fkeep-static-consts`
Emit variables declared `static const` when optimization isn't turned on, even if the variables aren't referenced.

GCC enables this option by default. If you want to force the compiler to check if a variable is referenced, regardless of whether or not optimization is turned on, use the '`-fno-keep-static-consts`' option.

`-fmerge-constants`
Attempt to merge identical constants (string constants and floating-point constants) across compilation units.

This option is the default for optimized compilation if the assembler and linker support it. Use '`-fno-merge-constants`' to inhibit this behavior.

Enabled at levels '`-O`', '`-O2`', '`-O3`', '`-Os`'.

`-fmerge-all-constants`

Attempt to merge identical constants and identical variables.

This option implies '`-fmerge-constants`'. In addition to '`-fmerge-constants`' this considers e.g. even constant initialized arrays or initialized constant variables with integral or floating-point types. Languages like C or C++ require each variable, including multiple instances of the same variable in recursive calls, to have distinct locations, so using this option results in non-conforming behavior.

`-fmodulo-sched`

Perform swing modulo scheduling immediately before the first scheduling pass. This pass looks at innermost loops and reorders their instructions by overlapping different iterations.

`-fmodulo-sched-allow-regmoves`

Perform more aggressive SMS-based modulo scheduling with register moves allowed. By setting this flag certain anti-dependences edges are deleted, which triggers the generation of reg-moves based on the life-range analysis. This option is effective only with '`-fmodulo-sched`' enabled.

`-fno-branch-count-reg`

Avoid running a pass scanning for opportunities to use "decrement and branch" instructions on a count register instead of generating sequences of instructions that decrement a register, compare it against zero, and then branch based upon the result. This option is only meaningful on architectures that support such instructions, which include x86, PowerPC, IA-64 and S/390. Note that the '`-fno-branch-count-reg`' option doesn't remove the decrement and branch instructions from the generated instruction stream introduced by other optimization passes.

Enabled by default at '`-O1`' and higher.

The default is '`-fbranch-count-reg`'.

`-fno-function-cse`

Do not put function addresses in registers; make each instruction that calls a constant function contain the function's address explicitly.

This option results in less efficient code, but some strange hacks that alter the assembler output may be confused by the optimizations performed when this option is not used.

The default is '`-ffunction-cse`'

`-fno-zero-initialized-in-bss`

If the target supports a BSS section, GCC by default puts variables that are initialized to zero into BSS. This can save space in the resulting code.

This option turns off this behavior because some programs explicitly rely on variables going to the data section—e.g., so that the resulting executable can find the beginning of that section and/or make assumptions based on that.

The default is '`-fzero-initialized-in-bss`'.

`-fthread-jumps`

Perform optimizations that check to see if a jump branches to a location where another comparison subsumed by the first is found. If so, the first branch is redirected to either the destination of the second branch or a point immediately following it, depending on whether the condition is known to be true or false.

Enabled at levels '`-O2`', '`-O3`', '`-Os`'.

`-fsplit-wide-types`
: When using a type that occupies multiple registers, such as `long long` on a 32-bit system, split the registers apart and allocate them independently. This normally generates better code for those types, but may make debugging more difficult.

  Enabled at levels '`-O`', '`-O2`', '`-O3`', '`-Os`'.

`-fcse-follow-jumps`
: In common subexpression elimination (CSE), scan through jump instructions when the target of the jump is not reached by any other path. For example, when CSE encounters an `if` statement with an `else` clause, CSE follows the jump when the condition tested is false.

  Enabled at levels '`-O2`', '`-O3`', '`-Os`'.

`-fcse-skip-blocks`
: This is similar to '`-fcse-follow-jumps`', but causes CSE to follow jumps that conditionally skip over blocks. When CSE encounters a simple `if` statement with no else clause, '`-fcse-skip-blocks`' causes CSE to follow the jump around the body of the `if`.

  Enabled at levels '`-O2`', '`-O3`', '`-Os`'.

`-frerun-cse-after-loop`
: Re-run common subexpression elimination after loop optimizations are performed.

  Enabled at levels '`-O2`', '`-O3`', '`-Os`'.

`-fgcse`
: Perform a global common subexpression elimination pass. This pass also performs global constant and copy propagation.

  Note: When compiling a program using computed gotos, a GCC extension, you may get better run-time performance if you disable the global common subexpression elimination pass by adding '`-fno-gcse`' to the command line.

  Enabled at levels '`-O2`', '`-O3`', '`-Os`'.

`-fgcse-lm`
: When '`-fgcse-lm`' is enabled, global common subexpression elimination attempts to move loads that are only killed by stores into themselves. This allows a loop containing a load/store sequence to be changed to a load outside the loop, and a copy/store within the loop.

  Enabled by default when '`-fgcse`' is enabled.

`-fgcse-sm`
: When '`-fgcse-sm`' is enabled, a store motion pass is run after global common subexpression elimination. This pass attempts to move stores out of loops. When used in conjunction with '`-fgcse-lm`', loops containing a load/store sequence can be changed to a load before the loop and a store after the loop.

  Not enabled at any optimization level.

`-fgcse-las`
: When '`-fgcse-las`' is enabled, the global common subexpression elimination pass eliminates redundant loads that come after stores to the same memory location (both partial and full redundancies).

  Not enabled at any optimization level.

`-fgcse-after-reload`
: When '`-fgcse-after-reload`' is enabled, a redundant load elimination pass is performed after reload. The purpose of this pass is to clean up redundant spilling.

`-faggressive-loop-optimizations`
: This option tells the loop optimizer to use language constraints to derive bounds for the number of iterations of a loop. This assumes that loop code does not invoke undefined behavior by for example causing signed integer overflows or out-of-bound array accesses. The bounds for the number of iterations of a loop are used to guide loop unrolling and peeling and loop exit test optimizations. This option is enabled by default.

`-funsafe-loop-optimizations`
: This option tells the loop optimizer to assume that loop indices do not overflow, and that loops with nontrivial exit condition are not infinite. This enables a wider range of loop optimizations even if the loop optimizer itself cannot prove that these assumptions are valid. If you use '`-Wunsafe-loop-optimizations`', the compiler warns you if it finds this kind of loop.

`-funconstrained-commons`
: This option tells the compiler that variables declared in common blocks (e.g. Fortran) may later be overridden with longer trailing arrays. This prevents certain optimizations that depend on knowing the array bounds.

`-fcrossjumping`
: Perform cross-jumping transformation. This transformation unifies equivalent code and saves code size. The resulting code may or may not perform better than without cross-jumping.

  Enabled at levels '`-O2`', '`-O3`', '`-Os`'.

`-fauto-inc-dec`
: Combine increments or decrements of addresses with memory accesses. This pass is always skipped on architectures that do not have instructions to support this. Enabled by default at '`-O`' and higher on architectures that support this.

`-fdce`
: Perform dead code elimination (DCE) on RTL. Enabled by default at '`-O`' and higher.

`-fdse`
: Perform dead store elimination (DSE) on RTL. Enabled by default at '`-O`' and higher.

`-fif-conversion`
: Attempt to transform conditional jumps into branch-less equivalents. This includes use of conditional moves, min, max, set flags and abs instructions, and

some tricks doable by standard arithmetics. The use of conditional execution on chips where it is available is controlled by '-fif-conversion2'.

Enabled at levels '-O', '-O2', '-O3', '-Os'.

`-fif-conversion2`
: Use conditional execution (where available) to transform conditional jumps into branch-less equivalents.

Enabled at levels '-O', '-O2', '-O3', '-Os'.

`-fdeclone-ctor-dtor`
: The C++ ABI requires multiple entry points for constructors and destructors: one for a base subobject, one for a complete object, and one for a virtual destructor that calls operator delete afterwards. For a hierarchy with virtual bases, the base and complete variants are clones, which means two copies of the function. With this option, the base and complete variants are changed to be thunks that call a common implementation.

Enabled by '-Os'.

`-fdelete-null-pointer-checks`
: Assume that programs cannot safely dereference null pointers, and that no code or data element resides at address zero. This option enables simple constant folding optimizations at all optimization levels. In addition, other optimization passes in GCC use this flag to control global dataflow analyses that eliminate useless checks for null pointers; these assume that a memory access to address zero always results in a trap, so that if a pointer is checked after it has already been dereferenced, it cannot be null.

Note however that in some environments this assumption is not true. Use '-fno-delete-null-pointer-checks' to disable this optimization for programs that depend on that behavior.

This option is enabled by default on most targets. On Nios II ELF, it defaults to off. On AVR and CR16, this option is completely disabled.

Passes that use the dataflow information are enabled independently at different optimization levels.

`-fdevirtualize`
: Attempt to convert calls to virtual functions to direct calls. This is done both within a procedure and interprocedurally as part of indirect inlining ('-findirect-inlining') and interprocedural constant propagation ('-fipa-cp'). Enabled at levels '-O2', '-O3', '-Os'.

`-fdevirtualize-speculatively`
: Attempt to convert calls to virtual functions to speculative direct calls. Based on the analysis of the type inheritance graph, determine for a given call the set of likely targets. If the set is small, preferably of size 1, change the call into a conditional deciding between direct and indirect calls. The speculative calls enable more optimizations, such as inlining. When they seem useless after further optimization, they are converted back into original form.

`-fdevirtualize-at-ltrans`
: Stream extra information needed for aggressive devirtualization when running the link-time optimizer in local transformation mode. This option enables more devirtualization but significantly increases the size of streamed data. For this reason it is disabled by default.

`-fexpensive-optimizations`
: Perform a number of minor optimizations that are relatively expensive.

  Enabled at levels '`-O2`', '`-O3`', '`-Os`'.

`-free`
: Attempt to remove redundant extension instructions. This is especially helpful for the x86-64 architecture, which implicitly zero-extends in 64-bit registers after writing to their lower 32-bit half.

  Enabled for Alpha, AArch64 and x86 at levels '`-O2`', '`-O3`', '`-Os`'.

`-fno-lifetime-dse`
: In C++ the value of an object is only affected by changes within its lifetime: when the constructor begins, the object has an indeterminate value, and any changes during the lifetime of the object are dead when the object is destroyed. Normally dead store elimination will take advantage of this; if your code relies on the value of the object storage persisting beyond the lifetime of the object, you can use this flag to disable this optimization. To preserve stores before the constructor starts (e.g. because your operator new clears the object storage) but still treat the object as dead after the destructor you, can use '`-flifetime-dse=1`'. The default behavior can be explicitly selected with '`-flifetime-dse=2`'. '`-flifetime-dse=0`' is equivalent to '`-fno-lifetime-dse`'.

`-flive-range-shrinkage`
: Attempt to decrease register pressure through register live range shrinkage. This is helpful for fast processors with small or moderate size register sets.

`-fira-algorithm=`*`algorithm`*
: Use the specified coloring algorithm for the integrated register allocator. The *algorithm* argument can be '`priority`', which specifies Chow's priority coloring, or '`CB`', which specifies Chaitin-Briggs coloring. Chaitin-Briggs coloring is not implemented for all architectures, but for those targets that do support it, it is the default because it generates better code.

`-fira-region=`*`region`*
: Use specified regions for the integrated register allocator. The *region* argument should be one of the following:

  '`all`'
  : Use all loops as register allocation regions. This can give the best results for machines with a small and/or irregular register set.

  '`mixed`'
  : Use all loops except for loops with small register pressure as the regions. This value usually gives the best results in most cases and for most architectures, and is enabled by default when compiling with optimization for speed ('`-O`', '`-O2`', ...).

'one' Use all functions as a single region. This typically results in the smallest code size, and is enabled by default for '-Os' or '-O0'.

-fira-hoist-pressure
: Use IRA to evaluate register pressure in the code hoisting pass for decisions to hoist expressions. This option usually results in smaller code, but it can slow the compiler down.

  This option is enabled at level '-Os' for all targets.

-fira-loop-pressure
: Use IRA to evaluate register pressure in loops for decisions to move loop invariants. This option usually results in generation of faster and smaller code on machines with large register files (>= 32 registers), but it can slow the compiler down.

  This option is enabled at level '-O3' for some targets.

-fno-ira-share-save-slots
: Disable sharing of stack slots used for saving call-used hard registers living through a call. Each hard register gets a separate stack slot, and as a result function stack frames are larger.

-fno-ira-share-spill-slots
: Disable sharing of stack slots allocated for pseudo-registers. Each pseudo-register that does not get a hard register gets a separate stack slot, and as a result function stack frames are larger.

-flra-remat
: Enable CFG-sensitive rematerialization in LRA. Instead of loading values of spilled pseudos, LRA tries to rematerialize (recalculate) values if it is profitable.

  Enabled at levels '-O2', '-O3', '-Os'.

-fdelayed-branch
: If supported for the target machine, attempt to reorder instructions to exploit instruction slots available after delayed branch instructions.

  Enabled at levels '-O', '-O2', '-O3', '-Os'.

-fschedule-insns
: If supported for the target machine, attempt to reorder instructions to eliminate execution stalls due to required data being unavailable. This helps machines that have slow floating point or memory load instructions by allowing other instructions to be issued until the result of the load or floating-point instruction is required.

  Enabled at levels '-O2', '-O3'.

-fschedule-insns2
: Similar to '-fschedule-insns', but requests an additional pass of instruction scheduling after register allocation has been done. This is especially useful on machines with a relatively small number of registers and where memory load instructions take more than one cycle.

  Enabled at levels '-O2', '-O3', '-Os'.

`-fno-sched-interblock`
: Don't schedule instructions across basic blocks. This is normally enabled by default when scheduling before register allocation, i.e. with '`-fschedule-insns`' or at '`-O2`' or higher.

`-fno-sched-spec`
: Don't allow speculative motion of non-load instructions. This is normally enabled by default when scheduling before register allocation, i.e. with '`-fschedule-insns`' or at '`-O2`' or higher.

`-fsched-pressure`
: Enable register pressure sensitive insn scheduling before register allocation. This only makes sense when scheduling before register allocation is enabled, i.e. with '`-fschedule-insns`' or at '`-O2`' or higher. Usage of this option can improve the generated code and decrease its size by preventing register pressure increase above the number of available hard registers and subsequent spills in register allocation.

`-fsched-spec-load`
: Allow speculative motion of some load instructions. This only makes sense when scheduling before register allocation, i.e. with '`-fschedule-insns`' or at '`-O2`' or higher.

`-fsched-spec-load-dangerous`
: Allow speculative motion of more load instructions. This only makes sense when scheduling before register allocation, i.e. with '`-fschedule-insns`' or at '`-O2`' or higher.

`-fsched-stalled-insns`
`-fsched-stalled-insns=`*n*
: Define how many insns (if any) can be moved prematurely from the queue of stalled insns into the ready list during the second scheduling pass. '`-fno-sched-stalled-insns`' means that no insns are moved prematurely, '`-fsched-stalled-insns=0`' means there is no limit on how many queued insns can be moved prematurely. '`-fsched-stalled-insns`' without a value is equivalent to '`-fsched-stalled-insns=1`'.

`-fsched-stalled-insns-dep`
`-fsched-stalled-insns-dep=`*n*
: Define how many insn groups (cycles) are examined for a dependency on a stalled insn that is a candidate for premature removal from the queue of stalled insns. This has an effect only during the second scheduling pass, and only if '`-fsched-stalled-insns`' is used. '`-fno-sched-stalled-insns-dep`' is equivalent to '`-fsched-stalled-insns-dep=0`'. '`-fsched-stalled-insns-dep`' without a value is equivalent to '`-fsched-stalled-insns-dep=1`'.

`-fsched2-use-superblocks`
: When scheduling after register allocation, use superblock scheduling. This allows motion across basic block boundaries, resulting in faster schedules. This

option is experimental, as not all machine descriptions used by GCC model the CPU closely enough to avoid unreliable results from the algorithm.

This only makes sense when scheduling after register allocation, i.e. with '-fschedule-insns2' or at '-O2' or higher.

`-fsched-group-heuristic`
: Enable the group heuristic in the scheduler. This heuristic favors the instruction that belongs to a schedule group. This is enabled by default when scheduling is enabled, i.e. with '-fschedule-insns' or '-fschedule-insns2' or at '-O2' or higher.

`-fsched-critical-path-heuristic`
: Enable the critical-path heuristic in the scheduler. This heuristic favors instructions on the critical path. This is enabled by default when scheduling is enabled, i.e. with '-fschedule-insns' or '-fschedule-insns2' or at '-O2' or higher.

`-fsched-spec-insn-heuristic`
: Enable the speculative instruction heuristic in the scheduler. This heuristic favors speculative instructions with greater dependency weakness. This is enabled by default when scheduling is enabled, i.e. with '-fschedule-insns' or '-fschedule-insns2' or at '-O2' or higher.

`-fsched-rank-heuristic`
: Enable the rank heuristic in the scheduler. This heuristic favors the instruction belonging to a basic block with greater size or frequency. This is enabled by default when scheduling is enabled, i.e. with '-fschedule-insns' or '-fschedule-insns2' or at '-O2' or higher.

`-fsched-last-insn-heuristic`
: Enable the last-instruction heuristic in the scheduler. This heuristic favors the instruction that is less dependent on the last instruction scheduled. This is enabled by default when scheduling is enabled, i.e. with '-fschedule-insns' or '-fschedule-insns2' or at '-O2' or higher.

`-fsched-dep-count-heuristic`
: Enable the dependent-count heuristic in the scheduler. This heuristic favors the instruction that has more instructions depending on it. This is enabled by default when scheduling is enabled, i.e. with '-fschedule-insns' or '-fschedule-insns2' or at '-O2' or higher.

`-freschedule-modulo-scheduled-loops`
: Modulo scheduling is performed before traditional scheduling. If a loop is modulo scheduled, later scheduling passes may change its schedule. Use this option to control that behavior.

`-fselective-scheduling`
: Schedule instructions using selective scheduling algorithm. Selective scheduling runs instead of the first scheduler pass.

`-fselective-scheduling2`
: Schedule instructions using selective scheduling algorithm. Selective scheduling runs instead of the second scheduler pass.

`-fsel-sched-pipelining`
: Enable software pipelining of innermost loops during selective scheduling. This option has no effect unless one of '`-fselective-scheduling`' or '`-fselective-scheduling2`' is turned on.

`-fsel-sched-pipelining-outer-loops`
: When pipelining loops during selective scheduling, also pipeline outer loops. This option has no effect unless '`-fsel-sched-pipelining`' is turned on.

`-fsemantic-interposition`
: Some object formats, like ELF, allow interposing of symbols by the dynamic linker. This means that for symbols exported from the DSO, the compiler cannot perform interprocedural propagation, inlining and other optimizations in anticipation that the function or variable in question may change. While this feature is useful, for example, to rewrite memory allocation functions by a debugging implementation, it is expensive in the terms of code quality. With '`-fno-semantic-interposition`' the compiler assumes that if interposition happens for functions the overwriting function will have precisely the same semantics (and side effects). Similarly if interposition happens for variables, the constructor of the variable will be the same. The flag has no effect for functions explicitly declared inline (where it is never allowed for interposition to change semantics) and for symbols explicitly declared weak.

`-fshrink-wrap`
: Emit function prologues only before parts of the function that need it, rather than at the top of the function. This flag is enabled by default at '`-O`' and higher.

`-fcaller-saves`
: Enable allocation of values to registers that are clobbered by function calls, by emitting extra instructions to save and restore the registers around such calls. Such allocation is done only when it seems to result in better code.

  This option is always enabled by default on certain machines, usually those which have no call-preserved registers to use instead.

  Enabled at levels '`-O2`', '`-O3`', '`-Os`'.

`-fcombine-stack-adjustments`
: Tracks stack adjustments (pushes and pops) and stack memory references and then tries to find ways to combine them.

  Enabled by default at '`-O1`' and higher.

`-fipa-ra`
: Use caller save registers for allocation if those registers are not used by any called function. In that case it is not necessary to save and restore them around calls. This is only possible if called functions are part of same compilation unit as current function and they are compiled before it.

  Enabled at levels '`-O2`', '`-O3`', '`-Os`'.

`-fconserve-stack`
: Attempt to minimize stack usage. The compiler attempts to use less stack space, even if that makes the program slower. This option implies setting the

'`large-stack-frame`' parameter to 100 and the '`large-stack-frame-growth`' parameter to 400.

`-ftree-reassoc`
: Perform reassociation on trees. This flag is enabled by default at '`-O`' and higher.

`-ftree-pre`
: Perform partial redundancy elimination (PRE) on trees. This flag is enabled by default at '`-O2`' and '`-O3`'.

`-ftree-partial-pre`
: Make partial redundancy elimination (PRE) more aggressive. This flag is enabled by default at '`-O3`'.

`-ftree-forwprop`
: Perform forward propagation on trees. This flag is enabled by default at '`-O`' and higher.

`-ftree-fre`
: Perform full redundancy elimination (FRE) on trees. The difference between FRE and PRE is that FRE only considers expressions that are computed on all paths leading to the redundant computation. This analysis is faster than PRE, though it exposes fewer redundancies. This flag is enabled by default at '`-O`' and higher.

`-ftree-phiprop`
: Perform hoisting of loads from conditional pointers on trees. This pass is enabled by default at '`-O`' and higher.

`-fhoist-adjacent-loads`
: Speculatively hoist loads from both branches of an if-then-else if the loads are from adjacent locations in the same structure and the target architecture has a conditional move instruction. This flag is enabled by default at '`-O2`' and higher.

`-ftree-copy-prop`
: Perform copy propagation on trees. This pass eliminates unnecessary copy operations. This flag is enabled by default at '`-O`' and higher.

`-fipa-pure-const`
: Discover which functions are pure or constant. Enabled by default at '`-O`' and higher.

`-fipa-reference`
: Discover which static variables do not escape the compilation unit. Enabled by default at '`-O`' and higher.

`-fipa-pta`
: Perform interprocedural pointer analysis and interprocedural modification and reference analysis. This option can cause excessive memory and compile-time usage on large compilation units. It is not enabled by default at any optimization level.

`-fipa-profile`
: Perform interprocedural profile propagation. The functions called only from cold functions are marked as cold. Also functions executed once (such as `cold`, `noreturn`, static constructors or destructors) are identified. Cold functions and loop less parts of functions executed once are then optimized for size. Enabled by default at '`-O`' and higher.

`-fipa-cp`
: Perform interprocedural constant propagation. This optimization analyzes the program to determine when values passed to functions are constants and then optimizes accordingly. This optimization can substantially increase performance if the application has constants passed to functions. This flag is enabled by default at '`-O2`', '`-Os`' and '`-O3`'.

`-fipa-cp-clone`
: Perform function cloning to make interprocedural constant propagation stronger. When enabled, interprocedural constant propagation performs function cloning when externally visible function can be called with constant arguments. Because this optimization can create multiple copies of functions, it may significantly increase code size (see '`--param ipcp-unit-growth=`*`value`*'). This flag is enabled by default at '`-O3`'.

`-fipa-cp-alignment`
: When enabled, this optimization propagates alignment of function parameters to support better vectorization and string operations.

  This flag is enabled by default at '`-O2`' and '`-Os`'. It requires that '`-fipa-cp`' is enabled.

`-fipa-icf`
: Perform Identical Code Folding for functions and read-only variables. The optimization reduces code size and may disturb unwind stacks by replacing a function by equivalent one with a different name. The optimization works more effectively with link time optimization enabled.

  Nevertheless the behavior is similar to Gold Linker ICF optimization, GCC ICF works on different levels and thus the optimizations are not same - there are equivalences that are found only by GCC and equivalences found only by Gold.

  This flag is enabled by default at '`-O2`' and '`-Os`'.

`-fisolate-erroneous-paths-dereference`
: Detect paths that trigger erroneous or undefined behavior due to dereferencing a null pointer. Isolate those paths from the main control flow and turn the statement with erroneous or undefined behavior into a trap. This flag is enabled by default at '`-O2`' and higher and depends on '`-fdelete-null-pointer-checks`' also being enabled.

`-fisolate-erroneous-paths-attribute`
: Detect paths that trigger erroneous or undefined behavior due a null value being used in a way forbidden by a `returns_nonnull` or `nonnull` attribute. Isolate those paths from the main control flow and turn the statement with erroneous or undefined behavior into a trap. This is not currently enabled, but may be enabled by '`-O2`' in the future.

`-ftree-sink`
Perform forward store motion on trees. This flag is enabled by default at '`-O`' and higher.

`-ftree-bit-ccp`
Perform sparse conditional bit constant propagation on trees and propagate pointer alignment information. This pass only operates on local scalar variables and is enabled by default at '`-O`' and higher. It requires that '`-ftree-ccp`' is enabled.

`-ftree-ccp`
Perform sparse conditional constant propagation (CCP) on trees. This pass only operates on local scalar variables and is enabled by default at '`-O`' and higher.

`-fssa-backprop`
Propagate information about uses of a value up the definition chain in order to simplify the definitions. For example, this pass strips sign operations if the sign of a value never matters. The flag is enabled by default at '`-O`' and higher.

`-fssa-phiopt`
Perform pattern matching on SSA PHI nodes to optimize conditional code. This pass is enabled by default at '`-O`' and higher.

`-ftree-switch-conversion`
Perform conversion of simple initializations in a switch to initializations from a scalar array. This flag is enabled by default at '`-O2`' and higher.

`-ftree-tail-merge`
Look for identical code sequences. When found, replace one with a jump to the other. This optimization is known as tail merging or cross jumping. This flag is enabled by default at '`-O2`' and higher. The compilation time in this pass can be limited using '`max-tail-merge-comparisons`' parameter and '`max-tail-merge-iterations`' parameter.

`-ftree-dce`
Perform dead code elimination (DCE) on trees. This flag is enabled by default at '`-O`' and higher.

`-ftree-builtin-call-dce`
Perform conditional dead code elimination (DCE) for calls to built-in functions that may set `errno` but are otherwise side-effect free. This flag is enabled by default at '`-O2`' and higher if '`-Os`' is not also specified.

`-ftree-dominator-opts`
Perform a variety of simple scalar cleanups (constant/copy propagation, redundancy elimination, range propagation and expression simplification) based on a dominator tree traversal. This also performs jump threading (to reduce jumps to jumps). This flag is enabled by default at '`-O`' and higher.

`-ftree-dse`
Perform dead store elimination (DSE) on trees. A dead store is a store into a memory location that is later overwritten by another store without any inter-

vening loads. In this case the earlier store can be deleted. This flag is enabled by default at '-O' and higher.

-ftree-ch
: Perform loop header copying on trees. This is beneficial since it increases effectiveness of code motion optimizations. It also saves one jump. This flag is enabled by default at '-O' and higher. It is not enabled for '-Os', since it usually increases code size.

-ftree-loop-optimize
: Perform loop optimizations on trees. This flag is enabled by default at '-O' and higher.

-ftree-loop-linear
-floop-interchange
-floop-strip-mine
-floop-block
-floop-unroll-and-jam
: Perform loop nest optimizations. Same as '-floop-nest-optimize'. To use this code transformation, GCC has to be configured with '--with-isl' to enable the Graphite loop transformation infrastructure.

-fgraphite-identity
: Enable the identity transformation for graphite. For every SCoP we generate the polyhedral representation and transform it back to gimple. Using '-fgraphite-identity' we can check the costs or benefits of the GIMPLE -> GRAPHITE -> GIMPLE transformation. Some minimal optimizations are also performed by the code generator isl, like index splitting and dead code elimination in loops.

-floop-nest-optimize
: Enable the isl based loop nest optimizer. This is a generic loop nest optimizer based on the Pluto optimization algorithms. It calculates a loop structure optimized for data-locality and parallelism. This option is experimental.

-floop-parallelize-all
: Use the Graphite data dependence analysis to identify loops that can be parallelized. Parallelize all the loops that can be analyzed to not contain loop carried dependences without checking that it is profitable to parallelize the loops.

-ftree-coalesce-vars
: While transforming the program out of the SSA representation, attempt to reduce copying by coalescing versions of different user-defined variables, instead of just compiler temporaries. This may severely limit the ability to debug an optimized program compiled with '-fno-var-tracking-assignments'. In the negated form, this flag prevents SSA coalescing of user variables. This option is enabled by default if optimization is enabled, and it does very little otherwise.

-ftree-loop-if-convert
: Attempt to transform conditional jumps in the innermost loops to branch-less equivalents. The intent is to remove control-flow from the innermost loops in

order to improve the ability of the vectorization pass to handle these loops. This is enabled by default if vectorization is enabled.

`-ftree-loop-if-convert-stores`

Attempt to also if-convert conditional jumps containing memory writes. This transformation can be unsafe for multi-threaded programs as it transforms conditional memory writes into unconditional memory writes. For example,

```
for (i = 0; i < N; i++)
  if (cond)
    A[i] = expr;
```

is transformed to

```
for (i = 0; i < N; i++)
  A[i] = cond ? expr : A[i];
```

potentially producing data races.

`-ftree-loop-distribution`

Perform loop distribution. This flag can improve cache performance on big loop bodies and allow further loop optimizations, like parallelization or vectorization, to take place. For example, the loop

```
DO I = 1, N
  A(I) = B(I) + C
  D(I) = E(I) * F
ENDDO
```

is transformed to

```
DO I = 1, N
   A(I) = B(I) + C
ENDDO
DO I = 1, N
   D(I) = E(I) * F
ENDDO
```

`-ftree-loop-distribute-patterns`

Perform loop distribution of patterns that can be code generated with calls to a library. This flag is enabled by default at '-O3'.

This pass distributes the initialization loops and generates a call to memset zero. For example, the loop

```
DO I = 1, N
  A(I) = 0
  B(I) = A(I) + I
ENDDO
```

is transformed to

```
DO I = 1, N
   A(I) = 0
ENDDO
DO I = 1, N
   B(I) = A(I) + I
ENDDO
```

and the initialization loop is transformed into a call to memset zero.

`-ftree-loop-im`

Perform loop invariant motion on trees. This pass moves only invariants that are hard to handle at RTL level (function calls, operations that expand to non-trivial sequences of insns). With '-funswitch-loops' it also moves operands of conditions that are invariant out of the loop, so that we can use just trivial invariantness analysis in loop unswitching. The pass also includes store motion.

`-ftree-loop-ivcanon`
: Create a canonical counter for number of iterations in loops for which determining number of iterations requires complicated analysis. Later optimizations then may determine the number easily. Useful especially in connection with unrolling.

`-fivopts`
: Perform induction variable optimizations (strength reduction, induction variable merging and induction variable elimination) on trees.

`-ftree-parallelize-loops=n`
: Parallelize loops, i.e., split their iteration space to run in n threads. This is only possible for loops whose iterations are independent and can be arbitrarily reordered. The optimization is only profitable on multiprocessor machines, for loops that are CPU-intensive, rather than constrained e.g. by memory bandwidth. This option implies '`-pthread`', and thus is only supported on targets that have support for '`-pthread`'.

`-ftree-pta`
: Perform function-local points-to analysis on trees. This flag is enabled by default at '`-O`' and higher.

`-ftree-sra`
: Perform scalar replacement of aggregates. This pass replaces structure references with scalars to prevent committing structures to memory too early. This flag is enabled by default at '`-O`' and higher.

`-ftree-ter`
: Perform temporary expression replacement during the SSA->normal phase. Single use/single def temporaries are replaced at their use location with their defining expression. This results in non-GIMPLE code, but gives the expanders much more complex trees to work on resulting in better RTL generation. This is enabled by default at '`-O`' and higher.

`-ftree-slsr`
: Perform straight-line strength reduction on trees. This recognizes related expressions involving multiplications and replaces them by less expensive calculations when possible. This is enabled by default at '`-O`' and higher.

`-ftree-vectorize`
: Perform vectorization on trees. This flag enables '`-ftree-loop-vectorize`' and '`-ftree-slp-vectorize`' if not explicitly specified.

`-ftree-loop-vectorize`
: Perform loop vectorization on trees. This flag is enabled by default at '`-O3`' and when '`-ftree-vectorize`' is enabled.

`-ftree-slp-vectorize`
: Perform basic block vectorization on trees. This flag is enabled by default at '`-O3`' and when '`-ftree-vectorize`' is enabled.

`-fvect-cost-model=model`

Alter the cost model used for vectorization. The *model* argument should be one of '`unlimited`', '`dynamic`' or '`cheap`'. With the '`unlimited`' model the vectorized code-path is assumed to be profitable while with the '`dynamic`' model a runtime check guards the vectorized code-path to enable it only for iteration counts that will likely execute faster than when executing the original scalar loop. The '`cheap`' model disables vectorization of loops where doing so would be cost prohibitive for example due to required runtime checks for data dependence or alignment but otherwise is equal to the '`dynamic`' model. The default cost model depends on other optimization flags and is either '`dynamic`' or '`cheap`'.

`-fsimd-cost-model=model`

Alter the cost model used for vectorization of loops marked with the OpenMP or Cilk Plus simd directive. The *model* argument should be one of '`unlimited`', '`dynamic`', '`cheap`'. All values of *model* have the same meaning as described in '`-fvect-cost-model`' and by default a cost model defined with '`-fvect-cost-model`' is used.

`-ftree-vrp`

Perform Value Range Propagation on trees. This is similar to the constant propagation pass, but instead of values, ranges of values are propagated. This allows the optimizers to remove unnecessary range checks like array bound checks and null pointer checks. This is enabled by default at '`-O2`' and higher. Null pointer check elimination is only done if '`-fdelete-null-pointer-checks`' is enabled.

`-fsplit-paths`

Split paths leading to loop backedges. This can improve dead code elimination and common subexpression elimination. This is enabled by default at '`-O2`' and above.

`-fsplit-ivs-in-unroller`

Enables expression of values of induction variables in later iterations of the unrolled loop using the value in the first iteration. This breaks long dependency chains, thus improving efficiency of the scheduling passes.

A combination of '`-fweb`' and CSE is often sufficient to obtain the same effect. However, that is not reliable in cases where the loop body is more complicated than a single basic block. It also does not work at all on some architectures due to restrictions in the CSE pass.

This optimization is enabled by default.

`-fvariable-expansion-in-unroller`

With this option, the compiler creates multiple copies of some local variables when unrolling a loop, which can result in superior code.

`-fpartial-inlining`

Inline parts of functions. This option has any effect only when inlining itself is turned on by the '`-finline-functions`' or '`-finline-small-functions`' options.

Enabled at level '`-O2`'.

`-fpredictive-commoning`
Perform predictive commoning optimization, i.e., reusing computations (especially memory loads and stores) performed in previous iterations of loops.

This option is enabled at level '`-O3`'.

`-fprefetch-loop-arrays`
If supported by the target machine, generate instructions to prefetch memory to improve the performance of loops that access large arrays.

This option may generate better or worse code; results are highly dependent on the structure of loops within the source code.

Disabled at level '`-Os`'.

`-fno-peephole`
`-fno-peephole2`
Disable any machine-specific peephole optimizations. The difference between '`-fno-peephole`' and '`-fno-peephole2`' is in how they are implemented in the compiler; some targets use one, some use the other, a few use both.

'`-fpeephole`' is enabled by default. '`-fpeephole2`' enabled at levels '`-O2`', '`-O3`', '`-Os`'.

`-fno-guess-branch-probability`
Do not guess branch probabilities using heuristics.

GCC uses heuristics to guess branch probabilities if they are not provided by profiling feedback ('`-fprofile-arcs`'). These heuristics are based on the control flow graph. If some branch probabilities are specified by `__builtin_expect`, then the heuristics are used to guess branch probabilities for the rest of the control flow graph, taking the `__builtin_expect` info into account. The interactions between the heuristics and `__builtin_expect` can be complex, and in some cases, it may be useful to disable the heuristics so that the effects of `__builtin_expect` are easier to understand.

The default is '`-fguess-branch-probability`' at levels '`-O`', '`-O2`', '`-O3`', '`-Os`'.

`-freorder-blocks`
Reorder basic blocks in the compiled function in order to reduce number of taken branches and improve code locality.

Enabled at levels '`-O`', '`-O2`', '`-O3`', '`-Os`'.

`-freorder-blocks-algorithm=`*`algorithm`*
Use the specified algorithm for basic block reordering. The *algorithm* argument can be '`simple`', which does not increase code size (except sometimes due to secondary effects like alignment), or '`stc`', the "software trace cache" algorithm, which tries to put all often executed code together, minimizing the number of branches executed by making extra copies of code.

The default is '`simple`' at levels '`-O`', '`-Os`', and '`stc`' at levels '`-O2`', '`-O3`'.

`-freorder-blocks-and-partition`
In addition to reordering basic blocks in the compiled function, in order to reduce number of taken branches, partitions hot and cold basic blocks into

separate sections of the assembly and '.o' files, to improve paging and cache locality performance.

This optimization is automatically turned off in the presence of exception handling, for linkonce sections, for functions with a user-defined section attribute and on any architecture that does not support named sections.

Enabled for x86 at levels '-O2', '-O3'.

`-freorder-functions`

Reorder functions in the object file in order to improve code locality. This is implemented by using special subsections `.text.hot` for most frequently executed functions and `.text.unlikely` for unlikely executed functions. Reordering is done by the linker so object file format must support named sections and linker must place them in a reasonable way.

Also profile feedback must be available to make this option effective. See '-fprofile-arcs' for details.

Enabled at levels '-O2', '-O3', '-Os'.

`-fstrict-aliasing`

Allow the compiler to assume the strictest aliasing rules applicable to the language being compiled. For C (and C++), this activates optimizations based on the type of expressions. In particular, an object of one type is assumed never to reside at the same address as an object of a different type, unless the types are almost the same. For example, an `unsigned int` can alias an `int`, but not a `void*` or a `double`. A character type may alias any other type.

Pay special attention to code like this:

```
union a_union {
  int i;
  double d;
};

int f() {
  union a_union t;
  t.d = 3.0;
  return t.i;
}
```

The practice of reading from a different union member than the one most recently written to (called "type-punning") is common. Even with '-fstrict-aliasing', type-punning is allowed, provided the memory is accessed through the union type. So, the code above works as expected. See Section 4.9 [Structures unions enumerations and bit-fields implementation], page 377. However, this code might not:

```
int f() {
  union a_union t;
  int* ip;
  t.d = 3.0;
  ip = &t.i;
  return *ip;
}
```

Similarly, access by taking the address, casting the resulting pointer and dereferencing the result has undefined behavior, even if the cast uses a union type, e.g.:

```
int f() {
  double d = 3.0;
  return ((union a_union *) &d)->i;
}
```

The '-fstrict-aliasing' option is enabled at levels '-O2', '-O3', '-Os'.

-fstrict-overflow

Allow the compiler to assume strict signed overflow rules, depending on the language being compiled. For C (and C++) this means that overflow when doing arithmetic with signed numbers is undefined, which means that the compiler may assume that it does not happen. This permits various optimizations. For example, the compiler assumes that an expression like `i + 10 > i` is always true for signed `i`. This assumption is only valid if signed overflow is undefined, as the expression is false if `i + 10` overflows when using twos complement arithmetic. When this option is in effect any attempt to determine whether an operation on signed numbers overflows must be written carefully to not actually involve overflow.

This option also allows the compiler to assume strict pointer semantics: given a pointer to an object, if adding an offset to that pointer does not produce a pointer to the same object, the addition is undefined. This permits the compiler to conclude that `p + u > p` is always true for a pointer `p` and unsigned integer `u`. This assumption is only valid because pointer wraparound is undefined, as the expression is false if `p + u` overflows using twos complement arithmetic.

See also the '-fwrapv' option. Using '-fwrapv' means that integer signed overflow is fully defined: it wraps. When '-fwrapv' is used, there is no difference between '-fstrict-overflow' and '-fno-strict-overflow' for integers. With '-fwrapv' certain types of overflow are permitted. For example, if the compiler gets an overflow when doing arithmetic on constants, the overflowed value can still be used with '-fwrapv', but not otherwise.

The '-fstrict-overflow' option is enabled at levels '-O2', '-O3', '-Os'.

-falign-functions
-falign-functions=*n*

Align the start of functions to the next power-of-two greater than *n*, skipping up to *n* bytes. For instance, '-falign-functions=32' aligns functions to the next 32-byte boundary, but '-falign-functions=24' aligns to the next 32-byte boundary only if this can be done by skipping 23 bytes or less.

'-fno-align-functions' and '-falign-functions=1' are equivalent and mean that functions are not aligned.

Some assemblers only support this flag when *n* is a power of two; in that case, it is rounded up.

If *n* is not specified or is zero, use a machine-dependent default.

Enabled at levels '-O2', '-O3'.

`-falign-labels`
`-falign-labels=`*n*

Align all branch targets to a power-of-two boundary, skipping up to *n* bytes like '`-falign-functions`'. This option can easily make code slower, because it must insert dummy operations for when the branch target is reached in the usual flow of the code.

'`-fno-align-labels`' and '`-falign-labels=1`' are equivalent and mean that labels are not aligned.

If '`-falign-loops`' or '`-falign-jumps`' are applicable and are greater than this value, then their values are used instead.

If *n* is not specified or is zero, use a machine-dependent default which is very likely to be '`1`', meaning no alignment.

Enabled at levels '`-O2`', '`-O3`'.

`-falign-loops`
`-falign-loops=`*n*

Align loops to a power-of-two boundary, skipping up to *n* bytes like '`-falign-functions`'. If the loops are executed many times, this makes up for any execution of the dummy operations.

'`-fno-align-loops`' and '`-falign-loops=1`' are equivalent and mean that loops are not aligned.

If *n* is not specified or is zero, use a machine-dependent default.

Enabled at levels '`-O2`', '`-O3`'.

`-falign-jumps`
`-falign-jumps=`*n*

Align branch targets to a power-of-two boundary, for branch targets where the targets can only be reached by jumping, skipping up to *n* bytes like '`-falign-functions`'. In this case, no dummy operations need be executed.

'`-fno-align-jumps`' and '`-falign-jumps=1`' are equivalent and mean that loops are not aligned.

If *n* is not specified or is zero, use a machine-dependent default.

Enabled at levels '`-O2`', '`-O3`'.

`-funit-at-a-time`

This option is left for compatibility reasons. '`-funit-at-a-time`' has no effect, while '`-fno-unit-at-a-time`' implies '`-fno-toplevel-reorder`' and '`-fno-section-anchors`'.

Enabled by default.

`-fno-toplevel-reorder`

Do not reorder top-level functions, variables, and `asm` statements. Output them in the same order that they appear in the input file. When this option is used, unreferenced static variables are not removed. This option is intended to support existing code that relies on a particular ordering. For new code, it is better to use attributes when possible.

Enabled at level '-O0'. When disabled explicitly, it also implies '-fno-section-anchors', which is otherwise enabled at '-O0' on some targets.

`-fweb` Constructs webs as commonly used for register allocation purposes and assign each web individual pseudo register. This allows the register allocation pass to operate on pseudos directly, but also strengthens several other optimization passes, such as CSE, loop optimizer and trivial dead code remover. It can, however, make debugging impossible, since variables no longer stay in a "home register".

Enabled by default with '-funroll-loops'.

`-fwhole-program`

Assume that the current compilation unit represents the whole program being compiled. All public functions and variables with the exception of `main` and those merged by attribute `externally_visible` become static functions and in effect are optimized more aggressively by interprocedural optimizers.

This option should not be used in combination with '-flto'. Instead relying on a linker plugin should provide safer and more precise information.

`-flto[=n]`

This option runs the standard link-time optimizer. When invoked with source code, it generates GIMPLE (one of GCC's internal representations) and writes it to special ELF sections in the object file. When the object files are linked together, all the function bodies are read from these ELF sections and instantiated as if they had been part of the same translation unit.

To use the link-time optimizer, '-flto' and optimization options should be specified at compile time and during the final link. It is recommended that you compile all the files participating in the same link with the same options and also specify those options at link time. For example:

```
gcc -c -O2 -flto foo.c
gcc -c -O2 -flto bar.c
gcc -o myprog -flto -O2 foo.o bar.o
```

The first two invocations to GCC save a bytecode representation of GIMPLE into special ELF sections inside 'foo.o' and 'bar.o'. The final invocation reads the GIMPLE bytecode from 'foo.o' and 'bar.o', merges the two files into a single internal image, and compiles the result as usual. Since both 'foo.o' and 'bar.o' are merged into a single image, this causes all the interprocedural analyses and optimizations in GCC to work across the two files as if they were a single one. This means, for example, that the inliner is able to inline functions in 'bar.o' into functions in 'foo.o' and vice-versa.

Another (simpler) way to enable link-time optimization is:

```
gcc -o myprog -flto -O2 foo.c bar.c
```

The above generates bytecode for 'foo.c' and 'bar.c', merges them together into a single GIMPLE representation and optimizes them as usual to produce 'myprog'.

The only important thing to keep in mind is that to enable link-time optimizations you need to use the GCC driver to perform the link step. GCC then automatically performs link-time optimization if any of the objects involved were compiled with the '-flto' command-line option. You generally should specify the optimization options to be used for link-time optimization though GCC tries to be clever at guessing an optimization level to use from the options used at compile time if you fail to specify one at link time. You can always override the automatic decision to do link-time optimization at link time by passing '-fno-lto' to the link command.

To make whole program optimization effective, it is necessary to make certain whole program assumptions. The compiler needs to know what functions and variables can be accessed by libraries and runtime outside of the link-time optimized unit. When supported by the linker, the linker plugin (see '-fuse-linker-plugin') passes information to the compiler about used and externally visible symbols. When the linker plugin is not available, '-fwhole-program' should be used to allow the compiler to make these assumptions, which leads to more aggressive optimization decisions.

When '-fuse-linker-plugin' is not enabled, when a file is compiled with '-flto', the generated object file is larger than a regular object file because it contains GIMPLE bytecodes and the usual final code (see '-ffat-lto-objects'. This means that object files with LTO information can be linked as normal object files; if '-fno-lto' is passed to the linker, no interprocedural optimizations are applied. Note that when '-fno-fat-lto-objects' is enabled the compile stage is faster but you cannot perform a regular, non-LTO link on them.

Additionally, the optimization flags used to compile individual files are not necessarily related to those used at link time. For instance,

```
gcc -c -O0 -ffat-lto-objects -flto foo.c
gcc -c -O0 -ffat-lto-objects -flto bar.c
gcc -o myprog -O3 foo.o bar.o
```

This produces individual object files with unoptimized assembler code, but the resulting binary 'myprog' is optimized at '-O3'. If, instead, the final binary is generated with '-fno-lto', then 'myprog' is not optimized.

When producing the final binary, GCC only applies link-time optimizations to those files that contain bytecode. Therefore, you can mix and match object files and libraries with GIMPLE bytecodes and final object code. GCC automatically selects which files to optimize in LTO mode and which files to link without further processing.

There are some code generation flags preserved by GCC when generating bytecodes, as they need to be used during the final link stage. Generally options specified at link time override those specified at compile time.

If you do not specify an optimization level option '-O' at link time, then GCC uses the highest optimization level used when compiling the object files.

Currently, the following options and their settings are taken from the first object file that explicitly specifies them: '-fPIC', '-fpic', '-fpie', '-fcommon', '-fexceptions', '-fnon-call-exceptions', '-fgnu-tm' and all the '-m' target flags.

Certain ABI-changing flags are required to match in all compilation units, and trying to override this at link time with a conflicting value is ignored. This includes options such as '-freg-struct-return' and '-fpcc-struct-return'.

Other options such as '-ffp-contract', '-fno-strict-overflow', '-fwrapv', '-fno-trapv' or '-fno-strict-aliasing' are passed through to the link stage and merged conservatively for conflicting translation units. Specifically '-fno-strict-overflow', '-fwrapv' and '-fno-trapv' take precedence; and for example '-ffp-contract=off' takes precedence over '-ffp-contract=fast'. You can override them at link time.

If LTO encounters objects with C linkage declared with incompatible types in separate translation units to be linked together (undefined behavior according to ISO C99 6.2.7), a non-fatal diagnostic may be issued. The behavior is still undefined at run time. Similar diagnostics may be raised for other languages.

Another feature of LTO is that it is possible to apply interprocedural optimizations on files written in different languages:

```
gcc -c -flto foo.c
g++ -c -flto bar.cc
gfortran -c -flto baz.f90
g++ -o myprog -flto -O3 foo.o bar.o baz.o -lgfortran
```

Notice that the final link is done with g++ to get the C++ runtime libraries and '-lgfortran' is added to get the Fortran runtime libraries. In general, when mixing languages in LTO mode, you should use the same link command options as when mixing languages in a regular (non-LTO) compilation.

If object files containing GIMPLE bytecode are stored in a library archive, say 'libfoo.a', it is possible to extract and use them in an LTO link if you are using a linker with plugin support. To create static libraries suitable for LTO, use gcc-ar and gcc-ranlib instead of ar and ranlib; to show the symbols of object files with GIMPLE bytecode, use gcc-nm. Those commands require that ar, ranlib and nm have been compiled with plugin support. At link time, use the the flag '-fuse-linker-plugin' to ensure that the library participates in the LTO optimization process:

```
gcc -o myprog -O2 -flto -fuse-linker-plugin a.o b.o -lfoo
```

With the linker plugin enabled, the linker extracts the needed GIMPLE files from 'libfoo.a' and passes them on to the running GCC to make them part of the aggregated GIMPLE image to be optimized.

If you are not using a linker with plugin support and/or do not enable the linker plugin, then the objects inside 'libfoo.a' are extracted and linked as usual, but they do not participate in the LTO optimization process. In order to make a static library suitable for both LTO optimization and usual linkage, compile its object files with '-flto' '-ffat-lto-objects'.

Link-time optimizations do not require the presence of the whole program to operate. If the program does not require any symbols to be exported, it is possible to combine '-flto' and '-fwhole-program' to allow the interprocedural optimizers to use more aggressive assumptions which may lead to improved optimization opportunities. Use of '-fwhole-program' is not needed when linker plugin is active (see '-fuse-linker-plugin').

The current implementation of LTO makes no attempt to generate bytecode that is portable between different types of hosts. The bytecode files are versioned and there is a strict version check, so bytecode files generated in one version of GCC do not work with an older or newer version of GCC.

Link-time optimization does not work well with generation of debugging information. Combining '`-flto`' with '`-g`' is currently experimental and expected to produce unexpected results.

If you specify the optional *n*, the optimization and code generation done at link time is executed in parallel using *n* parallel jobs by utilizing an installed `make` program. The environment variable `MAKE` may be used to override the program used. The default value for *n* is 1.

You can also specify '`-flto=jobserver`' to use GNU make's job server mode to determine the number of parallel jobs. This is useful when the Makefile calling GCC is already executing in parallel. You must prepend a '`+`' to the command recipe in the parent Makefile for this to work. This option likely only works if `MAKE` is GNU make.

`-flto-partition=`*`alg`*
: Specify the partitioning algorithm used by the link-time optimizer. The value is either '`1to1`' to specify a partitioning mirroring the original source files or '`balanced`' to specify partitioning into equally sized chunks (whenever possible) or '`max`' to create new partition for every symbol where possible. Specifying '`none`' as an algorithm disables partitioning and streaming completely. The default value is '`balanced`'. While '`1to1`' can be used as an workaround for various code ordering issues, the '`max`' partitioning is intended for internal testing only. The value '`one`' specifies that exactly one partition should be used while the value '`none`' bypasses partitioning and executes the link-time optimization step directly from the WPA phase.

`-flto-odr-type-merging`
: Enable streaming of mangled types names of C++ types and their unification at link time. This increases size of LTO object files, but enables diagnostics about One Definition Rule violations.

`-flto-compression-level=`*`n`*
: This option specifies the level of compression used for intermediate language written to LTO object files, and is only meaningful in conjunction with LTO mode ('`-flto`'). Valid values are 0 (no compression) to 9 (maximum compression). Values outside this range are clamped to either 0 or 9. If the option is not given, a default balanced compression setting is used.

`-fuse-linker-plugin`
: Enables the use of a linker plugin during link-time optimization. This option relies on plugin support in the linker, which is available in gold or in GNU ld 2.21 or newer.

This option enables the extraction of object files with GIMPLE bytecode out of library archives. This improves the quality of optimization by exposing more code to the link-time optimizer. This information specifies what symbols can be accessed externally (by non-LTO object or during dynamic linking). Resulting code quality improvements on binaries (and shared libraries that use hidden visibility) are similar to '`-fwhole-program`'. See '`-flto`' for a description of the effect of this flag and how to use it.

This option is enabled by default when LTO support in GCC is enabled and GCC was configured for use with a linker supporting plugins (GNU ld 2.21 or newer or gold).

`-ffat-lto-objects`

Fat LTO objects are object files that contain both the intermediate language and the object code. This makes them usable for both LTO linking and normal linking. This option is effective only when compiling with '`-flto`' and is ignored at link time.

'`-fno-fat-lto-objects`' improves compilation time over plain LTO, but requires the complete toolchain to be aware of LTO. It requires a linker with linker plugin support for basic functionality. Additionally, `nm`, `ar` and `ranlib` need to support linker plugins to allow a full-featured build environment (capable of building static libraries etc). GCC provides the `gcc-ar`, `gcc-nm`, `gcc-ranlib` wrappers to pass the right options to these tools. With non fat LTO makefiles need to be modified to use them.

The default is '`-fno-fat-lto-objects`' on targets with linker plugin support.

`-fcompare-elim`

After register allocation and post-register allocation instruction splitting, identify arithmetic instructions that compute processor flags similar to a comparison operation based on that arithmetic. If possible, eliminate the explicit comparison operation.

This pass only applies to certain targets that cannot explicitly represent the comparison operation before register allocation is complete.

Enabled at levels '`-O`', '`-O2`', '`-O3`', '`-Os`'.

`-fcprop-registers`

After register allocation and post-register allocation instruction splitting, perform a copy-propagation pass to try to reduce scheduling dependencies and occasionally eliminate the copy.

Enabled at levels '`-O`', '`-O2`', '`-O3`', '`-Os`'.

`-fprofile-correction`

Profiles collected using an instrumented binary for multi-threaded programs may be inconsistent due to missed counter updates. When this option is specified, GCC uses heuristics to correct or smooth out such inconsistencies. By default, GCC emits an error message when an inconsistent profile is detected.

`-fprofile-use`
`-fprofile-use=`*path*

Enable profile feedback-directed optimizations, and the following optimizations which are generally profitable only with profile feedback available: '`-fbranch-probabilities`', '`-fvpt`', '`-funroll-loops`', '`-fpeel-loops`', '`-ftracer`', '`-ftree-vectorize`', and '`ftree-loop-distribute-patterns`'.

Before you can use this option, you must first generate profiling information. See Section 3.10 [Optimize Options], page 93, for information about the '-fprofile-generate' option.

By default, GCC emits an error message if the feedback profiles do not match the source code. This error can be turned into a warning by using '-Wcoverage-mismatch'. Note this may result in poorly optimized code.

If *path* is specified, GCC looks at the *path* to find the profile feedback data files. See '-fprofile-dir'.

`-fauto-profile`
`-fauto-profile=`*path*

Enable sampling-based feedback-directed optimizations, and the following optimizations which are generally profitable only with profile feedback available: '-fbranch-probabilities', '-fvpt', '-funroll-loops', '-fpeel-loops', '-ftracer', '-ftree-vectorize', '-finline-functions', '-fipa-cp', '-fipa-cp-clone', '-fpredictive-commoning', '-funswitch-loops', '-fgcse-after-reload', and '-ftree-loop-distribute-patterns'.

path is the name of a file containing AutoFDO profile information. If omitted, it defaults to 'fbdata.afdo' in the current directory.

Producing an AutoFDO profile data file requires running your program with the `perf` utility on a supported GNU/Linux target system. For more information, see https://perf.wiki.kernel.org/.

E.g.

```
perf record -e br_inst_retired:near_taken -b -o perf.data \
    -- your_program
```

Then use the `create_gcov` tool to convert the raw profile data to a format that can be used by GCC. You must also supply the unstripped binary for your program to this tool. See https://github.com/google/autofdo.

E.g.

```
create_gcov --binary=your_program.unstripped --profile=perf.data \
    --gcov=profile.afdo
```

The following options control compiler behavior regarding floating-point arithmetic. These options trade off between speed and correctness. All must be specifically enabled.

`-ffloat-store`

Do not store floating-point variables in registers, and inhibit other options that might change whether a floating-point value is taken from a register or memory.

This option prevents undesirable excess precision on machines such as the 68000 where the floating registers (of the 68881) keep more precision than a `double` is supposed to have. Similarly for the x86 architecture. For most programs, the excess precision does only good, but a few programs rely on the precise definition of IEEE floating point. Use '-ffloat-store' for such programs, after modifying them to store all pertinent intermediate computations into variables.

`-fexcess-precision=`*style*

This option allows further control over excess precision on machines where floating-point registers have more precision than the IEEE `float` and `double` types and the processor does not support operations rounding to those types. By default, '-fexcess-precision=fast' is in effect; this means that operations are carried out in the precision of the registers and that it is unpredictable when rounding to the types specified in the source code takes place. When compiling C, if '-fexcess-precision=standard' is specified then excess precision follows the rules specified in ISO C99; in particular, both casts and assignments cause values to be rounded to their semantic types (whereas '-ffloat-store' only affects assignments). This option is enabled by default for C if a strict conformance option such as '-std=c99' is used.

'-fexcess-precision=standard' is not implemented for languages other than C, and has no effect if '-funsafe-math-optimizations' or '-ffast-math' is specified. On the x86, it also has no effect if '-mfpmath=sse' or '-mfpmath=sse+387' is specified; in the former case, IEEE semantics apply without excess precision, and in the latter, rounding is unpredictable.

`-ffast-math`

Sets the options '-fno-math-errno', '-funsafe-math-optimizations', '-ffinite-math-only', '-fno-rounding-math', '-fno-signaling-nans' and '-fcx-limited-range'.

This option causes the preprocessor macro `__FAST_MATH__` to be defined.

This option is not turned on by any '-O' option besides '-Ofast' since it can result in incorrect output for programs that depend on an exact implementation of IEEE or ISO rules/specifications for math functions. It may, however, yield faster code for programs that do not require the guarantees of these specifications.

`-fno-math-errno`

Do not set `errno` after calling math functions that are executed with a single instruction, e.g., `sqrt`. A program that relies on IEEE exceptions for math error handling may want to use this flag for speed while maintaining IEEE arithmetic compatibility.

This option is not turned on by any '-O' option since it can result in incorrect output for programs that depend on an exact implementation of IEEE or ISO rules/specifications for math functions. It may, however, yield faster code for programs that do not require the guarantees of these specifications.

The default is '-fmath-errno'.

On Darwin systems, the math library never sets `errno`. There is therefore no reason for the compiler to consider the possibility that it might, and '-fno-math-errno' is the default.

`-funsafe-math-optimizations`

Allow optimizations for floating-point arithmetic that (a) assume that arguments and results are valid and (b) may violate IEEE or ANSI standards. When used at link time, it may include libraries or startup files that change the default FPU control word or other similar optimizations.

This option is not turned on by any '-O' option since it can result in incorrect output for programs that depend on an exact implementation of IEEE or ISO rules/specifications for math functions. It may, however, yield faster code for programs that do not require the guarantees of these specifications. Enables '-fno-signed-zeros', '-fno-trapping-math', '-fassociative-math' and '-freciprocal-math'.

The default is '-fno-unsafe-math-optimizations'.

`-fassociative-math`
: Allow re-association of operands in series of floating-point operations. This violates the ISO C and C++ language standard by possibly changing computation result. NOTE: re-ordering may change the sign of zero as well as ignore NaNs and inhibit or create underflow or overflow (and thus cannot be used on code that relies on rounding behavior like `(x + 2**52) - 2**52`. May also reorder floating-point comparisons and thus may not be used when ordered comparisons are required. This option requires that both '-fno-signed-zeros' and '-fno-trapping-math' be in effect. Moreover, it doesn't make much sense with '-frounding-math'. For Fortran the option is automatically enabled when both '-fno-signed-zeros' and '-fno-trapping-math' are in effect.

The default is '-fno-associative-math'.

`-freciprocal-math`
: Allow the reciprocal of a value to be used instead of dividing by the value if this enables optimizations. For example `x / y` can be replaced with `x * (1/y)`, which is useful if `(1/y)` is subject to common subexpression elimination. Note that this loses precision and increases the number of flops operating on the value.

The default is '-fno-reciprocal-math'.

`-ffinite-math-only`
: Allow optimizations for floating-point arithmetic that assume that arguments and results are not NaNs or +-Infs.

This option is not turned on by any '-O' option since it can result in incorrect output for programs that depend on an exact implementation of IEEE or ISO rules/specifications for math functions. It may, however, yield faster code for programs that do not require the guarantees of these specifications.

The default is '-fno-finite-math-only'.

`-fno-signed-zeros`
: Allow optimizations for floating-point arithmetic that ignore the signedness of zero. IEEE arithmetic specifies the behavior of distinct +0.0 and −0.0 values, which then prohibits simplification of expressions such as x+0.0 or 0.0*x (even with '-ffinite-math-only'). This option implies that the sign of a zero result isn't significant.

The default is '-fsigned-zeros'.

`-fno-trapping-math`
: Compile code assuming that floating-point operations cannot generate user-visible traps. These traps include division by zero, overflow, underflow, inexact result and invalid operation. This option requires that '-fno-signaling-nans'

be in effect. Setting this option may allow faster code if one relies on "non-stop" IEEE arithmetic, for example.

This option should never be turned on by any '-O' option since it can result in incorrect output for programs that depend on an exact implementation of IEEE or ISO rules/specifications for math functions.

The default is '-ftrapping-math'.

-frounding-math
: Disable transformations and optimizations that assume default floating-point rounding behavior. This is round-to-zero for all floating point to integer conversions, and round-to-nearest for all other arithmetic truncations. This option should be specified for programs that change the FP rounding mode dynamically, or that may be executed with a non-default rounding mode. This option disables constant folding of floating-point expressions at compile time (which may be affected by rounding mode) and arithmetic transformations that are unsafe in the presence of sign-dependent rounding modes.

The default is '-fno-rounding-math'.

This option is experimental and does not currently guarantee to disable all GCC optimizations that are affected by rounding mode. Future versions of GCC may provide finer control of this setting using C99's FENV_ACCESS pragma. This command-line option will be used to specify the default state for FENV_ACCESS.

-fsignaling-nans
: Compile code assuming that IEEE signaling NaNs may generate user-visible traps during floating-point operations. Setting this option disables optimizations that may change the number of exceptions visible with signaling NaNs. This option implies '-ftrapping-math'.

This option causes the preprocessor macro __SUPPORT_SNAN__ to be defined.

The default is '-fno-signaling-nans'.

This option is experimental and does not currently guarantee to disable all GCC optimizations that affect signaling NaN behavior.

-fsingle-precision-constant
: Treat floating-point constants as single precision instead of implicitly converting them to double-precision constants.

-fcx-limited-range
: When enabled, this option states that a range reduction step is not needed when performing complex division. Also, there is no checking whether the result of a complex multiplication or division is NaN + I*NaN, with an attempt to rescue the situation in that case. The default is '-fno-cx-limited-range', but is enabled by '-ffast-math'.

This option controls the default setting of the ISO C99 CX_LIMITED_RANGE pragma. Nevertheless, the option applies to all languages.

-fcx-fortran-rules
: Complex multiplication and division follow Fortran rules. Range reduction is done as part of complex division, but there is no checking whether the result of

a complex multiplication or division is NaN + I*NaN, with an attempt to rescue the situation in that case.

The default is '-fno-cx-fortran-rules'.

The following options control optimizations that may improve performance, but are not enabled by any '-O' options. This section includes experimental options that may produce broken code.

-fbranch-probabilities
After running a program compiled with '-fprofile-arcs' (see Section 3.11 [Instrumentation Options], page 148), you can compile it a second time using '-fbranch-probabilities', to improve optimizations based on the number of times each branch was taken. When a program compiled with '-fprofile-arcs' exits, it saves arc execution counts to a file called '*sourcename*.gcda' for each source file. The information in this data file is very dependent on the structure of the generated code, so you must use the same source code and the same optimization options for both compilations.

With '-fbranch-probabilities', GCC puts a 'REG_BR_PROB' note on each 'JUMP_INSN' and 'CALL_INSN'. These can be used to improve optimization. Currently, they are only used in one place: in 'reorg.c', instead of guessing which path a branch is most likely to take, the 'REG_BR_PROB' values are used to exactly determine which path is taken more often.

-fprofile-values
If combined with '-fprofile-arcs', it adds code so that some data about values of expressions in the program is gathered.

With '-fbranch-probabilities', it reads back the data gathered from profiling values of expressions for usage in optimizations.

Enabled with '-fprofile-generate' and '-fprofile-use'.

-fprofile-reorder-functions
Function reordering based on profile instrumentation collects first time of execution of a function and orders these functions in ascending order.

Enabled with '-fprofile-use'.

-fvpt
If combined with '-fprofile-arcs', this option instructs the compiler to add code to gather information about values of expressions.

With '-fbranch-probabilities', it reads back the data gathered and actually performs the optimizations based on them. Currently the optimizations include specialization of division operations using the knowledge about the value of the denominator.

-frename-registers
Attempt to avoid false dependencies in scheduled code by making use of registers left over after register allocation. This optimization most benefits processors with lots of registers. Depending on the debug information format adopted by the target, however, it can make debugging impossible, since variables no longer stay in a "home register".

Enabled by default with '-funroll-loops' and '-fpeel-loops'.

`-fschedule-fusion`
: Performs a target dependent pass over the instruction stream to schedule instructions of same type together because target machine can execute them more efficiently if they are adjacent to each other in the instruction flow.

  Enabled at levels '`-O2`', '`-O3`', '`-Os`'.

`-ftracer`
: Perform tail duplication to enlarge superblock size. This transformation simplifies the control flow of the function allowing other optimizations to do a better job.

  Enabled with '`-fprofile-use`'.

`-funroll-loops`
: Unroll loops whose number of iterations can be determined at compile time or upon entry to the loop. '`-funroll-loops`' implies '`-frerun-cse-after-loop`', '`-fweb`' and '`-frename-registers`'. It also turns on complete loop peeling (i.e. complete removal of loops with a small constant number of iterations). This option makes code larger, and may or may not make it run faster.

  Enabled with '`-fprofile-use`'.

`-funroll-all-loops`
: Unroll all loops, even if their number of iterations is uncertain when the loop is entered. This usually makes programs run more slowly. '`-funroll-all-loops`' implies the same options as '`-funroll-loops`'.

`-fpeel-loops`
: Peels loops for which there is enough information that they do not roll much (from profile feedback). It also turns on complete loop peeling (i.e. complete removal of loops with small constant number of iterations).

  Enabled with '`-fprofile-use`'.

`-fmove-loop-invariants`
: Enables the loop invariant motion pass in the RTL loop optimizer. Enabled at level '`-O1`'

`-funswitch-loops`
: Move branches with loop invariant conditions out of the loop, with duplicates of the loop on both branches (modified according to result of the condition).

`-ffunction-sections`
`-fdata-sections`
: Place each function or data item into its own section in the output file if the target supports arbitrary sections. The name of the function or the name of the data item determines the section's name in the output file.

  Use these options on systems where the linker can perform optimizations to improve locality of reference in the instruction space. Most systems using the ELF object format and SPARC processors running Solaris 2 have linkers with such optimizations. AIX may have these optimizations in the future.

  Only use these options when there are significant benefits from doing so. When you specify these options, the assembler and linker create larger object and executable files and are also slower. You cannot use `gprof` on all systems if you specify this option, and you may have problems with debugging if you specify both this option and '`-g`'.

`-fbranch-target-load-optimize`
: Perform branch target register load optimization before prologue / epilogue threading. The use of target registers can typically be exposed only during reload, thus hoisting loads out of loops and doing inter-block scheduling needs a separate optimization pass.

`-fbranch-target-load-optimize2`
: Perform branch target register load optimization after prologue / epilogue threading.

`-fbtr-bb-exclusive`
: When performing branch target register load optimization, don't reuse branch target registers within any basic block.

`-fstdarg-opt`
: Optimize the prologue of variadic argument functions with respect to usage of those arguments.

`-fsection-anchors`
: Try to reduce the number of symbolic address calculations by using shared "anchor" symbols to address nearby objects. This transformation can help to reduce the number of GOT entries and GOT accesses on some targets.

For example, the implementation of the following function `foo`:

```
static int a, b, c;
int foo (void) { return a + b + c; }
```

usually calculates the addresses of all three variables, but if you compile it with '`-fsection-anchors`', it accesses the variables from a common anchor point instead. The effect is similar to the following pseudocode (which isn't valid C):

```
int foo (void)
{
  register int *xr = &x;
  return xr[&a - &x] + xr[&b - &x] + xr[&c - &x];
}
```

Not all targets support this option.

`--param` *`name=value`*
: In some places, GCC uses various constants to control the amount of optimization that is done. For example, GCC does not inline functions that contain more than a certain number of instructions. You can control some of these constants on the command line using the '`--param`' option.

The names of specific parameters, and the meaning of the values, are tied to the internals of the compiler, and are subject to change without notice in future releases.

In each case, the *value* is an integer. The allowable choices for *name* are:

`predictable-branch-outcome`
: When branch is predicted to be taken with probability lower than this threshold (in percent), then it is considered well predictable. The default is 10.

`max-rtl-if-conversion-insns`
: RTL if-conversion tries to remove conditional branches around a block and replace them with conditionally executed instructions. This parameter gives the maximum number of instructions in a block which should be considered for if-conversion. The default is 10, though the compiler will also use other heuristics to decide whether if-conversion is likely to be profitable.

`max-crossjump-edges`
: The maximum number of incoming edges to consider for cross-jumping. The algorithm used by '`-fcrossjumping`' is $O(N^2)$ in the number of edges incoming to each block. Increasing values mean more aggressive optimization, making the compilation time increase with probably small improvement in executable size.

`min-crossjump-insns`
: The minimum number of instructions that must be matched at the end of two blocks before cross-jumping is performed on them. This value is ignored in the case where all instructions in the block being cross-jumped from are matched. The default value is 5.

`max-grow-copy-bb-insns`
: The maximum code size expansion factor when copying basic blocks instead of jumping. The expansion is relative to a jump instruction. The default value is 8.

`max-goto-duplication-insns`
: The maximum number of instructions to duplicate to a block that jumps to a computed goto. To avoid $O(N^2)$ behavior in a number of passes, GCC factors computed gotos early in the compilation process, and unfactors them as late as possible. Only computed jumps at the end of a basic blocks with no more than max-goto-duplication-insns are unfactored. The default value is 8.

`max-delay-slot-insn-search`
: The maximum number of instructions to consider when looking for an instruction to fill a delay slot. If more than this arbitrary number of instructions are searched, the time savings from filling the delay slot are minimal, so stop searching. Increasing values mean more aggressive optimization, making the compilation time increase with probably small improvement in execution time.

`max-delay-slot-live-search`
: When trying to fill delay slots, the maximum number of instructions to consider when searching for a block with valid live register information. Increasing this arbitrarily chosen value means more

aggressive optimization, increasing the compilation time. This parameter should be removed when the delay slot code is rewritten to maintain the control-flow graph.

`max-gcse-memory`
: The approximate maximum amount of memory that can be allocated in order to perform the global common subexpression elimination optimization. If more memory than specified is required, the optimization is not done.

`max-gcse-insertion-ratio`
: If the ratio of expression insertions to deletions is larger than this value for any expression, then RTL PRE inserts or removes the expression and thus leaves partially redundant computations in the instruction stream. The default value is 20.

`max-pending-list-length`
: The maximum number of pending dependencies scheduling allows before flushing the current state and starting over. Large functions with few branches or calls can create excessively large lists which needlessly consume memory and resources.

`max-modulo-backtrack-attempts`
: The maximum number of backtrack attempts the scheduler should make when modulo scheduling a loop. Larger values can exponentially increase compilation time.

`max-inline-insns-single`
: Several parameters control the tree inliner used in GCC. This number sets the maximum number of instructions (counted in GCC's internal representation) in a single function that the tree inliner considers for inlining. This only affects functions declared inline and methods implemented in a class declaration (C++). The default value is 400.

`max-inline-insns-auto`
: When you use '`-finline-functions`' (included in '`-O3`'), a lot of functions that would otherwise not be considered for inlining by the compiler are investigated. To those functions, a different (more restrictive) limit compared to functions declared inline can be applied. The default value is 40.

`inline-min-speedup`
: When estimated performance improvement of caller + callee runtime exceeds this threshold (in precent), the function can be inlined regardless the limit on '`--param max-inline-insns-single`' and '`--param max-inline-insns-auto`'.

`large-function-insns`
: The limit specifying really large functions. For functions larger than this limit after inlining, inlining is constrained by '`--param`

large-function-growth'. This parameter is useful primarily to avoid extreme compilation time caused by non-linear algorithms used by the back end. The default value is 2700.

`large-function-growth`
: Specifies maximal growth of large function caused by inlining in percents. The default value is 100 which limits large function growth to 2.0 times the original size.

`large-unit-insns`
: The limit specifying large translation unit. Growth caused by inlining of units larger than this limit is limited by '--param inline-unit-growth'. For small units this might be too tight. For example, consider a unit consisting of function A that is inline and B that just calls A three times. If B is small relative to A, the growth of unit is 300\% and yet such inlining is very sane. For very large units consisting of small inlineable functions, however, the overall unit growth limit is needed to avoid exponential explosion of code size. Thus for smaller units, the size is increased to '--param large-unit-insns' before applying '--param inline-unit-growth'. The default is 10000.

`inline-unit-growth`
: Specifies maximal overall growth of the compilation unit caused by inlining. The default value is 20 which limits unit growth to 1.2 times the original size. Cold functions (either marked cold via an attribute or by profile feedback) are not accounted into the unit size.

`ipcp-unit-growth`
: Specifies maximal overall growth of the compilation unit caused by interprocedural constant propagation. The default value is 10 which limits unit growth to 1.1 times the original size.

`large-stack-frame`
: The limit specifying large stack frames. While inlining the algorithm is trying to not grow past this limit too much. The default value is 256 bytes.

`large-stack-frame-growth`
: Specifies maximal growth of large stack frames caused by inlining in percents. The default value is 1000 which limits large stack frame growth to 11 times the original size.

`max-inline-insns-recursive`
`max-inline-insns-recursive-auto`
: Specifies the maximum number of instructions an out-of-line copy of a self-recursive inline function can grow into by performing recursive inlining.

'--param max-inline-insns-recursive' applies to functions declared inline. For functions not declared inline, recursive inlining happens only when '-finline-functions' (included in '-O3') is enabled; '--param max-inline-insns-recursive-auto' applies instead. The default value is 450.

`max-inline-recursive-depth`
`max-inline-recursive-depth-auto`
: Specifies the maximum recursion depth used for recursive inlining.

  '--param max-inline-recursive-depth' applies to functions declared inline. For functions not declared inline, recursive inlining happens only when '-finline-functions' (included in '-O3') is enabled; '--param max-inline-recursive-depth-auto' applies instead. The default value is 8.

`min-inline-recursive-probability`
: Recursive inlining is profitable only for function having deep recursion in average and can hurt for function having little recursion depth by increasing the prologue size or complexity of function body to other optimizers.

  When profile feedback is available (see '-fprofile-generate') the actual recursion depth can be guessed from probability that function recurses via a given call expression. This parameter limits inlining only to call expressions whose probability exceeds the given threshold (in percents). The default value is 10.

`early-inlining-insns`
: Specify growth that the early inliner can make. In effect it increases the amount of inlining for code having a large abstraction penalty. The default value is 14.

`max-early-inliner-iterations`
: Limit of iterations of the early inliner. This basically bounds the number of nested indirect calls the early inliner can resolve. Deeper chains are still handled by late inlining.

`comdat-sharing-probability`
: Probability (in percent) that C++ inline function with comdat visibility are shared across multiple compilation units. The default value is 20.

`profile-func-internal-id`
: A parameter to control whether to use function internal id in profile database lookup. If the value is 0, the compiler uses an id that is based on function assembler name and filename, which makes old profile data more tolerant to source changes such as function reordering etc. The default value is 0.

`min-vect-loop-bound`
: The minimum number of iterations under which loops are not vectorized when '-ftree-vectorize' is used. The number of iterations after vectorization needs to be greater than the value specified by this option to allow vectorization. The default value is 0.

`gcse-cost-distance-ratio`
: Scaling factor in calculation of maximum distance an expression can be moved by GCSE optimizations. This is currently supported only in the code hoisting pass. The bigger the ratio, the more aggressive code hoisting is with simple expressions, i.e., the expressions that have cost less than '`gcse-unrestricted-cost`'. Specifying 0 disables hoisting of simple expressions. The default value is 10.

`gcse-unrestricted-cost`
: Cost, roughly measured as the cost of a single typical machine instruction, at which GCSE optimizations do not constrain the distance an expression can travel. This is currently supported only in the code hoisting pass. The lesser the cost, the more aggressive code hoisting is. Specifying 0 allows all expressions to travel unrestricted distances. The default value is 3.

`max-hoist-depth`
: The depth of search in the dominator tree for expressions to hoist. This is used to avoid quadratic behavior in hoisting algorithm. The value of 0 does not limit on the search, but may slow down compilation of huge functions. The default value is 30.

`max-tail-merge-comparisons`
: The maximum amount of similar bbs to compare a bb with. This is used to avoid quadratic behavior in tree tail merging. The default value is 10.

`max-tail-merge-iterations`
: The maximum amount of iterations of the pass over the function. This is used to limit compilation time in tree tail merging. The default value is 2.

`max-unrolled-insns`
: The maximum number of instructions that a loop may have to be unrolled. If a loop is unrolled, this parameter also determines how many times the loop code is unrolled.

`max-average-unrolled-insns`
: The maximum number of instructions biased by probabilities of their execution that a loop may have to be unrolled. If a loop is unrolled, this parameter also determines how many times the loop code is unrolled.

`max-unroll-times`
: The maximum number of unrollings of a single loop.

`max-peeled-insns`
: The maximum number of instructions that a loop may have to be peeled. If a loop is peeled, this parameter also determines how many times the loop code is peeled.

`max-peel-times`
: The maximum number of peelings of a single loop.

`max-peel-branches`
: The maximum number of branches on the hot path through the peeled sequence.

`max-completely-peeled-insns`
: The maximum number of insns of a completely peeled loop.

`max-completely-peel-times`
: The maximum number of iterations of a loop to be suitable for complete peeling.

`max-completely-peel-loop-nest-depth`
: The maximum depth of a loop nest suitable for complete peeling.

`max-unswitch-insns`
: The maximum number of insns of an unswitched loop.

`max-unswitch-level`
: The maximum number of branches unswitched in a single loop.

`lim-expensive`
: The minimum cost of an expensive expression in the loop invariant motion.

`iv-consider-all-candidates-bound`
: Bound on number of candidates for induction variables, below which all candidates are considered for each use in induction variable optimizations. If there are more candidates than this, only the most relevant ones are considered to avoid quadratic time complexity.

`iv-max-considered-uses`
: The induction variable optimizations give up on loops that contain more induction variable uses.

`iv-always-prune-cand-set-bound`
: If the number of candidates in the set is smaller than this value, always try to remove unnecessary ivs from the set when adding a new one.

`scev-max-expr-size`
: Bound on size of expressions used in the scalar evolutions analyzer. Large expressions slow the analyzer.

`scev-max-expr-complexity`
: Bound on the complexity of the expressions in the scalar evolutions analyzer. Complex expressions slow the analyzer.

`vect-max-version-for-alignment-checks`
: The maximum number of run-time checks that can be performed when doing loop versioning for alignment in the vectorizer.

`vect-max-version-for-alias-checks`
: The maximum number of run-time checks that can be performed when doing loop versioning for alias in the vectorizer.

`vect-max-peeling-for-alignment`
: The maximum number of loop peels to enhance access alignment for vectorizer. Value -1 means no limit.

`max-iterations-to-track`
: The maximum number of iterations of a loop the brute-force algorithm for analysis of the number of iterations of the loop tries to evaluate.

`hot-bb-count-ws-permille`
: A basic block profile count is considered hot if it contributes to the given permillage (i.e. 0...1000) of the entire profiled execution.

`hot-bb-frequency-fraction`
: Select fraction of the entry block frequency of executions of basic block in function given basic block needs to have to be considered hot.

`max-predicted-iterations`
: The maximum number of loop iterations we predict statically. This is useful in cases where a function contains a single loop with known bound and another loop with unknown bound. The known number of iterations is predicted correctly, while the unknown number of iterations average to roughly 10. This means that the loop without bounds appears artificially cold relative to the other one.

`builtin-expect-probability`
: Control the probability of the expression having the specified value. This parameter takes a percentage (i.e. 0 ... 100) as input. The default probability of 90 is obtained empirically.

`align-threshold`
: Select fraction of the maximal frequency of executions of a basic block in a function to align the basic block.

`align-loop-iterations`
: A loop expected to iterate at least the selected number of iterations is aligned.

`tracer-dynamic-coverage`
`tracer-dynamic-coverage-feedback`
: This value is used to limit superblock formation once the given percentage of executed instructions is covered. This limits unnecessary code size expansion.

: The '`tracer-dynamic-coverage-feedback`' parameter is used only when profile feedback is available. The real profiles (as opposed to statically estimated ones) are much less balanced allowing the threshold to be larger value.

`tracer-max-code-growth`
: Stop tail duplication once code growth has reached given percentage. This is a rather artificial limit, as most of the duplicates are

eliminated later in cross jumping, so it may be set to much higher values than is the desired code growth.

`tracer-min-branch-ratio`
: Stop reverse growth when the reverse probability of best edge is less than this threshold (in percent).

`tracer-min-branch-probability`
`tracer-min-branch-probability-feedback`
: Stop forward growth if the best edge has probability lower than this threshold.

Similarly to '`tracer-dynamic-coverage`' two parameters are provided. '`tracer-min-branch-probability-feedback`' is used for compilation with profile feedback and '`tracer-min-branch-probability`' compilation without. The value for compilation with profile feedback needs to be more conservative (higher) in order to make tracer effective.

`max-cse-path-length`
: The maximum number of basic blocks on path that CSE considers. The default is 10.

`max-cse-insns`
: The maximum number of instructions CSE processes before flushing. The default is 1000.

`ggc-min-expand`
: GCC uses a garbage collector to manage its own memory allocation. This parameter specifies the minimum percentage by which the garbage collector's heap should be allowed to expand between collections. Tuning this may improve compilation speed; it has no effect on code generation.

The default is 30% + 70% * (RAM/1GB) with an upper bound of 100% when RAM >= 1GB. If `getrlimit` is available, the notion of "RAM" is the smallest of actual RAM and `RLIMIT_DATA` or `RLIMIT_AS`. If GCC is not able to calculate RAM on a particular platform, the lower bound of 30% is used. Setting this parameter and '`ggc-min-heapsize`' to zero causes a full collection to occur at every opportunity. This is extremely slow, but can be useful for debugging.

`ggc-min-heapsize`
: Minimum size of the garbage collector's heap before it begins bothering to collect garbage. The first collection occurs after the heap expands by '`ggc-min-expand`'% beyond '`ggc-min-heapsize`'. Again, tuning this may improve compilation speed, and has no effect on code generation.

The default is the smaller of RAM/8, RLIMIT_RSS, or a limit that tries to ensure that RLIMIT_DATA or RLIMIT_AS are not exceeded, but with a lower bound of 4096 (four megabytes) and an upper bound of 131072 (128 megabytes). If GCC is not able to calculate RAM on a particular platform, the lower bound is used. Setting this parameter very large effectively disables garbage collection. Setting this parameter and '`ggc-min-expand`' to zero causes a full collection to occur at every opportunity.

`max-reload-search-insns`
: The maximum number of instruction reload should look backward for equivalent register. Increasing values mean more aggressive optimization, making the compilation time increase with probably slightly better performance. The default value is 100.

`max-cselib-memory-locations`
: The maximum number of memory locations cselib should take into account. Increasing values mean more aggressive optimization, making the compilation time increase with probably slightly better performance. The default value is 500.

`max-sched-ready-insns`
: The maximum number of instructions ready to be issued the scheduler should consider at any given time during the first scheduling pass. Increasing values mean more thorough searches, making the compilation time increase with probably little benefit. The default value is 100.

`max-sched-region-blocks`
: The maximum number of blocks in a region to be considered for interblock scheduling. The default value is 10.

`max-pipeline-region-blocks`
: The maximum number of blocks in a region to be considered for pipelining in the selective scheduler. The default value is 15.

`max-sched-region-insns`
: The maximum number of insns in a region to be considered for interblock scheduling. The default value is 100.

`max-pipeline-region-insns`
: The maximum number of insns in a region to be considered for pipelining in the selective scheduler. The default value is 200.

`min-spec-prob`
: The minimum probability (in percents) of reaching a source block for interblock speculative scheduling. The default value is 40.

`max-sched-extend-regions-iters`
: The maximum number of iterations through CFG to extend regions. A value of 0 (the default) disables region extensions.

`max-sched-insn-conflict-delay`
: The maximum conflict delay for an insn to be considered for speculative motion. The default value is 3.

`sched-spec-prob-cutoff`
: The minimal probability of speculation success (in percents), so that speculative insns are scheduled. The default value is 40.

`sched-state-edge-prob-cutoff`
: The minimum probability an edge must have for the scheduler to save its state across it. The default value is 10.

`sched-mem-true-dep-cost`
: Minimal distance (in CPU cycles) between store and load targeting same memory locations. The default value is 1.

`selsched-max-lookahead`
: The maximum size of the lookahead window of selective scheduling. It is a depth of search for available instructions. The default value is 50.

`selsched-max-sched-times`
: The maximum number of times that an instruction is scheduled during selective scheduling. This is the limit on the number of iterations through which the instruction may be pipelined. The default value is 2.

`selsched-insns-to-rename`
: The maximum number of best instructions in the ready list that are considered for renaming in the selective scheduler. The default value is 2.

`sms-min-sc`
: The minimum value of stage count that swing modulo scheduler generates. The default value is 2.

`max-last-value-rtl`
: The maximum size measured as number of RTLs that can be recorded in an expression in combiner for a pseudo register as last known value of that register. The default is 10000.

`max-combine-insns`
: The maximum number of instructions the RTL combiner tries to combine. The default value is 2 at '`-Og`' and 4 otherwise.

`integer-share-limit`
: Small integer constants can use a shared data structure, reducing the compiler's memory usage and increasing its speed. This sets the maximum value of a shared integer constant. The default value is 256.

`ssp-buffer-size`
: The minimum size of buffers (i.e. arrays) that receive stack smashing protection when '`-fstack-protection`' is used.

`min-size-for-stack-sharing`
: The minimum size of variables taking part in stack slot sharing when not optimizing. The default value is 32.

`max-jump-thread-duplication-stmts`
: Maximum number of statements allowed in a block that needs to be duplicated when threading jumps.

`max-fields-for-field-sensitive`
: Maximum number of fields in a structure treated in a field sensitive manner during pointer analysis. The default is zero for '-O0' and '-O1', and 100 for '-Os', '-O2', and '-O3'.

`prefetch-latency`
: Estimate on average number of instructions that are executed before prefetch finishes. The distance prefetched ahead is proportional to this constant. Increasing this number may also lead to less streams being prefetched (see '`simultaneous-prefetches`').

`simultaneous-prefetches`
: Maximum number of prefetches that can run at the same time.

`l1-cache-line-size`
: The size of cache line in L1 cache, in bytes.

`l1-cache-size`
: The size of L1 cache, in kilobytes.

`l2-cache-size`
: The size of L2 cache, in kilobytes.

`min-insn-to-prefetch-ratio`
: The minimum ratio between the number of instructions and the number of prefetches to enable prefetching in a loop.

`prefetch-min-insn-to-mem-ratio`
: The minimum ratio between the number of instructions and the number of memory references to enable prefetching in a loop.

`use-canonical-types`
: Whether the compiler should use the "canonical" type system. By default, this should always be 1, which uses a more efficient internal mechanism for comparing types in C++ and Objective-C++. However, if bugs in the canonical type system are causing compilation failures, set this value to 0 to disable canonical types.

`switch-conversion-max-branch-ratio`
: Switch initialization conversion refuses to create arrays that are bigger than '`switch-conversion-max-branch-ratio`' times the number of branches in the switch.

`max-partial-antic-length`
: Maximum length of the partial antic set computed during the tree partial redundancy elimination optimization ('`-ftree-pre`') when optimizing at '-O3' and above. For some sorts of source code the enhanced partial redundancy elimination optimization can run away, consuming all of the memory available on the host machine. This

parameter sets a limit on the length of the sets that are computed, which prevents the runaway behavior. Setting a value of 0 for this parameter allows an unlimited set length.

`sccvn-max-scc-size`
: Maximum size of a strongly connected component (SCC) during SCCVN processing. If this limit is hit, SCCVN processing for the whole function is not done and optimizations depending on it are disabled. The default maximum SCC size is 10000.

`sccvn-max-alias-queries-per-access`
: Maximum number of alias-oracle queries we perform when looking for redundancies for loads and stores. If this limit is hit the search is aborted and the load or store is not considered redundant. The number of queries is algorithmically limited to the number of stores on all paths from the load to the function entry. The default maximum number of queries is 1000.

`ira-max-loops-num`
: IRA uses regional register allocation by default. If a function contains more loops than the number given by this parameter, only at most the given number of the most frequently-executed loops form regions for regional register allocation. The default value of the parameter is 100.

`ira-max-conflict-table-size`
: Although IRA uses a sophisticated algorithm to compress the conflict table, the table can still require excessive amounts of memory for huge functions. If the conflict table for a function could be more than the size in MB given by this parameter, the register allocator instead uses a faster, simpler, and lower-quality algorithm that does not require building a pseudo-register conflict table. The default value of the parameter is 2000.

`ira-loop-reserved-regs`
: IRA can be used to evaluate more accurate register pressure in loops for decisions to move loop invariants (see '`-O3`'). The number of available registers reserved for some other purposes is given by this parameter. The default value of the parameter is 2, which is the minimal number of registers needed by typical instructions. This value is the best found from numerous experiments.

`lra-inheritance-ebb-probability-cutoff`
: LRA tries to reuse values reloaded in registers in subsequent insns. This optimization is called inheritance. EBB is used as a region to do this optimization. The parameter defines a minimal fall-through edge probability in percentage used to add BB to inheritance EBB in LRA. The default value of the parameter is 40. The value was chosen from numerous runs of SPEC2000 on x86-64.

`loop-invariant-max-bbs-in-loop`
: Loop invariant motion can be very expensive, both in compilation time and in amount of needed compile-time memory, with very large loops. Loops with more basic blocks than this parameter won't have loop invariant motion optimization performed on them. The default value of the parameter is 1000 for '`-O1`' and 10000 for '`-O2`' and above.

`loop-max-datarefs-for-datadeps`
: Building data dependencies is expensive for very large loops. This parameter limits the number of data references in loops that are considered for data dependence analysis. These large loops are no handled by the optimizations using loop data dependencies. The default value is 1000.

`max-vartrack-size`
: Sets a maximum number of hash table slots to use during variable tracking dataflow analysis of any function. If this limit is exceeded with variable tracking at assignments enabled, analysis for that function is retried without it, after removing all debug insns from the function. If the limit is exceeded even without debug insns, var tracking analysis is completely disabled for the function. Setting the parameter to zero makes it unlimited.

`max-vartrack-expr-depth`
: Sets a maximum number of recursion levels when attempting to map variable names or debug temporaries to value expressions. This trades compilation time for more complete debug information. If this is set too low, value expressions that are available and could be represented in debug information may end up not being used; setting this higher may enable the compiler to find more complex debug expressions, but compile time and memory use may grow. The default is 12.

`min-nondebug-insn-uid`
: Use uids starting at this parameter for nondebug insns. The range below the parameter is reserved exclusively for debug insns created by '**`-fvar-tracking-assignments`**', but debug insns may get (non-overlapping) uids above it if the reserved range is exhausted.

`ipa-sra-ptr-growth-factor`
: IPA-SRA replaces a pointer to an aggregate with one or more new parameters only when their cumulative size is less or equal to '`ipa-sra-ptr-growth-factor`' times the size of the original pointer parameter.

`sra-max-scalarization-size-Ospeed`
`sra-max-scalarization-size-Osize`
: The two Scalar Reduction of Aggregates passes (SRA and IPA-SRA) aim to replace scalar parts of aggregates with

uses of independent scalar variables. These parameters control the maximum size, in storage units, of aggregate which is considered for replacement when compiling for speed ('sra-max-scalarization-size-Ospeed') or size ('sra-max-scalarization-size-Osize') respectively.

`tm-max-aggregate-size`
: When making copies of thread-local variables in a transaction, this parameter specifies the size in bytes after which variables are saved with the logging functions as opposed to save/restore code sequence pairs. This option only applies when using '-fgnu-tm'.

`graphite-max-nb-scop-params`
: To avoid exponential effects in the Graphite loop transforms, the number of parameters in a Static Control Part (SCoP) is bounded. The default value is 10 parameters. A variable whose value is unknown at compilation time and defined outside a SCoP is a parameter of the SCoP.

`graphite-max-bbs-per-function`
: To avoid exponential effects in the detection of SCoPs, the size of the functions analyzed by Graphite is bounded. The default value is 100 basic blocks.

`loop-block-tile-size`
: Loop blocking or strip mining transforms, enabled with '-floop-block' or '-floop-strip-mine', strip mine each loop in the loop nest by a given number of iterations. The strip length can be changed using the 'loop-block-tile-size' parameter. The default value is 51 iterations.

`loop-unroll-jam-size`
: Specify the unroll factor for the '-floop-unroll-and-jam' option. The default value is 4.

`loop-unroll-jam-depth`
: Specify the dimension to be unrolled (counting from the most inner loop) for the '-floop-unroll-and-jam'. The default value is 2.

`ipa-cp-value-list-size`
: IPA-CP attempts to track all possible values and types passed to a function's parameter in order to propagate them and perform devirtualization. 'ipa-cp-value-list-size' is the maximum number of values and types it stores per one formal parameter of a function.

`ipa-cp-eval-threshold`
: IPA-CP calculates its own score of cloning profitability heuristics and performs those cloning opportunities with scores that exceed 'ipa-cp-eval-threshold'.

`ipa-cp-recursion-penalty`
: Percentage penalty the recursive functions will receive when they are evaluated for cloning.

`ipa-cp-single-call-penalty`
: Percentage penalty functions containg a single call to another function will receive when they are evaluated for cloning.

`ipa-max-agg-items`
: IPA-CP is also capable to propagate a number of scalar values passed in an aggregate. '`ipa-max-agg-items`' controls the maximum number of such values per one parameter.

`ipa-cp-loop-hint-bonus`
: When IPA-CP determines that a cloning candidate would make the number of iterations of a loop known, it adds a bonus of '`ipa-cp-loop-hint-bonus`' to the profitability score of the candidate.

`ipa-cp-array-index-hint-bonus`
: When IPA-CP determines that a cloning candidate would make the index of an array access known, it adds a bonus of '`ipa-cp-array-index-hint-bonus`' to the profitability score of the candidate.

`ipa-max-aa-steps`
: During its analysis of function bodies, IPA-CP employs alias analysis in order to track values pointed to by function parameters. In order not spend too much time analyzing huge functions, it gives up and consider all memory clobbered after examining '`ipa-max-aa-steps`' statements modifying memory.

`lto-partitions`
: Specify desired number of partitions produced during WHOPR compilation. The number of partitions should exceed the number of CPUs used for compilation. The default value is 32.

`lto-min-partition`
: Size of minimal partition for WHOPR (in estimated instructions). This prevents expenses of splitting very small programs into too many partitions.

`cxx-max-namespaces-for-diagnostic-help`
: The maximum number of namespaces to consult for suggestions when C++ name lookup fails for an identifier. The default is 1000.

`sink-frequency-threshold`
: The maximum relative execution frequency (in percents) of the target block relative to a statement's original block to allow statement sinking of a statement. Larger numbers result in more aggressive statement sinking. The default value is 75. A small positive adjustment is applied for statements with memory operands as those are even more profitable so sink.

`max-stores-to-sink`
: The maximum number of conditional store pairs that can be sunk. Set to 0 if either vectorization ('`-ftree-vectorize`')

or if-conversion ('-ftree-loop-if-convert') is disabled. The default is 2.

`allow-store-data-races`
: Allow optimizers to introduce new data races on stores. Set to 1 to allow, otherwise to 0. This option is enabled by default at optimization level '-Ofast'.

`case-values-threshold`
: The smallest number of different values for which it is best to use a jump-table instead of a tree of conditional branches. If the value is 0, use the default for the machine. The default is 0.

`tree-reassoc-width`
: Set the maximum number of instructions executed in parallel in reassociated tree. This parameter overrides target dependent heuristics used by default if has non zero value.

`sched-pressure-algorithm`
: Choose between the two available implementations of '-fsched-pressure'. Algorithm 1 is the original implementation and is the more likely to prevent instructions from being reordered. Algorithm 2 was designed to be a compromise between the relatively conservative approach taken by algorithm 1 and the rather aggressive approach taken by the default scheduler. It relies more heavily on having a regular register file and accurate register pressure classes. See 'haifa-sched.c' in the GCC sources for more details.

The default choice depends on the target.

`max-slsr-cand-scan`
: Set the maximum number of existing candidates that are considered when seeking a basis for a new straight-line strength reduction candidate.

`asan-globals`
: Enable buffer overflow detection for global objects. This kind of protection is enabled by default if you are using '-fsanitize=address' option. To disable global objects protection use '--param asan-globals=0'.

`asan-stack`
: Enable buffer overflow detection for stack objects. This kind of protection is enabled by default when using '-fsanitize=address'. To disable stack protection use '--param asan-stack=0' option.

`asan-instrument-reads`
: Enable buffer overflow detection for memory reads. This kind of protection is enabled by default when using '-fsanitize=address'. To disable memory reads protection use '--param asan-instrument-reads=0'.

`asan-instrument-writes`
: Enable buffer overflow detection for memory writes. This kind of protection is enabled by default when using '`-fsanitize=address`'. To disable memory writes protection use '`--param asan-instrument-writes=0`' option.

`asan-memintrin`
: Enable detection for built-in functions. This kind of protection is enabled by default when using '`-fsanitize=address`'. To disable built-in functions protection use '`--param asan-memintrin=0`'.

`asan-use-after-return`
: Enable detection of use-after-return. This kind of protection is enabled by default when using '`-fsanitize=address`' option. To disable use-after-return detection use '`--param asan-use-after-return=0`'.

`asan-instrumentation-with-call-threshold`
: If number of memory accesses in function being instrumented is greater or equal to this number, use callbacks instead of inline checks. E.g. to disable inline code use '`--param asan-instrumentation-with-call-threshold=0`'.

`chkp-max-ctor-size`
: Static constructors generated by Pointer Bounds Checker may become very large and significantly increase compile time at optimization level '`-O1`' and higher. This parameter is a maximum nubmer of statements in a single generated constructor. Default value is 5000.

`max-fsm-thread-path-insns`
: Maximum number of instructions to copy when duplicating blocks on a finite state automaton jump thread path. The default is 100.

`max-fsm-thread-length`
: Maximum number of basic blocks on a finite state automaton jump thread path. The default is 10.

`max-fsm-thread-paths`
: Maximum number of new jump thread paths to create for a finite state automaton. The default is 50.

`parloops-chunk-size`
: Chunk size of omp schedule for loops parallelized by parloops. The default is 0.

`parloops-schedule`
: Schedule type of omp schedule for loops parallelized by parloops (static, dynamic, guided, auto, runtime). The default is static.

`max-ssa-name-query-depth`
: Maximum depth of recursion when querying properties of SSA names in things like fold routines. One level of recursion corresponds to following a use-def chain.

`hsa-gen-debug-stores`
: Enable emission of special debug stores within HSA kernels which are then read and reported by libgomp plugin. Generation of these stores is disabled by default, use '`--param hsa-gen-debug-stores=1`' to enable it.

`max-speculative-devirt-maydefs`
: The maximum number of may-defs we analyze when looking for a must-def specifying the dynamic type of an object that invokes a virtual call we may be able to devirtualize speculatively.

3.11 Program Instrumentation Options

GCC supports a number of command-line options that control adding run-time instrumentation to the code it normally generates. For example, one purpose of instrumentation is collect profiling statistics for use in finding program hot spots, code coverage analysis, or profile-guided optimizations. Another class of program instrumentation is adding run-time checking to detect programming errors like invalid pointer dereferences or out-of-bounds array accesses, as well as deliberately hostile attacks such as stack smashing or C++ vtable hijacking. There is also a general hook which can be used to implement other forms of tracing or function-level instrumentation for debug or program analysis purposes.

`-p`
: Generate extra code to write profile information suitable for the analysis program `prof`. You must use this option when compiling the source files you want data about, and you must also use it when linking.

`-pg`
: Generate extra code to write profile information suitable for the analysis program `gprof`. You must use this option when compiling the source files you want data about, and you must also use it when linking.

`-fprofile-arcs`
: Add code so that program flow *arcs* are instrumented. During execution the program records how many times each branch and call is executed and how many times it is taken or returns. When the compiled program exits it saves this data to a file called '*auxname*`.gcda`' for each source file. The data may be used for profile-directed optimizations ('`-fbranch-probabilities`'), or for test coverage analysis ('`-ftest-coverage`'). Each object file's *auxname* is generated from the name of the output file, if explicitly specified and it is not the final executable, otherwise it is the basename of the source file. In both cases any suffix is removed (e.g. '`foo.gcda`' for input file '`dir/foo.c`', or '`dir/foo.gcda`' for output file specified as '`-o dir/foo.o`'). See Section 10.5 [Cross-profiling], page 725.

`--coverage`
: This option is used to compile and link code instrumented for coverage analysis. The option is a synonym for '`-fprofile-arcs`' '`-ftest-coverage`' (when com-

piling) and '-lgcov' (when linking). See the documentation for those options for more details.

- Compile the source files with '-fprofile-arcs' plus optimization and code generation options. For test coverage analysis, use the additional '-ftest-coverage' option. You do not need to profile every source file in a program.
- Link your object files with '-lgcov' or '-fprofile-arcs' (the latter implies the former).
- Run the program on a representative workload to generate the arc profile information. This may be repeated any number of times. You can run concurrent instances of your program, and provided that the file system supports locking, the data files will be correctly updated. Also `fork` calls are detected and correctly handled (double counting will not happen).
- For profile-directed optimizations, compile the source files again with the same optimization and code generation options plus '-fbranch-probabilities' (see Section 3.10 [Options that Control Optimization], page 93).
- For test coverage analysis, use `gcov` to produce human readable information from the '.gcno' and '.gcda' files. Refer to the `gcov` documentation for further information.

With '-fprofile-arcs', for each function of your program GCC creates a program flow graph, then finds a spanning tree for the graph. Only arcs that are not on the spanning tree have to be instrumented: the compiler adds code to count the number of times that these arcs are executed. When an arc is the only exit or only entrance to a block, the instrumentation code can be added to the block; otherwise, a new basic block must be created to hold the instrumentation code.

`-ftest-coverage`

Produce a notes file that the `gcov` code-coverage utility (see Chapter 10 [gcov—a Test Coverage Program], page 717) can use to show program coverage. Each source file's note file is called '*auxname*.gcno'. Refer to the '-fprofile-arcs' option above for a description of *auxname* and instructions on how to generate test coverage data. Coverage data matches the source files more closely if you do not optimize.

`-fprofile-dir=`*path*

Set the directory to search for the profile data files in to *path*. This option affects only the profile data generated by '-fprofile-generate', '-ftest-coverage', '-fprofile-arcs' and used by '-fprofile-use' and '-fbranch-probabilities' and its related options. Both absolute and relative paths can be used. By default, GCC uses the current directory as *path*, thus the profile data file appears in the same directory as the object file.

`-fprofile-generate`
`-fprofile-generate=`*path*

Enable options usually used for instrumenting application to produce profile useful for later recompilation with profile feedback based optimization. You must use '`-fprofile-generate`' both when compiling and when linking your program.

The following options are enabled: '`-fprofile-arcs`', '`-fprofile-values`', '`-fvpt`'.

If *path* is specified, GCC looks at the *path* to find the profile feedback data files. See '`-fprofile-dir`'.

To optimize the program based on the collected profile information, use '`-fprofile-use`'. See Section 3.10 [Optimize Options], page 93, for more information.

`-fsanitize=address`

Enable AddressSanitizer, a fast memory error detector. Memory access instructions are instrumented to detect out-of-bounds and use-after-free bugs. See `https://github.com/google/sanitizers/wiki/AddressSanitizer` for more details. The run-time behavior can be influenced using the `ASAN_OPTIONS` environment variable. When set to `help=1`, the available options are shown at startup of the instrumented program. See `https://github.com/google/sanitizers/wiki/AddressSanitizerFlags#run-time-flags` for a list of supported options.

`-fsanitize=kernel-address`

Enable AddressSanitizer for Linux kernel. See `https://github.com/google/kasan/wiki` for more details.

`-fsanitize=thread`

Enable ThreadSanitizer, a fast data race detector. Memory access instructions are instrumented to detect data race bugs. See `https://github.com/google/sanitizers/wiki#threadsanitizer` for more details. The run-time behavior can be influenced using the `TSAN_OPTIONS` environment variable; see `https://github.com/google/sanitizers/wiki/ThreadSanitizerFlags` for a list of supported options.

`-fsanitize=leak`

Enable LeakSanitizer, a memory leak detector. This option only matters for linking of executables and if neither '`-fsanitize=address`' nor '`-fsanitize=thread`' is used. In that case the executable is linked against a library that overrides `malloc` and other allocator functions. See `https://github.com/google/sanitizers/wiki/AddressSanitizerLeakSanitizer` for more details. The run-time behavior can be influenced using the `LSAN_OPTIONS` environment variable.

`-fsanitize=undefined`

Enable UndefinedBehaviorSanitizer, a fast undefined behavior detector. Various computations are instrumented to detect undefined behavior at runtime. Current suboptions are:

`-fsanitize=shift`

This option enables checking that the result of a shift operation is not undefined. Note that what exactly is considered undefined differs slightly between C and C++, as well as between ISO C90 and C99, etc.

`-fsanitize=integer-divide-by-zero`
: Detect integer division by zero as well as `INT_MIN / -1` division.

`-fsanitize=unreachable`
: With this option, the compiler turns the `__builtin_unreachable` call into a diagnostics message call instead. When reaching the `__builtin_unreachable` call, the behavior is undefined.

`-fsanitize=vla-bound`
: This option instructs the compiler to check that the size of a variable length array is positive.

`-fsanitize=null`
: This option enables pointer checking. Particularly, the application built with this option turned on will issue an error message when it tries to dereference a NULL pointer, or if a reference (possibly an rvalue reference) is bound to a NULL pointer, or if a method is invoked on an object pointed by a NULL pointer.

`-fsanitize=return`
: This option enables return statement checking. Programs built with this option turned on will issue an error message when the end of a non-void function is reached without actually returning a value. This option works in C++ only.

`-fsanitize=signed-integer-overflow`
: This option enables signed integer overflow checking. We check that the result of `+`, `*`, and both unary and binary `-` does not overflow in the signed arithmetics. Note, integer promotion rules must be taken into account. That is, the following is not an overflow:

```
signed char a = SCHAR_MAX;
a++;
```

`-fsanitize=bounds`
: This option enables instrumentation of array bounds. Various out of bounds accesses are detected. Flexible array members, flexible array member-like arrays, and initializers of variables with static storage are not instrumented.

`-fsanitize=bounds-strict`
: This option enables strict instrumentation of array bounds. Most out of bounds accesses are detected, including flexible array members and flexible array member-like arrays. Initializers of variables with static storage are not instrumented.

`-fsanitize=alignment`
: This option enables checking of alignment of pointers when they are dereferenced, or when a reference is bound to insufficiently aligned target, or when a method or constructor is invoked on insufficiently aligned object.

`-fsanitize=object-size`
: This option enables instrumentation of memory references using the `__builtin_object_size` function. Various out of bounds pointer accesses are detected.

`-fsanitize=float-divide-by-zero`
: Detect floating-point division by zero. Unlike other similar options, '`-fsanitize=float-divide-by-zero`' is not enabled by '`-fsanitize=undefined`', since floating-point division by zero can be a legitimate way of obtaining infinities and NaNs.

`-fsanitize=float-cast-overflow`
: This option enables floating-point type to integer conversion checking. We check that the result of the conversion does not overflow. Unlike other similar options, '`-fsanitize=float-cast-overflow`' is not enabled by '`-fsanitize=undefined`'. This option does not work well with `FE_INVALID` exceptions enabled.

`-fsanitize=nonnull-attribute`
: This option enables instrumentation of calls, checking whether null values are not passed to arguments marked as requiring a non-null value by the `nonnull` function attribute.

`-fsanitize=returns-nonnull-attribute`
: This option enables instrumentation of return statements in functions marked with `returns_nonnull` function attribute, to detect returning of null values from such functions.

`-fsanitize=bool`
: This option enables instrumentation of loads from bool. If a value other than 0/1 is loaded, a run-time error is issued.

`-fsanitize=enum`
: This option enables instrumentation of loads from an enum type. If a value outside the range of values for the enum type is loaded, a run-time error is issued.

`-fsanitize=vptr`
: This option enables instrumentation of C++ member function calls, member accesses and some conversions between pointers to base and derived classes, to verify the referenced object has the correct dynamic type.

While '`-ftrapv`' causes traps for signed overflows to be emitted, '`-fsanitize=undefined`' gives a diagnostic message. This currently works only for the C family of languages.

`-fno-sanitize=all`
: This option disables all previously enabled sanitizers. '`-fsanitize=all`' is not allowed, as some sanitizers cannot be used together.

`-fasan-shadow-offset=`*number*

This option forces GCC to use custom shadow offset in AddressSanitizer checks. It is useful for experimenting with different shadow memory layouts in Kernel AddressSanitizer.

`-fsanitize-sections=`*s1*`,`*s2*`,...`

Sanitize global variables in selected user-defined sections. *si* may contain wildcards.

`-fsanitize-recover`[`=`*opts*]

'`-fsanitize-recover=`' controls error recovery mode for sanitizers mentioned in comma-separated list of *opts*. Enabling this option for a sanitizer component causes it to attempt to continue running the program as if no error happened. This means multiple runtime errors can be reported in a single program run, and the exit code of the program may indicate success even when errors have been reported. The '`-fno-sanitize-recover=`' option can be used to alter this behavior: only the first detected error is reported and program then exits with a non-zero exit code.

Currently this feature only works for '`-fsanitize=undefined`' (and its suboptions except for '`-fsanitize=unreachable`' and '`-fsanitize=return`'), '`-fsanitize=float-cast-overflow`', '`-fsanitize=float-divide-by-zero`', '`-fsanitize=kernel-address`' and '`-fsanitize=address`'. For these sanitizers error recovery is turned on by default, except '`-fsanitize=address`', for which this feature is experimental. '`-fsanitize-recover=all`' and '`-fno-sanitize-recover=all`' is also accepted, the former enables recovery for all sanitizers that support it, the latter disables recovery for all sanitizers that support it.

Syntax without explicit *opts* parameter is deprecated. It is equivalent to

```
-fsanitize-recover=undefined,float-cast-overflow,float-divide-by-zero
```

Similarly '`-fno-sanitize-recover`' is equivalent to

```
-fno-sanitize-recover=undefined,float-cast-overflow,float-divide-by-zero
```

`-fsanitize-undefined-trap-on-error`

The '`-fsanitize-undefined-trap-on-error`' option instructs the compiler to report undefined behavior using `__builtin_trap` rather than a `libubsan` library routine. The advantage of this is that the `libubsan` library is not needed and is not linked in, so this is usable even in freestanding environments.

`-fsanitize-coverage=trace-pc`

Enable coverage-guided fuzzing code instrumentation. Inserts a call to `__sanitizer_cov_trace_pc` into every basic block.

`-fbounds-check`

For front ends that support it, generate additional code to check that indices used to access arrays are within the declared range. This is currently only supported by the Java and Fortran front ends, where this option defaults to true and false respectively.

`-fcheck-pointer-bounds`

Enable Pointer Bounds Checker instrumentation. Each memory reference is instrumented with checks of the pointer used for memory access against bounds associated with that pointer.

Currently there is only an implementation for Intel MPX available, thus x86 GNU/Linux target and '`-mmpx`' are required to enable this feature. MPX-based instrumentation requires a runtime library to enable MPX in hardware and handle bounds violation signals. By default when '`-fcheck-pointer-bounds`' and '`-mmpx`' options are used to link a program, the GCC driver links against the '`libmpx`' and '`libmpxwrappers`' libraries. Bounds checking on calls to dynamic libraries requires a linker with '`-z bndplt`' support; if GCC was configured with a linker without support for this option (including the Gold linker and older versions of ld), a warning is given if you link with '`-mmpx`' without also specifying '`-static`', since the overall effectiveness of the bounds checking protection is reduced. See also '`-static-libmpxwrappers`'.

MPX-based instrumentation may be used for debugging and also may be included in production code to increase program security. Depending on usage, you may have different requirements for the runtime library. The current version of the MPX runtime library is more oriented for use as a debugging tool. MPX runtime library usage implies '`-lpthread`'. See also '`-static-libmpx`'. The runtime library behavior can be influenced using various `CHKP_RT_*` environment variables. See `https://gcc.gnu.org/wiki/Intel%20MPX%20support%20in%20the%20GCC%20compiler` for more details.

Generated instrumentation may be controlled by various '`-fchkp-*`' options and by the `bnd_variable_size` structure field attribute (see Section 6.33 [Type Attributes], page 459) and `bnd_legacy`, and `bnd_instrument` function attributes (see Section 6.31 [Function Attributes], page 407). GCC also provides a number of built-in functions for controlling the Pointer Bounds Checker. See Section 6.56 [Pointer Bounds Checker builtins], page 542, for more information.

`-fchkp-check-incomplete-type`

Generate pointer bounds checks for variables with incomplete type. Enabled by default.

`-fchkp-narrow-bounds`

Controls bounds used by Pointer Bounds Checker for pointers to object fields. If narrowing is enabled then field bounds are used. Otherwise object bounds are used. See also '`-fchkp-narrow-to-innermost-array`' and '`-fchkp-first-field-has-own-bounds`'. Enabled by default.

`-fchkp-first-field-has-own-bounds`

Forces Pointer Bounds Checker to use narrowed bounds for the address of the first field in the structure. By default a pointer to the first field has the same bounds as a pointer to the whole structure.

`-fchkp-narrow-to-innermost-array`
: Forces Pointer Bounds Checker to use bounds of the innermost arrays in case of nested static array access. By default this option is disabled and bounds of the outermost array are used.

`-fchkp-optimize`
: Enables Pointer Bounds Checker optimizations. Enabled by default at optimization levels '`-O`', '`-O2`', '`-O3`'.

`-fchkp-use-fast-string-functions`
: Enables use of `*_nobnd` versions of string functions (not copying bounds) by Pointer Bounds Checker. Disabled by default.

`-fchkp-use-nochk-string-functions`
: Enables use of `*_nochk` versions of string functions (not checking bounds) by Pointer Bounds Checker. Disabled by default.

`-fchkp-use-static-bounds`
: Allow Pointer Bounds Checker to generate static bounds holding bounds of static variables. Enabled by default.

`-fchkp-use-static-const-bounds`
: Use statically-initialized bounds for constant bounds instead of generating them each time they are required. By default enabled when '`-fchkp-use-static-bounds`' is enabled.

`-fchkp-treat-zero-dynamic-size-as-infinite`
: With this option, objects with incomplete type whose dynamically-obtained size is zero are treated as having infinite size instead by Pointer Bounds Checker. This option may be helpful if a program is linked with a library missing size information for some symbols. Disabled by default.

`-fchkp-check-read`
: Instructs Pointer Bounds Checker to generate checks for all read accesses to memory. Enabled by default.

`-fchkp-check-write`
: Instructs Pointer Bounds Checker to generate checks for all write accesses to memory. Enabled by default.

`-fchkp-store-bounds`
: Instructs Pointer Bounds Checker to generate bounds stores for pointer writes. Enabled by default.

`-fchkp-instrument-calls`
: Instructs Pointer Bounds Checker to pass pointer bounds to calls. Enabled by default.

`-fchkp-instrument-marked-only`
: Instructs Pointer Bounds Checker to instrument only functions marked with the `bnd_instrument` attribute (see Section 6.31 [Function Attributes], page 407). Disabled by default.

`-fchkp-use-wrappers`
: Allows Pointer Bounds Checker to replace calls to built-in functions with calls to wrapper functions. When '`-fchkp-use-wrappers`' is used to link a program, the GCC driver automatically links against '`libmpxwrappers`'. See also '`-static-libmpxwrappers`'. Enabled by default.

`-fstack-protector`
: Emit extra code to check for buffer overflows, such as stack smashing attacks. This is done by adding a guard variable to functions with vulnerable objects. This includes functions that call `alloca`, and functions with buffers larger than 8 bytes. The guards are initialized when a function is entered and then checked when the function exits. If a guard check fails, an error message is printed and the program exits.

`-fstack-protector-all`
: Like '`-fstack-protector`' except that all functions are protected.

`-fstack-protector-strong`
: Like '`-fstack-protector`' but includes additional functions to be protected — those that have local array definitions, or have references to local frame addresses.

`-fstack-protector-explicit`
: Like '`-fstack-protector`' but only protects those functions which have the `stack_protect` attribute.

`-fstack-check`
: Generate code to verify that you do not go beyond the boundary of the stack. You should specify this flag if you are running in an environment with multiple threads, but you only rarely need to specify it in a single-threaded environment since stack overflow is automatically detected on nearly all systems if there is only one stack.

Note that this switch does not actually cause checking to be done; the operating system or the language runtime must do that. The switch causes generation of code to ensure that they see the stack being extended.

You can additionally specify a string parameter: '`no`' means no checking, '`generic`' means force the use of old-style checking, '`specific`' means use the best checking method and is equivalent to bare '`-fstack-check`'.

Old-style checking is a generic mechanism that requires no specific target support in the compiler but comes with the following drawbacks:

1. Modified allocation strategy for large objects: they are always allocated dynamically if their size exceeds a fixed threshold.
2. Fixed limit on the size of the static frame of functions: when it is topped by a particular function, stack checking is not reliable and a warning is issued by the compiler.
3. Inefficiency: because of both the modified allocation strategy and the generic implementation, code performance is hampered.

Note that old-style stack checking is also the fallback method for '`specific`' if no target support has been added in the compiler.

`-fstack-limit-register=reg`
`-fstack-limit-symbol=sym`
`-fno-stack-limit`

Generate code to ensure that the stack does not grow beyond a certain value, either the value of a register or the address of a symbol. If a larger stack is required, a signal is raised at run time. For most targets, the signal is raised before the stack overruns the boundary, so it is possible to catch the signal without taking special precautions.

For instance, if the stack starts at absolute address '0x80000000' and grows downwards, you can use the flags '-fstack-limit-symbol=__stack_limit' and '-Wl,--defsym,__stack_limit=0x7ffe0000' to enforce a stack limit of 128KB. Note that this may only work with the GNU linker.

You can locally override stack limit checking by using the no_stack_limit function attribute (see Section 6.31 [Function Attributes], page 407).

`-fsplit-stack`

Generate code to automatically split the stack before it overflows. The resulting program has a discontiguous stack which can only overflow if the program is unable to allocate any more memory. This is most useful when running threaded programs, as it is no longer necessary to calculate a good stack size to use for each thread. This is currently only implemented for the x86 targets running GNU/Linux.

When code compiled with '-fsplit-stack' calls code compiled without '-fsplit-stack', there may not be much stack space available for the latter code to run. If compiling all code, including library code, with '-fsplit-stack' is not an option, then the linker can fix up these calls so that the code compiled without '-fsplit-stack' always has a large stack. Support for this is implemented in the gold linker in GNU binutils release 2.21 and later.

`-fvtable-verify=[std|preinit|none]`

This option is only available when compiling C++ code. It turns on (or off, if using '-fvtable-verify=none') the security feature that verifies at run time, for every virtual call, that the vtable pointer through which the call is made is valid for the type of the object, and has not been corrupted or overwritten. If an invalid vtable pointer is detected at run time, an error is reported and execution of the program is immediately halted.

This option causes run-time data structures to be built at program startup, which are used for verifying the vtable pointers. The options 'std' and 'preinit' control the timing of when these data structures are built. In both cases the data structures are built before execution reaches main. Using '-fvtable-verify=std' causes the data structures to be built after shared libraries have been loaded and initialized. '-fvtable-verify=preinit' causes them to be built before shared libraries have been loaded and initialized.

If this option appears multiple times in the command line with different values specified, 'none' takes highest priority over both 'std' and 'preinit'; 'preinit' takes priority over 'std'.

`-fvtv-debug`

When used in conjunction with '`-fvtable-verify=std`' or '`-fvtable-verify=preinit`', causes debug versions of the runtime functions for the vtable verification feature to be called. This flag also causes the compiler to log information about which vtable pointers it finds for each class. This information is written to a file named '`vtv_set_ptr_data.log`' in the directory named by the environment variable `VTV_LOGS_DIR` if that is defined or the current working directory otherwise.

Note: This feature *appends* data to the log file. If you want a fresh log file, be sure to delete any existing one.

`-fvtv-counts`

This is a debugging flag. When used in conjunction with '`-fvtable-verify=std`' or '`-fvtable-verify=preinit`', this causes the compiler to keep track of the total number of virtual calls it encounters and the number of verifications it inserts. It also counts the number of calls to certain run-time library functions that it inserts and logs this information for each compilation unit. The compiler writes this information to a file named '`vtv_count_data.log`' in the directory named by the environment variable `VTV_LOGS_DIR` if that is defined or the current working directory otherwise. It also counts the size of the vtable pointer sets for each class, and writes this information to '`vtv_class_set_sizes.log`' in the same directory.

Note: This feature *appends* data to the log files. To get fresh log files, be sure to delete any existing ones.

`-finstrument-functions`

Generate instrumentation calls for entry and exit to functions. Just after function entry and just before function exit, the following profiling functions are called with the address of the current function and its call site. (On some platforms, `__builtin_return_address` does not work beyond the current function, so the call site information may not be available to the profiling functions otherwise.)

```
void __cyg_profile_func_enter (void *this_fn,
                               void *call_site);
void __cyg_profile_func_exit  (void *this_fn,
                               void *call_site);
```

The first argument is the address of the start of the current function, which may be looked up exactly in the symbol table.

This instrumentation is also done for functions expanded inline in other functions. The profiling calls indicate where, conceptually, the inline function is entered and exited. This means that addressable versions of such functions must be available. If all your uses of a function are expanded inline, this may mean an additional expansion of code size. If you use `extern inline` in your C code, an addressable version of such functions must be provided. (This is normally the case anyway, but if you get lucky and the optimizer always expands the functions inline, you might have gotten away without providing static copies.)

A function may be given the attribute no_instrument_function, in which case this instrumentation is not done. This can be used, for example, for the profiling functions listed above, high-priority interrupt routines, and any functions from which the profiling functions cannot safely be called (perhaps signal handlers, if the profiling routines generate output or allocate memory).

-finstrument-functions-exclude-file-list=*file*,*file*,...

Set the list of functions that are excluded from instrumentation (see the description of '-finstrument-functions'). If the file that contains a function definition matches with one of *file*, then that function is not instrumented. The match is done on substrings: if the *file* parameter is a substring of the file name, it is considered to be a match.

For example:

```
-finstrument-functions-exclude-file-list=/bits/stl,include/sys
```

excludes any inline function defined in files whose pathnames contain '/bits/stl' or 'include/sys'.

If, for some reason, you want to include letter ',' in one of *sym*, write '\,'. For example, '-finstrument-functions-exclude-file-list='\,\,tmp'' (note the single quote surrounding the option).

-finstrument-functions-exclude-function-list=*sym*,*sym*,...

This is similar to '-finstrument-functions-exclude-file-list', but this option sets the list of function names to be excluded from instrumentation. The function name to be matched is its user-visible name, such as vector<int> blah(const vector<int> &), not the internal mangled name (e.g., _Z4blahRSt6vectorIiSaIiEE). The match is done on substrings: if the *sym* parameter is a substring of the function name, it is considered to be a match. For C99 and C++ extended identifiers, the function name must be given in UTF-8, not using universal character names.

3.12 Options Controlling the Preprocessor

These options control the C preprocessor, which is run on each C source file before actual compilation.

If you use the '-E' option, nothing is done except preprocessing. Some of these options make sense only together with '-E' because they cause the preprocessor output to be unsuitable for actual compilation.

-Wp,*option*

You can use '-Wp,*option*' to bypass the compiler driver and pass *option* directly through to the preprocessor. If *option* contains commas, it is split into multiple options at the commas. However, many options are modified, translated or interpreted by the compiler driver before being passed to the preprocessor, and '-Wp' forcibly bypasses this phase. The preprocessor's direct interface is undocumented and subject to change, so whenever possible you should avoid using '-Wp' and let the driver handle the options instead.

`-Xpreprocessor` *option*
: Pass *option* as an option to the preprocessor. You can use this to supply system-specific preprocessor options that GCC does not recognize.

  If you want to pass an option that takes an argument, you must use '`-Xpreprocessor`' twice, once for the option and once for the argument.

`-no-integrated-cpp`
: Perform preprocessing as a separate pass before compilation. By default, GCC performs preprocessing as an integrated part of input tokenization and parsing. If this option is provided, the appropriate language front end (`cc1`, `cc1plus`, or `cc1obj` for C, C++, and Objective-C, respectively) is instead invoked twice, once for preprocessing only and once for actual compilation of the preprocessed input. This option may be useful in conjunction with the '`-B`' or '`-wrapper`' options to specify an alternate preprocessor or perform additional processing of the program source between normal preprocessing and compilation.

`-D` *name*
: Predefine *name* as a macro, with definition `1`.

`-D` *name=definition*
: The contents of *definition* are tokenized and processed as if they appeared during translation phase three in a '`#define`' directive. In particular, the definition will be truncated by embedded newline characters.

  If you are invoking the preprocessor from a shell or shell-like program you may need to use the shell's quoting syntax to protect characters such as spaces that have a meaning in the shell syntax.

  If you wish to define a function-like macro on the command line, write its argument list with surrounding parentheses before the equals sign (if any). Parentheses are meaningful to most shells, so you will need to quote the option. With `sh` and `csh`, '`-D'`*name*`(`*args...*`)=`*definition*`''` works.

  '`-D`' and '`-U`' options are processed in the order they are given on the command line. All '`-imacros` *file*' and '`-include` *file*' options are processed after all '`-D`' and '`-U`' options.

`-U` *name*
: Cancel any previous definition of *name*, either built in or provided with a '`-D`' option.

`-undef`
: Do not predefine any system-specific or GCC-specific macros. The standard predefined macros remain defined.

`-I` *dir*
: Add the directory *dir* to the list of directories to be searched for header files. Directories named by '`-I`' are searched before the standard system include directories. If the directory *dir* is a standard system include directory, the option is ignored to ensure that the default search order for system directories and the special treatment of system headers are not defeated . If *dir* begins with `=`, then the `=` will be replaced by the sysroot prefix; see '`--sysroot`' and '`-isysroot`'.

`-o` *file*
: Write output to *file*. This is the same as specifying *file* as the second non-option argument to `cpp`. `gcc` has a different interpretation of a second non-option argument, so you must use '`-o`' to specify the output file.

`-Wall` Turns on all optional warnings which are desirable for normal code. At present this is '`-Wcomment`', '`-Wtrigraphs`', '`-Wmultichar`' and a warning about integer promotion causing a change of sign in `#if` expressions. Note that many of the preprocessor's warnings are on by default and have no options to control them.

`-Wcomment`
`-Wcomments`
: Warn whenever a comment-start sequence '`/*`' appears in a '`/*`' comment, or whenever a backslash-newline appears in a '`//`' comment. (Both forms have the same effect.)

`-Wtrigraphs`
: Most trigraphs in comments cannot affect the meaning of the program. However, a trigraph that would form an escaped newline ('`??/`' at the end of a line) can, by changing where the comment begins or ends. Therefore, only trigraphs that would form escaped newlines produce warnings inside a comment.

  This option is implied by '`-Wall`'. If '`-Wall`' is not given, this option is still enabled unless trigraphs are enabled. To get trigraph conversion without warnings, but get the other '`-Wall`' warnings, use '`-trigraphs -Wall -Wno-trigraphs`'.

`-Wtraditional`
: Warn about certain constructs that behave differently in traditional and ISO C. Also warn about ISO C constructs that have no traditional C equivalent, and problematic constructs which should be avoided.

`-Wundef` Warn whenever an identifier which is not a macro is encountered in an '`#if`' directive, outside of '`defined`'. Such identifiers are replaced with zero.

`-Wunused-macros`
: Warn about macros defined in the main file that are unused. A macro is *used* if it is expanded or tested for existence at least once. The preprocessor will also warn if the macro has not been used at the time it is redefined or undefined.

  Built-in macros, macros defined on the command line, and macros defined in include files are not warned about.

  Note: If a macro is actually used, but only used in skipped conditional blocks, then CPP will report it as unused. To avoid the warning in such a case, you might improve the scope of the macro's definition by, for example, moving it into the first skipped block. Alternatively, you could provide a dummy use with something like:

```
#if defined the_macro_causing_the_warning
#endif
```

`-Wendif-labels`
: Warn whenever an '`#else`' or an '`#endif`' are followed by text. This usually happens in code of the form

```
#if FOO
...
#else FOO
...
```

```
#endif FOO
```

The second and third FOO should be in comments, but often are not in older programs. This warning is on by default.

-Werror
: Make all warnings into hard errors. Source code which triggers warnings will be rejected.

-Wsystem-headers
: Issue warnings for code in system headers. These are normally unhelpful in finding bugs in your own code, therefore suppressed. If you are responsible for the system library, you may want to see them.

-w
: Suppress all warnings, including those which GNU CPP issues by default.

-pedantic
: Issue all the mandatory diagnostics listed in the C standard. Some of them are left out by default, since they trigger frequently on harmless code.

-pedantic-errors
: Issue all the mandatory diagnostics, and make all mandatory diagnostics into errors. This includes mandatory diagnostics that GCC issues without '-pedantic' but treats as warnings.

-M
: Instead of outputting the result of preprocessing, output a rule suitable for make describing the dependencies of the main source file. The preprocessor outputs one make rule containing the object file name for that source file, a colon, and the names of all the included files, including those coming from '-include' or '-imacros' command-line options.

Unless specified explicitly (with '-MT' or '-MQ'), the object file name consists of the name of the source file with any suffix replaced with object file suffix and with any leading directory parts removed. If there are many included files then the rule is split into several lines using '\'-newline. The rule has no commands.

This option does not suppress the preprocessor's debug output, such as '-dM'. To avoid mixing such debug output with the dependency rules you should explicitly specify the dependency output file with '-MF', or use an environment variable like DEPENDENCIES_OUTPUT (see Section 3.20 [Environment Variables], page 367). Debug output will still be sent to the regular output stream as normal.

Passing '-M' to the driver implies '-E', and suppresses warnings with an implicit '-w'.

-MM
: Like '-M' but do not mention header files that are found in system header directories, nor header files that are included, directly or indirectly, from such a header.

This implies that the choice of angle brackets or double quotes in an '#include' directive does not in itself determine whether that header will appear in '-MM' dependency output. This is a slight change in semantics from GCC versions 3.0 and earlier.

`-MF file` When used with '-M' or '-MM', specifies a file to write the dependencies to. If no '-MF' switch is given the preprocessor sends the rules to the same place it would have sent preprocessed output.

When used with the driver options '-MD' or '-MMD', '-MF' overrides the default dependency output file.

`-MG` In conjunction with an option such as '-M' requesting dependency generation, '-MG' assumes missing header files are generated files and adds them to the dependency list without raising an error. The dependency filename is taken directly from the `#include` directive without prepending any path. '-MG' also suppresses preprocessed output, as a missing header file renders this useless.

This feature is used in automatic updating of makefiles.

`-MP` This option instructs CPP to add a phony target for each dependency other than the main file, causing each to depend on nothing. These dummy rules work around errors `make` gives if you remove header files without updating the 'Makefile' to match.

This is typical output:

```
test.o: test.c test.h

test.h:
```

`-MT target`

Change the target of the rule emitted by dependency generation. By default CPP takes the name of the main input file, deletes any directory components and any file suffix such as '.c', and appends the platform's usual object suffix. The result is the target.

An '-MT' option will set the target to be exactly the string you specify. If you want multiple targets, you can specify them as a single argument to '-MT', or use multiple '-MT' options.

For example, '-MT '$(objpfx)foo.o'' might give

```
$(objpfx)foo.o: foo.c
```

`-MQ target`

Same as '-MT', but it quotes any characters which are special to Make. '-MQ '$(objpfx)foo.o'' gives

```
$$(objpfx)foo.o: foo.c
```

The default target is automatically quoted, as if it were given with '-MQ'.

`-MD` '-MD' is equivalent to '-M -MF *file*', except that '-E' is not implied. The driver determines *file* based on whether an '-o' option is given. If it is, the driver uses its argument but with a suffix of '.d', otherwise it takes the name of the input file, removes any directory components and suffix, and applies a '.d' suffix.

If '-MD' is used in conjunction with '-E', any '-o' switch is understood to specify the dependency output file (see [-MF], page 162), but if used without '-E', each '-o' is understood to specify a target object file.

Since '-E' is not implied, '-MD' can be used to generate a dependency output file as a side-effect of the compilation process.

`-MMD` Like '`-MD`' except mention only user header files, not system header files.

`-fpch-deps`
: When using precompiled headers (see Section 3.21 [Precompiled Headers], page 370), this flag will cause the dependency-output flags to also list the files from the precompiled header's dependencies. If not specified only the precompiled header would be listed and not the files that were used to create it because those files are not consulted when a precompiled header is used.

`-fpch-preprocess`
: This option allows use of a precompiled header (see Section 3.21 [Precompiled Headers], page 370) together with '`-E`'. It inserts a special **`#pragma`**, **`#pragma GCC pch_preprocess "`*`filename`*`"`** in the output to mark the place where the precompiled header was found, and its *filename*. When '`-fpreprocessed`' is in use, GCC recognizes this **`#pragma`** and loads the PCH.

  This option is off by default, because the resulting preprocessed output is only really suitable as input to GCC. It is switched on by '`-save-temps`'.

  You should not write this **`#pragma`** in your own code, but it is safe to edit the filename if the PCH file is available in a different location. The filename may be absolute or it may be relative to GCC's current directory.

`-x c`
`-x c++`
`-x objective-c`
`-x assembler-with-cpp`
: Specify the source language: C, C++, Objective-C, or assembly. This has nothing to do with standards conformance or extensions; it merely selects which base syntax to expect. If you give none of these options, cpp will deduce the language from the extension of the source file: '`.c`', '`.cc`', '`.m`', or '`.S`'. Some other common extensions for C++ and assembly are also recognized. If cpp does not recognize the extension, it will treat the file as C; this is the most generic mode.

  Note: Previous versions of cpp accepted a '`-lang`' option which selected both the language and the standards conformance level. This option has been removed, because it conflicts with the '`-l`' option.

`-std=`*`standard`*
`-ansi` Specify the standard to which the code should conform. Currently CPP knows about C and C++ standards; others may be added in the future.

  standard may be one of:

  `c90`
  `c89`
  `iso9899:1990`
  : The ISO C standard from 1990. '`c90`' is the customary shorthand for this version of the standard.

    The '`-ansi`' option is equivalent to '`-std=c90`'.

  `iso9899:199409`
  : The 1990 C standard, as amended in 1994.

`iso9899:1999`
`c99`
`iso9899:199x`
`c9x` The revised ISO C standard, published in December 1999. Before publication, this was known as C9X.

`iso9899:2011`
`c11`
`c1x` The revised ISO C standard, published in December 2011. Before publication, this was known as C1X.

`gnu90`
`gnu89` The 1990 C standard plus GNU extensions. This is the default.

`gnu99`
`gnu9x` The 1999 C standard plus GNU extensions.

`gnu11`
`gnu1x` The 2011 C standard plus GNU extensions.

`c++98` The 1998 ISO C++ standard plus amendments.

`gnu++98` The same as '`-std=c++98`' plus GNU extensions. This is the default for C++ code.

`-I-` Split the include path. Any directories specified with '`-I`' options before '`-I-`' are searched only for headers requested with `#include "file"`; they are not searched for `#include <file>`. If additional directories are specified with '`-I`' options after the '`-I-`', those directories are searched for all '`#include`' directives.

In addition, '`-I-`' inhibits the use of the directory of the current file directory as the first search directory for `#include "file"`. This option has been deprecated.

`-nostdinc`
Do not search the standard system directories for header files. Only the directories you have specified with '`-I`' options (and the directory of the current file, if appropriate) are searched.

`-nostdinc++`
Do not search for header files in the C++-specific standard directories, but do still search the other standard directories. (This option is used when building the C++ library.)

`-include` *`file`*
Process *file* as if `#include "file"` appeared as the first line of the primary source file. However, the first directory searched for *file* is the preprocessor's working directory *instead of* the directory containing the main source file. If not found there, it is searched for in the remainder of the `#include "..."` search chain as normal.

If multiple '`-include`' options are given, the files are included in the order they appear on the command line.

`-imacros file`
: Exactly like '`-include`', except that any output produced by scanning *file* is thrown away. Macros it defines remain defined. This allows you to acquire all the macros from a header without also processing its declarations.

  All files specified by '`-imacros`' are processed before all files specified by '`-include`'.

`-idirafter dir`
: Search *dir* for header files, but do it *after* all directories specified with '`-I`' and the standard system directories have been exhausted. *dir* is treated as a system include directory. If *dir* begins with `=`, then the `=` will be replaced by the sysroot prefix; see '`--sysroot`' and '`-isysroot`'.

`-iprefix prefix`
: Specify *prefix* as the prefix for subsequent '`-iwithprefix`' options. If the prefix represents a directory, you should include the final '`/`'.

`-iwithprefix dir`
`-iwithprefixbefore dir`
: Append *dir* to the prefix specified previously with '`-iprefix`', and add the resulting directory to the include search path. '`-iwithprefixbefore`' puts it in the same place '`-I`' would; '`-iwithprefix`' puts it where '`-idirafter`' would.

`-isysroot dir`
: This option is like the '`--sysroot`' option, but applies only to header files (except for Darwin targets, where it applies to both header files and libraries). See the '`--sysroot`' option for more information.

`-imultilib dir`
: Use *dir* as a subdirectory of the directory containing target-specific C++ headers.

`-isystem dir`
: Search *dir* for header files, after all directories specified by '`-I`' but before the standard system directories. Mark it as a system directory, so that it gets the same special treatment as is applied to the standard system directories. If *dir* begins with `=`, then the `=` will be replaced by the sysroot prefix; see '`--sysroot`' and '`-isysroot`'.

`-iquote dir`
: Search *dir* only for header files requested with `#include "file"`; they are not searched for `#include <file>`, before all directories specified by '`-I`' and before the standard system directories. If *dir* begins with `=`, then the `=` will be replaced by the sysroot prefix; see '`--sysroot`' and '`-isysroot`'.

`-fdirectives-only`
: When preprocessing, handle directives, but do not expand macros.

  The option's behavior depends on the '`-E`' and '`-fpreprocessed`' options.

  With '`-E`', preprocessing is limited to the handling of directives such as `#define`, `#ifdef`, and `#error`. Other preprocessor operations, such as macro expansion and trigraph conversion are not performed. In addition, the '`-dD`' option is implicitly enabled.

With '-fpreprocessed', predefinition of command line and most builtin macros is disabled. Macros such as __LINE__, which are contextually dependent, are handled normally. This enables compilation of files previously preprocessed with -E -fdirectives-only.

With both '-E' and '-fpreprocessed', the rules for '-fpreprocessed' take precedence. This enables full preprocessing of files previously preprocessed with -E -fdirectives-only.

-fdollars-in-identifiers
: Accept '$' in identifiers.

-fextended-identifiers
: Accept universal character names in identifiers. This option is enabled by default for C99 (and later C standard versions) and C++.

-fno-canonical-system-headers
: When preprocessing, do not shorten system header paths with canonicalization.

-fpreprocessed
: Indicate to the preprocessor that the input file has already been preprocessed. This suppresses things like macro expansion, trigraph conversion, escaped newline splicing, and processing of most directives. The preprocessor still recognizes and removes comments, so that you can pass a file preprocessed with '-C' to the compiler without problems. In this mode the integrated preprocessor is little more than a tokenizer for the front ends.

'-fpreprocessed' is implicit if the input file has one of the extensions '.i', '.ii' or '.mi'. These are the extensions that GCC uses for preprocessed files created by '-save-temps'.

-ftabstop=*width*
: Set the distance between tab stops. This helps the preprocessor report correct column numbers in warnings or errors, even if tabs appear on the line. If the value is less than 1 or greater than 100, the option is ignored. The default is 8.

-fdebug-cpp
: This option is only useful for debugging GCC. When used with '-E', dumps debugging information about location maps. Every token in the output is preceded by the dump of the map its location belongs to. The dump of the map holding the location of a token would be:

```
{'P':'/file/path';'F':'/includer/path';'L':line_num;'C':col_num;'S':system_header_p;'M':map_a
```

When used without '-E', this option has no effect.

-ftrack-macro-expansion[=*level*]
: Track locations of tokens across macro expansions. This allows the compiler to emit diagnostic about the current macro expansion stack when a compilation error occurs in a macro expansion. Using this option makes the preprocessor and the compiler consume more memory. The *level* parameter can be used to choose the level of precision of token location tracking thus decreasing the memory consumption if necessary. Value '0' of *level* de-activates this option just as if no '-ftrack-macro-expansion' was present on the command line.

Value '1' tracks tokens locations in a degraded mode for the sake of minimal memory overhead. In this mode all tokens resulting from the expansion of an argument of a function-like macro have the same location. Value '2' tracks tokens locations completely. This value is the most memory hungry. When this option is given no argument, the default parameter value is '2'.

Note that `-ftrack-macro-expansion=2` is activated by default.

`-fexec-charset=`*`charset`*
: Set the execution character set, used for string and character constants. The default is UTF-8. *charset* can be any encoding supported by the system's `iconv` library routine.

`-fwide-exec-charset=`*`charset`*
: Set the wide execution character set, used for wide string and character constants. The default is UTF-32 or UTF-16, whichever corresponds to the width of `wchar_t`. As with '`-fexec-charset`', *charset* can be any encoding supported by the system's `iconv` library routine; however, you will have problems with encodings that do not fit exactly in `wchar_t`.

`-finput-charset=`*`charset`*
: Set the input character set, used for translation from the character set of the input file to the source character set used by GCC. If the locale does not specify, or GCC cannot get this information from the locale, the default is UTF-8. This can be overridden by either the locale or this command-line option. Currently the command-line option takes precedence if there's a conflict. *charset* can be any encoding supported by the system's `iconv` library routine.

`-fworking-directory`
: Enable generation of linemarkers in the preprocessor output that will let the compiler know the current working directory at the time of preprocessing. When this option is enabled, the preprocessor will emit, after the initial linemarker, a second linemarker with the current working directory followed by two slashes. GCC will use this directory, when it's present in the preprocessed input, as the directory emitted as the current working directory in some debugging information formats. This option is implicitly enabled if debugging information is enabled, but this can be inhibited with the negated form '`-fno-working-directory`'. If the '`-P`' flag is present in the command line, this option has no effect, since no `#line` directives are emitted whatsoever.

`-fno-show-column`
: Do not print column numbers in diagnostics. This may be necessary if diagnostics are being scanned by a program that does not understand the column numbers, such as `dejagnu`.

`-A` *`predicate=answer`*
: Make an assertion with the predicate *predicate* and answer *answer*. This form is preferred to the older form '`-A` *`predicate(answer)`*', which is still supported, because it does not use shell special characters.

`-A` *`-predicate=answer`*
: Cancel an assertion with the predicate *predicate* and answer *answer*.

-dCHARS *CHARS* is a sequence of one or more of the following characters, and must not be preceded by a space. Other characters are interpreted by the compiler proper, or reserved for future versions of GCC, and so are silently ignored. If you specify characters whose behavior conflicts, the result is undefined.

'M' Instead of the normal output, generate a list of '#define' directives for all the macros defined during the execution of the preprocessor, including predefined macros. This gives you a way of finding out what is predefined in your version of the preprocessor. Assuming you have no file 'foo.h', the command

```
touch foo.h; cpp -dM foo.h
```

will show all the predefined macros.

If you use '-dM' without the '-E' option, '-dM' is interpreted as a synonym for '-fdump-rtl-mach'. See Section "Developer Options" in gcc.

'D' Like 'M' except in two respects: it does *not* include the predefined macros, and it outputs *both* the '#define' directives and the result of preprocessing. Both kinds of output go to the standard output file.

'N' Like 'D', but emit only the macro names, not their expansions.

'I' Output '#include' directives in addition to the result of preprocessing.

'U' Like 'D' except that only macros that are expanded, or whose definedness is tested in preprocessor directives, are output; the output is delayed until the use or test of the macro; and '#undef' directives are also output for macros tested but undefined at the time.

-P Inhibit generation of linemarkers in the output from the preprocessor. This might be useful when running the preprocessor on something that is not C code, and will be sent to a program which might be confused by the linemarkers.

-C Do not discard comments. All comments are passed through to the output file, except for comments in processed directives, which are deleted along with the directive.

You should be prepared for side effects when using '-C'; it causes the preprocessor to treat comments as tokens in their own right. For example, comments appearing at the start of what would be a directive line have the effect of turning that line into an ordinary source line, since the first token on the line is no longer a '#'.

-CC Do not discard comments, including during macro expansion. This is like '-C', except that comments contained within macros are also passed through to the output file where the macro is expanded.

In addition to the side-effects of the '-C' option, the '-CC' option causes all C++-style comments inside a macro to be converted to C-style comments. This is to prevent later use of that macro from inadvertently commenting out the remainder of the source line.

The '-CC' option is generally used to support lint comments.

-traditional-cpp
: Try to imitate the behavior of old-fashioned C preprocessors, as opposed to ISO C preprocessors.

-trigraphs
: Process trigraph sequences. These are three-character sequences, all starting with '??', that are defined by ISO C to stand for single characters. For example, '??/' stands for '\', so ''??/n'' is a character constant for a newline. By default, GCC ignores trigraphs, but in standard-conforming modes it converts them. See the '-std' and '-ansi' options.

The nine trigraphs and their replacements are

```
Trigraph:       ??(  ??)  ??<  ??>  ??=  ??/  ??'  ??!  ??-
Replacement:     [    ]    {    }    #    \    ^    |    ~
```

-remap
: Enable special code to work around file systems which only permit very short file names, such as MS-DOS.

--help
--target-help
: Print text describing all the command-line options instead of preprocessing anything.

-v
: Verbose mode. Print out GNU CPP's version number at the beginning of execution, and report the final form of the include path.

-H
: Print the name of each header file used, in addition to other normal activities. Each name is indented to show how deep in the '#include' stack it is. Precompiled header files are also printed, even if they are found to be invalid; an invalid precompiled header file is printed with '...x' and a valid one with '...!' .

-version
--version
: Print out GNU CPP's version number. With one dash, proceed to preprocess as normal. With two dashes, exit immediately.

3.13 Passing Options to the Assembler

You can pass options to the assembler.

-Wa,*option*
: Pass *option* as an option to the assembler. If *option* contains commas, it is split into multiple options at the commas.

-Xassembler *option*
: Pass *option* as an option to the assembler. You can use this to supply system-specific assembler options that GCC does not recognize.

If you want to pass an option that takes an argument, you must use '-Xassembler' twice, once for the option and once for the argument.

3.14 Options for Linking

These options come into play when the compiler links object files into an executable output file. They are meaningless if the compiler is not doing a link step.

object-file-name
: A file name that does not end in a special recognized suffix is considered to name an object file or library. (Object files are distinguished from libraries by the linker according to the file contents.) If linking is done, these object files are used as input to the linker.

`-c`
`-S`
`-E`
: If any of these options is used, then the linker is not run, and object file names should not be used as arguments. See Section 3.2 [Overall Options], page 27.

`-fuse-ld=bfd`
: Use the `bfd` linker instead of the default linker.

`-fuse-ld=gold`
: Use the `gold` linker instead of the default linker.

`-l`*library*
`-l` *library*
: Search the library named *library* when linking. (The second alternative with the library as a separate argument is only for POSIX compliance and is not recommended.)

It makes a difference where in the command you write this option; the linker searches and processes libraries and object files in the order they are specified. Thus, '`foo.o -lz bar.o`' searches library '`z`' after file '`foo.o`' but before '`bar.o`'. If '`bar.o`' refers to functions in '`z`', those functions may not be loaded.

The linker searches a standard list of directories for the library, which is actually a file named '`lib`*library*`.a`'. The linker then uses this file as if it had been specified precisely by name.

The directories searched include several standard system directories plus any that you specify with '`-L`'.

Normally the files found this way are library files—archive files whose members are object files. The linker handles an archive file by scanning through it for members which define symbols that have so far been referenced but not defined. But if the file that is found is an ordinary object file, it is linked in the usual fashion. The only difference between using an '`-l`' option and specifying a file name is that '`-l`' surrounds *library* with '`lib`' and '`.a`' and searches several directories.

`-lobjc`
: You need this special case of the '`-l`' option in order to link an Objective-C or Objective-C++ program.

`-nostartfiles`
: Do not use the standard system startup files when linking. The standard system libraries are used normally, unless '`-nostdlib`' or '`-nodefaultlibs`' is used.

`-nodefaultlibs`
: Do not use the standard system libraries when linking. Only the libraries you specify are passed to the linker, and options specifying linkage of the system libraries, such as '`-static-libgcc`' or '`-shared-libgcc`', are ignored. The standard startup files are used normally, unless '`-nostartfiles`' is used.

  The compiler may generate calls to `memcmp`, `memset`, `memcpy` and `memmove`. These entries are usually resolved by entries in libc. These entry points should be supplied through some other mechanism when this option is specified.

`-nostdlib`
: Do not use the standard system startup files or libraries when linking. No startup files and only the libraries you specify are passed to the linker, and options specifying linkage of the system libraries, such as '`-static-libgcc`' or '`-shared-libgcc`', are ignored.

  The compiler may generate calls to `memcmp`, `memset`, `memcpy` and `memmove`. These entries are usually resolved by entries in libc. These entry points should be supplied through some other mechanism when this option is specified.

  One of the standard libraries bypassed by '`-nostdlib`' and '`-nodefaultlibs`' is '`libgcc.a`', a library of internal subroutines which GCC uses to overcome shortcomings of particular machines, or special needs for some languages. (See Section "Interfacing to GCC Output" in *GNU Compiler Collection (GCC) Internals*, for more discussion of '`libgcc.a`'.) In most cases, you need '`libgcc.a`' even when you want to avoid other standard libraries. In other words, when you specify '`-nostdlib`' or '`-nodefaultlibs`' you should usually specify '`-lgcc`' as well. This ensures that you have no unresolved references to internal GCC library subroutines. (An example of such an internal subroutine is `__main`, used to ensure C++ constructors are called; see Section "`collect2`" in *GNU Compiler Collection (GCC) Internals*.)

`-pie`
: Produce a position independent executable on targets that support it. For predictable results, you must also specify the same set of options used for compilation ('`-fpie`', '`-fPIE`', or model suboptions) when you specify this linker option.

`-no-pie`
: Don't produce a position independent executable.

`-rdynamic`
: Pass the flag '`-export-dynamic`' to the ELF linker, on targets that support it. This instructs the linker to add all symbols, not only used ones, to the dynamic symbol table. This option is needed for some uses of `dlopen` or to allow obtaining backtraces from within a program.

`-s`
: Remove all symbol table and relocation information from the executable.

`-static`
: On systems that support dynamic linking, this prevents linking with the shared libraries. On other systems, this option has no effect.

`-shared`
: Produce a shared object which can then be linked with other objects to form an executable. Not all systems support this option. For predictable results,

you must also specify the same set of options used for compilation ('-fpic', '-fPIC', or model suboptions) when you specify this linker option.[1]

-shared-libgcc
-static-libgcc
: On systems that provide 'libgcc' as a shared library, these options force the use of either the shared or static version, respectively. If no shared version of 'libgcc' was built when the compiler was configured, these options have no effect.

There are several situations in which an application should use the shared 'libgcc' instead of the static version. The most common of these is when the application wishes to throw and catch exceptions across different shared libraries. In that case, each of the libraries as well as the application itself should use the shared 'libgcc'.

Therefore, the G++ and GCJ drivers automatically add '-shared-libgcc' whenever you build a shared library or a main executable, because C++ and Java programs typically use exceptions, so this is the right thing to do.

If, instead, you use the GCC driver to create shared libraries, you may find that they are not always linked with the shared 'libgcc'. If GCC finds, at its configuration time, that you have a non-GNU linker or a GNU linker that does not support option '--eh-frame-hdr', it links the shared version of 'libgcc' into shared libraries by default. Otherwise, it takes advantage of the linker and optimizes away the linking with the shared version of 'libgcc', linking with the static version of libgcc by default. This allows exceptions to propagate through such shared libraries, without incurring relocation costs at library load time.

However, if a library or main executable is supposed to throw or catch exceptions, you must link it using the G++ or GCJ driver, as appropriate for the languages used in the program, or using the option '-shared-libgcc', such that it is linked with the shared 'libgcc'.

-static-libasan
: When the '-fsanitize=address' option is used to link a program, the GCC driver automatically links against 'libasan'. If 'libasan' is available as a shared library, and the '-static' option is not used, then this links against the shared version of 'libasan'. The '-static-libasan' option directs the GCC driver to link 'libasan' statically, without necessarily linking other libraries statically.

-static-libtsan
: When the '-fsanitize=thread' option is used to link a program, the GCC driver automatically links against 'libtsan'. If 'libtsan' is available as a shared library, and the '-static' option is not used, then this links against the shared version of 'libtsan'. The '-static-libtsan' option directs the GCC

[1] On some systems, 'gcc -shared' needs to build supplementary stub code for constructors to work. On multi-libbed systems, 'gcc -shared' must select the correct support libraries to link against. Failing to supply the correct flags may lead to subtle defects. Supplying them in cases where they are not necessary is innocuous.

driver to link '`libtsan`' statically, without necessarily linking other libraries statically.

`-static-liblsan`
: When the '`-fsanitize=leak`' option is used to link a program, the GCC driver automatically links against '`liblsan`'. If '`liblsan`' is available as a shared library, and the '`-static`' option is not used, then this links against the shared version of '`liblsan`'. The '`-static-liblsan`' option directs the GCC driver to link '`liblsan`' statically, without necessarily linking other libraries statically.

`-static-libubsan`
: When the '`-fsanitize=undefined`' option is used to link a program, the GCC driver automatically links against '`libubsan`'. If '`libubsan`' is available as a shared library, and the '`-static`' option is not used, then this links against the shared version of '`libubsan`'. The '`-static-libubsan`' option directs the GCC driver to link '`libubsan`' statically, without necessarily linking other libraries statically.

`-static-libmpx`
: When the '`-fcheck-pointer bounds`' and '`-mmpx`' options are used to link a program, the GCC driver automatically links against '`libmpx`'. If '`libmpx`' is available as a shared library, and the '`-static`' option is not used, then this links against the shared version of '`libmpx`'. The '`-static-libmpx`' option directs the GCC driver to link '`libmpx`' statically, without necessarily linking other libraries statically.

`-static-libmpxwrappers`
: When the '`-fcheck-pointer bounds`' and '`-mmpx`' options are used to link a program without also using '`-fno-chkp-use-wrappers`', the GCC driver automatically links against '`libmpxwrappers`'. If '`libmpxwrappers`' is available as a shared library, and the '`-static`' option is not used, then this links against the shared version of '`libmpxwrappers`'. The '`-static-libmpxwrappers`' option directs the GCC driver to link '`libmpxwrappers`' statically, without necessarily linking other libraries statically.

`-static-libstdc++`
: When the `g++` program is used to link a C++ program, it normally automatically links against '`libstdc++`'. If '`libstdc++`' is available as a shared library, and the '`-static`' option is not used, then this links against the shared version of '`libstdc++`'. That is normally fine. However, it is sometimes useful to freeze the version of '`libstdc++`' used by the program without going all the way to a fully static link. The '`-static-libstdc++`' option directs the `g++` driver to link '`libstdc++`' statically, without necessarily linking other libraries statically.

`-symbolic`
: Bind references to global symbols when building a shared object. Warn about any unresolved references (unless overridden by the link editor option '`-Xlinker -z -Xlinker defs`'). Only a few systems support this option.

`-T` *`script`*
: Use *script* as the linker script. This option is supported by most systems using the GNU linker. On some targets, such as bare-board targets without an oper-

ating system, the '-T' option may be required when linking to avoid references to undefined symbols.

`-Xlinker option`
: Pass *option* as an option to the linker. You can use this to supply system-specific linker options that GCC does not recognize.

  If you want to pass an option that takes a separate argument, you must use '-Xlinker' twice, once for the option and once for the argument. For example, to pass '-assert definitions', you must write '-Xlinker -assert -Xlinker definitions'. It does not work to write '-Xlinker "-assert definitions"', because this passes the entire string as a single argument, which is not what the linker expects.

  When using the GNU linker, it is usually more convenient to pass arguments to linker options using the '*option*=*value*' syntax than as separate arguments. For example, you can specify '-Xlinker -Map=output.map' rather than '-Xlinker -Map -Xlinker output.map'. Other linkers may not support this syntax for command-line options.

`-Wl,option`
: Pass *option* as an option to the linker. If *option* contains commas, it is split into multiple options at the commas. You can use this syntax to pass an argument to the option. For example, '-Wl,-Map,output.map' passes '-Map output.map' to the linker. When using the GNU linker, you can also get the same effect with '-Wl,-Map=output.map'.

`-u symbol`
: Pretend the symbol *symbol* is undefined, to force linking of library modules to define it. You can use '-u' multiple times with different symbols to force loading of additional library modules.

`-z keyword`
: '-z' is passed directly on to the linker along with the keyword *keyword*. See the section in the documentation of your linker for permitted values and their meanings.

3.15 Options for Directory Search

These options specify directories to search for header files, for libraries and for parts of the compiler:

`-Idir`
: Add the directory *dir* to the head of the list of directories to be searched for header files. This can be used to override a system header file, substituting your own version, since these directories are searched before the system header file directories. However, you should not use this option to add directories that contain vendor-supplied system header files (use '-isystem' for that). If you use more than one '-I' option, the directories are scanned in left-to-right order; the standard system directories come after.

  If a standard system include directory, or a directory specified with '-isystem', is also specified with '-I', the '-I' option is ignored. The directory is still searched but as a system directory at its normal position in the system include chain. This is to ensure that GCC's procedure to fix buggy system headers and the ordering for the `include_next` directive are not inadvertently changed. If you really need to change the search order for system directories, use the '`-nostdinc`' and/or '`-isystem`' options.

`-iplugindir=`*dir*
: Set the directory to search for plugins that are passed by '`-fplugin=`*name*' instead of '`-fplugin=`*path*/*name*`.so`'. This option is not meant to be used by the user, but only passed by the driver.

`-iquote`*dir*
: Add the directory *dir* to the head of the list of directories to be searched for header files only for the case of `#include "`*file*`"`; they are not searched for `#include <`*file*`>`, otherwise just like '`-I`'.

`-L`*dir*
: Add directory *dir* to the list of directories to be searched for '`-l`'.

`-B`*prefix*
: This option specifies where to find the executables, libraries, include files, and data files of the compiler itself.

The compiler driver program runs one or more of the subprograms `cpp`, `cc1`, `as` and `ld`. It tries *prefix* as a prefix for each program it tries to run, both with and without '*machine*/*version*/' for the corresponding target machine and compiler version.

For each subprogram to be run, the compiler driver first tries the '`-B`' prefix, if any. If that name is not found, or if '`-B`' is not specified, the driver tries two standard prefixes, '`/usr/lib/gcc/`' and '`/usr/local/lib/gcc/`'. If neither of those results in a file name that is found, the unmodified program name is searched for using the directories specified in your `PATH` environment variable.

The compiler checks to see if the path provided by '`-B`' refers to a directory, and if necessary it adds a directory separator character at the end of the path.

'`-B`' prefixes that effectively specify directory names also apply to libraries in the linker, because the compiler translates these options into '`-L`' options for the linker. They also apply to include files in the preprocessor, because the compiler translates these options into '`-isystem`' options for the preprocessor. In this case, the compiler appends '`include`' to the prefix.

The runtime support file '`libgcc.a`' can also be searched for using the '`-B`' prefix, if needed. If it is not found there, the two standard prefixes above are tried, and that is all. The file is left out of the link if it is not found by those means.

Another way to specify a prefix much like the '`-B`' prefix is to use the environment variable `GCC_EXEC_PREFIX`. See Section 3.20 [Environment Variables], page 367.

As a special kludge, if the path provided by '`-B`' is '`[dir/]stage`*N*`/`', where *N* is a number in the range 0 to 9, then it is replaced by '`[dir/]include`'. This is to help with boot-strapping the compiler.

`-no-canonical-prefixes`
: Do not expand any symbolic links, resolve references to '`/../`' or '`/./`', or make the path absolute when generating a relative prefix.

`--sysroot=dir`
: Use *dir* as the logical root directory for headers and libraries. For example, if the compiler normally searches for headers in '/usr/include' and libraries in '/usr/lib', it instead searches '*dir*/usr/include' and '*dir*/usr/lib'.

  If you use both this option and the '-isysroot' option, then the '--sysroot' option applies to libraries, but the '-isysroot' option applies to header files.

  The GNU linker (beginning with version 2.16) has the necessary support for this option. If your linker does not support this option, the header file aspect of '--sysroot' still works, but the library aspect does not.

`--no-sysroot-suffix`
: For some targets, a suffix is added to the root directory specified with '--sysroot', depending on the other options used, so that headers may for example be found in '*dir*/*suffix*/usr/include' instead of '*dir*/usr/include'. This option disables the addition of such a suffix.

`-I-`
: This option has been deprecated. Please use '-iquote' instead for '-I' directories before the '-I-' and remove the '-I-' option. Any directories you specify with '-I' options before the '-I-' option are searched only for the case of `#include "file"`; they are not searched for `#include <file>`.

  If additional directories are specified with '-I' options after the '-I-' option, these directories are searched for all `#include` directives. (Ordinarily *all* '-I' directories are used this way.)

  In addition, the '-I-' option inhibits the use of the current directory (where the current input file came from) as the first search directory for `#include "file"`. There is no way to override this effect of '-I-'. With '-I.' you can specify searching the directory that is current when the compiler is invoked. That is not exactly the same as what the preprocessor does by default, but it is often satisfactory.

  '-I-' does not inhibit the use of the standard system directories for header files. Thus, '-I-' and '-nostdinc' are independent.

3.16 Options for Code Generation Conventions

These machine-independent options control the interface conventions used in code generation.

Most of them have both positive and negative forms; the negative form of '-ffoo' is '-fno-foo'. In the table below, only one of the forms is listed—the one that is not the default. You can figure out the other form by either removing 'no-' or adding it.

`-fstack-reuse=reuse-level`
: This option controls stack space reuse for user declared local/auto variables and compiler generated temporaries. *reuse_level* can be 'all', 'named_vars', or 'none'. 'all' enables stack reuse for all local variables and temporaries, 'named_vars' enables the reuse only for user defined local variables with names, and 'none' disables stack reuse completely. The default value is 'all'. The option is needed when the program extends the lifetime of a scoped local variable

or a compiler generated temporary beyond the end point defined by the language. When a lifetime of a variable ends, and if the variable lives in memory, the optimizing compiler has the freedom to reuse its stack space with other temporaries or scoped local variables whose live range does not overlap with it. Legacy code extending local lifetime is likely to break with the stack reuse optimization.

For example,

```
int *p;
{
  int local1;

  p = &local1;
  local1 = 10;
  ....
}
{
   int local2;
   local2 = 20;
   ...
}

if (*p == 10)  // out of scope use of local1
  {

  }
```

Another example:

```
struct A
{
    A(int k) : i(k), j(k) { }
    int i;
    int j;
};

A *ap;

void foo(const A& ar)
{
   ap = &ar;
}

void bar()
{
   foo(A(10)); // temp object's lifetime ends when foo returns

   {
     A a(20);
     ....
   }
   ap->i+= 10;  // ap references out of scope temp whose space
                // is reused with a. What is the value of ap->i?
}
```

The lifetime of a compiler generated temporary is well defined by the C++ standard. When a lifetime of a temporary ends, and if the temporary lives in memory, the optimizing compiler has the freedom to reuse its stack space with other temporaries or scoped local variables whose live range does not overlap with it. However some of the legacy code relies on the behavior of older compilers in which temporaries' stack space is not reused, the aggressive stack reuse can lead to runtime errors. This option is used to control the temporary stack reuse optimization.

`-ftrapv`
: This option generates traps for signed overflow on addition, subtraction, multiplication operations. The options '`-ftrapv`' and '`-fwrapv`' override each other, so using '`-ftrapv`' '`-fwrapv`' on the command-line results in '`-fwrapv`' being effective. Note that only active options override, so using '`-ftrapv`' '`-fwrapv`' '`-fno-wrapv`' on the command-line results in '`-ftrapv`' being effective.

`-fwrapv`
: This option instructs the compiler to assume that signed arithmetic overflow of addition, subtraction and multiplication wraps around using twos-complement representation. This flag enables some optimizations and disables others. This option is enabled by default for the Java front end, as required by the Java language specification. The options '`-ftrapv`' and '`-fwrapv`' override each other, so using '`-ftrapv`' '`-fwrapv`' on the command-line results in '`-fwrapv`' being effective. Note that only active options override, so using '`-ftrapv`' '`-fwrapv`' '`-fno-wrapv`' on the command-line results in '`-ftrapv`' being effective.

`-fexceptions`
: Enable exception handling. Generates extra code needed to propagate exceptions. For some targets, this implies GCC generates frame unwind information for all functions, which can produce significant data size overhead, although it does not affect execution. If you do not specify this option, GCC enables it by default for languages like C++ that normally require exception handling, and disables it for languages like C that do not normally require it. However, you may need to enable this option when compiling C code that needs to interoperate properly with exception handlers written in C++. You may also wish to disable this option if you are compiling older C++ programs that don't use exception handling.

`-fnon-call-exceptions`
: Generate code that allows trapping instructions to throw exceptions. Note that this requires platform-specific runtime support that does not exist everywhere. Moreover, it only allows *trapping* instructions to throw exceptions, i.e. memory references or floating-point instructions. It does not allow exceptions to be thrown from arbitrary signal handlers such as `SIGALRM`.

`-fdelete-dead-exceptions`
: Consider that instructions that may throw exceptions but don't otherwise contribute to the execution of the program can be optimized away. This option is enabled by default for the Ada front end, as permitted by the Ada language specification. Optimization passes that cause dead exceptions to be removed are enabled independently at different optimization levels.

`-funwind-tables`
: Similar to '`-fexceptions`', except that it just generates any needed static data, but does not affect the generated code in any other way. You normally do

not need to enable this option; instead, a language processor that needs this handling enables it on your behalf.

`-fasynchronous-unwind-tables`
: Generate unwind table in DWARF format, if supported by target machine. The table is exact at each instruction boundary, so it can be used for stack unwinding from asynchronous events (such as debugger or garbage collector).

`-fno-gnu-unique`
: On systems with recent GNU assembler and C library, the C++ compiler uses the `STB_GNU_UNIQUE` binding to make sure that definitions of template static data members and static local variables in inline functions are unique even in the presence of `RTLD_LOCAL`; this is necessary to avoid problems with a library used by two different `RTLD_LOCAL` plugins depending on a definition in one of them and therefore disagreeing with the other one about the binding of the symbol. But this causes `dlclose` to be ignored for affected DSOs; if your program relies on reinitialization of a DSO via `dlclose` and `dlopen`, you can use '`-fno-gnu-unique`'.

`-fpcc-struct-return`
: Return "short" `struct` and `union` values in memory like longer ones, rather than in registers. This convention is less efficient, but it has the advantage of allowing intercallability between GCC-compiled files and files compiled with other compilers, particularly the Portable C Compiler (pcc).

The precise convention for returning structures in memory depends on the target configuration macros.

Short structures and unions are those whose size and alignment match that of some integer type.

Warning: code compiled with the '`-fpcc-struct-return`' switch is not binary compatible with code compiled with the '`-freg-struct-return`' switch. Use it to conform to a non-default application binary interface.

`-freg-struct-return`
: Return `struct` and `union` values in registers when possible. This is more efficient for small structures than '`-fpcc-struct-return`'.

If you specify neither '`-fpcc-struct-return`' nor '`-freg-struct-return`', GCC defaults to whichever convention is standard for the target. If there is no standard convention, GCC defaults to '`-fpcc-struct-return`', except on targets where GCC is the principal compiler. In those cases, we can choose the standard, and we chose the more efficient register return alternative.

Warning: code compiled with the '`-freg-struct-return`' switch is not binary compatible with code compiled with the '`-fpcc-struct-return`' switch. Use it to conform to a non-default application binary interface.

`-fshort-enums`
: Allocate to an `enum` type only as many bytes as it needs for the declared range of possible values. Specifically, the `enum` type is equivalent to the smallest integer type that has enough room.

Warning: the '-fshort-enums' switch causes GCC to generate code that is not binary compatible with code generated without that switch. Use it to conform to a non-default application binary interface.

-fshort-wchar
: Override the underlying type for `wchar_t` to be `short unsigned int` instead of the default for the target. This option is useful for building programs to run under WINE.

  Warning: the '-fshort-wchar' switch causes GCC to generate code that is not binary compatible with code generated without that switch. Use it to conform to a non-default application binary interface.

-fno-common
: In C code, controls the placement of uninitialized global variables. Unix C compilers have traditionally permitted multiple definitions of such variables in different compilation units by placing the variables in a common block. This is the behavior specified by '-fcommon', and is the default for GCC on most targets. On the other hand, this behavior is not required by ISO C, and on some targets may carry a speed or code size penalty on variable references. The '-fno-common' option specifies that the compiler should place uninitialized global variables in the data section of the object file, rather than generating them as common blocks. This has the effect that if the same variable is declared (without `extern`) in two different compilations, you get a multiple-definition error when you link them. In this case, you must compile with '-fcommon' instead. Compiling with '-fno-common' is useful on targets for which it provides better performance, or if you wish to verify that the program will work on other systems that always treat uninitialized variable declarations this way.

-fno-ident
: Ignore the `#ident` directive.

-finhibit-size-directive
: Don't output a `.size` assembler directive, or anything else that would cause trouble if the function is split in the middle, and the two halves are placed at locations far apart in memory. This option is used when compiling 'crtstuff.c'; you should not need to use it for anything else.

-fverbose-asm
: Put extra commentary information in the generated assembly code to make it more readable. This option is generally only of use to those who actually need to read the generated assembly code (perhaps while debugging the compiler itself).

  '-fno-verbose-asm', the default, causes the extra information to be omitted and is useful when comparing two assembler files.

-frecord-gcc-switches
: This switch causes the command line used to invoke the compiler to be recorded into the object file that is being created. This switch is only implemented on some targets and the exact format of the recording is target and binary file format dependent, but it usually takes the form of a section containing ASCII

text. This switch is related to the '-fverbose-asm' switch, but that switch only records information in the assembler output file as comments, so it never reaches the object file. See also '-grecord-gcc-switches' for another way of storing compiler options into the object file.

-fpic
: Generate position-independent code (PIC) suitable for use in a shared library, if supported for the target machine. Such code accesses all constant addresses through a global offset table (GOT). The dynamic loader resolves the GOT entries when the program starts (the dynamic loader is not part of GCC; it is part of the operating system). If the GOT size for the linked executable exceeds a machine-specific maximum size, you get an error message from the linker indicating that '-fpic' does not work; in that case, recompile with '-fPIC' instead. (These maximums are 8k on the SPARC, 28k on AArch64 and 32k on the m68k and RS/6000. The x86 has no such limit.)

  Position-independent code requires special support, and therefore works only on certain machines. For the x86, GCC supports PIC for System V but not for the Sun 386i. Code generated for the IBM RS/6000 is always position-independent.

  When this flag is set, the macros `__pic__` and `__PIC__` are defined to 1.

-fPIC
: If supported for the target machine, emit position-independent code, suitable for dynamic linking and avoiding any limit on the size of the global offset table. This option makes a difference on AArch64, m68k, PowerPC and SPARC.

  Position-independent code requires special support, and therefore works only on certain machines.

  When this flag is set, the macros `__pic__` and `__PIC__` are defined to 2.

-fpie
-fPIE
: These options are similar to '-fpic' and '-fPIC', but generated position independent code can be only linked into executables. Usually these options are used when '-pie' GCC option is used during linking.

  '-fpie' and '-fPIE' both define the macros `__pie__` and `__PIE__`. The macros have the value 1 for '-fpie' and 2 for '-fPIE'.

-fno-plt
: Do not use the PLT for external function calls in position-independent code. Instead, load the callee address at call sites from the GOT and branch to it. This leads to more efficient code by eliminating PLT stubs and exposing GOT loads to optimizations. On architectures such as 32-bit x86 where PLT stubs expect the GOT pointer in a specific register, this gives more register allocation freedom to the compiler. Lazy binding requires use of the PLT; with '-fno-plt' all external symbols are resolved at load time.

  Alternatively, the function attribute `noplt` can be used to avoid calls through the PLT for specific external functions.

  In position-dependent code, a few targets also convert calls to functions that are marked to not use the PLT to use the GOT instead.

-fno-jump-tables
: Do not use jump tables for switch statements even where it would be more efficient than other code generation strategies. This option is of use in conjunction

with '-fpic' or '-fPIC' for building code that forms part of a dynamic linker and cannot reference the address of a jump table. On some targets, jump tables do not require a GOT and this option is not needed.

`-ffixed-reg`
: Treat the register named *reg* as a fixed register; generated code should never refer to it (except perhaps as a stack pointer, frame pointer or in some other fixed role).

reg must be the name of a register. The register names accepted are machine-specific and are defined in the `REGISTER_NAMES` macro in the machine description macro file.

This flag does not have a negative form, because it specifies a three-way choice.

`-fcall-used-reg`
: Treat the register named *reg* as an allocable register that is clobbered by function calls. It may be allocated for temporaries or variables that do not live across a call. Functions compiled this way do not save and restore the register *reg*.

It is an error to use this flag with the frame pointer or stack pointer. Use of this flag for other registers that have fixed pervasive roles in the machine's execution model produces disastrous results.

This flag does not have a negative form, because it specifies a three-way choice.

`-fcall-saved-reg`
: Treat the register named *reg* as an allocable register saved by functions. It may be allocated even for temporaries or variables that live across a call. Functions compiled this way save and restore the register *reg* if they use it.

It is an error to use this flag with the frame pointer or stack pointer. Use of this flag for other registers that have fixed pervasive roles in the machine's execution model produces disastrous results.

A different sort of disaster results from the use of this flag for a register in which function values may be returned.

This flag does not have a negative form, because it specifies a three-way choice.

`-fpack-struct[=n]`
: Without a value specified, pack all structure members together without holes. When a value is specified (which must be a small power of two), pack structure members according to this value, representing the maximum alignment (that is, objects with default alignment requirements larger than this are output potentially unaligned at the next fitting location.

Warning: the '-fpack-struct' switch causes GCC to generate code that is not binary compatible with code generated without that switch. Additionally, it makes the code suboptimal. Use it to conform to a non-default application binary interface.

`-fleading-underscore`
: This option and its counterpart, '-fno-leading-underscore', forcibly change the way C symbols are represented in the object file. One use is to help link with legacy assembly code.

Warning: the '`-fleading-underscore`' switch causes GCC to generate code that is not binary compatible with code generated without that switch. Use it to conform to a non-default application binary interface. Not all targets provide complete support for this switch.

`-ftls-model=`*`model`*

Alter the thread-local storage model to be used (see Section 6.63 [Thread-Local], page 677). The *model* argument should be one of '`global-dynamic`', '`local-dynamic`', '`initial-exec`' or '`local-exec`'. Note that the choice is subject to optimization: the compiler may use a more efficient model for symbols not visible outside of the translation unit, or if '`-fpic`' is not given on the command line.

The default without '`-fpic`' is '`initial-exec`'; with '`-fpic`' the default is '`global-dynamic`'.

`-fvisibility=[default|internal|hidden|protected]`

Set the default ELF image symbol visibility to the specified option—all symbols are marked with this unless overridden within the code. Using this feature can very substantially improve linking and load times of shared object libraries, produce more optimized code, provide near-perfect API export and prevent symbol clashes. It is **strongly** recommended that you use this in any shared objects you distribute.

Despite the nomenclature, '`default`' always means public; i.e., available to be linked against from outside the shared object. '`protected`' and '`internal`' are pretty useless in real-world usage so the only other commonly used option is '`hidden`'. The default if '`-fvisibility`' isn't specified is '`default`', i.e., make every symbol public.

A good explanation of the benefits offered by ensuring ELF symbols have the correct visibility is given by "How To Write Shared Libraries" by Ulrich Drepper (which can be found at `http://www.akkadia.org/drepper/`)—however a superior solution made possible by this option to marking things hidden when the default is public is to make the default hidden and mark things public. This is the norm with DLLs on Windows and with '`-fvisibility=hidden`' and `__attribute__ ((visibility("default")))` instead of `__declspec(dllexport)` you get almost identical semantics with identical syntax. This is a great boon to those working with cross-platform projects.

For those adding visibility support to existing code, you may find `#pragma GCC visibility` of use. This works by you enclosing the declarations you wish to set visibility for with (for example) `#pragma GCC visibility push(hidden)` and `#pragma GCC visibility pop`. Bear in mind that symbol visibility should be viewed **as part of the API interface contract** and thus all new code should always specify visibility when it is not the default; i.e., declarations only for use within the local DSO should **always** be marked explicitly as hidden as so to avoid PLT indirection overheads—making this abundantly clear also aids readability and self-documentation of the code. Note that due to ISO C++

specification requirements, `operator new` and `operator delete` must always be of default visibility.

Be aware that headers from outside your project, in particular system headers and headers from any other library you use, may not be expecting to be compiled with visibility other than the default. You may need to explicitly say `#pragma GCC visibility push(default)` before including any such headers.

`extern` declarations are not affected by '`-fvisibility`', so a lot of code can be recompiled with '`-fvisibility=hidden`' with no modifications. However, this means that calls to `extern` functions with no explicit visibility use the PLT, so it is more effective to use `__attribute ((visibility))` and/or `#pragma GCC visibility` to tell the compiler which `extern` declarations should be treated as hidden.

Note that '`-fvisibility`' does affect C++ vague linkage entities. This means that, for instance, an exception class that is be thrown between DSOs must be explicitly marked with default visibility so that the '`type_info`' nodes are unified between the DSOs.

An overview of these techniques, their benefits and how to use them is at `http://gcc.gnu.org/wiki/Visibility`.

`-fstrict-volatile-bitfields`

This option should be used if accesses to volatile bit-fields (or other structure fields, although the compiler usually honors those types anyway) should use a single access of the width of the field's type, aligned to a natural alignment if possible. For example, targets with memory-mapped peripheral registers might require all such accesses to be 16 bits wide; with this flag you can declare all peripheral bit-fields as `unsigned short` (assuming short is 16 bits on these targets) to force GCC to use 16-bit accesses instead of, perhaps, a more efficient 32-bit access.

If this option is disabled, the compiler uses the most efficient instruction. In the previous example, that might be a 32-bit load instruction, even though that accesses bytes that do not contain any portion of the bit-field, or memory-mapped registers unrelated to the one being updated.

In some cases, such as when the `packed` attribute is applied to a structure field, it may not be possible to access the field with a single read or write that is correctly aligned for the target machine. In this case GCC falls back to generating multiple accesses rather than code that will fault or truncate the result at run time.

Note: Due to restrictions of the C/C++11 memory model, write accesses are not allowed to touch non bit-field members. It is therefore recommended to define all bits of the field's type as bit-field members.

The default value of this option is determined by the application binary interface for the target processor.

`-fsync-libcalls`

This option controls whether any out-of-line instance of the `__sync` family of functions may be used to implement the C++11 `__atomic` family of functions.

The default value of this option is enabled, thus the only useful form of the option is '`-fno-sync-libcalls`'. This option is used in the implementation of the '`libatomic`' runtime library.

3.17 GCC Developer Options

This section describes command-line options that are primarily of interest to GCC developers, including options to support compiler testing and investigation of compiler bugs and compile-time performance problems. This includes options that produce debug dumps at various points in the compilation; that print statistics such as memory use and execution time; and that print information about GCC's configuration, such as where it searches for libraries. You should rarely need to use any of these options for ordinary compilation and linking tasks.

`-d`*`letters`*
`-fdump-rtl-`*`pass`*
`-fdump-rtl-`*`pass`*`=`*`filename`*

Says to make debugging dumps during compilation at times specified by *letters*. This is used for debugging the RTL-based passes of the compiler. The file names for most of the dumps are made by appending a pass number and a word to the *dumpname*, and the files are created in the directory of the output file. In case of '`=`*`filename`*' option, the dump is output on the given file instead of the pass numbered dump files. Note that the pass number is assigned as passes are registered into the pass manager. Most passes are registered in the order that they will execute and for these passes the number corresponds to the pass execution order. However, passes registered by plugins, passes specific to compilation targets, or passes that are otherwise registered after all the other passes are numbered higher than a pass named "final", even if they are executed earlier. *dumpname* is generated from the name of the output file if explicitly specified and not an executable, otherwise it is the basename of the source file. These switches may have different effects when '`-E`' is used for preprocessing.

Debug dumps can be enabled with a '`-fdump-rtl`' switch or some '`-d`' option *letters*. Here are the possible letters for use in *pass* and *letters*, and their meanings:

`-fdump-rtl-alignments`
Dump after branch alignments have been computed.

`-fdump-rtl-asmcons`
Dump after fixing rtl statements that have unsatisfied in/out constraints.

`-fdump-rtl-auto_inc_dec`
Dump after auto-inc-dec discovery. This pass is only run on architectures that have auto inc or auto dec instructions.

`-fdump-rtl-barriers`
Dump after cleaning up the barrier instructions.

`-fdump-rtl-bbpart`
Dump after partitioning hot and cold basic blocks.

`-fdump-rtl-bbro`
: Dump after block reordering.

`-fdump-rtl-btl1`
`-fdump-rtl-btl2`
: '-fdump-rtl-btl1' and '-fdump-rtl-btl2' enable dumping after the two branch target load optimization passes.

`-fdump-rtl-bypass`
: Dump after jump bypassing and control flow optimizations.

`-fdump-rtl-combine`
: Dump after the RTL instruction combination pass.

`-fdump-rtl-compgotos`
: Dump after duplicating the computed gotos.

`-fdump-rtl-ce1`
`-fdump-rtl-ce2`
`-fdump-rtl-ce3`
: '-fdump-rtl-ce1', '-fdump-rtl-ce2', and '-fdump-rtl-ce3' enable dumping after the three if conversion passes.

`-fdump-rtl-cprop_hardreg`
: Dump after hard register copy propagation.

`-fdump-rtl-csa`
: Dump after combining stack adjustments.

`-fdump-rtl-cse1`
`-fdump-rtl-cse2`
: '-fdump-rtl-cse1' and '-fdump-rtl-cse2' enable dumping after the two common subexpression elimination passes.

`-fdump-rtl-dce`
: Dump after the standalone dead code elimination passes.

`-fdump-rtl-dbr`
: Dump after delayed branch scheduling.

`-fdump-rtl-dce1`
`-fdump-rtl-dce2`
: '-fdump-rtl-dce1' and '-fdump-rtl-dce2' enable dumping after the two dead store elimination passes.

`-fdump-rtl-eh`
: Dump after finalization of EH handling code.

`-fdump-rtl-eh_ranges`
: Dump after conversion of EH handling range regions.

`-fdump-rtl-expand`
: Dump after RTL generation.

`-fdump-rtl-fwprop1`
`-fdump-rtl-fwprop2`
: '-fdump-rtl-fwprop1' and '-fdump-rtl-fwprop2' enable dumping after the two forward propagation passes.

`-fdump-rtl-gcse1`
`-fdump-rtl-gcse2`
: '-fdump-rtl-gcse1' and '-fdump-rtl-gcse2' enable dumping after global common subexpression elimination.

`-fdump-rtl-init-regs`
: Dump after the initialization of the registers.

`-fdump-rtl-initvals`
: Dump after the computation of the initial value sets.

`-fdump-rtl-into_cfglayout`
: Dump after converting to cfglayout mode.

`-fdump-rtl-ira`
: Dump after iterated register allocation.

`-fdump-rtl-jump`
: Dump after the second jump optimization.

`-fdump-rtl-loop2`
: '-fdump-rtl-loop2' enables dumping after the rtl loop optimization passes.

`-fdump-rtl-mach`
: Dump after performing the machine dependent reorganization pass, if that pass exists.

`-fdump-rtl-mode_sw`
: Dump after removing redundant mode switches.

`-fdump-rtl-rnreg`
: Dump after register renumbering.

`-fdump-rtl-outof_cfglayout`
: Dump after converting from cfglayout mode.

`-fdump-rtl-peephole2`
: Dump after the peephole pass.

`-fdump-rtl-postreload`
: Dump after post-reload optimizations.

`-fdump-rtl-pro_and_epilogue`
: Dump after generating the function prologues and epilogues.

`-fdump-rtl-sched1`
`-fdump-rtl-sched2`
: '-fdump-rtl-sched1' and '-fdump-rtl-sched2' enable dumping after the basic block scheduling passes.

`-fdump-rtl-ree`
: Dump after sign/zero extension elimination.

`-fdump-rtl-seqabstr`
: Dump after common sequence discovery.

`-fdump-rtl-shorten`
: Dump after shortening branches.

`-fdump-rtl-sibling`
: Dump after sibling call optimizations.

`-fdump-rtl-split1`
`-fdump-rtl-split2`
`-fdump-rtl-split3`
`-fdump-rtl-split4`
`-fdump-rtl-split5`
: These options enable dumping after five rounds of instruction splitting.

`-fdump-rtl-sms`
: Dump after modulo scheduling. This pass is only run on some architectures.

`-fdump-rtl-stack`
: Dump after conversion from GCC's "flat register file" registers to the x87's stack-like registers. This pass is only run on x86 variants.

`-fdump-rtl-subreg1`
`-fdump-rtl-subreg2`
: '`-fdump-rtl-subreg1`' and '`-fdump-rtl-subreg2`' enable dumping after the two subreg expansion passes.

`-fdump-rtl-unshare`
: Dump after all rtl has been unshared.

`-fdump-rtl-vartrack`
: Dump after variable tracking.

`-fdump-rtl-vregs`
: Dump after converting virtual registers to hard registers.

`-fdump-rtl-web`
: Dump after live range splitting.

`-fdump-rtl-regclass`
`-fdump-rtl-subregs_of_mode_init`
`-fdump-rtl-subregs_of_mode_finish`
`-fdump-rtl-dfinit`
`-fdump-rtl-dfinish`
: These dumps are defined but always produce empty files.

`-da`
`-fdump-rtl-all`
: Produce all the dumps listed above.

`-dA` Annotate the assembler output with miscellaneous debugging information.

`-dD` Dump all macro definitions, at the end of preprocessing, in addition to normal output.

`-dH` Produce a core dump whenever an error occurs.

`-dp` Annotate the assembler output with a comment indicating which pattern and alternative is used. The length of each instruction is also printed.

`-dP` Dump the RTL in the assembler output as a comment before each instruction. Also turns on '`-dp`' annotation.

`-dx` Just generate RTL for a function instead of compiling it. Usually used with '`-fdump-rtl-expand`'.

`-fdump-noaddr`
When doing debugging dumps, suppress address output. This makes it more feasible to use diff on debugging dumps for compiler invocations with different compiler binaries and/or different text / bss / data / heap / stack / dso start locations.

`-freport-bug`
Collect and dump debug information into a temporary file if an internal compiler error (ICE) occurs.

`-fdump-unnumbered`
When doing debugging dumps, suppress instruction numbers and address output. This makes it more feasible to use diff on debugging dumps for compiler invocations with different options, in particular with and without '`-g`'.

`-fdump-unnumbered-links`
When doing debugging dumps (see '`-d`' option above), suppress instruction numbers for the links to the previous and next instructions in a sequence.

`-fdump-translation-unit` (C++ only)
`-fdump-translation-unit-`*`options`* (C++ only)
Dump a representation of the tree structure for the entire translation unit to a file. The file name is made by appending '`.tu`' to the source file name, and the file is created in the same directory as the output file. If the '`-`*`options`*' form is used, *options* controls the details of the dump as described for the '`-fdump-tree`' options.

`-fdump-class-hierarchy` (C++ only)
`-fdump-class-hierarchy-`*`options`* (C++ only)
Dump a representation of each class's hierarchy and virtual function table layout to a file. The file name is made by appending '`.class`' to the source file name, and the file is created in the same directory as the output file. If the '`-`*`options`*' form is used, *options* controls the details of the dump as described for the '`-fdump-tree`' options.

`-fdump-ipa-switch`
Control the dumping at various stages of inter-procedural analysis language tree to a file. The file name is generated by appending a switch specific suffix to the source file name, and the file is created in the same directory as the output file. The following dumps are possible:

'all' Enables all inter-procedural analysis dumps.

'cgraph' Dumps information about call-graph optimization, unused function removal, and inlining decisions.

'inline' Dump after function inlining.

`-fdump-passes`
Dump the list of optimization passes that are turned on and off by the current command-line options.

`-fdump-statistics-option`
Enable and control dumping of pass statistics in a separate file. The file name is generated by appending a suffix ending in '.statistics' to the source file name, and the file is created in the same directory as the output file. If the '-option' form is used, '-stats' causes counters to be summed over the whole compilation unit while '-details' dumps every event as the passes generate them. The default with no option is to sum counters for each function compiled.

`-fdump-tree-switch`
`-fdump-tree-switch-options`
`-fdump-tree-switch-options=filename`
Control the dumping at various stages of processing the intermediate language tree to a file. The file name is generated by appending a switch-specific suffix to the source file name, and the file is created in the same directory as the output file. In case of '=filename' option, the dump is output on the given file instead of the auto named dump files. If the '-options' form is used, *options* is a list of '-' separated options which control the details of the dump. Not all options are applicable to all dumps; those that are not meaningful are ignored. The following options are available

'address' Print the address of each node. Usually this is not meaningful as it changes according to the environment and source file. Its primary use is for tying up a dump file with a debug environment.

'asmname' If DECL_ASSEMBLER_NAME has been set for a given decl, use that in the dump instead of DECL_NAME. Its primary use is ease of use working backward from mangled names in the assembly file.

'slim' When dumping front-end intermediate representations, inhibit dumping of members of a scope or body of a function merely because that scope has been reached. Only dump such items when they are directly reachable by some other path.

When dumping pretty-printed trees, this option inhibits dumping the bodies of control structures.

When dumping RTL, print the RTL in slim (condensed) form instead of the default LISP-like representation.

'raw' Print a raw representation of the tree. By default, trees are pretty-printed into a C-like representation.

'details' Enable more detailed dumps (not honored by every dump option). Also include information from the optimization passes.

'stats' Enable dumping various statistics about the pass (not honored by every dump option).

'blocks' Enable showing basic block boundaries (disabled in raw dumps).

'graph' For each of the other indicated dump files ('-fdump-rtl-*pass*'), dump a representation of the control flow graph suitable for viewing with GraphViz to '*file.passid.pass*.dot'. Each function in the file is pretty-printed as a subgraph, so that GraphViz can render them all in a single plot.

This option currently only works for RTL dumps, and the RTL is always dumped in slim form.

'vops' Enable showing virtual operands for every statement.

'lineno' Enable showing line numbers for statements.

'uid' Enable showing the unique ID (DECL_UID) for each variable.

'verbose' Enable showing the tree dump for each statement.

'eh' Enable showing the EH region number holding each statement.

'scev' Enable showing scalar evolution analysis details.

'optimized'
Enable showing optimization information (only available in certain passes).

'missed' Enable showing missed optimization information (only available in certain passes).

'note' Enable other detailed optimization information (only available in certain passes).

'=*filename*'
Instead of an auto named dump file, output into the given file name. The file names 'stdout' and 'stderr' are treated specially and are considered already open standard streams. For example,

```
gcc -O2 -ftree-vectorize -fdump-tree-vect-blocks=foo.dump
     -fdump-tree-pre=stderr file.c
```

outputs vectorizer dump into 'foo.dump', while the PRE dump is output on to 'stderr'. If two conflicting dump filenames are given for the same pass, then the latter option overrides the earlier one.

'split-paths'
: Dump each function after splitting paths to loop backedges. The file name is made by appending '.split-paths' to the source file name.

'all'
: Turn on all options, except 'raw', 'slim', 'verbose' and 'lineno'.

'optall'
: Turn on all optimization options, i.e., 'optimized', 'missed', and 'note'.

The following tree dumps are possible:

'original'
: Dump before any tree based optimization, to '*file*.original'.

'optimized'
: Dump after all tree based optimization, to '*file*.optimized'.

'gimple'
: Dump each function before and after the gimplification pass to a file. The file name is made by appending '.gimple' to the source file name.

'cfg'
: Dump the control flow graph of each function to a file. The file name is made by appending '.cfg' to the source file name.

'ch'
: Dump each function after copying loop headers. The file name is made by appending '.ch' to the source file name.

'ssa'
: Dump SSA related information to a file. The file name is made by appending '.ssa' to the source file name.

'alias'
: Dump aliasing information for each function. The file name is made by appending '.alias' to the source file name.

'ccp'
: Dump each function after CCP. The file name is made by appending '.ccp' to the source file name.

'storeccp'
: Dump each function after STORE-CCP. The file name is made by appending '.storeccp' to the source file name.

'pre'
: Dump trees after partial redundancy elimination. The file name is made by appending '.pre' to the source file name.

'fre'
: Dump trees after full redundancy elimination. The file name is made by appending '.fre' to the source file name.

'copyprop'
: Dump trees after copy propagation. The file name is made by appending '.copyprop' to the source file name.

'store_copyprop'
: Dump trees after store copy-propagation. The file name is made by appending '.store_copyprop' to the source file name.

'dce'
: Dump each function after dead code elimination. The file name is made by appending '.dce' to the source file name.

'sra' Dump each function after performing scalar replacement of aggregates. The file name is made by appending '.sra' to the source file name.

'sink' Dump each function after performing code sinking. The file name is made by appending '.sink' to the source file name.

'dom' Dump each function after applying dominator tree optimizations. The file name is made by appending '.dom' to the source file name.

'dse' Dump each function after applying dead store elimination. The file name is made by appending '.dse' to the source file name.

'phiopt' Dump each function after optimizing PHI nodes into straightline code. The file name is made by appending '.phiopt' to the source file name.

'backprop'
Dump each function after back-propagating use information up the definition chain. The file name is made by appending '.backprop' to the source file name.

'forwprop'
Dump each function after forward propagating single use variables. The file name is made by appending '.forwprop' to the source file name.

'nrv' Dump each function after applying the named return value optimization on generic trees. The file name is made by appending '.nrv' to the source file name.

'vect' Dump each function after applying vectorization of loops. The file name is made by appending '.vect' to the source file name.

'slp' Dump each function after applying vectorization of basic blocks. The file name is made by appending '.slp' to the source file name.

'vrp' Dump each function after Value Range Propagation (VRP). The file name is made by appending '.vrp' to the source file name.

'oaccdevlow'
Dump each function after applying device-specific OpenACC transformations. The file name is made by appending '.oaccdevlow' to the source file name.

'all' Enable all the available tree dumps with the flags provided in this option.

-fopt-info
-fopt-info-*options*
-fopt-info-*options*=*filename*
Controls optimization dumps from various optimization passes. If the '-*options*' form is used, *options* is a list of '-' separated option keywords to select the dump details and optimizations.

The *options* can be divided into two groups: options describing the verbosity of the dump, and options describing which optimizations should be included. The options from both the groups can be freely mixed as they are non-overlapping. However, in case of any conflicts, the later options override the earlier options on the command line.

The following options control the dump verbosity:

'`optimized`'
: Print information when an optimization is successfully applied. It is up to a pass to decide which information is relevant. For example, the vectorizer passes print the source location of loops which are successfully vectorized.

'`missed`'
: Print information about missed optimizations. Individual passes control which information to include in the output.

'`note`'
: Print verbose information about optimizations, such as certain transformations, more detailed messages about decisions etc.

'`all`'
: Print detailed optimization information. This includes '`optimized`', '`missed`', and '`note`'.

One or more of the following option keywords can be used to describe a group of optimizations:

'`ipa`'
: Enable dumps from all interprocedural optimizations.

'`loop`'
: Enable dumps from all loop optimizations.

'`inline`'
: Enable dumps from all inlining optimizations.

'`vec`'
: Enable dumps from all vectorization optimizations.

'`optall`'
: Enable dumps from all optimizations. This is a superset of the optimization groups listed above.

If *options* is omitted, it defaults to '`optimized-optall`', which means to dump all info about successful optimizations from all the passes.

If the *filename* is provided, then the dumps from all the applicable optimizations are concatenated into the *filename*. Otherwise the dump is output onto '`stderr`'. Though multiple '`-fopt-info`' options are accepted, only one of them can include a *filename*. If other filenames are provided then all but the first such option are ignored.

Note that the output *filename* is overwritten in case of multiple translation units. If a combined output from multiple translation units is desired, '`stderr`' should be used instead.

In the following example, the optimization info is output to '`stderr`':

```
gcc -O3 -fopt-info
```

This example:

```
gcc -O3 -fopt-info-missed=missed.all
```

outputs missed optimization report from all the passes into '`missed.all`', and this one:

```
gcc -O2 -ftree-vectorize -fopt-info-vec-missed
```

prints information about missed optimization opportunities from vectorization passes on '`stderr`'. Note that '`-fopt-info-vec-missed`' is equivalent to '`-fopt-info-missed-vec`'.

As another example,

```
gcc -O3 -fopt-info-inline-optimized-missed=inline.txt
```

outputs information about missed optimizations as well as optimized locations from all the inlining passes into '`inline.txt`'.

Finally, consider:

```
gcc -fopt-info-vec-missed=vec.miss -fopt-info-loop-optimized=loop.opt
```

Here the two output filenames '`vec.miss`' and '`loop.opt`' are in conflict since only one output file is allowed. In this case, only the first option takes effect and the subsequent options are ignored. Thus only '`vec.miss`' is produced which contains dumps from the vectorizer about missed opportunities.

`-fsched-verbose=`*`n`*

On targets that use instruction scheduling, this option controls the amount of debugging output the scheduler prints to the dump files.

For *n* greater than zero, '`-fsched-verbose`' outputs the same information as '`-fdump-rtl-sched1`' and '`-fdump-rtl-sched2`'. For *n* greater than one, it also output basic block probabilities, detailed ready list information and unit/insn info. For *n* greater than two, it includes RTL at abort point, control-flow and regions info. And for *n* over four, '`-fsched-verbose`' also includes dependence info.

`-fenable-`*`kind-pass`*

`-fdisable-`*`kind-pass=range-list`*

This is a set of options that are used to explicitly disable/enable optimization passes. These options are intended for use for debugging GCC. Compiler users should use regular options for enabling/disabling passes instead.

`-fdisable-ipa-`*`pass`*

Disable IPA pass *pass*. *pass* is the pass name. If the same pass is statically invoked in the compiler multiple times, the pass name should be appended with a sequential number starting from 1.

`-fdisable-rtl-`*`pass`*

`-fdisable-rtl-`*`pass=range-list`*

Disable RTL pass *pass*. *pass* is the pass name. If the same pass is statically invoked in the compiler multiple times, the pass name should be appended with a sequential number starting from 1. *range-list* is a comma-separated list of function ranges or assembler names. Each range is a number pair separated by a colon. The range is inclusive in both ends. If the range is trivial, the number pair can be simplified as a single number. If the function's call graph node's *uid* falls within one of the specified ranges, the *pass* is disabled for that function. The *uid* is shown in the function header of a dump file, and the pass names can be dumped by using option '`-fdump-passes`'.

`-fdisable-tree-`*pass*
`-fdisable-tree-`*pass*`=`*range-list*
: Disable tree pass *pass*. See '`-fdisable-rtl`' for the description of option arguments.

`-fenable-ipa-`*pass*
: Enable IPA pass *pass*. *pass* is the pass name. If the same pass is statically invoked in the compiler multiple times, the pass name should be appended with a sequential number starting from 1.

`-fenable-rtl-`*pass*
`-fenable-rtl-`*pass*`=`*range-list*
: Enable RTL pass *pass*. See '`-fdisable-rtl`' for option argument description and examples.

`-fenable-tree-`*pass*
`-fenable-tree-`*pass*`=`*range-list*
: Enable tree pass *pass*. See '`-fdisable-rtl`' for the description of option arguments.

Here are some examples showing uses of these options.

```
# disable ccp1 for all functions
   -fdisable-tree-ccp1
# disable complete unroll for function whose cgraph node uid is 1
   -fenable-tree-cunroll=1
# disable gcse2 for functions at the following ranges [1,1],
# [300,400], and [400,1000]
# disable gcse2 for functions foo and foo2
   -fdisable-rtl-gcse2=foo,foo2
# disable early inlining
   -fdisable-tree-einline
# disable ipa inlining
   -fdisable-ipa-inline
# enable tree full unroll
   -fenable-tree-unroll
```

`-fchecking`
: Enable internal consistency checking. The default depends on the compiler configuration.

`-frandom-seed=`*string*
: This option provides a seed that GCC uses in place of random numbers in generating certain symbol names that have to be different in every compiled file. It is also used to place unique stamps in coverage data files and the object files that produce them. You can use the '`-frandom-seed`' option to produce reproducibly identical object files.

The *string* can either be a number (decimal, octal or hex) or an arbitrary string (in which case it's converted to a number by computing CRC32).

The *string* should be different for every file you compile.

`-save-temps`
`-save-temps=cwd`

Store the usual "temporary" intermediate files permanently; place them in the current directory and name them based on the source file. Thus, compiling '`foo.c`' with '`-c -save-temps`' produces files '`foo.i`' and '`foo.s`', as well as '`foo.o`'. This creates a preprocessed '`foo.i`' output file even though the compiler now normally uses an integrated preprocessor.

When used in combination with the '`-x`' command-line option, '`-save-temps`' is sensible enough to avoid over writing an input source file with the same extension as an intermediate file. The corresponding intermediate file may be obtained by renaming the source file before using '`-save-temps`'.

If you invoke GCC in parallel, compiling several different source files that share a common base name in different subdirectories or the same source file compiled for multiple output destinations, it is likely that the different parallel compilers will interfere with each other, and overwrite the temporary files. For instance:

```
gcc -save-temps -o outdir1/foo.o indir1/foo.c&
gcc -save-temps -o outdir2/foo.o indir2/foo.c&
```

may result in '`foo.i`' and '`foo.o`' being written to simultaneously by both compilers.

`-save-temps=obj`

Store the usual "temporary" intermediate files permanently. If the '`-o`' option is used, the temporary files are based on the object file. If the '`-o`' option is not used, the '`-save-temps=obj`' switch behaves like '`-save-temps`'.

For example:

```
gcc -save-temps=obj -c foo.c
gcc -save-temps=obj -c bar.c -o dir/xbar.o
gcc -save-temps=obj foobar.c -o dir2/yfoobar
```

creates '`foo.i`', '`foo.s`', '`dir/xbar.i`', '`dir/xbar.s`', '`dir2/yfoobar.i`', '`dir2/yfoobar.s`', and '`dir2/yfoobar.o`'.

`-time[=`*`file`*`]`

Report the CPU time taken by each subprocess in the compilation sequence. For C source files, this is the compiler proper and assembler (plus the linker if linking is done).

Without the specification of an output file, the output looks like this:

```
# cc1 0.12 0.01
# as 0.00 0.01
```

The first number on each line is the "user time", that is time spent executing the program itself. The second number is "system time", time spent executing operating system routines on behalf of the program. Both numbers are in seconds.

With the specification of an output file, the output is appended to the named file, and it looks like this:

```
0.12 0.01 cc1 options
0.00 0.01 as options
```

The "user time" and the "system time" are moved before the program name, and the options passed to the program are displayed, so that one can later tell what file was being compiled, and with which options.

`-fdump-final-insns[=file]`
: Dump the final internal representation (RTL) to *file*. If the optional argument is omitted (or if *file* is `.`), the name of the dump file is determined by appending `.gkd` to the compilation output file name.

`-fcompare-debug[=opts]`
: If no error occurs during compilation, run the compiler a second time, adding *opts* and '`-fcompare-debug-second`' to the arguments passed to the second compilation. Dump the final internal representation in both compilations, and print an error if they differ.

  If the equal sign is omitted, the default '`-gtoggle`' is used.

  The environment variable `GCC_COMPARE_DEBUG`, if defined, non-empty and nonzero, implicitly enables '`-fcompare-debug`'. If `GCC_COMPARE_DEBUG` is defined to a string starting with a dash, then it is used for *opts*, otherwise the default '`-gtoggle`' is used.

  '`-fcompare-debug=`', with the equal sign but without *opts*, is equivalent to '`-fno-compare-debug`', which disables the dumping of the final representation and the second compilation, preventing even `GCC_COMPARE_DEBUG` from taking effect.

  To verify full coverage during '`-fcompare-debug`' testing, set `GCC_COMPARE_DEBUG` to say '`-fcompare-debug-not-overridden`', which GCC rejects as an invalid option in any actual compilation (rather than preprocessing, assembly or linking). To get just a warning, setting `GCC_COMPARE_DEBUG` to '`-w%n-fcompare-debug not overridden`' will do.

`-fcompare-debug-second`
: This option is implicitly passed to the compiler for the second compilation requested by '`-fcompare-debug`', along with options to silence warnings, and omitting other options that would cause side-effect compiler outputs to files or to the standard output. Dump files and preserved temporary files are renamed so as to contain the `.gk` additional extension during the second compilation, to avoid overwriting those generated by the first.

  When this option is passed to the compiler driver, it causes the *first* compilation to be skipped, which makes it useful for little other than debugging the compiler proper.

`-gtoggle`
: Turn off generation of debug info, if leaving out this option generates it, or turn it on at level 2 otherwise. The position of this argument in the command line does not matter; it takes effect after all other options are processed, and it does so only once, no matter how many times it is given. This is mainly intended to be used with '`-fcompare-debug`'.

`-fvar-tracking-assignments-toggle`
: Toggle '`-fvar-tracking-assignments`', in the same way that '`-gtoggle`' toggles '`-g`'.

`-Q` Makes the compiler print out each function name as it is compiled, and print some statistics about each pass when it finishes.

`-ftime-report`
: Makes the compiler print some statistics about the time consumed by each pass when it finishes.

`-fira-verbose=`*n*
: Control the verbosity of the dump file for the integrated register allocator. The default value is 5. If the value *n* is greater or equal to 10, the dump output is sent to stderr using the same format as *n* minus 10.

`-flto-report`
: Prints a report with internal details on the workings of the link-time optimizer. The contents of this report vary from version to version. It is meant to be useful to GCC developers when processing object files in LTO mode (via '`-flto`').

  Disabled by default.

`-flto-report-wpa`
: Like '`-flto-report`', but only print for the WPA phase of Link Time Optimization.

`-fmem-report`
: Makes the compiler print some statistics about permanent memory allocation when it finishes.

`-fmem-report-wpa`
: Makes the compiler print some statistics about permanent memory allocation for the WPA phase only.

`-fpre-ipa-mem-report`
`-fpost-ipa-mem-report`
: Makes the compiler print some statistics about permanent memory allocation before or after interprocedural optimization.

`-fprofile-report`
: Makes the compiler print some statistics about consistency of the (estimated) profile and effect of individual passes.

`-fstack-usage`
: Makes the compiler output stack usage information for the program, on a per-function basis. The filename for the dump is made by appending '`.su`' to the *auxname*. *auxname* is generated from the name of the output file, if explicitly specified and it is not an executable, otherwise it is the basename of the source file. An entry is made up of three fields:

  - The name of the function.
  - A number of bytes.
  - One or more qualifiers: `static`, `dynamic`, `bounded`.

  The qualifier `static` means that the function manipulates the stack statically: a fixed number of bytes are allocated for the frame on function entry and released on function exit; no stack adjustments are otherwise made in the function. The second field is this fixed number of bytes.

The qualifier `dynamic` means that the function manipulates the stack dynamically: in addition to the static allocation described above, stack adjustments are made in the body of the function, for example to push/pop arguments around function calls. If the qualifier `bounded` is also present, the amount of these adjustments is bounded at compile time and the second field is an upper bound of the total amount of stack used by the function. If it is not present, the amount of these adjustments is not bounded at compile time and the second field only represents the bounded part.

`-fstats` Emit statistics about front-end processing at the end of the compilation. This option is supported only by the C++ front end, and the information is generally only useful to the G++ development team.

`-fdbg-cnt-list`
Print the name and the counter upper bound for all debug counters.

`-fdbg-cnt=`*`counter-value-list`*
Set the internal debug counter upper bound. *counter-value-list* is a comma-separated list of *name*:*value* pairs which sets the upper bound of each debug counter *name* to *value*. All debug counters have the initial upper bound of `UINT_MAX`; thus `dbg_cnt` returns true always unless the upper bound is set by this option. For example, with '`-fdbg-cnt=dce:10,tail_call:0`', `dbg_cnt(dce)` returns true only for first 10 invocations.

`-print-file-name=`*`library`*
Print the full absolute name of the library file *library* that would be used when linking—and don't do anything else. With this option, GCC does not compile or link anything; it just prints the file name.

`-print-multi-directory`
Print the directory name corresponding to the multilib selected by any other switches present in the command line. This directory is supposed to exist in `GCC_EXEC_PREFIX`.

`-print-multi-lib`
Print the mapping from multilib directory names to compiler switches that enable them. The directory name is separated from the switches by '`;`', and each switch starts with an '`@`' instead of the '`-`', without spaces between multiple switches. This is supposed to ease shell processing.

`-print-multi-os-directory`
Print the path to OS libraries for the selected multilib, relative to some '`lib`' subdirectory. If OS libraries are present in the '`lib`' subdirectory and no multilibs are used, this is usually just '`.`', if OS libraries are present in '`lib`*`suffix`*' sibling directories this prints e.g. '`../lib64`', '`../lib`' or '`../lib32`', or if OS libraries are present in '`lib/`*`subdir`*' subdirectories it prints e.g. '`amd64`', '`sparcv9`' or '`ev6`'.

`-print-multiarch`
: Print the path to OS libraries for the selected multiarch, relative to some '`lib`' subdirectory.

`-print-prog-name=`*`program`*
: Like '`-print-file-name`', but searches for a program such as `cpp`.

`-print-libgcc-file-name`
: Same as '`-print-file-name=libgcc.a`'.

This is useful when you use '`-nostdlib`' or '`-nodefaultlibs`' but you do want to link with '`libgcc.a`'. You can do:

```
gcc -nostdlib files... `gcc -print-libgcc-file-name`
```

`-print-search-dirs`
: Print the name of the configured installation directory and a list of program and library directories `gcc` searches—and don't do anything else.

This is useful when `gcc` prints the error message '`installation problem, cannot exec cpp0: No such file or directory`'. To resolve this you either need to put '`cpp0`' and the other compiler components where `gcc` expects to find them, or you can set the environment variable `GCC_EXEC_PREFIX` to the directory where you installed them. Don't forget the trailing '`/`'. See Section 3.20 [Environment Variables], page 367.

`-print-sysroot`
: Print the target sysroot directory that is used during compilation. This is the target sysroot specified either at configure time or using the '`--sysroot`' option, possibly with an extra suffix that depends on compilation options. If no target sysroot is specified, the option prints nothing.

`-print-sysroot-headers-suffix`
: Print the suffix added to the target sysroot when searching for headers, or give an error if the compiler is not configured with such a suffix—and don't do anything else.

`-dumpmachine`
: Print the compiler's target machine (for example, '`i686-pc-linux-gnu`')—and don't do anything else.

`-dumpversion`
: Print the compiler version (for example, `3.0`)—and don't do anything else.

`-dumpspecs`
: Print the compiler's built-in specs—and don't do anything else. (This is used when GCC itself is being built.) See Section 3.19 [Spec Files], page 360.

3.18 Machine-Dependent Options

Each target machine supported by GCC can have its own options—for example, to allow you to compile for a particular processor variant or ABI, or to control optimizations specific to that machine. By convention, the names of machine-specific options start with '`-m`'.

Some configurations of the compiler also support additional target-specific options, usually for compatibility with other compilers on the same platform.

3.18.1 AArch64 Options

These options are defined for AArch64 implementations:

`-mabi=name`
: Generate code for the specified data model. Permissible values are '`ilp32`' for SysV-like data model where int, long int and pointer are 32-bit, and '`lp64`' for SysV-like data model where int is 32-bit, but long int and pointer are 64-bit.

  The default depends on the specific target configuration. Note that the LP64 and ILP32 ABIs are not link-compatible; you must compile your entire program with the same ABI, and link with a compatible set of libraries.

`-mbig-endian`
: Generate big-endian code. This is the default when GCC is configured for an '`aarch64_be-*-*`' target.

`-mgeneral-regs-only`
: Generate code which uses only the general-purpose registers. This will prevent the compiler from using floating-point and Advanced SIMD registers but will not impose any restrictions on the assembler.

`-mlittle-endian`
: Generate little-endian code. This is the default when GCC is configured for an '`aarch64-*-*`' but not an '`aarch64_be-*-*`' target.

`-mcmodel=tiny`
: Generate code for the tiny code model. The program and its statically defined symbols must be within 1GB of each other. Pointers are 64 bits. Programs can be statically or dynamically linked. This model is not fully implemented and mostly treated as '`small`'.

`-mcmodel=small`
: Generate code for the small code model. The program and its statically defined symbols must be within 4GB of each other. Pointers are 64 bits. Programs can be statically or dynamically linked. This is the default code model.

`-mcmodel=large`
: Generate code for the large code model. This makes no assumptions about addresses and sizes of sections. Pointers are 64 bits. Programs can be statically linked only.

`-mstrict-align`
: Do not assume that unaligned memory references are handled by the system.

`-momit-leaf-frame-pointer`
`-mno-omit-leaf-frame-pointer`
: Omit or keep the frame pointer in leaf functions. The former behavior is the default.

`-mtls-dialect=desc`
: Use TLS descriptors as the thread-local storage mechanism for dynamic accesses of TLS variables. This is the default.

`-mtls-dialect=traditional`
: Use traditional TLS as the thread-local storage mechanism for dynamic accesses of TLS variables.

`-mtls-size=`*size*
: Specify bit size of immediate TLS offsets. Valid values are 12, 24, 32, 48. This option depends on binutils higher than 2.25.

`-mfix-cortex-a53-835769`
`-mno-fix-cortex-a53-835769`
: Enable or disable the workaround for the ARM Cortex-A53 erratum number 835769. This involves inserting a NOP instruction between memory instructions and 64-bit integer multiply-accumulate instructions.

`-mfix-cortex-a53-843419`
`-mno-fix-cortex-a53-843419`
: Enable or disable the workaround for the ARM Cortex-A53 erratum number 843419. This erratum workaround is made at link time and this will only pass the corresponding flag to the linker.

`-mlow-precision-recip-sqrt`
`-mno-low-precision-recip-sqrt`
: When calculating the reciprocal square root approximation, uses one less step than otherwise, thus reducing latency and precision. This is only relevant if '`-ffast-math`' enables the reciprocal square root approximation, which in turn depends on the target processor.

`-march=`*name*
: Specify the name of the target architecture and, optionally, one or more feature modifiers. This option has the form '`-march=`*arch*{`+`[`no`]*feature*}*'.

The permissible values for *arch* are '`armv8-a`', '`armv8.1-a`' or *native*.

The value '`armv8.1-a`' implies '`armv8-a`' and enables compiler support for the ARMv8.1 architecture extension. In particular, it enables the '`+crc`' and '`+lse`' features.

The value '`native`' is available on native AArch64 GNU/Linux and causes the compiler to pick the architecture of the host system. This option has no effect if the compiler is unable to recognize the architecture of the host system,

The permissible values for *feature* are listed in the sub-section on ['`-march`' and '`-mcpu`' Feature Modifiers], page 205. Where conflicting feature modifiers are specified, the right-most feature is used.

GCC uses *name* to determine what kind of instructions it can emit when generating assembly code. If '`-march`' is specified without either of '`-mtune`' or '`-mcpu`' also being specified, the code is tuned to perform well across a range of target processors implementing the target architecture.

`-mtune=`*name*
: Specify the name of the target processor for which GCC should tune the performance of the code. Permissible values for this option are: '`generic`', '`cortex-a35`', '`cortex-a53`', '`cortex-a57`', '`cortex-a72`', '`exynos-m1`', '`qdf24xx`', '`thunderx`', '`xgene1`'.

Additionally, this option can specify that GCC should tune the performance of the code for a big.LITTLE system. Permissible values for this option are: '`cortex-a57.cortex-a53`', '`cortex-a72.cortex-a53`'.

Additionally on native AArch64 GNU/Linux systems the value '`native`' is available. This option causes the compiler to pick the architecture of and tune the performance of the code for the processor of the host system. This option has no effect if the compiler is unable to recognize the architecture of the host system.

Where none of '`-mtune=`', '`-mcpu=`' or '`-march=`' are specified, the code is tuned to perform well across a range of target processors.

This option cannot be suffixed by feature modifiers.

`-mcpu=`*`name`*
: Specify the name of the target processor, optionally suffixed by one or more feature modifiers. This option has the form '`-mcpu=`*cpu*{+[no]*`feature`*}*', where the permissible values for *cpu* are the same as those available for '`-mtune`'. The permissible values for *feature* are documented in the sub-section on ['`-march`' and '`-mcpu`' Feature Modifiers], page 205. Where conflicting feature modifiers are specified, the right-most feature is used.

  Additionally on native AArch64 GNU/Linux systems the value '`native`' is available. This option causes the compiler to tune the performance of the code for the processor of the host system. This option has no effect if the compiler is unable to recognize the architecture of the host system.

  GCC uses *name* to determine what kind of instructions it can emit when generating assembly code (as if by '`-march`') and to determine the target processor for which to tune for performance (as if by '`-mtune`'). Where this option is used in conjunction with '`-march`' or '`-mtune`', those options take precedence over the appropriate part of this option.

`-moverride=`*`string`*
: Override tuning decisions made by the back-end in response to a '`-mtune=`' switch. The syntax, semantics, and accepted values for *string* in this option are not guaranteed to be consistent across releases.

  This option is only intended to be useful when developing GCC.

`-mpc-relative-literal-loads`
: Enable PC relative literal loads. If this option is used, literal pools are assumed to have a range of up to 1MiB and an appropriate instruction sequence is used. This option has no impact when used with '`-mcmodel=tiny`'.

3.18.1.1 '`-march`' and '`-mcpu`' Feature Modifiers

Feature modifiers used with '`-march`' and '`-mcpu`' can be any of the following and their inverses '`no`*`feature`*':

'`crc`'
: Enable CRC extension. This is on by default for '`-march=armv8.1-a`'.

'`crypto`'
: Enable Crypto extension. This also enables Advanced SIMD and floating-point instructions.

'`fp`'
: Enable floating-point instructions. This is on by default for all possible values for options '`-march`' and '`-mcpu`'.

'simd' Enable Advanced SIMD instructions. This also enables floating-point instructions. This is on by default for all possible values for options '-march' and '-mcpu'.

'lse' Enable Large System Extension instructions. This is on by default for '-march=armv8.1-a'.

That is, 'crypto' implies 'simd' implies 'fp'. Conversely, 'nofp' (or equivalently, '-mgeneral-regs-only') implies 'nosimd' implies 'nocrypto'.

3.18.2 Adapteva Epiphany Options

These '-m' options are defined for Adapteva Epiphany:

-mhalf-reg-file
: Don't allocate any register in the range r32...r63. That allows code to run on hardware variants that lack these registers.

-mprefer-short-insn-regs
: Preferentially allocate registers that allow short instruction generation. This can result in increased instruction count, so this may either reduce or increase overall code size.

-mbranch-cost=*num*
: Set the cost of branches to roughly *num* "simple" instructions. This cost is only a heuristic and is not guaranteed to produce consistent results across releases.

-mcmove
: Enable the generation of conditional moves.

-mnops=*num*
: Emit *num* NOPs before every other generated instruction.

-mno-soft-cmpsf
: For single-precision floating-point comparisons, emit an fsub instruction and test the flags. This is faster than a software comparison, but can get incorrect results in the presence of NaNs, or when two different small numbers are compared such that their difference is calculated as zero. The default is '-msoft-cmpsf', which uses slower, but IEEE-compliant, software comparisons.

-mstack-offset=*num*
: Set the offset between the top of the stack and the stack pointer. E.g., a value of 8 means that the eight bytes in the range sp+0...sp+7 can be used by leaf functions without stack allocation. Values other than '8' or '16' are untested and unlikely to work. Note also that this option changes the ABI; compiling a program with a different stack offset than the libraries have been compiled with generally does not work. This option can be useful if you want to evaluate if a different stack offset would give you better code, but to actually use a different stack offset to build working programs, it is recommended to configure the toolchain with the appropriate '--with-stack-offset=*num*' option.

-mno-round-nearest
: Make the scheduler assume that the rounding mode has been set to truncating. The default is '-mround-nearest'.

`-mlong-calls`
: If not otherwise specified by an attribute, assume all calls might be beyond the offset range of the `b` / `bl` instructions, and therefore load the function address into a register before performing a (otherwise direct) call. This is the default.

`-mshort-calls`
: If not otherwise specified by an attribute, assume all direct calls are in the range of the `b` / `bl` instructions, so use these instructions for direct calls. The default is '`-mlong-calls`'.

`-msmall16`
: Assume addresses can be loaded as 16-bit unsigned values. This does not apply to function addresses for which '`-mlong-calls`' semantics are in effect.

`-mfp-mode=`*`mode`*
: Set the prevailing mode of the floating-point unit. This determines the floating-point mode that is provided and expected at function call and return time. Making this mode match the mode you predominantly need at function start can make your programs smaller and faster by avoiding unnecessary mode switches.

  mode can be set to one the following values:

  '`caller`' Any mode at function entry is valid, and retained or restored when the function returns, and when it calls other functions. This mode is useful for compiling libraries or other compilation units you might want to incorporate into different programs with different prevailing FPU modes, and the convenience of being able to use a single object file outweighs the size and speed overhead for any extra mode switching that might be needed, compared with what would be needed with a more specific choice of prevailing FPU mode.

  '`truncate`'
  : This is the mode used for floating-point calculations with truncating (i.e. round towards zero) rounding mode. That includes conversion from floating point to integer.

  '`round-nearest`'
  : This is the mode used for floating-point calculations with round-to-nearest-or-even rounding mode.

  '`int`' This is the mode used to perform integer calculations in the FPU, e.g. integer multiply, or integer multiply-and-accumulate.

  The default is '`-mfp-mode=caller`'

`-mnosplit-lohi`
`-mno-postinc`
`-mno-postmodify`
: Code generation tweaks that disable, respectively, splitting of 32-bit loads, generation of post-increment addresses, and generation of post-modify addresses. The defaults are '`msplit-lohi`', '`-mpost-inc`', and '`-mpost-modify`'.

`-mnovect-double`
: Change the preferred SIMD mode to SImode. The default is '`-mvect-double`', which uses DImode as preferred SIMD mode.

`-max-vect-align=`*num*
: The maximum alignment for SIMD vector mode types. *num* may be 4 or 8. The default is 8. Note that this is an ABI change, even though many library function interfaces are unaffected if they don't use SIMD vector modes in places that affect size and/or alignment of relevant types.

`-msplit-vecmove-early`
: Split vector moves into single word moves before reload. In theory this can give better register allocation, but so far the reverse seems to be generally the case.

`-m1reg-`*reg*
: Specify a register to hold the constant −1, which makes loading small negative constants and certain bitmasks faster. Allowable values for *reg* are '`r43`' and '`r63`', which specify use of that register as a fixed register, and '`none`', which means that no register is used for this purpose. The default is '`-m1reg-none`'.

3.18.3 ARC Options

The following options control the architecture variant for which code is being compiled:

`-mbarrel-shifter`
: Generate instructions supported by barrel shifter. This is the default unless '`-mcpu=ARC601`' or '`-mcpu=ARCEM`' is in effect.

`-mcpu=`*cpu*
: Set architecture type, register usage, and instruction scheduling parameters for *cpu*. There are also shortcut alias options available for backward compatibility and convenience. Supported values for *cpu* are

  '`ARC600`'
  '`arc600`' Compile for ARC600. Aliases: '`-mA6`', '`-mARC600`'.

  '`ARC601`'
  '`arc601`' Compile for ARC601. Alias: '`-mARC601`'.

  '`ARC700`'
  '`arc700`' Compile for ARC700. Aliases: '`-mA7`', '`-mARC700`'. This is the default when configured with '`--with-cpu=arc700`'.

  '`ARCEM`'
  '`arcem`' Compile for ARC EM.

  '`ARCHS`'
  '`archs`' Compile for ARC HS.

`-mdpfp`
`-mdpfp-compact`
: FPX: Generate Double Precision FPX instructions, tuned for the compact implementation.

`-mdpfp-fast`
: FPX: Generate Double Precision FPX instructions, tuned for the fast implementation.

`-mno-dpfp-lrsr`
: Disable LR and SR instructions from using FPX extension aux registers.

`-mea`
: Generate Extended arithmetic instructions. Currently only `divaw`, `adds`, `subs`, and `sat16` are supported. This is always enabled for '`-mcpu=ARC700`'.

`-mno-mpy`
: Do not generate mpy instructions for ARC700.

`-mmul32x16`
: Generate 32x16 bit multiply and mac instructions.

`-mmul64`
: Generate mul64 and mulu64 instructions. Only valid for '`-mcpu=ARC600`'.

`-mnorm`
: Generate norm instruction. This is the default if '`-mcpu=ARC700`' is in effect.

`-mspfp`
`-mspfp-compact`
: FPX: Generate Single Precision FPX instructions, tuned for the compact implementation.

`-mspfp-fast`
: FPX: Generate Single Precision FPX instructions, tuned for the fast implementation.

`-msimd`
: Enable generation of ARC SIMD instructions via target-specific builtins. Only valid for '`-mcpu=ARC700`'.

`-msoft-float`
: This option ignored; it is provided for compatibility purposes only. Software floating point code is emitted by default, and this default can overridden by FPX options; '`mspfp`', '`mspfp-compact`', or '`mspfp-fast`' for single precision, and '`mdpfp`', '`mdpfp-compact`', or '`mdpfp-fast`' for double precision.

`-mswap`
: Generate swap instructions.

`-matomic`
: This enables Locked Load/Store Conditional extension to implement atomic memopry built-in functions. Not available for ARC 6xx or ARC EM cores.

`-mdiv-rem`
: Enable DIV/REM instructions for ARCv2 cores.

`-mcode-density`
: Enable code density instructions for ARC EM, default on for ARC HS.

`-mll64`
: Enable double load/store operations for ARC HS cores.

`-mmpy-option=`*multo*
: Compile ARCv2 code with a multiplier design option. '`wlh1`' is the default value. The recognized values for *multo* are:

  '`0`'
  : No multiplier available.

  '`1`'
  : The multiply option is set to w: 16x16 multiplier, fully pipelined. The following instructions are enabled: MPYW, and MPYUW.

'2' The multiply option is set to wlh1: 32x32 multiplier, fully pipelined (1 stage). The following instructions are additionally enabled: MPY, MPYU, MPYM, MPYMU, and MPY_S.

'3' The multiply option is set to wlh2: 32x32 multiplier, fully pipelined (2 stages). The following instructions are additionally enabled: MPY, MPYU, MPYM, MPYMU, and MPY_S.

'4' The multiply option is set to wlh3: Two 16x16 multiplier, blocking, sequential. The following instructions are additionally enabled: MPY, MPYU, MPYM, MPYMU, and MPY_S.

'5' The multiply option is set to wlh4: One 16x16 multiplier, blocking, sequential. The following instructions are additionally enabled: MPY, MPYU, MPYM, MPYMU, and MPY_S.

'6' The multiply option is set to wlh5: One 32x4 multiplier, blocking, sequential. The following instructions are additionally enabled: MPY, MPYU, MPYM, MPYMU, and MPY_S.

This option is only available for ARCv2 cores.

`-mfpu=`*fpu*

Enables specific floating-point hardware extension for ARCv2 core. Supported values for *fpu* are:

'`fpus`' Enables support for single precision floating point hardware extensions.

'`fpud`' Enables support for double precision floating point hardware extensions. The single precision floating point extension is also enabled. Not available for ARC EM.

'`fpuda`' Enables support for double precision floating point hardware extensions using double precision assist instructions. The single precision floating point extension is also enabled. This option is only available for ARC EM.

'`fpuda_div`'
Enables support for double precision floating point hardware extensions using double precision assist instructions, and simple precision square-root and divide hardware extensions. The single precision floating point extension is also enabled. This option is only available for ARC EM.

'`fpuda_fma`'
Enables support for double precision floating point hardware extensions using double precision assist instructions, and simple precision fused multiple and add hardware extension. The single precision floating point extension is also enabled. This option is only available for ARC EM.

'`fpuda_all`'
Enables support for double precision floating point hardware extensions using double precision assist instructions, and all simple

precision hardware extensions. The single precision floating point extension is also enabled. This option is only available for ARC EM.

'fpus_div'
: Enables support for single precision floating point, and single precision square-root and divide hardware extensions.

'fpud_div'
: Enables support for double precision floating point, and double precision square-root and divide hardware extensions. This option includes option 'fpus_div'. Not available for ARC EM.

'fpus_fma'
: Enables support for single precision floating point, and single precision fused multiple and add hardware extensions.

'fpud_fma'
: Enables support for double precision floating point, and double precision fused multiple and add hardware extensions. This option includes option 'fpus_fma'. Not available for ARC EM.

'fpus_all'
: Enables support for all single precision floating point hardware extensions.

'fpud_all'
: Enables support for all single and double precision floating point hardware extensions. Not available for ARC EM.

The following options are passed through to the assembler, and also define preprocessor macro symbols.

-mdsp-packa
: Passed down to the assembler to enable the DSP Pack A extensions. Also sets the preprocessor symbol __Xdsp_packa.

-mdvbf
: Passed down to the assembler to enable the dual viterbi butterfly extension. Also sets the preprocessor symbol __Xdvbf.

-mlock
: Passed down to the assembler to enable the Locked Load/Store Conditional extension. Also sets the preprocessor symbol __Xlock.

-mmac-d16
: Passed down to the assembler. Also sets the preprocessor symbol __Xxmac_d16.

-mmac-24
: Passed down to the assembler. Also sets the preprocessor symbol __Xxmac_24.

-mrtsc
: Passed down to the assembler to enable the 64-bit Time-Stamp Counter extension instruction. Also sets the preprocessor symbol __Xrtsc.

-mswape
: Passed down to the assembler to enable the swap byte ordering extension instruction. Also sets the preprocessor symbol __Xswape.

`-mtelephony`
: Passed down to the assembler to enable dual and single operand instructions for telephony. Also sets the preprocessor symbol `__Xtelephony`.

`-mxy`
: Passed down to the assembler to enable the XY Memory extension. Also sets the preprocessor symbol `__Xxy`.

The following options control how the assembly code is annotated:

`-misize`
: Annotate assembler instructions with estimated addresses.

`-mannotate-align`
: Explain what alignment considerations lead to the decision to make an instruction short or long.

The following options are passed through to the linker:

`-marclinux`
: Passed through to the linker, to specify use of the `arclinux` emulation. This option is enabled by default in tool chains built for `arc-linux-uclibc` and `arceb-linux-uclibc` targets when profiling is not requested.

`-marclinux_prof`
: Passed through to the linker, to specify use of the `arclinux_prof` emulation. This option is enabled by default in tool chains built for `arc-linux-uclibc` and `arceb-linux-uclibc` targets when profiling is requested.

The following options control the semantics of generated code:

`-mlong-calls`
: Generate call insns as register indirect calls, thus providing access to the full 32-bit address range.

`-mmedium-calls`
: Don't use less than 25 bit addressing range for calls, which is the offset available for an unconditional branch-and-link instruction. Conditional execution of function calls is suppressed, to allow use of the 25-bit range, rather than the 21-bit range with conditional branch-and-link. This is the default for tool chains built for `arc-linux-uclibc` and `arceb-linux-uclibc` targets.

`-mno-sdata`
: Do not generate sdata references. This is the default for tool chains built for `arc-linux-uclibc` and `arceb-linux-uclibc` targets.

`-mucb-mcount`
: Instrument with mcount calls as used in UCB code. I.e. do the counting in the callee, not the caller. By default ARC instrumentation counts in the caller.

`-mvolatile-cache`
: Use ordinarily cached memory accesses for volatile references. This is the default.

`-mno-volatile-cache`
: Enable cache bypass for volatile references.

The following options fine tune code generation:

`-malign-call`
: Do alignment optimizations for call instructions.

`-mauto-modify-reg`
: Enable the use of pre/post modify with register displacement.

`-mbbit-peephole`
: Enable bbit peephole2.

`-mno-brcc`
: This option disables a target-specific pass in '`arc_reorg`' to generate `BRcc` instructions. It has no effect on `BRcc` generation driven by the combiner pass.

`-mcase-vector-pcrel`
: Use pc-relative switch case tables - this enables case table shortening. This is the default for '`-Os`'.

`-mcompact-casesi`
: Enable compact casesi pattern. This is the default for '`-Os`'.

`-mno-cond-exec`
: Disable ARCompact specific pass to generate conditional execution instructions. Due to delay slot scheduling and interactions between operand numbers, literal sizes, instruction lengths, and the support for conditional execution, the target-independent pass to generate conditional execution is often lacking, so the ARC port has kept a special pass around that tries to find more conditional execution generating opportunities after register allocation, branch shortening, and delay slot scheduling have been done. This pass generally, but not always, improves performance and code size, at the cost of extra compilation time, which is why there is an option to switch it off. If you have a problem with call instructions exceeding their allowable offset range because they are conditionalized, you should consider using '`-mmedium-calls`' instead.

`-mearly-cbranchsi`
: Enable pre-reload use of the cbranchsi pattern.

`-mexpand-adddi`
: Expand `adddi3` and `subdi3` at rtl generation time into `add.f`, `adc` etc.

`-mindexed-loads`
: Enable the use of indexed loads. This can be problematic because some optimizers then assume that indexed stores exist, which is not the case.

`-mlra`
: Enable Local Register Allocation. This is still experimental for ARC, so by default the compiler uses standard reload (i.e. '`-mno-lra`').

`-mlra-priority-none`
: Don't indicate any priority for target registers.

`-mlra-priority-compact`
: Indicate target register priority for r0..r3 / r12..r15.

`-mlra-priority-noncompact`
: Reduce target register priority for r0..r3 / r12..r15.

`-mno-millicode`
: When optimizing for size (using '`-Os`'), prologues and epilogues that have to save or restore a large number of registers are often shortened by using call to a special function in libgcc; this is referred to as a *millicode* call. As these calls can pose performance issues, and/or cause linking issues when linking in a nonstandard way, this option is provided to turn off millicode call generation.

`-mmixed-code`
: Tweak register allocation to help 16-bit instruction generation. This generally has the effect of decreasing the average instruction size while increasing the instruction count.

`-mq-class`
: Enable 'q' instruction alternatives. This is the default for '`-Os`'.

`-mRcq`
: Enable Rcq constraint handling - most short code generation depends on this. This is the default.

`-mRcw`
: Enable Rcw constraint handling - ccfsm condexec mostly depends on this. This is the default.

`-msize-level=`*level*
: Fine-tune size optimization with regards to instruction lengths and alignment. The recognized values for *level* are:

  '`0`' No size optimization. This level is deprecated and treated like '`1`'.

  '`1`' Short instructions are used opportunistically.

  '`2`' In addition, alignment of loops and of code after barriers are dropped.

  '`3`' In addition, optional data alignment is dropped, and the option '`Os`' is enabled.

  This defaults to '`3`' when '`-Os`' is in effect. Otherwise, the behavior when this is not set is equivalent to level '`1`'.

`-mtune=`*cpu*
: Set instruction scheduling parameters for *cpu*, overriding any implied by '`-mcpu=`'.

  Supported values for *cpu* are

  '`ARC600`' Tune for ARC600 cpu.

  '`ARC601`' Tune for ARC601 cpu.

  '`ARC700`' Tune for ARC700 cpu with standard multiplier block.

  '`ARC700-xmac`'
  Tune for ARC700 cpu with XMAC block.

  '`ARC725D`' Tune for ARC725D cpu.

'ARC750D' Tune for ARC750D cpu.

-mmultcost=*num*
: Cost to assume for a multiply instruction, with '4' being equal to a normal instruction.

-munalign-prob-threshold=*probability*
: Set probability threshold for unaligning branches. When tuning for 'ARC700' and optimizing for speed, branches without filled delay slot are preferably emitted unaligned and long, unless profiling indicates that the probability for the branch to be taken is below *probability*. See Section 10.5 [Cross-profiling], page 725. The default is (REG_BR_PROB_BASE/2), i.e. 5000.

The following options are maintained for backward compatibility, but are now deprecated and will be removed in a future release:

-margonaut
: Obsolete FPX.

-mbig-endian
-EB
: Compile code for big endian targets. Use of these options is now deprecated. Users wanting big-endian code, should use the arceb-elf32 and arceb-linux-uclibc targets when building the tool chain, for which big-endian is the default.

-mlittle-endian
-EL
: Compile code for little endian targets. Use of these options is now deprecated. Users wanting little-endian code should use the arc-elf32 and arc-linux-uclibc targets when building the tool chain, for which little-endian is the default.

-mbarrel_shifter
: Replaced by '-mbarrel-shifter'.

-mdpfp_compact
: Replaced by '-mdpfp-compact'.

-mdpfp_fast
: Replaced by '-mdpfp-fast'.

-mdsp_packa
: Replaced by '-mdsp-packa'.

-mEA
: Replaced by '-mea'.

-mmac_24
: Replaced by '-mmac-24'.

-mmac_d16
: Replaced by '-mmac-d16'.

-mspfp_compact
: Replaced by '-mspfp-compact'.

-mspfp_fast
: Replaced by '-mspfp-fast'.

`-mtune=cpu`
: Values 'arc600', 'arc601', 'arc700' and 'arc700-xmac' for *cpu* are replaced by 'ARC600', 'ARC601', 'ARC700' and 'ARC700-xmac' respectively

`-multcost=num`
: Replaced by '-mmultcost'.

3.18.4 ARM Options

These '-m' options are defined for the ARM port:

`-mabi=name`
: Generate code for the specified ABI. Permissible values are: 'apcs-gnu', 'atpcs', 'aapcs', 'aapcs-linux' and 'iwmmxt'.

`-mapcs-frame`
: Generate a stack frame that is compliant with the ARM Procedure Call Standard for all functions, even if this is not strictly necessary for correct execution of the code. Specifying '-fomit-frame-pointer' with this option causes the stack frames not to be generated for leaf functions. The default is '-mno-apcs-frame'. This option is deprecated.

`-mapcs`
: This is a synonym for '-mapcs-frame' and is deprecated.

`-mthumb-interwork`
: Generate code that supports calling between the ARM and Thumb instruction sets. Without this option, on pre-v5 architectures, the two instruction sets cannot be reliably used inside one program. The default is '-mno-thumb-interwork', since slightly larger code is generated when '-mthumb-interwork' is specified. In AAPCS configurations this option is meaningless.

`-mno-sched-prolog`
: Prevent the reordering of instructions in the function prologue, or the merging of those instruction with the instructions in the function's body. This means that all functions start with a recognizable set of instructions (or in fact one of a choice from a small set of different function prologues), and this information can be used to locate the start of functions inside an executable piece of code. The default is '-msched-prolog'.

`-mfloat-abi=name`
: Specifies which floating-point ABI to use. Permissible values are: 'soft', 'softfp' and 'hard'.

  Specifying 'soft' causes GCC to generate output containing library calls for floating-point operations. 'softfp' allows the generation of code using hardware floating-point instructions, but still uses the soft-float calling conventions. 'hard' allows generation of floating-point instructions and uses FPU-specific calling conventions.

  The default depends on the specific target configuration. Note that the hard-float and soft-float ABIs are not link-compatible; you must compile your entire program with the same ABI, and link with a compatible set of libraries.

`-mlittle-endian`
: Generate code for a processor running in little-endian mode. This is the default for all standard configurations.

`-mbig-endian`
: Generate code for a processor running in big-endian mode; the default is to compile code for a little-endian processor.

`-march=`*name*
: This specifies the name of the target ARM architecture. GCC uses this name to determine what kind of instructions it can emit when generating assembly code. This option can be used in conjunction with or instead of the '`-mcpu=`' option. Permissible names are: '`armv2`', '`armv2a`', '`armv3`', '`armv3m`', '`armv4`', '`armv4t`', '`armv5`', '`armv5t`', '`armv5e`', '`armv5te`', '`armv6`', '`armv6j`', '`armv6t2`', '`armv6z`', '`armv6kz`', '`armv6-m`', '`armv7`', '`armv7-a`', '`armv7-r`', '`armv7-m`', '`armv7e-m`', '`armv7ve`', '`armv8-a`', '`armv8-a+crc`', '`armv8.1-a`', '`armv8.1-a+crc`', '`iwmmxt`', '`iwmmxt2`', '`ep9312`'.

  Architecture revisions older than '`armv4t`' are deprecated.

  '`-march=armv7ve`' is the armv7-a architecture with virtualization extensions.

  '`-march=armv8-a+crc`' enables code generation for the ARMv8-A architecture together with the optional CRC32 extensions.

  '`-march=native`' causes the compiler to auto-detect the architecture of the build computer. At present, this feature is only supported on GNU/Linux, and not all architectures are recognized. If the auto-detect is unsuccessful the option has no effect.

`-mtune=`*name*
: This option specifies the name of the target ARM processor for which GCC should tune the performance of the code. For some ARM implementations better performance can be obtained by using this option. Permissible names are: '`arm2`', '`arm250`', '`arm3`', '`arm6`', '`arm60`', '`arm600`', '`arm610`', '`arm620`', '`arm7`', '`arm7m`', '`arm7d`', '`arm7dm`', '`arm7di`', '`arm7dmi`', '`arm70`', '`arm700`', '`arm700i`', '`arm710`', '`arm710c`', '`arm7100`', '`arm720`', '`arm7500`', '`arm7500fe`', '`arm7tdmi`', '`arm7tdmi-s`', '`arm710t`', '`arm720t`', '`arm740t`', '`strongarm`', '`strongarm110`', '`strongarm1100`', '`strongarm1110`', '`arm8`', '`arm810`', '`arm9`', '`arm9e`', '`arm920`', '`arm920t`', '`arm922t`', '`arm946e-s`', '`arm966e-s`', '`arm968e-s`', '`arm926ej-s`', '`arm940t`', '`arm9tdmi`', '`arm10tdmi`', '`arm1020t`', '`arm1026ej-s`', '`arm10e`', '`arm1020e`', '`arm1022e`', '`arm1136j-s`', '`arm1136jf-s`', '`mpcore`', '`mpcorenovfp`', '`arm1156t2-s`', '`arm1156t2f-s`', '`arm1176jz-s`', '`arm1176jzf-s`', '`generic-armv7-a`', '`cortex-a5`', '`cortex-a7`', '`cortex-a8`', '`cortex-a9`', '`cortex-a12`', '`cortex-a15`', '`cortex-a17`', '`cortex-a32`', '`cortex-a35`', '`cortex-a53`', '`cortex-a57`', '`cortex-a72`', '`cortex-r4`', '`cortex-r4f`', '`cortex-r5`', '`cortex-r7`', '`cortex-r8`', '`cortex-m7`', '`cortex-m4`', '`cortex-m3`', '`cortex-m1`', '`cortex-m0`', '`cortex-m0plus`', '`cortex-m1.small-multiply`', '`cortex-m0.small-multiply`', '`cortex-m0plus.small-multiply`', '`exynos-m1`', '`qdf24xx`', '`marvell-pj4`', '`xscale`', '`iwmmxt`', '`iwmmxt2`',

'ep9312', 'fa526', 'fa626', 'fa606te', 'fa626te', 'fmp626', 'fa726te', 'xgene1'.

Additionally, this option can specify that GCC should tune the performance of the code for a big.LITTLE system. Permissible names are: 'cortex-a15.cortex-a7', 'cortex-a17.cortex-a7', 'cortex-a57.cortex-a53', 'cortex-a72.cortex-a53'.

'-mtune=generic-*arch*' specifies that GCC should tune the performance for a blend of processors within architecture *arch*. The aim is to generate code that run well on the current most popular processors, balancing between optimizations that benefit some CPUs in the range, and avoiding performance pitfalls of other CPUs. The effects of this option may change in future GCC versions as CPU models come and go.

'-mtune=native' causes the compiler to auto-detect the CPU of the build computer. At present, this feature is only supported on GNU/Linux, and not all architectures are recognized. If the auto-detect is unsuccessful the option has no effect.

-mcpu=*name*

This specifies the name of the target ARM processor. GCC uses this name to derive the name of the target ARM architecture (as if specified by '-march') and the ARM processor type for which to tune for performance (as if specified by '-mtune'). Where this option is used in conjunction with '-march' or '-mtune', those options take precedence over the appropriate part of this option.

Permissible names for this option are the same as those for '-mtune'.

'-mcpu=generic-*arch*' is also permissible, and is equivalent to '-march=*arch* -mtune=generic-*arch*'. See '-mtune' for more information.

'-mcpu=native' causes the compiler to auto-detect the CPU of the build computer. At present, this feature is only supported on GNU/Linux, and not all architectures are recognized. If the auto-detect is unsuccessful the option has no effect.

-mfpu=*name*

This specifies what floating-point hardware (or hardware emulation) is available on the target. Permissible names are: 'vfp', 'vfpv3', 'vfpv3-fp16', 'vfpv3-d16', 'vfpv3-d16-fp16', 'vfpv3xd', 'vfpv3xd-fp16', 'neon', 'neon-fp16', 'vfpv4', 'vfpv4-d16', 'fpv4-sp-d16', 'neon-vfpv4', 'fpv5-d16', 'fpv5-sp-d16', 'fp-armv8', 'neon-fp-armv8' and 'crypto-neon-fp-armv8'.

If '-msoft-float' is specified this specifies the format of floating-point values.

If the selected floating-point hardware includes the NEON extension (e.g. '-mfpu'='neon'), note that floating-point operations are not generated by GCC's auto-vectorization pass unless '-funsafe-math-optimizations' is also specified. This is because NEON hardware does not fully implement the IEEE 754 standard for floating-point arithmetic (in particular denormal values are treated as zero), so the use of NEON instructions may lead to a loss of precision.

You can also set the fpu name at function level by using the `target("fpu=")` function attributes (see Section 6.31.4 [ARM Function Attributes], page 425) or pragmas (see Section 6.61.15 [Function Specific Option Pragmas], page 675).

`-mfp16-format=`*name*
: Specify the format of the `__fp16` half-precision floating-point type. Permissible names are '`none`', '`ieee`', and '`alternative`'; the default is '`none`', in which case the `__fp16` type is not defined. See Section 6.12 [Half-Precision], page 394, for more information.

`-mstructure-size-boundary=`*n*
: The sizes of all structures and unions are rounded up to a multiple of the number of bits set by this option. Permissible values are 8, 32 and 64. The default value varies for different toolchains. For the COFF targeted toolchain the default value is 8. A value of 64 is only allowed if the underlying ABI supports it.

Specifying a larger number can produce faster, more efficient code, but can also increase the size of the program. Different values are potentially incompatible. Code compiled with one value cannot necessarily expect to work with code or libraries compiled with another value, if they exchange information using structures or unions.

`-mabort-on-noreturn`
: Generate a call to the function `abort` at the end of a `noreturn` function. It is executed if the function tries to return.

`-mlong-calls`
`-mno-long-calls`
: Tells the compiler to perform function calls by first loading the address of the function into a register and then performing a subroutine call on this register. This switch is needed if the target function lies outside of the 64-megabyte addressing range of the offset-based version of subroutine call instruction.

Even if this switch is enabled, not all function calls are turned into long calls. The heuristic is that static functions, functions that have the `short_call` attribute, functions that are inside the scope of a `#pragma no_long_calls` directive, and functions whose definitions have already been compiled within the current compilation unit are not turned into long calls. The exceptions to this rule are that weak function definitions, functions with the `long_call` attribute or the `section` attribute, and functions that are within the scope of a `#pragma long_calls` directive are always turned into long calls.

This feature is not enabled by default. Specifying '`-mno-long-calls`' restores the default behavior, as does placing the function calls within the scope of a `#pragma long_calls_off` directive. Note these switches have no effect on how the compiler generates code to handle function calls via function pointers.

`-msingle-pic-base`
: Treat the register used for PIC addressing as read-only, rather than loading it in the prologue for each function. The runtime system is responsible for initializing this register with an appropriate value before execution begins.

`-mpic-register=`*reg*
: Specify the register to be used for PIC addressing. For standard PIC base case, the default is any suitable register determined by compiler. For single PIC base case, the default is '`R9`' if target is EABI based or stack-checking is enabled, otherwise the default is '`R10`'.

`-mpic-data-is-text-relative`
: Assume that each data segments are relative to text segment at load time. Therefore, it permits addressing data using PC-relative operations. This option is on by default for targets other than VxWorks RTP.

`-mpoke-function-name`
: Write the name of each function into the text section, directly preceding the function prologue. The generated code is similar to this:

```
t0
    .ascii "arm_poke_function_name", 0
    .align
t1
    .word 0xff000000 + (t1 - t0)
arm_poke_function_name
    mov     ip, sp
    stmfd   sp!, {fp, ip, lr, pc}
    sub     fp, ip, #4
```

When performing a stack backtrace, code can inspect the value of `pc` stored at `fp + 0`. If the trace function then looks at location `pc - 12` and the top 8 bits are set, then we know that there is a function name embedded immediately preceding this location and has length `((pc[-3]) & 0xff000000)`.

`-mthumb`
`-marm`
: Select between generating code that executes in ARM and Thumb states. The default for most configurations is to generate code that executes in ARM state, but the default can be changed by configuring GCC with the '`--with-mode=`*state*' configure option.

You can also override the ARM and Thumb mode for each function by using the `target("thumb")` and `target("arm")` function attributes (see Section 6.31.4 [ARM Function Attributes], page 425) or pragmas (see Section 6.61.15 [Function Specific Option Pragmas], page 675).

`-mtpcs-frame`
: Generate a stack frame that is compliant with the Thumb Procedure Call Standard for all non-leaf functions. (A leaf function is one that does not call any other functions.) The default is '`-mno-tpcs-frame`'.

`-mtpcs-leaf-frame`
: Generate a stack frame that is compliant with the Thumb Procedure Call Standard for all leaf functions. (A leaf function is one that does not call any other functions.) The default is '`-mno-apcs-leaf-frame`'.

`-mcallee-super-interworking`
: Gives all externally visible functions in the file being compiled an ARM instruction set header which switches to Thumb mode before executing the rest

of the function. This allows these functions to be called from non-interworking code. This option is not valid in AAPCS configurations because interworking is enabled by default.

`-mcaller-super-interworking`
: Allows calls via function pointers (including virtual functions) to execute correctly regardless of whether the target code has been compiled for interworking or not. There is a small overhead in the cost of executing a function pointer if this option is enabled. This option is not valid in AAPCS configurations because interworking is enabled by default.

`-mtp=`*name*
: Specify the access model for the thread local storage pointer. The valid models are '`soft`', which generates calls to `__aeabi_read_tp`, '`cp15`', which fetches the thread pointer from `cp15` directly (supported in the arm6k architecture), and '`auto`', which uses the best available method for the selected processor. The default setting is '`auto`'.

`-mtls-dialect=`*dialect*
: Specify the dialect to use for accessing thread local storage. Two *dialects* are supported—'`gnu`' and '`gnu2`'. The '`gnu`' dialect selects the original GNU scheme for supporting local and global dynamic TLS models. The '`gnu2`' dialect selects the GNU descriptor scheme, which provides better performance for shared libraries. The GNU descriptor scheme is compatible with the original scheme, but does require new assembler, linker and library support. Initial and local exec TLS models are unaffected by this option and always use the original scheme.

`-mword-relocations`
: Only generate absolute relocations on word-sized values (i.e. R_ARM_ABS32). This is enabled by default on targets (uClinux, SymbianOS) where the runtime loader imposes this restriction, and when '`-fpic`' or '`-fPIC`' is specified.

`-mfix-cortex-m3-ldrd`
: Some Cortex-M3 cores can cause data corruption when `ldrd` instructions with overlapping destination and base registers are used. This option avoids generating these instructions. This option is enabled by default when '`-mcpu=cortex-m3`' is specified.

`-munaligned-access`
`-mno-unaligned-access`
: Enables (or disables) reading and writing of 16- and 32- bit values from addresses that are not 16- or 32- bit aligned. By default unaligned access is disabled for all pre-ARMv6 and all ARMv6-M architectures, and enabled for all other architectures. If unaligned access is not enabled then words in packed data structures are accessed a byte at a time.

  The ARM attribute `Tag_CPU_unaligned_access` is set in the generated object file to either true or false, depending upon the setting of this option. If unaligned access is enabled then the preprocessor symbol `__ARM_FEATURE_UNALIGNED` is also defined.

`-mneon-for-64bits`
: Enables using Neon to handle scalar 64-bits operations. This is disabled by default since the cost of moving data from core registers to Neon is high.

`-mslow-flash-data`
: Assume loading data from flash is slower than fetching instruction. Therefore literal load is minimized for better performance. This option is only supported when compiling for ARMv7 M-profile and off by default.

`-masm-syntax-unified`
: Assume inline assembler is using unified asm syntax. The default is currently off which implies divided syntax. This option has no impact on Thumb2. However, this may change in future releases of GCC. Divided syntax should be considered deprecated.

`-mrestrict-it`
: Restricts generation of IT blocks to conform to the rules of ARMv8. IT blocks can only contain a single 16-bit instruction from a select set of instructions. This option is on by default for ARMv8 Thumb mode.

`-mprint-tune-info`
: Print CPU tuning information as comment in assembler file. This is an option used only for regression testing of the compiler and not intended for ordinary use in compiling code. This option is disabled by default.

3.18.5 AVR Options

These options are defined for AVR implementations:

`-mmcu=`*`mcu`*
: Specify Atmel AVR instruction set architectures (ISA) or MCU type.

The default for this option is '`avr2`'.

GCC supports the following AVR devices and ISAs:

`avr2` "Classic" devices with up to 8 KiB of program memory.
mcu = `attiny22`, `attiny26`, `at90c8534`, `at90s2313`, `at90s2323`, `at90s2333`, `at90s2343`, `at90s4414`, `at90s4433`, `at90s4434`, `at90s8515`, `at90s8535`.

`avr25` "Classic" devices with up to 8 KiB of program memory and with the `MOVW` instruction.
mcu = `ata5272`, `ata6616c`, `attiny13`, `attiny13a`, `attiny2313`, `attiny2313a`, `attiny24`, `attiny24a`, `attiny25`, `attiny261`, `attiny261a`, `attiny43u`, `attiny4313`, `attiny44`, `attiny44a`, `attiny441`, `attiny45`, `attiny461`, `attiny461a`, `attiny48`, `attiny828`, `attiny84`, `attiny84a`, `attiny841`, `attiny85`, `attiny861`, `attiny861a`, `attiny87`, `attiny88`, `at86rf401`.

`avr3` "Classic" devices with 16 KiB up to 64 KiB of program memory.
mcu = `at43usb355`, `at76c711`.

`avr31` "Classic" devices with 128 KiB of program memory.
mcu = `atmega103`, `at43usb320`.

`avr35` "Classic" devices with 16 KiB up to 64 KiB of program memory and with the `MOVW` instruction.
mcu = `ata5505`, `ata6617c`, `ata664251`, `atmega16u2`, `atmega32u2`, `atmega8u2`, `attiny1634`, `attiny167`, `at90usb162`, `at90usb82`.

`avr4` "Enhanced" devices with up to 8 KiB of program memory.
mcu = `ata6285`, `ata6286`, `ata6289`, `ata6612c`, `atmega48`, `atmega48a`, `atmega48p`, `atmega48pa`, `atmega48pb`, `atmega8`, `atmega8a`, `atmega8hva`, `atmega8515`, `atmega8535`, `atmega88`, `atmega88a`, `atmega88p`, `atmega88pa`, `atmega88pb`, `at90pwm1`, `at90pwm2`, `at90pwm2b`, `at90pwm3`, `at90pwm3b`, `at90pwm81`.

`avr5` "Enhanced" devices with 16 KiB up to 64 KiB of program memory.
mcu = `ata5702m322`, `ata5782`, `ata5790`, `ata5790n`, `ata5791`, `ata5795`, `ata5831`, `ata6613c`, `ata6614q`, `ata8210`, `ata8510`, `atmega16`, `atmega16a`, `atmega16hva`, `atmega16hva2`, `atmega16hvb`, `atmega16hvbrevb`, `atmega16m1`, `atmega16u4`, `atmega161`, `atmega162`, `atmega163`, `atmega164a`, `atmega164p`, `atmega164pa`, `atmega165`, `atmega165a`, `atmega165p`, `atmega165pa`, `atmega168`, `atmega168a`, `atmega168p`, `atmega168pa`, `atmega168pb`, `atmega169`, `atmega169a`, `atmega169p`, `atmega169pa`, `atmega32`, `atmega32a`, `atmega32c1`, `atmega32hvb`, `atmega32hvbrevb`, `atmega32m1`, `atmega32u4`, `atmega32u6`, `atmega323`, `atmega324a`, `atmega324p`, `atmega324pa`, `atmega325`, `atmega325a`, `atmega325p`, `atmega325pa`, `atmega3250`, `atmega3250a`, `atmega3250p`, `atmega3250pa`, `atmega328`, `atmega328p`, `atmega328pb`, `atmega329`, `atmega329a`, `atmega329p`, `atmega329pa`, `atmega3290`, `atmega3290a`, `atmega3290p`, `atmega3290pa`, `atmega406`, `atmega64`, `atmega64a`, `atmega64c1`, `atmega64hve`, `atmega64hve2`, `atmega64m1`, `atmega64rfr2`, `atmega640`, `atmega644`, `atmega644a`, `atmega644p`, `atmega644pa`, `atmega644rfr2`, `atmega645`, `atmega645a`, `atmega645p`, `atmega6450`, `atmega6450a`, `atmega6450p`, `atmega649`, `atmega649a`, `atmega649p`, `atmega6490`, `atmega6490a`, `atmega6490p`, `at90can32`, `at90can64`, `at90pwm161`, `at90pwm216`, `at90pwm316`, `at90scr100`, `at90usb646`, `at90usb647`, `at94k`, `m3000`.

`avr51` "Enhanced" devices with 128 KiB of program memory.
mcu = `atmega128`, `atmega128a`, `atmega128rfa1`, `atmega128rfr2`, `atmega1280`, `atmega1281`, `atmega1284`, `atmega1284p`, `atmega1284rfr2`, `at90can128`, `at90usb1286`, `at90usb1287`.

`avr6` "Enhanced" devices with 3-byte PC, i.e. with more than 128 KiB of program memory.
mcu = `atmega256rfr2`, `atmega2560`, `atmega2561`, `atmega2564rfr2`.

`avrxmega2`
: "XMEGA" devices with more than 8 KiB and up to 64 KiB of program memory.
mcu = `atxmega16a4`, `atxmega16a4u`, `atxmega16c4`, `atxmega16d4`, `atxmega16e5`, `atxmega32a4`, `atxmega32a4u`, `atxmega32c3`, `atxmega32c4`, `atxmega32d3`, `atxmega32d4`, `atxmega32e5`, `atxmega8e5`.

`avrxmega4`
: "XMEGA" devices with more than 64 KiB and up to 128 KiB of program memory.
mcu = `atxmega64a3`, `atxmega64a3u`, `atxmega64a4u`, `atxmega64b1`, `atxmega64b3`, `atxmega64c3`, `atxmega64d3`, `atxmega64d4`.

`avrxmega5`
: "XMEGA" devices with more than 64 KiB and up to 128 KiB of program memory and more than 64 KiB of RAM.
mcu = `atxmega64a1`, `atxmega64a1u`.

`avrxmega6`
: "XMEGA" devices with more than 128 KiB of program memory.
mcu = `atxmega128a3`, `atxmega128a3u`, `atxmega128b1`, `atxmega128b3`, `atxmega128c3`, `atxmega128d3`, `atxmega128d4`, `atxmega192a3`, `atxmega192a3u`, `atxmega192c3`, `atxmega192d3`, `atxmega256a3`, `atxmega256a3b`, `atxmega256a3bu`, `atxmega256a3u`, `atxmega256c3`, `atxmega256d3`, `atxmega384c3`, `atxmega384d3`.

`avrxmega7`
: "XMEGA" devices with more than 128 KiB of program memory and more than 64 KiB of RAM.
mcu = `atxmega128a1`, `atxmega128a1u`, `atxmega128a4u`.

`avrtiny`
: "TINY" Tiny core devices with 512 B up to 4 KiB of program memory.
mcu = `attiny10`, `attiny20`, `attiny4`, `attiny40`, `attiny5`, `attiny9`.

`avr1`
: This ISA is implemented by the minimal AVR core and supported for assembler only.
mcu = `attiny11`, `attiny12`, `attiny15`, `attiny28`, `at90s1200`.

`-maccumulate-args`
: Accumulate outgoing function arguments and acquire/release the needed stack space for outgoing function arguments once in function prologue/epilogue. Without this option, outgoing arguments are pushed before calling a function and popped afterwards.

Popping the arguments after the function call can be expensive on AVR so that accumulating the stack space might lead to smaller executables because arguments need not to be removed from the stack after such a function call.

This option can lead to reduced code size for functions that perform several calls to functions that get their arguments on the stack like calls to printf-like functions.

`-mbranch-cost=`*cost*
: Set the branch costs for conditional branch instructions to *cost*. Reasonable values for *cost* are small, non-negative integers. The default branch cost is 0.

`-mcall-prologues`
: Functions prologues/epilogues are expanded as calls to appropriate subroutines. Code size is smaller.

`-mint8`
: Assume `int` to be 8-bit integer. This affects the sizes of all types: a `char` is 1 byte, an `int` is 1 byte, a `long` is 2 bytes, and `long long` is 4 bytes. Please note that this option does not conform to the C standards, but it results in smaller code size.

`-mn-flash=`*num*
: Assume that the flash memory has a size of *num* times 64 KiB.

`-mno-interrupts`
: Generated code is not compatible with hardware interrupts. Code size is smaller.

`-mrelax`
: Try to replace `CALL` resp. `JMP` instruction by the shorter `RCALL` resp. `RJMP` instruction if applicable. Setting '`-mrelax`' just adds the '`--mlink-relax`' option to the assembler's command line and the '`--relax`' option to the linker's command line.

Jump relaxing is performed by the linker because jump offsets are not known before code is located. Therefore, the assembler code generated by the compiler is the same, but the instructions in the executable may differ from instructions in the assembler code.

Relaxing must be turned on if linker stubs are needed, see the section on `EIND` and linker stubs below.

`-mrmw`
: Assume that the device supports the Read-Modify-Write instructions `XCH`, `LAC`, `LAS` and `LAT`.

`-msp8`
: Treat the stack pointer register as an 8-bit register, i.e. assume the high byte of the stack pointer is zero. In general, you don't need to set this option by hand.

This option is used internally by the compiler to select and build multilibs for architectures `avr2` and `avr25`. These architectures mix devices with and without `SPH`. For any setting other than '`-mmcu=avr2`' or '`-mmcu=avr25`' the compiler driver adds or removes this option from the compiler proper's command line, because the compiler then knows if the device or architecture has an 8-bit stack pointer and thus no `SPH` register or not.

`-mstrict-X`
: Use address register `X` in a way proposed by the hardware. This means that `X` is only used in indirect, post-increment or pre-decrement addressing.

Without this option, the `X` register may be used in the same way as `Y` or `Z` which then is emulated by additional instructions. For example, loading a value with

`X+const` addressing with a small non-negative `const < 64` to a register *Rn* is performed as

```
adiw r26, const    ; X += const
ld   Rn, X         ; Rn = *X
sbiw r26, const    ; X -= const
```

`-mtiny-stack`
: Only change the lower 8 bits of the stack pointer.

`-nodevicelib`
: Don't link against AVR-LibC's device specific library `libdev.a`.

`-Waddr-space-convert`
: Warn about conversions between address spaces in the case where the resulting address space is not contained in the incoming address space.

3.18.5.1 `EIND` and Devices with More Than 128 Ki Bytes of Flash

Pointers in the implementation are 16 bits wide. The address of a function or label is represented as word address so that indirect jumps and calls can target any code address in the range of 64 Ki words.

In order to facilitate indirect jump on devices with more than 128 Ki bytes of program memory space, there is a special function register called `EIND` that serves as most significant part of the target address when `EICALL` or `EIJMP` instructions are used.

Indirect jumps and calls on these devices are handled as follows by the compiler and are subject to some limitations:

- The compiler never sets `EIND`.
- The compiler uses `EIND` implicitly in `EICALL`/`EIJMP` instructions or might read `EIND` directly in order to emulate an indirect call/jump by means of a `RET` instruction.
- The compiler assumes that `EIND` never changes during the startup code or during the application. In particular, `EIND` is not saved/restored in function or interrupt service routine prologue/epilogue.
- For indirect calls to functions and computed goto, the linker generates *stubs*. Stubs are jump pads sometimes also called *trampolines*. Thus, the indirect call/jump jumps to such a stub. The stub contains a direct jump to the desired address.
- Linker relaxation must be turned on so that the linker generates the stubs correctly in all situations. See the compiler option '`-mrelax`' and the linker option '`--relax`'. There are corner cases where the linker is supposed to generate stubs but aborts without relaxation and without a helpful error message.
- The default linker script is arranged for code with `EIND = 0`. If code is supposed to work for a setup with `EIND != 0`, a custom linker script has to be used in order to place the sections whose name start with `.trampolines` into the segment where `EIND` points to.
- The startup code from libgcc never sets `EIND`. Notice that startup code is a blend of code from libgcc and AVR-LibC. For the impact of AVR-LibC on `EIND`, see the AVR-LibC user manual.

- It is legitimate for user-specific startup code to set up `EIND` early, for example by means of initialization code located in section `.init3`. Such code runs prior to general startup code that initializes RAM and calls constructors, but after the bit of startup code from AVR-LibC that sets `EIND` to the segment where the vector table is located.

```
#include <avr/io.h>

static void
__attribute__((section(".init3"),naked,used,no_instrument_function))
init3_set_eind (void)
{
  __asm volatile ("ldi r24,pm_hh8(__trampolines_start)\n\t"
                  "out %i0,r24" :: "n" (&EIND) : "r24","memory");
}
```

  The `__trampolines_start` symbol is defined in the linker script.
- Stubs are generated automatically by the linker if the following two conditions are met:
  - The address of a label is taken by means of the `gs` modifier (short for *generate stubs*) like so:

    ```
    LDI r24, lo8(gs(func))
    LDI r25, hi8(gs(func))
    ```

  - The final location of that label is in a code segment *outside* the segment where the stubs are located.
- The compiler emits such `gs` modifiers for code labels in the following situations:
  - Taking address of a function or code label.
  - Computed goto.
  - If prologue-save function is used, see '`-mcall-prologues`' command-line option.
  - Switch/case dispatch tables. If you do not want such dispatch tables you can specify the '`-fno-jump-tables`' command-line option.
  - C and C++ constructors/destructors called during startup/shutdown.
  - If the tools hit a `gs()` modifier explained above.
- Jumping to non-symbolic addresses like so is *not* supported:

```
int main (void)
{
    /* Call function at word address 0x2 */
    return ((int(*)(void)) 0x2)();
}
```

  Instead, a stub has to be set up, i.e. the function has to be called through a symbol (`func_4` in the example):

```
int main (void)
{
    extern int func_4 (void);

    /* Call function at byte address 0x4 */
    return func_4();
```

```
}
```

and the application be linked with '-Wl,--defsym,func_4=0x4'. Alternatively, `func_4` can be defined in the linker script.

3.18.5.2 Handling of the RAMPD, RAMPX, RAMPY and RAMPZ Special Function Registers

Some AVR devices support memories larger than the 64 KiB range that can be accessed with 16-bit pointers. To access memory locations outside this 64 KiB range, the contentent of a `RAMP` register is used as high part of the address: The `X`, `Y`, `Z` address register is concatenated with the `RAMPX`, `RAMPY`, `RAMPZ` special function register, respectively, to get a wide address. Similarly, `RAMPD` is used together with direct addressing.

- The startup code initializes the `RAMP` special function registers with zero.
- If a [AVR Named Address Spaces], page 396 other than generic or `__flash` is used, then `RAMPZ` is set as needed before the operation.
- If the device supports RAM larger than 64 KiB and the compiler needs to change `RAMPZ` to accomplish an operation, `RAMPZ` is reset to zero after the operation.
- If the device comes with a specific `RAMP` register, the ISR prologue/epilogue saves/restores that SFR and initializes it with zero in case the ISR code might (implicitly) use it.
- RAM larger than 64 KiB is not supported by GCC for AVR targets. If you use inline assembler to read from locations outside the 16-bit address range and change one of the `RAMP` registers, you must reset it to zero after the access.

3.18.5.3 AVR Built-in Macros

GCC defines several built-in macros so that the user code can test for the presence or absence of features. Almost any of the following built-in macros are deduced from device capabilities and thus triggered by the '-mmcu=' command-line option.

For even more AVR-specific built-in macros see [AVR Named Address Spaces], page 396 and Section 6.59.9 [AVR Built-in Functions], page 568.

`__AVR_ARCH__`

Build-in macro that resolves to a decimal number that identifies the architecture and depends on the '-mmcu=*mcu*' option. Possible values are:

`2, 25, 3, 31, 35, 4, 5, 51, 6`

for *mcu*=`avr2`, `avr25`, `avr3`, `avr31`, `avr35`, `avr4`, `avr5`, `avr51`, `avr6`,

respectively and

`100, 102, 104, 105, 106, 107`

for *mcu*=`avrtiny`, `avrxmega2`, `avrxmega4`, `avrxmega5`, `avrxmega6`, `avrxmega7`, respectively. If *mcu* specifies a device, this built-in macro is set accordingly. For example, with '-mmcu=atmega8' the macro is defined to `4`.

`__AVR_`*`Device`*`__`

Setting '-mmcu=*device*' defines this built-in macro which reflects the device's name. For example, '-mmcu=atmega8' defines the built-in macro `__AVR_ATmega8__`, '-mmcu=attiny261a' defines `__AVR_ATtiny261A__`, etc.

The built-in macros' names follow the scheme `__AVR_`*`Device`*`__` where *Device* is the device name as from the AVR user manual. The difference between *Device* in the built-in macro and *device* in '`-mmcu=`*`device`*' is that the latter is always lowercase.

If *device* is not a device but only a core architecture like '`avr51`', this macro is not defined.

`__AVR_DEVICE_NAME__`
: Setting '`-mmcu=`*`device`*' defines this built-in macro to the device's name. For example, with '`-mmcu=atmega8`' the macro is defined to `atmega8`.

  If *device* is not a device but only a core architecture like '`avr51`', this macro is not defined.

`__AVR_XMEGA__`
: The device / architecture belongs to the XMEGA family of devices.

`__AVR_HAVE_ELPM__`
: The device has the `ELPM` instruction.

`__AVR_HAVE_ELPMX__`
: The device has the `ELPM R`*`n`*`,Z` and `ELPM R`*`n`*`,Z+` instructions.

`__AVR_HAVE_MOVW__`
: The device has the `MOVW` instruction to perform 16-bit register-register moves.

`__AVR_HAVE_LPMX__`
: The device has the `LPM R`*`n`*`,Z` and `LPM R`*`n`*`,Z+` instructions.

`__AVR_HAVE_MUL__`
: The device has a hardware multiplier.

`__AVR_HAVE_JMP_CALL__`
: The device has the `JMP` and `CALL` instructions. This is the case for devices with at least 16 KiB of program memory.

`__AVR_HAVE_EIJMP_EICALL__`
`__AVR_3_BYTE_PC__`
: The device has the `EIJMP` and `EICALL` instructions. This is the case for devices with more than 128 KiB of program memory. This also means that the program counter (PC) is 3 bytes wide.

`__AVR_2_BYTE_PC__`
: The program counter (PC) is 2 bytes wide. This is the case for devices with up to 128 KiB of program memory.

`__AVR_HAVE_8BIT_SP__`
`__AVR_HAVE_16BIT_SP__`
: The stack pointer (SP) register is treated as 8-bit respectively 16-bit register by the compiler. The definition of these macros is affected by '`-mtiny-stack`'.

`__AVR_HAVE_SPH__`
`__AVR_SP8__`
: The device has the SPH (high part of stack pointer) special function register or has an 8-bit stack pointer, respectively. The definition of these macros is

affected by '-mmcu=' and in the cases of '-mmcu=avr2' and '-mmcu=avr25' also by '-msp8'.

__AVR_HAVE_RAMPD__
__AVR_HAVE_RAMPX__
__AVR_HAVE_RAMPY__
__AVR_HAVE_RAMPZ__
: The device has the RAMPD, RAMPX, RAMPY, RAMPZ special function register, respectively.

__NO_INTERRUPTS__
: This macro reflects the '-mno-interrupts' command-line option.

__AVR_ERRATA_SKIP__
__AVR_ERRATA_SKIP_JMP_CALL__
: Some AVR devices (AT90S8515, ATmega103) must not skip 32-bit instructions because of a hardware erratum. Skip instructions are SBRS, SBRC, SBIS, SBIC and CPSE. The second macro is only defined if __AVR_HAVE_JMP_CALL__ is also set.

__AVR_ISA_RMW__
: The device has Read-Modify-Write instructions (XCH, LAC, LAS and LAT).

__AVR_SFR_OFFSET__=*offset*
: Instructions that can address I/O special function registers directly like IN, OUT, SBI, etc. may use a different address as if addressed by an instruction to access RAM like LD or STS. This offset depends on the device architecture and has to be subtracted from the RAM address in order to get the respective I/O address.

__WITH_AVRLIBC__
: The compiler is configured to be used together with AVR-Libc. See the '--with-avrlibc' configure option.

3.18.6 Blackfin Options

-mcpu=*cpu*[-*sirevision*]
: Specifies the name of the target Blackfin processor. Currently, *cpu* can be one of 'bf512', 'bf514', 'bf516', 'bf518', 'bf522', 'bf523', 'bf524', 'bf525', 'bf526', 'bf527', 'bf531', 'bf532', 'bf533', 'bf534', 'bf536', 'bf537', 'bf538', 'bf539', 'bf542', 'bf544', 'bf547', 'bf548', 'bf549', 'bf542m', 'bf544m', 'bf547m', 'bf548m', 'bf549m', 'bf561', 'bf592'.

  The optional *sirevision* specifies the silicon revision of the target Blackfin processor. Any workarounds available for the targeted silicon revision are enabled. If *sirevision* is 'none', no workarounds are enabled. If *sirevision* is 'any', all workarounds for the targeted processor are enabled. The __SILICON_REVISION__ macro is defined to two hexadecimal digits representing the major and minor numbers in the silicon revision. If *sirevision* is 'none', the __SILICON_REVISION__ is not defined. If *sirevision* is 'any', the __SILICON_REVISION__ is defined to be 0xffff. If this optional *sirevision* is not used, GCC assumes the latest known silicon revision of the targeted Blackfin processor.

GCC defines a preprocessor macro for the specified *cpu*. For the '`bfin-elf`' toolchain, this option causes the hardware BSP provided by libgloss to be linked in if '`-msim`' is not given.

Without this option, '`bf532`' is used as the processor by default.

Note that support for '`bf561`' is incomplete. For '`bf561`', only the preprocessor macro is defined.

`-msim` Specifies that the program will be run on the simulator. This causes the simulator BSP provided by libgloss to be linked in. This option has effect only for '`bfin-elf`' toolchain. Certain other options, such as '`-mid-shared-library`' and '`-mfdpic`', imply '`-msim`'.

`-momit-leaf-frame-pointer`
Don't keep the frame pointer in a register for leaf functions. This avoids the instructions to save, set up and restore frame pointers and makes an extra register available in leaf functions. The option '`-fomit-frame-pointer`' removes the frame pointer for all functions, which might make debugging harder.

`-mspecld-anomaly`
When enabled, the compiler ensures that the generated code does not contain speculative loads after jump instructions. If this option is used, `__WORKAROUND_SPECULATIVE_LOADS` is defined.

`-mno-specld-anomaly`
Don't generate extra code to prevent speculative loads from occurring.

`-mcsync-anomaly`
When enabled, the compiler ensures that the generated code does not contain CSYNC or SSYNC instructions too soon after conditional branches. If this option is used, `__WORKAROUND_SPECULATIVE_SYNCS` is defined.

`-mno-csync-anomaly`
Don't generate extra code to prevent CSYNC or SSYNC instructions from occurring too soon after a conditional branch.

`-mlow-64k`
When enabled, the compiler is free to take advantage of the knowledge that the entire program fits into the low 64k of memory.

`-mno-low-64k`
Assume that the program is arbitrarily large. This is the default.

`-mstack-check-l1`
Do stack checking using information placed into L1 scratchpad memory by the uClinux kernel.

`-mid-shared-library`
Generate code that supports shared libraries via the library ID method. This allows for execute in place and shared libraries in an environment without virtual memory management. This option implies '`-fPIC`'. With a '`bfin-elf`' target, this option implies '`-msim`'.

`-mno-id-shared-library`
: Generate code that doesn't assume ID-based shared libraries are being used. This is the default.

`-mleaf-id-shared-library`
: Generate code that supports shared libraries via the library ID method, but assumes that this library or executable won't link against any other ID shared libraries. That allows the compiler to use faster code for jumps and calls.

`-mno-leaf-id-shared-library`
: Do not assume that the code being compiled won't link against any ID shared libraries. Slower code is generated for jump and call insns.

`-mshared-library-id=n`
: Specifies the identification number of the ID-based shared library being compiled. Specifying a value of 0 generates more compact code; specifying other values forces the allocation of that number to the current library but is no more space- or time-efficient than omitting this option.

`-msep-data`
: Generate code that allows the data segment to be located in a different area of memory from the text segment. This allows for execute in place in an environment without virtual memory management by eliminating relocations against the text section.

`-mno-sep-data`
: Generate code that assumes that the data segment follows the text segment. This is the default.

`-mlong-calls`
`-mno-long-calls`
: Tells the compiler to perform function calls by first loading the address of the function into a register and then performing a subroutine call on this register. This switch is needed if the target function lies outside of the 24-bit addressing range of the offset-based version of subroutine call instruction.

  This feature is not enabled by default. Specifying '`-mno-long-calls`' restores the default behavior. Note these switches have no effect on how the compiler generates code to handle function calls via function pointers.

`-mfast-fp`
: Link with the fast floating-point library. This library relaxes some of the IEEE floating-point standard's rules for checking inputs against Not-a-Number (NAN), in the interest of performance.

`-minline-plt`
: Enable inlining of PLT entries in function calls to functions that are not known to bind locally. It has no effect without '`-mfdpic`'.

`-mmulticore`
: Build a standalone application for multicore Blackfin processors. This option causes proper start files and link scripts supporting multicore to be

used, and defines the macro `__BFIN_MULTICORE`. It can only be used with '`-mcpu=bf561[-sirevision]`'.

This option can be used with '`-mcorea`' or '`-mcoreb`', which selects the one-application-per-core programming model. Without '`-mcorea`' or '`-mcoreb`', the single-application/dual-core programming model is used. In this model, the main function of Core B should be named as `coreb_main`.

If this option is not used, the single-core application programming model is used.

`-mcorea` Build a standalone application for Core A of BF561 when using the one-application-per-core programming model. Proper start files and link scripts are used to support Core A, and the macro `__BFIN_COREA` is defined. This option can only be used in conjunction with '`-mmulticore`'.

`-mcoreb` Build a standalone application for Core B of BF561 when using the one-application-per-core programming model. Proper start files and link scripts are used to support Core B, and the macro `__BFIN_COREB` is defined. When this option is used, `coreb_main` should be used instead of `main`. This option can only be used in conjunction with '`-mmulticore`'.

`-msdram` Build a standalone application for SDRAM. Proper start files and link scripts are used to put the application into SDRAM, and the macro `__BFIN_SDRAM` is defined. The loader should initialize SDRAM before loading the application.

`-micplb` Assume that ICPLBs are enabled at run time. This has an effect on certain anomaly workarounds. For Linux targets, the default is to assume ICPLBs are enabled; for standalone applications the default is off.

3.18.7 C6X Options

`-march=name`

This specifies the name of the target architecture. GCC uses this name to determine what kind of instructions it can emit when generating assembly code. Permissible names are: '`c62x`', '`c64x`', '`c64x+`', '`c67x`', '`c67x+`', '`c674x`'.

`-mbig-endian`

Generate code for a big-endian target.

`-mlittle-endian`

Generate code for a little-endian target. This is the default.

`-msim` Choose startup files and linker script suitable for the simulator.

`-msdata=default`

Put small global and static data in the `.neardata` section, which is pointed to by register `B14`. Put small uninitialized global and static data in the `.bss` section, which is adjacent to the `.neardata` section. Put small read-only data into the `.rodata` section. The corresponding sections used for large pieces of data are `.fardata`, `.far` and `.const`.

`-msdata=all`

Put all data, not just small objects, into the sections reserved for small data, and use addressing relative to the `B14` register to access them.

`-msdata=none`
: Make no use of the sections reserved for small data, and use absolute addresses to access all data. Put all initialized global and static data in the `.fardata` section, and all uninitialized data in the `.far` section. Put all constant data into the `.const` section.

3.18.8 CRIS Options

These options are defined specifically for the CRIS ports.

`-march=`*`architecture-type`*
`-mcpu=`*`architecture-type`*
: Generate code for the specified architecture. The choices for *architecture-type* are '`v3`', '`v8`' and '`v10`' for respectively ETRAX 4, ETRAX 100, and ETRAX 100 LX. Default is '`v0`' except for cris-axis-linux-gnu, where the default is '`v10`'.

`-mtune=`*`architecture-type`*
: Tune to *architecture-type* everything applicable about the generated code, except for the ABI and the set of available instructions. The choices for *architecture-type* are the same as for '`-march=`*`architecture-type`*'.

`-mmax-stack-frame=`*`n`*
: Warn when the stack frame of a function exceeds *n* bytes.

`-metrax4`
`-metrax100`
: The options '`-metrax4`' and '`-metrax100`' are synonyms for '`-march=v3`' and '`-march=v8`' respectively.

`-mmul-bug-workaround`
`-mno-mul-bug-workaround`
: Work around a bug in the `muls` and `mulu` instructions for CPU models where it applies. This option is active by default.

`-mpdebug`
: Enable CRIS-specific verbose debug-related information in the assembly code. This option also has the effect of turning off the '`#NO_APP`' formatted-code indicator to the assembler at the beginning of the assembly file.

`-mcc-init`
: Do not use condition-code results from previous instruction; always emit compare and test instructions before use of condition codes.

`-mno-side-effects`
: Do not emit instructions with side effects in addressing modes other than post-increment.

`-mstack-align`
`-mno-stack-align`
`-mdata-align`
`-mno-data-align`
`-mconst-align`
`-mno-const-align`

These options ('`no-`' options) arrange (eliminate arrangements) for the stack frame, individual data and constants to be aligned for the maximum single data access size for the chosen CPU model. The default is to arrange for 32-bit alignment. ABI details such as structure layout are not affected by these options.

`-m32-bit`
`-m16-bit`
`-m8-bit`

Similar to the stack- data- and const-align options above, these options arrange for stack frame, writable data and constants to all be 32-bit, 16-bit or 8-bit aligned. The default is 32-bit alignment.

`-mno-prologue-epilogue`
`-mprologue-epilogue`

With '`-mno-prologue-epilogue`', the normal function prologue and epilogue which set up the stack frame are omitted and no return instructions or return sequences are generated in the code. Use this option only together with visual inspection of the compiled code: no warnings or errors are generated when call-saved registers must be saved, or storage for local variables needs to be allocated.

`-mno-gotplt`
`-mgotplt`

With '`-fpic`' and '`-fPIC`', don't generate (do generate) instruction sequences that load addresses for functions from the PLT part of the GOT rather than (traditional on other architectures) calls to the PLT. The default is '`-mgotplt`'.

`-melf`

Legacy no-op option only recognized with the cris-axis-elf and cris-axis-linux-gnu targets.

`-mlinux`

Legacy no-op option only recognized with the cris-axis-linux-gnu target.

`-sim`

This option, recognized for the cris-axis-elf, arranges to link with input-output functions from a simulator library. Code, initialized data and zero-initialized data are allocated consecutively.

`-sim2`

Like '`-sim`', but pass linker options to locate initialized data at 0x40000000 and zero-initialized data at 0x80000000.

3.18.9 CR16 Options

These options are defined specifically for the CR16 ports.

`-mmac`

Enable the use of multiply-accumulate instructions. Disabled by default.

`-mcr16cplus`
`-mcr16c`

Generate code for CR16C or CR16C+ architecture. CR16C+ architecture is default.

`-msim` Links the library libsim.a which is in compatible with simulator. Applicable to ELF compiler only.

`-mint32` Choose integer type as 32-bit wide.

`-mbit-ops`
Generates `sbit/cbit` instructions for bit manipulations.

`-mdata-model=`*model*
Choose a data model. The choices for *model* are '`near`', '`far`' or '`medium`'. '`medium`' is default. However, '`far`' is not valid with '`-mcr16c`', as the CR16C architecture does not support the far data model.

3.18.10 Darwin Options

These options are defined for all architectures running the Darwin operating system.

FSF GCC on Darwin does not create "fat" object files; it creates an object file for the single architecture that GCC was built to target. Apple's GCC on Darwin does create "fat" files if multiple '`-arch`' options are used; it does so by running the compiler or linker multiple times and joining the results together with '`lipo`'.

The subtype of the file created (like '`ppc7400`' or '`ppc970`' or '`i686`') is determined by the flags that specify the ISA that GCC is targeting, like '`-mcpu`' or '`-march`'. The '`-force_cpusubtype_ALL`' option can be used to override this.

The Darwin tools vary in their behavior when presented with an ISA mismatch. The assembler, '`as`', only permits instructions to be used that are valid for the subtype of the file it is generating, so you cannot put 64-bit instructions in a '`ppc750`' object file. The linker for shared libraries, '`/usr/bin/libtool`', fails and prints an error if asked to create a shared library with a less restrictive subtype than its input files (for instance, trying to put a '`ppc970`' object file in a '`ppc7400`' library). The linker for executables, `ld`, quietly gives the executable the most restrictive subtype of any of its input files.

`-F`*dir* Add the framework directory *dir* to the head of the list of directories to be searched for header files. These directories are interleaved with those specified by '`-I`' options and are scanned in a left-to-right order.

A framework directory is a directory with frameworks in it. A framework is a directory with a '`Headers`' and/or '`PrivateHeaders`' directory contained directly in it that ends in '`.framework`'. The name of a framework is the name of this directory excluding the '`.framework`'. Headers associated with the framework are found in one of those two directories, with '`Headers`' being searched first. A subframework is a framework directory that is in a framework's '`Frameworks`' directory. Includes of subframework headers can only appear in a header of a framework that contains the subframework, or in a sibling subframework header. Two subframeworks are siblings if they occur in the same framework. A subframework should not have the same name as a framework; a warning is issued if this is violated. Currently a subframework cannot have subframeworks; in the future, the mechanism may be extended to support this. The standard frameworks can be found in '`/System/Library/Frameworks`' and '`/Library/Frameworks`'. An example include looks like `#include <Framework/header.h>`, where

'`Framework`' denotes the name of the framework and '`header.h`' is found in the '`PrivateHeaders`' or '`Headers`' directory.

`-iframework`*`dir`*
: Like '`-F`' except the directory is a treated as a system directory. The main difference between this '`-iframework`' and '`-F`' is that with '`-iframework`' the compiler does not warn about constructs contained within header files found via *dir*. This option is valid only for the C family of languages.

`-gused`
: Emit debugging information for symbols that are used. For stabs debugging format, this enables '`-feliminate-unused-debug-symbols`'. This is by default ON.

`-gfull`
: Emit debugging information for all symbols and types.

`-mmacosx-version-min=`*`version`*
: The earliest version of MacOS X that this executable will run on is *version*. Typical values of *version* include `10.1`, `10.2`, and `10.3.9`.

If the compiler was built to use the system's headers by default, then the default for this option is the system version on which the compiler is running, otherwise the default is to make choices that are compatible with as many systems and code bases as possible.

`-mkernel`
: Enable kernel development mode. The '`-mkernel`' option sets '`-static`', '`-fno-common`', '`-fno-use-cxa-atexit`', '`-fno-exceptions`', '`-fno-non-call-exceptions`', '`-fapple-kext`', '`-fno-weak`' and '`-fno-rtti`' where applicable. This mode also sets '`-mno-altivec`', '`-msoft-float`', '`-fno-builtin`' and '`-mlong-branch`' for PowerPC targets.

`-mone-byte-bool`
: Override the defaults for `bool` so that `sizeof(bool)==1`. By default `sizeof(bool)` is `4` when compiling for Darwin/PowerPC and `1` when compiling for Darwin/x86, so this option has no effect on x86.

Warning: The '`-mone-byte-bool`' switch causes GCC to generate code that is not binary compatible with code generated without that switch. Using this switch may require recompiling all other modules in a program, including system libraries. Use this switch to conform to a non-default data model.

`-mfix-and-continue`
`-ffix-and-continue`
`-findirect-data`
: Generate code suitable for fast turnaround development, such as to allow GDB to dynamically load '`.o`' files into already-running programs. '`-findirect-data`' and '`-ffix-and-continue`' are provided for backwards compatibility.

`-all_load`
: Loads all members of static archive libraries. See man ld(1) for more information.

`-arch_errors_fatal`
: Cause the errors having to do with files that have the wrong architecture to be fatal.

`-bind_at_load`
: Causes the output file to be marked such that the dynamic linker will bind all undefined references when the file is loaded or launched.

`-bundle`
: Produce a Mach-o bundle format file. See man ld(1) for more information.

`-bundle_loader` *executable*
: This option specifies the *executable* that will load the build output file being linked. See man ld(1) for more information.

`-dynamiclib`
: When passed this option, GCC produces a dynamic library instead of an executable when linking, using the Darwin '`libtool`' command.

`-force_cpusubtype_ALL`
: This causes GCC's output file to have the '`ALL`' subtype, instead of one controlled by the '`-mcpu`' or '`-march`' option.

`-allowable_client` *client_name*
`-client_name`
`-compatibility_version`
`-current_version`
`-dead_strip`
`-dependency-file`
`-dylib_file`
`-dylinker_install_name`
`-dynamic`
`-exported_symbols_list`
`-filelist`
`-flat_namespace`
`-force_flat_namespace`
`-headerpad_max_install_names`
`-image_base`
`-init`
`-install_name`
`-keep_private_externs`
`-multi_module`
`-multiply_defined`
`-multiply_defined_unused`

-noall_load
-no_dead_strip_inits_and_terms
-nofixprebinding
-nomultidefs
-noprebind
-noseglinkedit
-pagezero_size
-prebind
-prebind_all_twolevel_modules
-private_bundle
-read_only_relocs
-sectalign
-sectobjectsymbols
-whyload
-seg1addr
-sectcreate
-sectobjectsymbols
-sectorder
-segaddr
-segs_read_only_addr
-segs_read_write_addr
-seg_addr_table
-seg_addr_table_filename
-seglinkedit
-segprot
-segs_read_only_addr
-segs_read_write_addr
-single_module
-static
-sub_library
-sub_umbrella
-twolevel_namespace
-umbrella
-undefined
-unexported_symbols_list
-weak_reference_mismatches
-whatsloaded

These options are passed to the Darwin linker. The Darwin linker man page describes them in detail.

3.18.11 DEC Alpha Options

These '-m' options are defined for the DEC Alpha implementations:

-mno-soft-float
-msoft-float

Use (do not use) the hardware floating-point instructions for floating-point operations. When '-msoft-float' is specified, functions in 'libgcc.a' are used to perform floating-point operations. Unless they are replaced by routines that emulate the floating-point operations, or compiled in such a way as to call such emulations routines, these routines issue floating-point operations. If you are compiling for an Alpha without floating-point operations, you must ensure that the library is built so as not to call them.

Note that Alpha implementations without floating-point operations are required to have floating-point registers.

`-mfp-reg`
`-mno-fp-regs`
: Generate code that uses (does not use) the floating-point register set. '`-mno-fp-regs`' implies '`-msoft-float`'. If the floating-point register set is not used, floating-point operands are passed in integer registers as if they were integers and floating-point results are passed in `$0` instead of `$f0`. This is a non-standard calling sequence, so any function with a floating-point argument or return value called by code compiled with '`-mno-fp-regs`' must also be compiled with that option.

  A typical use of this option is building a kernel that does not use, and hence need not save and restore, any floating-point registers.

`-mieee`
: The Alpha architecture implements floating-point hardware optimized for maximum performance. It is mostly compliant with the IEEE floating-point standard. However, for full compliance, software assistance is required. This option generates code fully IEEE-compliant code *except* that the *inexact-flag* is not maintained (see below). If this option is turned on, the preprocessor macro `_IEEE_FP` is defined during compilation. The resulting code is less efficient but is able to correctly support denormalized numbers and exceptional IEEE values such as not-a-number and plus/minus infinity. Other Alpha compilers call this option '`-ieee_with_no_inexact`'.

`-mieee-with-inexact`
: This is like '`-mieee`' except the generated code also maintains the IEEE *inexact-flag*. Turning on this option causes the generated code to implement fully-compliant IEEE math. In addition to `_IEEE_FP`, `_IEEE_FP_EXACT` is defined as a preprocessor macro. On some Alpha implementations the resulting code may execute significantly slower than the code generated by default. Since there is very little code that depends on the *inexact-flag*, you should normally not specify this option. Other Alpha compilers call this option '`-ieee_with_inexact`'.

`-mfp-trap-mode=`*`trap-mode`*
: This option controls what floating-point related traps are enabled. Other Alpha compilers call this option '`-fptm` *`trap-mode`*'. The trap mode can be set to one of four values:

  '`n`'
  : This is the default (normal) setting. The only traps that are enabled are the ones that cannot be disabled in software (e.g., division by zero trap).

  '`u`'
  : In addition to the traps enabled by '`n`', underflow traps are enabled as well.

'su' Like 'u', but the instructions are marked to be safe for software completion (see Alpha architecture manual for details).

'sui' Like 'su', but inexact traps are enabled as well.

-mfp-rounding-mode=*rounding-mode*
Selects the IEEE rounding mode. Other Alpha compilers call this option '-fprm *rounding-mode*'. The *rounding-mode* can be one of:

'n' Normal IEEE rounding mode. Floating-point numbers are rounded towards the nearest machine number or towards the even machine number in case of a tie.

'm' Round towards minus infinity.

'c' Chopped rounding mode. Floating-point numbers are rounded towards zero.

'd' Dynamic rounding mode. A field in the floating-point control register (*fpcr*, see Alpha architecture reference manual) controls the rounding mode in effect. The C library initializes this register for rounding towards plus infinity. Thus, unless your program modifies the *fpcr*, 'd' corresponds to round towards plus infinity.

-mtrap-precision=*trap-precision*
In the Alpha architecture, floating-point traps are imprecise. This means without software assistance it is impossible to recover from a floating trap and program execution normally needs to be terminated. GCC can generate code that can assist operating system trap handlers in determining the exact location that caused a floating-point trap. Depending on the requirements of an application, different levels of precisions can be selected:

'p' Program precision. This option is the default and means a trap handler can only identify which program caused a floating-point exception.

'f' Function precision. The trap handler can determine the function that caused a floating-point exception.

'i' Instruction precision. The trap handler can determine the exact instruction that caused a floating-point exception.

Other Alpha compilers provide the equivalent options called '-scope_safe' and '-resumption_safe'.

-mieee-conformant
This option marks the generated code as IEEE conformant. You must not use this option unless you also specify '-mtrap-precision=i' and either '-mfp-trap-mode=su' or '-mfp-trap-mode=sui'. Its only effect is to emit the line '.eflag 48' in the function prologue of the generated assembly file.

-mbuild-constants
Normally GCC examines a 32- or 64-bit integer constant to see if it can construct it from smaller constants in two or three instructions. If it cannot, it outputs

the constant as a literal and generates code to load it from the data segment at run time.

Use this option to require GCC to construct *all* integer constants using code, even if it takes more instructions (the maximum is six).

You typically use this option to build a shared library dynamic loader. Itself a shared library, it must relocate itself in memory before it can find the variables and constants in its own data segment.

`-mbwx`
`-mno-bwx`
`-mcix`
`-mno-cix`
`-mfix`
`-mno-fix`
`-mmax`
`-mno-max` Indicate whether GCC should generate code to use the optional BWX, CIX, FIX and MAX instruction sets. The default is to use the instruction sets supported by the CPU type specified via '`-mcpu=`' option or that of the CPU on which GCC was built if none is specified.

`-mfloat-vax`
`-mfloat-ieee`
Generate code that uses (does not use) VAX F and G floating-point arithmetic instead of IEEE single and double precision.

`-mexplicit-relocs`
`-mno-explicit-relocs`
Older Alpha assemblers provided no way to generate symbol relocations except via assembler macros. Use of these macros does not allow optimal instruction scheduling. GNU binutils as of version 2.12 supports a new syntax that allows the compiler to explicitly mark which relocations should apply to which instructions. This option is mostly useful for debugging, as GCC detects the capabilities of the assembler when it is built and sets the default accordingly.

`-msmall-data`
`-mlarge-data`
When '`-mexplicit-relocs`' is in effect, static data is accessed via *gp-relative* relocations. When '`-msmall-data`' is used, objects 8 bytes long or smaller are placed in a *small data area* (the `.sdata` and `.sbss` sections) and are accessed via 16-bit relocations off of the `$gp` register. This limits the size of the small data area to 64KB, but allows the variables to be directly accessed via a single instruction.

The default is '`-mlarge-data`'. With this option the data area is limited to just below 2GB. Programs that require more than 2GB of data must use `malloc` or `mmap` to allocate the data in the heap instead of in the program's data segment.

When generating code for shared libraries, '`-fpic`' implies '`-msmall-data`' and '`-fPIC`' implies '`-mlarge-data`'.

`-msmall-text`
`-mlarge-text`

When '`-msmall-text`' is used, the compiler assumes that the code of the entire program (or shared library) fits in 4MB, and is thus reachable with a branch instruction. When '`-msmall-data`' is used, the compiler can assume that all local symbols share the same `$gp` value, and thus reduce the number of instructions required for a function call from 4 to 1.

The default is '`-mlarge-text`'.

`-mcpu=`*`cpu_type`*

Set the instruction set and instruction scheduling parameters for machine type *cpu_type*. You can specify either the '`EV`' style name or the corresponding chip number. GCC supports scheduling parameters for the EV4, EV5 and EV6 family of processors and chooses the default values for the instruction set from the processor you specify. If you do not specify a processor type, GCC defaults to the processor on which the compiler was built.

Supported values for *cpu_type* are

'`ev4`'
'`ev45`'
'`21064`' Schedules as an EV4 and has no instruction set extensions.

'`ev5`'
'`21164`' Schedules as an EV5 and has no instruction set extensions.

'`ev56`'
'`21164a`' Schedules as an EV5 and supports the BWX extension.

'`pca56`'
'`21164pc`'
'`21164PC`' Schedules as an EV5 and supports the BWX and MAX extensions.

'`ev6`'
'`21264`' Schedules as an EV6 and supports the BWX, FIX, and MAX extensions.

'`ev67`'
'`21264a`' Schedules as an EV6 and supports the BWX, CIX, FIX, and MAX extensions.

Native toolchains also support the value '`native`', which selects the best architecture option for the host processor. '`-mcpu=native`' has no effect if GCC does not recognize the processor.

`-mtune=`*`cpu_type`*

Set only the instruction scheduling parameters for machine type *cpu_type*. The instruction set is not changed.

Native toolchains also support the value '`native`', which selects the best architecture option for the host processor. '`-mtune=native`' has no effect if GCC does not recognize the processor.

`-mmemory-latency=`*`time`*
: Sets the latency the scheduler should assume for typical memory references as seen by the application. This number is highly dependent on the memory access patterns used by the application and the size of the external cache on the machine.

  Valid options for *time* are

  '*`number`*' A decimal number representing clock cycles.

  '`L1`'
  '`L2`'
  '`L3`'
  '`main`' The compiler contains estimates of the number of clock cycles for "typical" EV4 & EV5 hardware for the Level 1, 2 & 3 caches (also called Dcache, Scache, and Bcache), as well as to main memory. Note that L3 is only valid for EV5.

3.18.12 FR30 Options

These options are defined specifically for the FR30 port.

`-msmall-model`
: Use the small address space model. This can produce smaller code, but it does assume that all symbolic values and addresses fit into a 20-bit range.

`-mno-lsim`
: Assume that runtime support has been provided and so there is no need to include the simulator library ('`libsim.a`') on the linker command line.

3.18.13 FT32 Options

These options are defined specifically for the FT32 port.

`-msim` Specifies that the program will be run on the simulator. This causes an alternate runtime startup and library to be linked. You must not use this option when generating programs that will run on real hardware; you must provide your own runtime library for whatever I/O functions are needed.

`-mlra` Enable Local Register Allocation. This is still experimental for FT32, so by default the compiler uses standard reload.

`-mnodiv` Do not use div and mod instructions.

3.18.14 FRV Options

`-mgpr-32`
: Only use the first 32 general-purpose registers.

`-mgpr-64`
: Use all 64 general-purpose registers.

`-mfpr-32`
: Use only the first 32 floating-point registers.

`-mfpr-64`
: Use all 64 floating-point registers.

`-mhard-float`
: Use hardware instructions for floating-point operations.

`-msoft-float`
: Use library routines for floating-point operations.

`-malloc-cc`
: Dynamically allocate condition code registers.

`-mfixed-cc`
: Do not try to dynamically allocate condition code registers, only use `icc0` and `fcc0`.

`-mdword`
: Change ABI to use double word insns.

`-mno-dword`
: Do not use double word instructions.

`-mdouble`
: Use floating-point double instructions.

`-mno-double`
: Do not use floating-point double instructions.

`-mmedia`
: Use media instructions.

`-mno-media`
: Do not use media instructions.

`-mmuladd`
: Use multiply and add/subtract instructions.

`-mno-muladd`
: Do not use multiply and add/subtract instructions.

`-mfdpic`
: Select the FDPIC ABI, which uses function descriptors to represent pointers to functions. Without any PIC/PIE-related options, it implies '`-fPIE`'. With '`-fpic`' or '`-fpie`', it assumes GOT entries and small data are within a 12-bit range from the GOT base address; with '`-fPIC`' or '`-fPIE`', GOT offsets are computed with 32 bits. With a '`bfin-elf`' target, this option implies '`-msim`'.

`-minline-plt`
: Enable inlining of PLT entries in function calls to functions that are not known to bind locally. It has no effect without '`-mfdpic`'. It's enabled by default if optimizing for speed and compiling for shared libraries (i.e., '`-fPIC`' or '`-fpic`'), or when an optimization option such as '`-O3`' or above is present in the command line.

`-mTLS`
: Assume a large TLS segment when generating thread-local code.

`-mtls`
: Do not assume a large TLS segment when generating thread-local code.

`-mgprel-ro`
: Enable the use of `GPREL` relocations in the FDPIC ABI for data that is known to be in read-only sections. It's enabled by default, except for '`-fpic`' or '`-fpie`': even though it may help make the global offset table smaller, it trades 1 instruction for 4. With '`-fPIC`' or '`-fPIE`', it trades 3 instructions for 4, one of which may be shared by multiple symbols, and it avoids the need for a GOT entry for the referenced symbol, so it's more likely to be a win. If it is not, '`-mno-gprel-ro`' can be used to disable it.

`-multilib-library-pic`
: Link with the (library, not FD) pic libraries. It's implied by '`-mlibrary-pic`', as well as by '`-fPIC`' and '`-fpic`' without '`-mfdpic`'. You should never have to use it explicitly.

`-mlinked-fp`
: Follow the EABI requirement of always creating a frame pointer whenever a stack frame is allocated. This option is enabled by default and can be disabled with '`-mno-linked-fp`'.

`-mlong-calls`
: Use indirect addressing to call functions outside the current compilation unit. This allows the functions to be placed anywhere within the 32-bit address space.

`-malign-labels`
: Try to align labels to an 8-byte boundary by inserting NOPs into the previous packet. This option only has an effect when VLIW packing is enabled. It doesn't create new packets; it merely adds NOPs to existing ones.

`-mlibrary-pic`
: Generate position-independent EABI code.

`-macc-4`
: Use only the first four media accumulator registers.

`-macc-8`
: Use all eight media accumulator registers.

`-mpack`
: Pack VLIW instructions.

`-mno-pack`
: Do not pack VLIW instructions.

`-mno-eflags`
: Do not mark ABI switches in e_flags.

`-mcond-move`
: Enable the use of conditional-move instructions (default).

  This switch is mainly for debugging the compiler and will likely be removed in a future version.

`-mno-cond-move`
: Disable the use of conditional-move instructions.

  This switch is mainly for debugging the compiler and will likely be removed in a future version.

`-mscc`
: Enable the use of conditional set instructions (default).

  This switch is mainly for debugging the compiler and will likely be removed in a future version.

`-mno-scc`
: Disable the use of conditional set instructions.

  This switch is mainly for debugging the compiler and will likely be removed in a future version.

`-mcond-exec`
: Enable the use of conditional execution (default).

  This switch is mainly for debugging the compiler and will likely be removed in a future version.

`-mno-cond-exec`
: Disable the use of conditional execution.

  This switch is mainly for debugging the compiler and will likely be removed in a future version.

`-mvliw-branch`
: Run a pass to pack branches into VLIW instructions (default).

  This switch is mainly for debugging the compiler and will likely be removed in a future version.

`-mno-vliw-branch`
: Do not run a pass to pack branches into VLIW instructions.

  This switch is mainly for debugging the compiler and will likely be removed in a future version.

`-mmulti-cond-exec`
: Enable optimization of `&&` and `||` in conditional execution (default).

  This switch is mainly for debugging the compiler and will likely be removed in a future version.

`-mno-multi-cond-exec`
: Disable optimization of `&&` and `||` in conditional execution.

  This switch is mainly for debugging the compiler and will likely be removed in a future version.

`-mnested-cond-exec`
: Enable nested conditional execution optimizations (default).

  This switch is mainly for debugging the compiler and will likely be removed in a future version.

`-mno-nested-cond-exec`
: Disable nested conditional execution optimizations.

  This switch is mainly for debugging the compiler and will likely be removed in a future version.

`-moptimize-membar`
: This switch removes redundant `membar` instructions from the compiler-generated code. It is enabled by default.

`-mno-optimize-membar`
: This switch disables the automatic removal of redundant `membar` instructions from the generated code.

`-mtomcat-stats`
: Cause gas to print out tomcat statistics.

`-mcpu=`*`cpu`*
: Select the processor type for which to generate code. Possible values are '`frv`', '`fr550`', '`tomcat`', '`fr500`', '`fr450`', '`fr405`', '`fr400`', '`fr300`' and '`simple`'.

3.18.15 GNU/Linux Options

These '`-m`' options are defined for GNU/Linux targets:

`-mglibc`
: Use the GNU C library. This is the default except on '`*-*-linux-*uclibc*`', '`*-*-linux-*musl*`' and '`*-*-linux-*android*`' targets.

`-muclibc`
: Use uClibc C library. This is the default on '`*-*-linux-*uclibc*`' targets.

`-mmusl`
: Use the musl C library. This is the default on '`*-*-linux-*musl*`' targets.

`-mbionic`
: Use Bionic C library. This is the default on '`*-*-linux-*android*`' targets.

`-mandroid`
: Compile code compatible with Android platform. This is the default on '`*-*-linux-*android*`' targets.

  When compiling, this option enables '`-mbionic`', '`-fPIC`', '`-fno-exceptions`' and '`-fno-rtti`' by default. When linking, this option makes the GCC driver pass Android-specific options to the linker. Finally, this option causes the preprocessor macro `__ANDROID__` to be defined.

`-tno-android-cc`
: Disable compilation effects of '`-mandroid`', i.e., do not enable '`-mbionic`', '`-fPIC`', '`-fno-exceptions`' and '`-fno-rtti`' by default.

`-tno-android-ld`
: Disable linking effects of '`-mandroid`', i.e., pass standard Linux linking options to the linker.

3.18.16 H8/300 Options

These '-m' options are defined for the H8/300 implementations:

-mrelax
: Shorten some address references at link time, when possible; uses the linker option '-relax'. See Section "ld and the H8/300" in *Using ld*, for a fuller description.

-mh
: Generate code for the H8/300H.

-ms
: Generate code for the H8S.

-mn
: Generate code for the H8S and H8/300H in the normal mode. This switch must be used either with '-mh' or '-ms'.

-ms2600
: Generate code for the H8S/2600. This switch must be used with '-ms'.

-mexr
: Extended registers are stored on stack before execution of function with monitor attribute. Default option is '-mexr'. This option is valid only for H8S targets.

-mno-exr
: Extended registers are not stored on stack before execution of function with monitor attribute. Default option is '-mno-exr'. This option is valid only for H8S targets.

-mint32
: Make int data 32 bits by default.

-malign-300
: On the H8/300H and H8S, use the same alignment rules as for the H8/300. The default for the H8/300H and H8S is to align longs and floats on 4-byte boundaries. '-malign-300' causes them to be aligned on 2-byte boundaries. This option has no effect on the H8/300.

3.18.17 HPPA Options

These '-m' options are defined for the HPPA family of computers:

-march=*architecture-type*
: Generate code for the specified architecture. The choices for *architecture-type* are '1.0' for PA 1.0, '1.1' for PA 1.1, and '2.0' for PA 2.0 processors. Refer to '/usr/lib/sched.models' on an HP-UX system to determine the proper architecture option for your machine. Code compiled for lower numbered architectures runs on higher numbered architectures, but not the other way around.

-mpa-risc-1-0
-mpa-risc-1-1
-mpa-risc-2-0
: Synonyms for '-march=1.0', '-march=1.1', and '-march=2.0' respectively.

-mjump-in-delay
: This option is ignored and provided for compatibility purposes only.

-mdisable-fpregs
: Prevent floating-point registers from being used in any manner. This is necessary for compiling kernels that perform lazy context switching of floating-point registers. If you use this option and attempt to perform floating-point operations, the compiler aborts.

`-mdisable-indexing`
: Prevent the compiler from using indexing address modes. This avoids some rather obscure problems when compiling MIG generated code under MACH.

`-mno-space-regs`
: Generate code that assumes the target has no space registers. This allows GCC to generate faster indirect calls and use unscaled index address modes.

  Such code is suitable for level 0 PA systems and kernels.

`-mfast-indirect-calls`
: Generate code that assumes calls never cross space boundaries. This allows GCC to emit code that performs faster indirect calls.

  This option does not work in the presence of shared libraries or nested functions.

`-mfixed-range=`*`register-range`*
: Generate code treating the given register range as fixed registers. A fixed register is one that the register allocator cannot use. This is useful when compiling kernel code. A register range is specified as two registers separated by a dash. Multiple register ranges can be specified separated by a comma.

`-mlong-load-store`
: Generate 3-instruction load and store sequences as sometimes required by the HP-UX 10 linker. This is equivalent to the '`+k`' option to the HP compilers.

`-mportable-runtime`
: Use the portable calling conventions proposed by HP for ELF systems.

`-mgas`
: Enable the use of assembler directives only GAS understands.

`-mschedule=`*`cpu-type`*
: Schedule code according to the constraints for the machine type *cpu-type*. The choices for *cpu-type* are '`700`' '`7100`', '`7100LC`', '`7200`', '`7300`' and '`8000`'. Refer to '`/usr/lib/sched.models`' on an HP-UX system to determine the proper scheduling option for your machine. The default scheduling is '`8000`'.

`-mlinker-opt`
: Enable the optimization pass in the HP-UX linker. Note this makes symbolic debugging impossible. It also triggers a bug in the HP-UX 8 and HP-UX 9 linkers in which they give bogus error messages when linking some programs.

`-msoft-float`
: Generate output containing library calls for floating point. **Warning:** the requisite libraries are not available for all HPPA targets. Normally the facilities of the machine's usual C compiler are used, but this cannot be done directly in cross-compilation. You must make your own arrangements to provide suitable library functions for cross-compilation.

  '`-msoft-float`' changes the calling convention in the output file; therefore, it is only useful if you compile *all* of a program with this option. In particular, you need to compile '`libgcc.a`', the library that comes with GCC, with '`-msoft-float`' in order for this to work.

`-msio` Generate the predefine, `_SIO`, for server IO. The default is '`-mwsio`'. This generates the predefines, `__hp9000s700`, `__hp9000s700__` and `_WSIO`, for workstation IO. These options are available under HP-UX and HI-UX.

`-mgnu-ld` Use options specific to GNU `ld`. This passes '`-shared`' to `ld` when building a shared library. It is the default when GCC is configured, explicitly or implicitly, with the GNU linker. This option does not affect which `ld` is called; it only changes what parameters are passed to that `ld`. The `ld` that is called is determined by the '`--with-ld`' configure option, GCC's program search path, and finally by the user's `PATH`. The linker used by GCC can be printed using '`which `gcc -print-prog-name=ld``'. This option is only available on the 64-bit HP-UX GCC, i.e. configured with '`hppa*64*-*-hpux*`'.

`-mhp-ld` Use options specific to HP `ld`. This passes '`-b`' to `ld` when building a shared library and passes '`+Accept TypeMismatch`' to `ld` on all links. It is the default when GCC is configured, explicitly or implicitly, with the HP linker. This option does not affect which `ld` is called; it only changes what parameters are passed to that `ld`. The `ld` that is called is determined by the '`--with-ld`' configure option, GCC's program search path, and finally by the user's `PATH`. The linker used by GCC can be printed using '`which `gcc -print-prog-name=ld``'. This option is only available on the 64-bit HP-UX GCC, i.e. configured with '`hppa*64*-*-hpux*`'.

`-mlong-calls`
Generate code that uses long call sequences. This ensures that a call is always able to reach linker generated stubs. The default is to generate long calls only when the distance from the call site to the beginning of the function or translation unit, as the case may be, exceeds a predefined limit set by the branch type being used. The limits for normal calls are 7,600,000 and 240,000 bytes, respectively for the PA 2.0 and PA 1.X architectures. Sibcalls are always limited at 240,000 bytes.

Distances are measured from the beginning of functions when using the '`-ffunction-sections`' option, or when using the '`-mgas`' and '`-mno-portable-runtime`' options together under HP-UX with the SOM linker.

It is normally not desirable to use this option as it degrades performance. However, it may be useful in large applications, particularly when partial linking is used to build the application.

The types of long calls used depends on the capabilities of the assembler and linker, and the type of code being generated. The impact on systems that support long absolute calls, and long pic symbol-difference or pc-relative calls should be relatively small. However, an indirect call is used on 32-bit ELF systems in pic code and it is quite long.

`-munix=`*`unix-std`*
Generate compiler predefines and select a startfile for the specified UNIX standard. The choices for *unix-std* are '`93`', '`95`' and '`98`'. '`93`' is supported on all HP-UX versions. '`95`' is available on HP-UX 10.10 and later. '`98`' is available

on HP-UX 11.11 and later. The default values are '93' for HP-UX 10.00, '95' for HP-UX 10.10 though to 11.00, and '98' for HP-UX 11.11 and later.

'-munix=93' provides the same predefines as GCC 3.3 and 3.4. '-munix=95' provides additional predefines for XOPEN_UNIX and _XOPEN_SOURCE_EXTENDED, and the startfile 'unix95.o'. '-munix=98' provides additional predefines for _XOPEN_UNIX, _XOPEN_SOURCE_EXTENDED, _INCLUDE__STDC_A1_SOURCE and _INCLUDE_XOPEN_SOURCE_500, and the startfile 'unix98.o'.

It is *important* to note that this option changes the interfaces for various library routines. It also affects the operational behavior of the C library. Thus, *extreme* care is needed in using this option.

Library code that is intended to operate with more than one UNIX standard must test, set and restore the variable __xpg4_extended_mask as appropriate. Most GNU software doesn't provide this capability.

-nolibdld
: Suppress the generation of link options to search libdld.sl when the '-static' option is specified on HP-UX 10 and later.

-static
: The HP-UX implementation of setlocale in libc has a dependency on libdld.sl. There isn't an archive version of libdld.sl. Thus, when the '-static' option is specified, special link options are needed to resolve this dependency.

On HP-UX 10 and later, the GCC driver adds the necessary options to link with libdld.sl when the '-static' option is specified. This causes the resulting binary to be dynamic. On the 64-bit port, the linkers generate dynamic binaries by default in any case. The '-nolibdld' option can be used to prevent the GCC driver from adding these link options.

-threads
: Add support for multithreading with the *dce thread* library under HP-UX. This option sets flags for both the preprocessor and linker.

3.18.18 IA-64 Options

These are the '-m' options defined for the Intel IA-64 architecture.

-mbig-endian
: Generate code for a big-endian target. This is the default for HP-UX.

-mlittle-endian
: Generate code for a little-endian target. This is the default for AIX5 and GNU/Linux.

-mgnu-as
-mno-gnu-as
: Generate (or don't) code for the GNU assembler. This is the default.

-mgnu-ld
-mno-gnu-ld
: Generate (or don't) code for the GNU linker. This is the default.

-mno-pic
: Generate code that does not use a global pointer register. The result is not position independent code, and violates the IA-64 ABI.

`-mvolatile-asm-stop`
`-mno-volatile-asm-stop`
Generate (or don't) a stop bit immediately before and after volatile asm statements.

`-mregister-names`
`-mno-register-names`
Generate (or don't) '`in`', '`loc`', and '`out`' register names for the stacked registers. This may make assembler output more readable.

`-mno-sdata`
`-msdata` Disable (or enable) optimizations that use the small data section. This may be useful for working around optimizer bugs.

`-mconstant-gp`
Generate code that uses a single constant global pointer value. This is useful when compiling kernel code.

`-mauto-pic`
Generate code that is self-relocatable. This implies '`-mconstant-gp`'. This is useful when compiling firmware code.

`-minline-float-divide-min-latency`
Generate code for inline divides of floating-point values using the minimum latency algorithm.

`-minline-float-divide-max-throughput`
Generate code for inline divides of floating-point values using the maximum throughput algorithm.

`-mno-inline-float-divide`
Do not generate inline code for divides of floating-point values.

`-minline-int-divide-min-latency`
Generate code for inline divides of integer values using the minimum latency algorithm.

`-minline-int-divide-max-throughput`
Generate code for inline divides of integer values using the maximum throughput algorithm.

`-mno-inline-int-divide`
Do not generate inline code for divides of integer values.

`-minline-sqrt-min-latency`
Generate code for inline square roots using the minimum latency algorithm.

`-minline-sqrt-max-throughput`
Generate code for inline square roots using the maximum throughput algorithm.

`-mno-inline-sqrt`
Do not generate inline code for `sqrt`.

`-mfused-madd`
`-mno-fused-madd`
Do (don't) generate code that uses the fused multiply/add or multiply/subtract instructions. The default is to use these instructions.

`-mno-dwarf2-asm`
`-mdwarf2-asm`
Don't (or do) generate assembler code for the DWARF line number debugging info. This may be useful when not using the GNU assembler.

`-mearly-stop-bits`
`-mno-early-stop-bits`
Allow stop bits to be placed earlier than immediately preceding the instruction that triggered the stop bit. This can improve instruction scheduling, but does not always do so.

`-mfixed-range=`*`register-range`*
Generate code treating the given register range as fixed registers. A fixed register is one that the register allocator cannot use. This is useful when compiling kernel code. A register range is specified as two registers separated by a dash. Multiple register ranges can be specified separated by a comma.

`-mtls-size=`*`tls-size`*
Specify bit size of immediate TLS offsets. Valid values are 14, 22, and 64.

`-mtune=`*`cpu-type`*
Tune the instruction scheduling for a particular CPU, Valid values are '`itanium`', '`itanium1`', '`merced`', '`itanium2`', and '`mckinley`'.

`-milp32`
`-mlp64` Generate code for a 32-bit or 64-bit environment. The 32-bit environment sets int, long and pointer to 32 bits. The 64-bit environment sets int to 32 bits and long and pointer to 64 bits. These are HP-UX specific flags.

`-mno-sched-br-data-spec`
`-msched-br-data-spec`
(Dis/En)able data speculative scheduling before reload. This results in generation of `ld.a` instructions and the corresponding check instructions (`ld.c` / `chk.a`). The default setting is disabled.

`-msched-ar-data-spec`
`-mno-sched-ar-data-spec`
(En/Dis)able data speculative scheduling after reload. This results in generation of `ld.a` instructions and the corresponding check instructions (`ld.c` / `chk.a`). The default setting is enabled.

`-mno-sched-control-spec`
`-msched-control-spec`
(Dis/En)able control speculative scheduling. This feature is available only during region scheduling (i.e. before reload). This results in generation of the `ld.s` instructions and the corresponding check instructions `chk.s`. The default setting is disabled.

`-msched-br-in-data-spec`
`-mno-sched-br-in-data-spec`
: (En/Dis)able speculative scheduling of the instructions that are dependent on the data speculative loads before reload. This is effective only with '`-msched-br-data-spec`' enabled. The default setting is enabled.

`-msched-ar-in-data-spec`
`-mno-sched-ar-in-data-spec`
: (En/Dis)able speculative scheduling of the instructions that are dependent on the data speculative loads after reload. This is effective only with '`-msched-ar-data-spec`' enabled. The default setting is enabled.

`-msched-in-control-spec`
`-mno-sched-in-control-spec`
: (En/Dis)able speculative scheduling of the instructions that are dependent on the control speculative loads. This is effective only with '`-msched-control-spec`' enabled. The default setting is enabled.

`-mno-sched-prefer-non-data-spec-insns`
`-msched-prefer-non-data-spec-insns`
: If enabled, data-speculative instructions are chosen for schedule only if there are no other choices at the moment. This makes the use of the data speculation much more conservative. The default setting is disabled.

`-mno-sched-prefer-non-control-spec-insns`
`-msched-prefer-non-control-spec-insns`
: If enabled, control-speculative instructions are chosen for schedule only if there are no other choices at the moment. This makes the use of the control speculation much more conservative. The default setting is disabled.

`-mno-sched-count-spec-in-critical-path`
`-msched-count-spec-in-critical-path`
: If enabled, speculative dependencies are considered during computation of the instructions priorities. This makes the use of the speculation a bit more conservative. The default setting is disabled.

`-msched-spec-ldc`
: Use a simple data speculation check. This option is on by default.

`-msched-control-spec-ldc`
: Use a simple check for control speculation. This option is on by default.

`-msched-stop-bits-after-every-cycle`
: Place a stop bit after every cycle when scheduling. This option is on by default.

`-msched-fp-mem-deps-zero-cost`
: Assume that floating-point stores and loads are not likely to cause a conflict when placed into the same instruction group. This option is disabled by default.

`-msel-sched-dont-check-control-spec`
: Generate checks for control speculation in selective scheduling. This flag is disabled by default.

`-msched-max-memory-insns=max-insns`
: Limit on the number of memory insns per instruction group, giving lower priority to subsequent memory insns attempting to schedule in the same instruction group. Frequently useful to prevent cache bank conflicts. The default value is 1.

`-msched-max-memory-insns-hard-limit`
: Makes the limit specified by 'msched-max-memory-insns' a hard limit, disallowing more than that number in an instruction group. Otherwise, the limit is "soft", meaning that non-memory operations are preferred when the limit is reached, but memory operations may still be scheduled.

3.18.19 LM32 Options

These '-m' options are defined for the LatticeMico32 architecture:

`-mbarrel-shift-enabled`
: Enable barrel-shift instructions.

`-mdivide-enabled`
: Enable divide and modulus instructions.

`-mmultiply-enabled`
: Enable multiply instructions.

`-msign-extend-enabled`
: Enable sign extend instructions.

`-muser-enabled`
: Enable user-defined instructions.

3.18.20 M32C Options

`-mcpu=name`
: Select the CPU for which code is generated. *name* may be one of 'r8c' for the R8C/Tiny series, 'm16c' for the M16C (up to /60) series, 'm32cm' for the M16C/80 series, or 'm32c' for the M32C/80 series.

`-msim`
: Specifies that the program will be run on the simulator. This causes an alternate runtime library to be linked in which supports, for example, file I/O. You must not use this option when generating programs that will run on real hardware; you must provide your own runtime library for whatever I/O functions are needed.

`-memregs=number`
: Specifies the number of memory-based pseudo-registers GCC uses during code generation. These pseudo-registers are used like real registers, so there is a tradeoff between GCC's ability to fit the code into available registers, and the performance penalty of using memory instead of registers. Note that all modules in a program must be compiled with the same value for this option. Because of that, you must not use this option with GCC's default runtime libraries.

3.18.21 M32R/D Options

These '-m' options are defined for Renesas M32R/D architectures:

`-m32r2` Generate code for the M32R/2.

`-m32rx` Generate code for the M32R/X.

`-m32r` Generate code for the M32R. This is the default.

`-mmodel=small`
: Assume all objects live in the lower 16MB of memory (so that their addresses can be loaded with the `ld24` instruction), and assume all subroutines are reachable with the `bl` instruction. This is the default.

  The addressability of a particular object can be set with the `model` attribute.

`-mmodel=medium`
: Assume objects may be anywhere in the 32-bit address space (the compiler generates `seth/add3` instructions to load their addresses), and assume all subroutines are reachable with the `bl` instruction.

`-mmodel=large`
: Assume objects may be anywhere in the 32-bit address space (the compiler generates `seth/add3` instructions to load their addresses), and assume subroutines may not be reachable with the `bl` instruction (the compiler generates the much slower `seth/add3/jl` instruction sequence).

`-msdata=none`
: Disable use of the small data area. Variables are put into one of `.data`, `.bss`, or `.rodata` (unless the `section` attribute has been specified). This is the default.

  The small data area consists of sections `.sdata` and `.sbss`. Objects may be explicitly put in the small data area with the `section` attribute using one of these sections.

`-msdata=sdata`
: Put small global and static data in the small data area, but do not generate special code to reference them.

`-msdata=use`
: Put small global and static data in the small data area, and generate special instructions to reference them.

`-G num` Put global and static objects less than or equal to *num* bytes into the small data or BSS sections instead of the normal data or BSS sections. The default value of *num* is 8. The '`-msdata`' option must be set to one of '`sdata`' or '`use`' for this option to have any effect.

  All modules should be compiled with the same '`-G num`' value. Compiling with different values of *num* may or may not work; if it doesn't the linker gives an error message—incorrect code is not generated.

`-mdebug` Makes the M32R-specific code in the compiler display some statistics that might help in debugging programs.

`-malign-loops`
: Align all loops to a 32-byte boundary.

`-mno-align-loops`
: Do not enforce a 32-byte alignment for loops. This is the default.

`-missue-rate=`*number*
: Issue *number* instructions per cycle. *number* can only be 1 or 2.

`-mbranch-cost=`*number*
: *number* can only be 1 or 2. If it is 1 then branches are preferred over conditional code, if it is 2, then the opposite applies.

`-mflush-trap=`*number*
: Specifies the trap number to use to flush the cache. The default is 12. Valid numbers are between 0 and 15 inclusive.

`-mno-flush-trap`
: Specifies that the cache cannot be flushed by using a trap.

`-mflush-func=`*name*
: Specifies the name of the operating system function to call to flush the cache. The default is '`_flush_cache`', but a function call is only used if a trap is not available.

`-mno-flush-func`
: Indicates that there is no OS function for flushing the cache.

3.18.22 M680x0 Options

These are the '`-m`' options defined for M680x0 and ColdFire processors. The default settings depend on which architecture was selected when the compiler was configured; the defaults for the most common choices are given below.

`-march=`*arch*
: Generate code for a specific M680x0 or ColdFire instruction set architecture. Permissible values of *arch* for M680x0 architectures are: '`68000`', '`68010`', '`68020`', '`68030`', '`68040`', '`68060`' and '`cpu32`'. ColdFire architectures are selected according to Freescale's ISA classification and the permissible values are: '`isaa`', '`isaaplus`', '`isab`' and '`isac`'.

  GCC defines a macro `__mcf`*`arch`*`__` whenever it is generating code for a ColdFire target. The *arch* in this macro is one of the '`-march`' arguments given above.

  When used together, '`-march`' and '`-mtune`' select code that runs on a family of similar processors but that is optimized for a particular microarchitecture.

`-mcpu=`*cpu*
: Generate code for a specific M680x0 or ColdFire processor. The M680x0 *cpus* are: '`68000`', '`68010`', '`68020`', '`68030`', '`68040`', '`68060`', '`68302`', '`68332`' and '`cpu32`'. The ColdFire *cpus* are given by the table below, which also classifies the CPUs into families:

Family	**'`-mcpu`' arguments**
'`51`'	'`51`' '`51ac`' '`51ag`' '`51cn`' '`51em`' '`51je`' '`51jf`' '`51jg`' '`51jm`' '`51mm`' '`51qe`' '`51qm`'

'5206'	'5202' '5204' '5206'
'5206e'	'5206e'
'5208'	'5207' '5208'
'5211a'	'5210a' '5211a'
'5213'	'5211' '5212' '5213'
'5216'	'5214' '5216'
'52235'	'52230' '52231' '52232' '52233' '52234' '52235'
'5225'	'5224' '5225'
'52259'	'52252' '52254' '52255' '52256' '52258' '52259'
'5235'	'5232' '5233' '5234' '5235' '523x'
'5249'	'5249'
'5250'	'5250'
'5271'	'5270' '5271'
'5272'	'5272'
'5275'	'5274' '5275'
'5282'	'5280' '5281' '5282' '528x'
'53017'	'53011' '53012' '53013' '53014' '53015' '53016' '53017'
'5307'	'5307'
'5329'	'5327' '5328' '5329' '532x'
'5373'	'5372' '5373' '537x'
'5407'	'5407'
'5475'	'5470' '5471' '5472' '5473' '5474' '5475' '547x' '5480' '5481' '5482' '5483' '5484' '5485'

'-mcpu=*cpu*' overrides '-march=*arch*' if *arch* is compatible with *cpu*. Other combinations of '-mcpu' and '-march' are rejected.

GCC defines the macro __mcf_cpu_*cpu* when ColdFire target *cpu* is selected. It also defines __mcf_family_*family*, where the value of *family* is given by the table above.

-mtune=*tune*

Tune the code for a particular microarchitecture within the constraints set by '-march' and '-mcpu'. The M680x0 microarchitectures are: '68000', '68010', '68020', '68030', '68040', '68060' and 'cpu32'. The ColdFire microarchitectures are: 'cfv1', 'cfv2', 'cfv3', 'cfv4' and 'cfv4e'.

You can also use '-mtune=68020-40' for code that needs to run relatively well on 68020, 68030 and 68040 targets. '-mtune=68020-60' is similar but includes 68060 targets as well. These two options select the same tuning decisions as '-m68020-40' and '-m68020-60' respectively.

GCC defines the macros __mc*arch* and __mc*arch*__ when tuning for 680x0 architecture *arch*. It also defines mc*arch* unless either '-ansi' or a non-GNU '-std' option is used. If GCC is tuning for a range of architectures, as selected by '-mtune=68020-40' or '-mtune=68020-60', it defines the macros for every architecture in the range.

GCC also defines the macro __m*uarch*__ when tuning for ColdFire microarchitecture *uarch*, where *uarch* is one of the arguments given above.

-m68000

-mc68000 Generate output for a 68000. This is the default when the compiler is configured for 68000-based systems. It is equivalent to '-march=68000'.

Use this option for microcontrollers with a 68000 or EC000 core, including the 68008, 68302, 68306, 68307, 68322, 68328 and 68356.

-m68010 Generate output for a 68010. This is the default when the compiler is configured for 68010-based systems. It is equivalent to '-march=68010'.

-m68020

-mc68020 Generate output for a 68020. This is the default when the compiler is configured for 68020-based systems. It is equivalent to '-march=68020'.

-m68030 Generate output for a 68030. This is the default when the compiler is configured for 68030-based systems. It is equivalent to '-march=68030'.

-m68040 Generate output for a 68040. This is the default when the compiler is configured for 68040-based systems. It is equivalent to '-march=68040'.

This option inhibits the use of 68881/68882 instructions that have to be emulated by software on the 68040. Use this option if your 68040 does not have code to emulate those instructions.

-m68060 Generate output for a 68060. This is the default when the compiler is configured for 68060-based systems. It is equivalent to '-march=68060'.

This option inhibits the use of 68020 and 68881/68882 instructions that have to be emulated by software on the 68060. Use this option if your 68060 does not have code to emulate those instructions.

-mcpu32 Generate output for a CPU32. This is the default when the compiler is configured for CPU32-based systems. It is equivalent to '-march=cpu32'.

Use this option for microcontrollers with a CPU32 or CPU32+ core, including the 68330, 68331, 68332, 68333, 68334, 68336, 68340, 68341, 68349 and 68360.

-m5200 Generate output for a 520X ColdFire CPU. This is the default when the compiler is configured for 520X-based systems. It is equivalent to '-mcpu=5206', and is now deprecated in favor of that option.

Use this option for microcontroller with a 5200 core, including the MCF5202, MCF5203, MCF5204 and MCF5206.

-m5206e Generate output for a 5206e ColdFire CPU. The option is now deprecated in favor of the equivalent '-mcpu=5206e'.

-m528x Generate output for a member of the ColdFire 528X family. The option is now deprecated in favor of the equivalent '-mcpu=528x'.

-m5307 Generate output for a ColdFire 5307 CPU. The option is now deprecated in favor of the equivalent '-mcpu=5307'.

-m5407 Generate output for a ColdFire 5407 CPU. The option is now deprecated in favor of the equivalent '-mcpu=5407'.

-mcfv4e Generate output for a ColdFire V4e family CPU (e.g. 547x/548x). This includes use of hardware floating-point instructions. The option is equivalent to '-mcpu=547x', and is now deprecated in favor of that option.

-m68020-40
: Generate output for a 68040, without using any of the new instructions. This results in code that can run relatively efficiently on either a 68020/68881 or a 68030 or a 68040. The generated code does use the 68881 instructions that are emulated on the 68040.

  The option is equivalent to '-march=68020' '-mtune=68020-40'.

-m68020-60
: Generate output for a 68060, without using any of the new instructions. This results in code that can run relatively efficiently on either a 68020/68881 or a 68030 or a 68040. The generated code does use the 68881 instructions that are emulated on the 68060.

  The option is equivalent to '-march=68020' '-mtune=68020-60'.

-mhard-float
-m68881
: Generate floating-point instructions. This is the default for 68020 and above, and for ColdFire devices that have an FPU. It defines the macro __HAVE_68881__ on M680x0 targets and __mcffpu__ on ColdFire targets.

-msoft-float
: Do not generate floating-point instructions; use library calls instead. This is the default for 68000, 68010, and 68832 targets. It is also the default for ColdFire devices that have no FPU.

-mdiv
-mno-div
: Generate (do not generate) ColdFire hardware divide and remainder instructions. If '-march' is used without '-mcpu', the default is "on" for ColdFire architectures and "off" for M680x0 architectures. Otherwise, the default is taken from the target CPU (either the default CPU, or the one specified by '-mcpu'). For example, the default is "off" for '-mcpu=5206' and "on" for '-mcpu=5206e'.

  GCC defines the macro __mcfhwdiv__ when this option is enabled.

-mshort
: Consider type int to be 16 bits wide, like short int. Additionally, parameters passed on the stack are also aligned to a 16-bit boundary even on targets whose API mandates promotion to 32-bit.

-mno-short
: Do not consider type int to be 16 bits wide. This is the default.

-mnobitfield
-mno-bitfield
: Do not use the bit-field instructions. The '-m68000', '-mcpu32' and '-m5200' options imply '-mnobitfield'.

-mbitfield
: Do use the bit-field instructions. The '-m68020' option implies '-mbitfield'. This is the default if you use a configuration designed for a 68020.

-mrtd
: Use a different function-calling convention, in which functions that take a fixed number of arguments return with the rtd instruction, which pops their arguments while returning. This saves one instruction in the caller since there is no need to pop the arguments there.

This calling convention is incompatible with the one normally used on Unix, so you cannot use it if you need to call libraries compiled with the Unix compiler.

Also, you must provide function prototypes for all functions that take variable numbers of arguments (including `printf`); otherwise incorrect code is generated for calls to those functions.

In addition, seriously incorrect code results if you call a function with too many arguments. (Normally, extra arguments are harmlessly ignored.)

The `rtd` instruction is supported by the 68010, 68020, 68030, 68040, 68060 and CPU32 processors, but not by the 68000 or 5200.

`-mno-rtd` Do not use the calling conventions selected by '`-mrtd`'. This is the default.

`-malign-int`
`-mno-align-int`
Control whether GCC aligns `int`, `long`, `long long`, `float`, `double`, and `long double` variables on a 32-bit boundary ('`-malign-int`') or a 16-bit boundary ('`-mno-align-int`'). Aligning variables on 32-bit boundaries produces code that runs somewhat faster on processors with 32-bit busses at the expense of more memory.

Warning: if you use the '`-malign-int`' switch, GCC aligns structures containing the above types differently than most published application binary interface specifications for the m68k.

`-mpcrel` Use the pc-relative addressing mode of the 68000 directly, instead of using a global offset table. At present, this option implies '`-fpic`', allowing at most a 16-bit offset for pc-relative addressing. '`-fPIC`' is not presently supported with '`-mpcrel`', though this could be supported for 68020 and higher processors.

`-mno-strict-align`
`-mstrict-align`
Do not (do) assume that unaligned memory references are handled by the system.

`-msep-data`
Generate code that allows the data segment to be located in a different area of memory from the text segment. This allows for execute-in-place in an environment without virtual memory management. This option implies '`-fPIC`'.

`-mno-sep-data`
Generate code that assumes that the data segment follows the text segment. This is the default.

`-mid-shared-library`
Generate code that supports shared libraries via the library ID method. This allows for execute-in-place and shared libraries in an environment without virtual memory management. This option implies '`-fPIC`'.

`-mno-id-shared-library`
Generate code that doesn't assume ID-based shared libraries are being used. This is the default.

`-mshared-library-id=n`
: Specifies the identification number of the ID-based shared library being compiled. Specifying a value of 0 generates more compact code; specifying other values forces the allocation of that number to the current library, but is no more space- or time-efficient than omitting this option.

`-mxgot`
`-mno-xgot`
: When generating position-independent code for ColdFire, generate code that works if the GOT has more than 8192 entries. This code is larger and slower than code generated without this option. On M680x0 processors, this option is not needed; '`-fPIC`' suffices.

GCC normally uses a single instruction to load values from the GOT. While this is relatively efficient, it only works if the GOT is smaller than about 64k. Anything larger causes the linker to report an error such as:

```
relocation truncated to fit: R_68K_GOT16O foobar
```

If this happens, you should recompile your code with '`-mxgot`'. It should then work with very large GOTs. However, code generated with '`-mxgot`' is less efficient, since it takes 4 instructions to fetch the value of a global symbol.

Note that some linkers, including newer versions of the GNU linker, can create multiple GOTs and sort GOT entries. If you have such a linker, you should only need to use '`-mxgot`' when compiling a single object file that accesses more than 8192 GOT entries. Very few do.

These options have no effect unless GCC is generating position-independent code.

3.18.23 MCore Options

These are the '`-m`' options defined for the Motorola M*Core processors.

`-mhardlit`
`-mno-hardlit`
: Inline constants into the code stream if it can be done in two instructions or less.

`-mdiv`
`-mno-div` Use the divide instruction. (Enabled by default).

`-mrelax-immediate`
`-mno-relax-immediate`
: Allow arbitrary-sized immediates in bit operations.

`-mwide-bitfields`
`-mno-wide-bitfields`
: Always treat bit-fields as `int`-sized.

`-m4byte-functions`
`-mno-4byte-functions`
: Force all functions to be aligned to a 4-byte boundary.

`-mcallgraph-data`
`-mno-callgraph-data`
: Emit callgraph information.

`-mslow-bytes`
`-mno-slow-bytes`
: Prefer word access when reading byte quantities.

`-mlittle-endian`
`-mbig-endian`
: Generate code for a little-endian target.

`-m210`
`-m340`
: Generate code for the 210 processor.

`-mno-lsim`
: Assume that runtime support has been provided and so omit the simulator library ('`libsim.a)`' from the linker command line.

`-mstack-increment=`*`size`*
: Set the maximum amount for a single stack increment operation. Large values can increase the speed of programs that contain functions that need a large amount of stack space, but they can also trigger a segmentation fault if the stack is extended too much. The default value is 0x1000.

3.18.24 MeP Options

`-mabsdiff`
: Enables the `abs` instruction, which is the absolute difference between two registers.

`-mall-opts`
: Enables all the optional instructions—average, multiply, divide, bit operations, leading zero, absolute difference, min/max, clip, and saturation.

`-maverage`
: Enables the `ave` instruction, which computes the average of two registers.

`-mbased=`*`n`*
: Variables of size *n* bytes or smaller are placed in the `.based` section by default. Based variables use the `$tp` register as a base register, and there is a 128-byte limit to the `.based` section.

`-mbitops`
: Enables the bit operation instructions—bit test (`btstm`), set (`bsetm`), clear (`bclrm`), invert (`bnotm`), and test-and-set (`tas`).

`-mc=`*`name`*
: Selects which section constant data is placed in. *name* may be '`tiny`', '`near`', or '`far`'.

`-mclip`
: Enables the `clip` instruction. Note that '`-mclip`' is not useful unless you also provide '`-mminmax`'.

`-mconfig=`*`name`*
: Selects one of the built-in core configurations. Each MeP chip has one or more modules in it; each module has a core CPU and a variety of coprocessors,

optional instructions, and peripherals. The MeP-Integrator tool, not part of GCC, provides these configurations through this option; using this option is the same as using all the corresponding command-line options. The default configuration is 'default'.

-mcop
: Enables the coprocessor instructions. By default, this is a 32-bit coprocessor. Note that the coprocessor is normally enabled via the '-mconfig=' option.

-mcop32
: Enables the 32-bit coprocessor's instructions.

-mcop64
: Enables the 64-bit coprocessor's instructions.

-mivc2
: Enables IVC2 scheduling. IVC2 is a 64-bit VLIW coprocessor.

-mdc
: Causes constant variables to be placed in the .near section.

-mdiv
: Enables the div and divu instructions.

-meb
: Generate big-endian code.

-mel
: Generate little-endian code.

-mio-volatile
: Tells the compiler that any variable marked with the io attribute is to be considered volatile.

-ml
: Causes variables to be assigned to the .far section by default.

-mleadz
: Enables the leadz (leading zero) instruction.

-mm
: Causes variables to be assigned to the .near section by default.

-mminmax
: Enables the min and max instructions.

-mmult
: Enables the multiplication and multiply-accumulate instructions.

-mno-opts
: Disables all the optional instructions enabled by '-mall-opts'.

-mrepeat
: Enables the repeat and erepeat instructions, used for low-overhead looping.

-ms
: Causes all variables to default to the .tiny section. Note that there is a 65536-byte limit to this section. Accesses to these variables use the %gp base register.

-msatur
: Enables the saturation instructions. Note that the compiler does not currently generate these itself, but this option is included for compatibility with other tools, like as.

-msdram
: Link the SDRAM-based runtime instead of the default ROM-based runtime.

-msim
: Link the simulator run-time libraries.

-msimnovec
: Link the simulator runtime libraries, excluding built-in support for reset and exception vectors and tables.

-mtf
: Causes all functions to default to the .far section. Without this option, functions default to the .near section.

-mtiny=*n*
: Variables that are *n* bytes or smaller are allocated to the .tiny section. These variables use the $gp base register. The default for this option is 4, but note that there's a 65536-byte limit to the .tiny section.

3.18.25 MicroBlaze Options

`-msoft-float`
: Use software emulation for floating point (default).

`-mhard-float`
: Use hardware floating-point instructions.

`-mmemcpy`
: Do not optimize block moves, use `memcpy`.

`-mno-clearbss`
: This option is deprecated. Use '`-fno-zero-initialized-in-bss`' instead.

`-mcpu=`*`cpu-type`*
: Use features of, and schedule code for, the given CPU. Supported values are in the format '`v`*`X`*`.`*`YY`*`.`*`Z`*', where *X* is a major version, *YY* is the minor version, and *Z* is compatibility code. Example values are '`v3.00.a`', '`v4.00.b`', '`v5.00.a`', '`v5.00.b`', '`v5.00.b`', '`v6.00.a`'.

`-mxl-soft-mul`
: Use software multiply emulation (default).

`-mxl-soft-div`
: Use software emulation for divides (default).

`-mxl-barrel-shift`
: Use the hardware barrel shifter.

`-mxl-pattern-compare`
: Use pattern compare instructions.

`-msmall-divides`
: Use table lookup optimization for small signed integer divisions.

`-mxl-stack-check`
: This option is deprecated. Use '`-fstack-check`' instead.

`-mxl-gp-opt`
: Use GP-relative `.sdata`/`.sbss` sections.

`-mxl-multiply-high`
: Use multiply high instructions for high part of 32x32 multiply.

`-mxl-float-convert`
: Use hardware floating-point conversion instructions.

`-mxl-float-sqrt`
: Use hardware floating-point square root instruction.

`-mbig-endian`
: Generate code for a big-endian target.

`-mlittle-endian`
: Generate code for a little-endian target.

`-mxl-reorder`
: Use reorder instructions (swap and byte reversed load/store).

`-mxl-mode-app-model`

Select application model *app-model*. Valid models are

'executable'
: normal executable (default), uses startup code 'crt0.o'.

'xmdstub'
: for use with Xilinx Microprocessor Debugger (XMD) based software intrusive debug agent called xmdstub. This uses startup file 'crt1.o' and sets the start address of the program to 0x800.

'bootstrap'
: for applications that are loaded using a bootloader. This model uses startup file 'crt2.o' which does not contain a processor reset vector handler. This is suitable for transferring control on a processor reset to the bootloader rather than the application.

'novectors'
: for applications that do not require any of the MicroBlaze vectors. This option may be useful for applications running within a monitoring application. This model uses 'crt3.o' as a startup file.

Option '-xl-mode-*app-model*' is a deprecated alias for '-mxl-mode-*app-model*'.

3.18.26 MIPS Options

`-EB` Generate big-endian code.

`-EL` Generate little-endian code. This is the default for 'mips*el-*-*' configurations.

`-march=arch`

Generate code that runs on *arch*, which can be the name of a generic MIPS ISA, or the name of a particular processor. The ISA names are: 'mips1', 'mips2', 'mips3', 'mips4', 'mips32', 'mips32r2', 'mips32r3', 'mips32r5', 'mips32r6', 'mips64', 'mips64r2', 'mips64r3', 'mips64r5' and 'mips64r6'. The processor names are: '4kc', '4km', '4kp', '4ksc', '4kec', '4kem', '4kep', '4ksd', '5kc', '5kf', '20kc', '24kc', '24kf2_1', '24kf1_1', '24kec', '24kef2_1', '24kef1_1', '34kc', '34kf2_1', '34kf1_1', '34kn', '74kc', '74kf2_1', '74kf1_1', '74kf3_2', '1004kc', '1004kf2_1', '1004kf1_1', 'i6400', 'interaptiv', 'loongson2e', 'loongson2f', 'loongson3a', 'm4k', 'm14k', 'm14kc', 'm14ke', 'm14kec', 'm5100', 'm5101', 'octeon', 'octeon+', 'octeon2', 'octeon3', 'orion', 'p5600', 'r2000', 'r3000', 'r3900', 'r4000', 'r4400', 'r4600', 'r4650', 'r4700', 'r6000', 'r8000', 'rm7000', 'rm9000', 'r10000', 'r12000', 'r14000', 'r16000', 'sb1', 'sr71000', 'vr4100', 'vr4111', 'vr4120', 'vr4130', 'vr4300', 'vr5000', 'vr5400', 'vr5500', 'xlr' and 'xlp'. The special value 'from-abi' selects the most compatible architecture for the selected ABI (that is, 'mips1' for 32-bit ABIs and 'mips3' for 64-bit ABIs).

The native Linux/GNU toolchain also supports the value 'native', which selects the best architecture option for the host processor. '-march=native' has no effect if GCC does not recognize the processor.

In processor names, a final '000' can be abbreviated as 'k' (for example, '-march=r2k'). Prefixes are optional, and 'vr' may be written 'r'.

Names of the form 'nf2_1' refer to processors with FPUs clocked at half the rate of the core, names of the form 'nf1_1' refer to processors with FPUs clocked at the same rate as the core, and names of the form 'nf3_2' refer to processors with FPUs clocked a ratio of 3:2 with respect to the core. For compatibility reasons, 'nf' is accepted as a synonym for 'nf2_1' while 'nx' and 'bfx' are accepted as synonyms for 'nf1_1'.

GCC defines two macros based on the value of this option. The first is _MIPS_ARCH, which gives the name of target architecture, as a string. The second has the form _MIPS_ARCH_*foo*, where *foo* is the capitalized value of _MIPS_ARCH. For example, '-march=r2000' sets _MIPS_ARCH to "r2000" and defines the macro _MIPS_ARCH_R2000.

Note that the _MIPS_ARCH macro uses the processor names given above. In other words, it has the full prefix and does not abbreviate '000' as 'k'. In the case of 'from-abi', the macro names the resolved architecture (either "mips1" or "mips3"). It names the default architecture when no '-march' option is given.

-mtune=*arch*

Optimize for *arch*. Among other things, this option controls the way instructions are scheduled, and the perceived cost of arithmetic operations. The list of *arch* values is the same as for '-march'.

When this option is not used, GCC optimizes for the processor specified by '-march'. By using '-march' and '-mtune' together, it is possible to generate code that runs on a family of processors, but optimize the code for one particular member of that family.

'-mtune' defines the macros _MIPS_TUNE and _MIPS_TUNE_*foo*, which work in the same way as the '-march' ones described above.

-mips1 Equivalent to '-march=mips1'.

-mips2 Equivalent to '-march=mips2'.

-mips3 Equivalent to '-march=mips3'.

-mips4 Equivalent to '-march=mips4'.

-mips32 Equivalent to '-march=mips32'.

-mips32r3

Equivalent to '-march=mips32r3'.

-mips32r5

Equivalent to '-march=mips32r5'.

-mips32r6

Equivalent to '-march=mips32r6'.

-mips64 Equivalent to '-march=mips64'.

-mips64r2

Equivalent to '-march=mips64r2'.

`-mips64r3`
Equivalent to '`-march=mips64r3`'.

`-mips64r5`
Equivalent to '`-march=mips64r5`'.

`-mips64r6`
Equivalent to '`-march=mips64r6`'.

`-mips16`
`-mno-mips16`
Generate (do not generate) MIPS16 code. If GCC is targeting a MIPS32 or MIPS64 architecture, it makes use of the MIPS16e ASE.

MIPS16 code generation can also be controlled on a per-function basis by means of `mips16` and `nomips16` attributes. See Section 6.31 [Function Attributes], page 407, for more information.

`-mflip-mips16`
Generate MIPS16 code on alternating functions. This option is provided for regression testing of mixed MIPS16/non-MIPS16 code generation, and is not intended for ordinary use in compiling user code.

`-minterlink-compressed`
`-mno-interlink-compressed`
Require (do not require) that code using the standard (uncompressed) MIPS ISA be link-compatible with MIPS16 and microMIPS code, and vice versa.

For example, code using the standard ISA encoding cannot jump directly to MIPS16 or microMIPS code; it must either use a call or an indirect jump. '`-minterlink-compressed`' therefore disables direct jumps unless GCC knows that the target of the jump is not compressed.

`-minterlink-mips16`
`-mno-interlink-mips16`
Aliases of '`-minterlink-compressed`' and '`-mno-interlink-compressed`'. These options predate the microMIPS ASE and are retained for backwards compatibility.

`-mabi=32`
`-mabi=o64`
`-mabi=n32`
`-mabi=64`
`-mabi=eabi`
Generate code for the given ABI.

Note that the EABI has a 32-bit and a 64-bit variant. GCC normally generates 64-bit code when you select a 64-bit architecture, but you can use '`-mgp32`' to get 32-bit code instead.

For information about the O64 ABI, see `http://gcc.gnu.org/projects/mipso64-abi.html`.

GCC supports a variant of the o32 ABI in which floating-point registers are 64 rather than 32 bits wide. You can select this combination with '`-mabi=32`'

'-mfp64'. This ABI relies on the mthc1 and mfhc1 instructions and is therefore only supported for MIPS32R2, MIPS32R3 and MIPS32R5 processors.

The register assignments for arguments and return values remain the same, but each scalar value is passed in a single 64-bit register rather than a pair of 32-bit registers. For example, scalar floating-point values are returned in '$f0' only, not a '$f0'/'$f1' pair. The set of call-saved registers also remains the same in that the even-numbered double-precision registers are saved.

Two additional variants of the o32 ABI are supported to enable a transition from 32-bit to 64-bit registers. These are FPXX ('-mfpxx') and FP64A ('-mfp64' '-mno-odd-spreg'). The FPXX extension mandates that all code must execute correctly when run using 32-bit or 64-bit registers. The code can be interlinked with either FP32 or FP64, but not both. The FP64A extension is similar to the FP64 extension but forbids the use of odd-numbered single-precision registers. This can be used in conjunction with the FRE mode of FPUs in MIPS32R5 processors and allows both FP32 and FP64A code to interlink and run in the same process without changing FPU modes.

-mabicalls
-mno-abicalls
Generate (do not generate) code that is suitable for SVR4-style dynamic objects. '-mabicalls' is the default for SVR4-based systems.

-mshared
-mno-shared
Generate (do not generate) code that is fully position-independent, and that can therefore be linked into shared libraries. This option only affects '-mabicalls'.

All '-mabicalls' code has traditionally been position-independent, regardless of options like '-fPIC' and '-fpic'. However, as an extension, the GNU toolchain allows executables to use absolute accesses for locally-binding symbols. It can also use shorter GP initialization sequences and generate direct calls to locally-defined functions. This mode is selected by '-mno-shared'.

'-mno-shared' depends on binutils 2.16 or higher and generates objects that can only be linked by the GNU linker. However, the option does not affect the ABI of the final executable; it only affects the ABI of relocatable objects. Using '-mno-shared' generally makes executables both smaller and quicker.

'-mshared' is the default.

-mplt
-mno-plt
Assume (do not assume) that the static and dynamic linkers support PLTs and copy relocations. This option only affects '-mno-shared -mabicalls'. For the n64 ABI, this option has no effect without '-msym32'.

You can make '-mplt' the default by configuring GCC with '--with-mips-plt'. The default is '-mno-plt' otherwise.

-mxgot
-mno-xgot
Lift (do not lift) the usual restrictions on the size of the global offset table.

GCC normally uses a single instruction to load values from the GOT. While this is relatively efficient, it only works if the GOT is smaller than about 64k. Anything larger causes the linker to report an error such as:

```
relocation truncated to fit: R_MIPS_GOT16 foobar
```

If this happens, you should recompile your code with '`-mxgot`'. This works with very large GOTs, although the code is also less efficient, since it takes three instructions to fetch the value of a global symbol.

Note that some linkers can create multiple GOTs. If you have such a linker, you should only need to use '`-mxgot`' when a single object file accesses more than 64k's worth of GOT entries. Very few do.

These options have no effect unless GCC is generating position independent code.

`-mgp32` Assume that general-purpose registers are 32 bits wide.

`-mgp64` Assume that general-purpose registers are 64 bits wide.

`-mfp32` Assume that floating-point registers are 32 bits wide.

`-mfp64` Assume that floating-point registers are 64 bits wide.

`-mfpxx` Do not assume the width of floating-point registers.

`-mhard-float`
: Use floating-point coprocessor instructions.

`-msoft-float`
: Do not use floating-point coprocessor instructions. Implement floating-point calculations using library calls instead.

`-mno-float`
: Equivalent to '`-msoft-float`', but additionally asserts that the program being compiled does not perform any floating-point operations. This option is presently supported only by some bare-metal MIPS configurations, where it may select a special set of libraries that lack all floating-point support (including, for example, the floating-point `printf` formats). If code compiled with '`-mno-float`' accidentally contains floating-point operations, it is likely to suffer a link-time or run-time failure.

`-msingle-float`
: Assume that the floating-point coprocessor only supports single-precision operations.

`-mdouble-float`
: Assume that the floating-point coprocessor supports double-precision operations. This is the default.

`-modd-spreg`
`-mno-odd-spreg`
: Enable the use of odd-numbered single-precision floating-point registers for the o32 ABI. This is the default for processors that are known to support these registers. When using the o32 FPXX ABI, '`-mno-odd-spreg`' is set by default.

`-mabs=2008`
`-mabs=legacy`

These options control the treatment of the special not-a-number (NaN) IEEE 754 floating-point data with the `abs.`*`fmt`* and `neg.`*`fmt`* machine instructions.

By default or when '`-mabs=legacy`' is used the legacy treatment is selected. In this case these instructions are considered arithmetic and avoided where correct operation is required and the input operand might be a NaN. A longer sequence of instructions that manipulate the sign bit of floating-point datum manually is used instead unless the '`-ffinite-math-only`' option has also been specified.

The '`-mabs=2008`' option selects the IEEE 754-2008 treatment. In this case these instructions are considered non-arithmetic and therefore operating correctly in all cases, including in particular where the input operand is a NaN. These instructions are therefore always used for the respective operations.

`-mnan=2008`
`-mnan=legacy`

These options control the encoding of the special not-a-number (NaN) IEEE 754 floating-point data.

The '`-mnan=legacy`' option selects the legacy encoding. In this case quiet NaNs (qNaNs) are denoted by the first bit of their trailing significand field being 0, whereas signalling NaNs (sNaNs) are denoted by the first bit of their trailing significand field being 1.

The '`-mnan=2008`' option selects the IEEE 754-2008 encoding. In this case qNaNs are denoted by the first bit of their trailing significand field being 1, whereas sNaNs are denoted by the first bit of their trailing significand field being 0.

The default is '`-mnan=legacy`' unless GCC has been configured with '`--with-nan=2008`'.

`-mllsc`
`-mno-llsc`

Use (do not use) '`ll`', '`sc`', and '`sync`' instructions to implement atomic memory built-in functions. When neither option is specified, GCC uses the instructions if the target architecture supports them.

'`-mllsc`' is useful if the runtime environment can emulate the instructions and '`-mno-llsc`' can be useful when compiling for nonstandard ISAs. You can make either option the default by configuring GCC with '`--with-llsc`' and '`--without-llsc`' respectively. '`--with-llsc`' is the default for some configurations; see the installation documentation for details.

`-mdsp`
`-mno-dsp`

Use (do not use) revision 1 of the MIPS DSP ASE. See Section 6.59.12 [MIPS DSP Built-in Functions], page 573. This option defines the preprocessor macro `__mips_dsp`. It also defines `__mips_dsp_rev` to 1.

`-mdspr2`
`-mno-dspr2`
Use (do not use) revision 2 of the MIPS DSP ASE. See Section 6.59.12 [MIPS DSP Built-in Functions], page 573. This option defines the preprocessor macros `__mips_dsp` and `__mips_dspr2`. It also defines `__mips_dsp_rev` to 2.

`-msmartmips`
`-mno-smartmips`
Use (do not use) the MIPS SmartMIPS ASE.

`-mpaired-single`
`-mno-paired-single`
Use (do not use) paired-single floating-point instructions. See Section 6.59.13 [MIPS Paired-Single Support], page 577. This option requires hardware floating-point support to be enabled.

`-mdmx`
`-mno-mdmx`
Use (do not use) MIPS Digital Media Extension instructions. This option can only be used when generating 64-bit code and requires hardware floating-point support to be enabled.

`-mips3d`
`-mno-mips3d`
Use (do not use) the MIPS-3D ASE. See Section 6.59.14.3 [MIPS-3D Built-in Functions], page 581. The option '`-mips3d`' implies '`-mpaired-single`'.

`-mmicromips`
`-mno-micromips`
Generate (do not generate) microMIPS code.

MicroMIPS code generation can also be controlled on a per-function basis by means of `micromips` and `nomicromips` attributes. See Section 6.31 [Function Attributes], page 407, for more information.

`-mmt`
`-mno-mt` Use (do not use) MT Multithreading instructions.

`-mmcu`
`-mno-mcu` Use (do not use) the MIPS MCU ASE instructions.

`-meva`
`-mno-eva` Use (do not use) the MIPS Enhanced Virtual Addressing instructions.

`-mvirt`
`-mno-virt`
Use (do not use) the MIPS Virtualization Application Specific instructions.

`-mxpa`
`-mno-xpa` Use (do not use) the MIPS eXtended Physical Address (XPA) instructions.

`-mlong64` Force `long` types to be 64 bits wide. See '`-mlong32`' for an explanation of the default and the way that the pointer size is determined.

`-mlong32` Force `long`, `int`, and pointer types to be 32 bits wide.

The default size of `int`s, `long`s and pointers depends on the ABI. All the supported ABIs use 32-bit `int`s. The n64 ABI uses 64-bit `long`s, as does the 64-bit EABI; the others use 32-bit `long`s. Pointers are the same size as `long`s, or the same size as integer registers, whichever is smaller.

`-msym32`
`-mno-sym32`
Assume (do not assume) that all symbols have 32-bit values, regardless of the selected ABI. This option is useful in combination with '`-mabi=64`' and '`-mno-abicalls`' because it allows GCC to generate shorter and faster references to symbolic addresses.

`-G` *num* Put definitions of externally-visible data in a small data section if that data is no bigger than *num* bytes. GCC can then generate more efficient accesses to the data; see '`-mgpopt`' for details.

The default '`-G`' option depends on the configuration.

`-mlocal-sdata`
`-mno-local-sdata`
Extend (do not extend) the '`-G`' behavior to local data too, such as to static variables in C. '`-mlocal-sdata`' is the default for all configurations.

If the linker complains that an application is using too much small data, you might want to try rebuilding the less performance-critical parts with '`-mno-local-sdata`'. You might also want to build large libraries with '`-mno-local-sdata`', so that the libraries leave more room for the main program.

`-mextern-sdata`
`-mno-extern-sdata`
Assume (do not assume) that externally-defined data is in a small data section if the size of that data is within the '`-G`' limit. '`-mextern-sdata`' is the default for all configurations.

If you compile a module *Mod* with '`-mextern-sdata`' '`-G` *num*' '`-mgpopt`', and *Mod* references a variable *Var* that is no bigger than *num* bytes, you must make sure that *Var* is placed in a small data section. If *Var* is defined by another module, you must either compile that module with a high-enough '`-G`' setting or attach a `section` attribute to *Var*'s definition. If *Var* is common, you must link the application with a high-enough '`-G`' setting.

The easiest way of satisfying these restrictions is to compile and link every module with the same '`-G`' option. However, you may wish to build a library that supports several different small data limits. You can do this by compiling the library with the highest supported '`-G`' setting and additionally using '`-mno-extern-sdata`' to stop the library from making assumptions about externally-defined data.

`-mgpopt`
`-mno-gpopt`
Use (do not use) GP-relative accesses for symbols that are known to be in a small data section; see '`-G`', '`-mlocal-sdata`' and '`-mextern-sdata`'. '`-mgpopt`' is the default for all configurations.

'`-mno-gpopt`' is useful for cases where the `$gp` register might not hold the value of `_gp`. For example, if the code is part of a library that might be used in a boot monitor, programs that call boot monitor routines pass an unknown value in `$gp`. (In such situations, the boot monitor itself is usually compiled with '`-G0`'.)

'`-mno-gpopt`' implies '`-mno-local-sdata`' and '`-mno-extern-sdata`'.

`-membedded-data`
`-mno-embedded-data`
Allocate variables to the read-only data section first if possible, then next in the small data section if possible, otherwise in data. This gives slightly slower code than the default, but reduces the amount of RAM required when executing, and thus may be preferred for some embedded systems.

`-muninit-const-in-rodata`
`-mno-uninit-const-in-rodata`
Put uninitialized `const` variables in the read-only data section. This option is only meaningful in conjunction with '`-membedded-data`'.

`-mcode-readable=`*`setting`*
Specify whether GCC may generate code that reads from executable sections. There are three possible settings:

`-mcode-readable=yes`
Instructions may freely access executable sections. This is the default setting.

`-mcode-readable=pcrel`
MIPS16 PC-relative load instructions can access executable sections, but other instructions must not do so. This option is useful on 4KSc and 4KSd processors when the code TLBs have the Read Inhibit bit set. It is also useful on processors that can be configured to have a dual instruction/data SRAM interface and that, like the M4K, automatically redirect PC-relative loads to the instruction RAM.

`-mcode-readable=no`
Instructions must not access executable sections. This option can be useful on targets that are configured to have a dual instruction/data SRAM interface but that (unlike the M4K) do not automatically redirect PC-relative loads to the instruction RAM.

`-msplit-addresses`
`-mno-split-addresses`
Enable (disable) use of the `%hi()` and `%lo()` assembler relocation operators. This option has been superseded by '`-mexplicit-relocs`' but is retained for backwards compatibility.

`-mexplicit-relocs`
`-mno-explicit-relocs`
Use (do not use) assembler relocation operators when dealing with symbolic addresses. The alternative, selected by '`-mno-explicit-relocs`', is to use assembler macros instead.

'`-mexplicit-relocs`' is the default if GCC was configured to use an assembler that supports relocation operators.

`-mcheck-zero-division`
`-mno-check-zero-division`
Trap (do not trap) on integer division by zero.

The default is '`-mcheck-zero-division`'.

`-mdivide-traps`
`-mdivide-breaks`
MIPS systems check for division by zero by generating either a conditional trap or a break instruction. Using traps results in smaller code, but is only supported on MIPS II and later. Also, some versions of the Linux kernel have a bug that prevents trap from generating the proper signal (`SIGFPE`). Use '`-mdivide-traps`' to allow conditional traps on architectures that support them and '`-mdivide-breaks`' to force the use of breaks.

The default is usually '`-mdivide-traps`', but this can be overridden at configure time using '`--with-divide=breaks`'. Divide-by-zero checks can be completely disabled using '`-mno-check-zero-division`'.

`-mmemcpy`
`-mno-memcpy`
Force (do not force) the use of `memcpy` for non-trivial block moves. The default is '`-mno-memcpy`', which allows GCC to inline most constant-sized copies.

`-mlong-calls`
`-mno-long-calls`
Disable (do not disable) use of the `jal` instruction. Calling functions using `jal` is more efficient but requires the caller and callee to be in the same 256 megabyte segment.

This option has no effect on abicalls code. The default is '`-mno-long-calls`'.

`-mmad`
`-mno-mad` Enable (disable) use of the `mad`, `madu` and `mul` instructions, as provided by the R4650 ISA.

`-mimadd`
`-mno-imadd`
Enable (disable) use of the `madd` and `msub` integer instructions. The default is '`-mimadd`' on architectures that support `madd` and `msub` except for the 74k architecture where it was found to generate slower code.

`-mfused-madd`
`-mno-fused-madd`
Enable (disable) use of the floating-point multiply-accumulate instructions, when they are available. The default is '`-mfused-madd`'.

On the R8000 CPU when multiply-accumulate instructions are used, the intermediate product is calculated to infinite precision and is not subject to the FCSR Flush to Zero bit. This may be undesirable in some circumstances. On other processors the result is numerically identical to the equivalent computation using separate multiply, add, subtract and negate instructions.

`-nocpp` Tell the MIPS assembler to not run its preprocessor over user assembler files (with a '`.s`' suffix) when assembling them.

`-mfix-24k`
`-mno-fix-24k`
Work around the 24K E48 (lost data on stores during refill) errata. The workarounds are implemented by the assembler rather than by GCC.

`-mfix-r4000`
`-mno-fix-r4000`
Work around certain R4000 CPU errata:

- A double-word or a variable shift may give an incorrect result if executed immediately after starting an integer division.
- A double-word or a variable shift may give an incorrect result if executed while an integer multiplication is in progress.
- An integer division may give an incorrect result if started in a delay slot of a taken branch or a jump.

`-mfix-r4400`
`-mno-fix-r4400`
Work around certain R4400 CPU errata:

- A double-word or a variable shift may give an incorrect result if executed immediately after starting an integer division.

`-mfix-r10000`
`-mno-fix-r10000`
Work around certain R10000 errata:

- `ll`/`sc` sequences may not behave atomically on revisions prior to 3.0. They may deadlock on revisions 2.6 and earlier.

This option can only be used if the target architecture supports branch-likely instructions. '`-mfix-r10000`' is the default when '`-march=r10000`' is used; '`-mno-fix-r10000`' is the default otherwise.

`-mfix-rm7000`
`-mno-fix-rm7000`
Work around the RM7000 `dmult`/`dmultu` errata. The workarounds are implemented by the assembler rather than by GCC.

`-mfix-vr4120`
`-mno-fix-vr4120`
Work around certain VR4120 errata:

- `dmultu` does not always produce the correct result.
- `div` and `ddiv` do not always produce the correct result if one of the operands is negative.

The workarounds for the division errata rely on special functions in '`libgcc.a`'. At present, these functions are only provided by the `mips64vr*-elf` configurations.

Other VR4120 errata require a NOP to be inserted between certain pairs of instructions. These errata are handled by the assembler, not by GCC itself.

`-mfix-vr4130`
Work around the VR4130 `mflo`/`mfhi` errata. The workarounds are implemented by the assembler rather than by GCC, although GCC avoids using `mflo` and `mfhi` if the VR4130 `macc`, `macchi`, `dmacc` and `dmacchi` instructions are available instead.

`-mfix-sb1`
`-mno-fix-sb1`
Work around certain SB-1 CPU core errata. (This flag currently works around the SB-1 revision 2 "F1" and "F2" floating-point errata.)

`-mr10k-cache-barrier=`*`setting`*
Specify whether GCC should insert cache barriers to avoid the side-effects of speculation on R10K processors.

In common with many processors, the R10K tries to predict the outcome of a conditional branch and speculatively executes instructions from the "taken" branch. It later aborts these instructions if the predicted outcome is wrong. However, on the R10K, even aborted instructions can have side effects.

This problem only affects kernel stores and, depending on the system, kernel loads. As an example, a speculatively-executed store may load the target memory into cache and mark the cache line as dirty, even if the store itself is later aborted. If a DMA operation writes to the same area of memory before the "dirty" line is flushed, the cached data overwrites the DMA-ed data. See the R10K processor manual for a full description, including other potential problems.

One workaround is to insert cache barrier instructions before every memory access that might be speculatively executed and that might have side effects even if aborted. '`-mr10k-cache-barrier=`*`setting`*' controls GCC's implementation of this workaround. It assumes that aborted accesses to any byte in the following regions does not have side effects:

1. the memory occupied by the current function's stack frame;
2. the memory occupied by an incoming stack argument;
3. the memory occupied by an object with a link-time-constant address.

It is the kernel's responsibility to ensure that speculative accesses to these regions are indeed safe.

If the input program contains a function declaration such as:

```
void foo (void);
```

then the implementation of `foo` must allow `j foo` and `jal foo` to be executed speculatively. GCC honors this restriction for functions it compiles itself. It expects non-GCC functions (such as hand-written assembly code) to do the same.

The option has three forms:

`-mr10k-cache-barrier=load-store`
: Insert a cache barrier before a load or store that might be speculatively executed and that might have side effects even if aborted.

`-mr10k-cache-barrier=store`
: Insert a cache barrier before a store that might be speculatively executed and that might have side effects even if aborted.

`-mr10k-cache-barrier=none`
: Disable the insertion of cache barriers. This is the default setting.

`-mflush-func=`*`func`*
`-mno-flush-func`
: Specifies the function to call to flush the I and D caches, or to not call any such function. If called, the function must take the same arguments as the common `_flush_func`, that is, the address of the memory range for which the cache is being flushed, the size of the memory range, and the number 3 (to flush both caches). The default depends on the target GCC was configured for, but commonly is either `_flush_func` or `__cpu_flush`.

`mbranch-cost=`*`num`*
: Set the cost of branches to roughly *num* "simple" instructions. This cost is only a heuristic and is not guaranteed to produce consistent results across releases. A zero cost redundantly selects the default, which is based on the '`-mtune`' setting.

`-mbranch-likely`
`-mno-branch-likely`
: Enable or disable use of Branch Likely instructions, regardless of the default for the selected architecture. By default, Branch Likely instructions may be generated if they are supported by the selected architecture. An exception is for the MIPS32 and MIPS64 architectures and processors that implement those architectures; for those, Branch Likely instructions are not be generated by default because the MIPS32 and MIPS64 architectures specifically deprecate their use.

`-mcompact-branches=never`
`-mcompact-branches=optimal`
`-mcompact-branches=always`

These options control which form of branches will be generated. The default is '-mcompact-branches=optimal'.

The '-mcompact-branches=never' option ensures that compact branch instructions will never be generated.

The '-mcompact-branches=always' option ensures that a compact branch instruction will be generated if available. If a compact branch instruction is not available, a delay slot form of the branch will be used instead.

This option is supported from MIPS Release 6 onwards.

The '-mcompact-branches=optimal' option will cause a delay slot branch to be used if one is available in the current ISA and the delay slot is successfully filled. If the delay slot is not filled, a compact branch will be chosen if one is available.

`-mfp-exceptions`
`-mno-fp-exceptions`

Specifies whether FP exceptions are enabled. This affects how FP instructions are scheduled for some processors. The default is that FP exceptions are enabled.

For instance, on the SB-1, if FP exceptions are disabled, and we are emitting 64-bit code, then we can use both FP pipes. Otherwise, we can only use one FP pipe.

`-mvr4130-align`
`-mno-vr4130-align`

The VR4130 pipeline is two-way superscalar, but can only issue two instructions together if the first one is 8-byte aligned. When this option is enabled, GCC aligns pairs of instructions that it thinks should execute in parallel.

This option only has an effect when optimizing for the VR4130. It normally makes code faster, but at the expense of making it bigger. It is enabled by default at optimization level '-O3'.

`-msynci`
`-mno-synci`

Enable (disable) generation of `synci` instructions on architectures that support it. The `synci` instructions (if enabled) are generated when `__builtin___clear_cache` is compiled.

This option defaults to '-mno-synci', but the default can be overridden by configuring GCC with '--with-synci'.

When compiling code for single processor systems, it is generally safe to use `synci`. However, on many multi-core (SMP) systems, it does not invalidate the instruction caches on all cores and may lead to undefined behavior.

-mrelax-pic-calls
-mno-relax-pic-calls

Try to turn PIC calls that are normally dispatched via register $25 into direct calls. This is only possible if the linker can resolve the destination at link time and if the destination is within range for a direct call.

'-mrelax-pic-calls' is the default if GCC was configured to use an assembler and a linker that support the .reloc assembly directive and '-mexplicit-relocs' is in effect. With '-mno-explicit-relocs', this optimization can be performed by the assembler and the linker alone without help from the compiler.

-mmcount-ra-address
-mno-mcount-ra-address

Emit (do not emit) code that allows _mcount to modify the calling function's return address. When enabled, this option extends the usual _mcount interface with a new *ra-address* parameter, which has type intptr_t * and is passed in register $12. _mcount can then modify the return address by doing both of the following:

- Returning the new address in register $31.
- Storing the new address in *ra-address, if *ra-address* is nonnull.

The default is '-mno-mcount-ra-address'.

-mframe-header-opt
-mno-frame-header-opt

Enable (disable) frame header optimization in the o32 ABI. When using the o32 ABI, calling functions will allocate 16 bytes on the stack for the called function to write out register arguments. When enabled, this optimization will suppress the allocation of the frame header if it can be determined that it is unused.

This optimization is off by default at all optimization levels.

3.18.27 MMIX Options

These options are defined for the MMIX:

-mlibfuncs
-mno-libfuncs

Specify that intrinsic library functions are being compiled, passing all values in registers, no matter the size.

-mepsilon
-mno-epsilon

Generate floating-point comparison instructions that compare with respect to the rE epsilon register.

-mabi=mmixware
-mabi=gnu

Generate code that passes function parameters and return values that (in the called function) are seen as registers $0 and up, as opposed to the GNU ABI which uses global registers $231 and up.

`-mzero-extend`
`-mno-zero-extend`
: When reading data from memory in sizes shorter than 64 bits, use (do not use) zero-extending load instructions by default, rather than sign-extending ones.

`-mknuthdiv`
`-mno-knuthdiv`
: Make the result of a division yielding a remainder have the same sign as the divisor. With the default, '`-mno-knuthdiv`', the sign of the remainder follows the sign of the dividend. Both methods are arithmetically valid, the latter being almost exclusively used.

`-mtoplevel-symbols`
`-mno-toplevel-symbols`
: Prepend (do not prepend) a '`:`' to all global symbols, so the assembly code can be used with the `PREFIX` assembly directive.

`-melf`
: Generate an executable in the ELF format, rather than the default '`mmo`' format used by the `mmix` simulator.

`-mbranch-predict`
`-mno-branch-predict`
: Use (do not use) the probable-branch instructions, when static branch prediction indicates a probable branch.

`-mbase-addresses`
`-mno-base-addresses`
: Generate (do not generate) code that uses *base addresses*. Using a base address automatically generates a request (handled by the assembler and the linker) for a constant to be set up in a global register. The register is used for one or more base address requests within the range 0 to 255 from the value held in the register. The generally leads to short and fast code, but the number of different data items that can be addressed is limited. This means that a program that uses lots of static data may require '`-mno-base-addresses`'.

`-msingle-exit`
`-mno-single-exit`
: Force (do not force) generated code to have a single exit point in each function.

3.18.28 MN10300 Options

These '`-m`' options are defined for Matsushita MN10300 architectures:

`-mmult-bug`
: Generate code to avoid bugs in the multiply instructions for the MN10300 processors. This is the default.

`-mno-mult-bug`
: Do not generate code to avoid bugs in the multiply instructions for the MN10300 processors.

`-mam33`
: Generate code using features specific to the AM33 processor.

`-mno-am33`
: Do not generate code using features specific to the AM33 processor. This is the default.

`-mam33-2` Generate code using features specific to the AM33/2.0 processor.

`-mam34` Generate code using features specific to the AM34 processor.

`-mtune=`*cpu-type*
: Use the timing characteristics of the indicated CPU type when scheduling instructions. This does not change the targeted processor type. The CPU type must be one of 'mn10300', 'am33', 'am33-2' or 'am34'.

`-mreturn-pointer-on-d0`
: When generating a function that returns a pointer, return the pointer in both a0 and d0. Otherwise, the pointer is returned only in a0, and attempts to call such functions without a prototype result in errors. Note that this option is on by default; use '-mno-return-pointer-on-d0' to disable it.

`-mno-crt0`
: Do not link in the C run-time initialization object file.

`-mrelax` Indicate to the linker that it should perform a relaxation optimization pass to shorten branches, calls and absolute memory addresses. This option only has an effect when used on the command line for the final link step.

This option makes symbolic debugging impossible.

`-mliw` Allow the compiler to generate *Long Instruction Word* instructions if the target is the 'AM33' or later. This is the default. This option defines the preprocessor macro __LIW__.

`-mnoliw` Do not allow the compiler to generate *Long Instruction Word* instructions. This option defines the preprocessor macro __NO_LIW__.

`-msetlb` Allow the compiler to generate the *SETLB* and *Lcc* instructions if the target is the 'AM33' or later. This is the default. This option defines the preprocessor macro __SETLB__.

`-mnosetlb`
: Do not allow the compiler to generate *SETLB* or *Lcc* instructions. This option defines the preprocessor macro __NO_SETLB__.

3.18.29 Moxie Options

`-meb` Generate big-endian code. This is the default for 'moxie-*-*' configurations.

`-mel` Generate little-endian code.

`-mmul.x` Generate mul.x and umul.x instructions. This is the default for 'moxiebox-*-*' configurations.

`-mno-crt0`
: Do not link in the C run-time initialization object file.

3.18.30 MSP430 Options

These options are defined for the MSP430:

`-masm-hex`
: Force assembly output to always use hex constants. Normally such constants are signed decimals, but this option is available for testsuite and/or aesthetic purposes.

`-mmcu=`
: Select the MCU to target. This is used to create a C preprocessor symbol based upon the MCU name, converted to upper case and pre- and post-fixed with '`__`'. This in turn is used by the '`msp430.h`' header file to select an MCU-specific supplementary header file.

  The option also sets the ISA to use. If the MCU name is one that is known to only support the 430 ISA then that is selected, otherwise the 430X ISA is selected. A generic MCU name of '`msp430`' can also be used to select the 430 ISA. Similarly the generic '`msp430x`' MCU name selects the 430X ISA.

  In addition an MCU-specific linker script is added to the linker command line. The script's name is the name of the MCU with '`.ld`' appended. Thus specifying '`-mmcu=xxx`' on the `gcc` command line defines the C preprocessor symbol `__XXX__` and cause the linker to search for a script called '`xxx.ld`'.

  This option is also passed on to the assembler.

`-mwarn-mcu`
`-mno-warn-mcu`
: This option enables or disables warnings about conflicts between the MCU name specified by the '`-mmcu`' option and the ISA set by the '`-mcpu`' option and/or the hardware multiply support set by the '`-mhwmult`' option. It also toggles warnings about unrecognized MCU names. This option is on by default.

`-mcpu=`
: Specifies the ISA to use. Accepted values are '`msp430`', '`msp430x`' and '`msp430xv2`'. This option is deprecated. The '`-mmcu=`' option should be used to select the ISA.

`-msim`
: Link to the simulator runtime libraries and linker script. Overrides any scripts that would be selected by the '`-mmcu=`' option.

`-mlarge`
: Use large-model addressing (20-bit pointers, 32-bit `size_t`).

`-msmall`
: Use small-model addressing (16-bit pointers, 16-bit `size_t`).

`-mrelax`
: This option is passed to the assembler and linker, and allows the linker to perform certain optimizations that cannot be done until the final link.

`mhwmult=`
: Describes the type of hardware multiply supported by the target. Accepted values are '`none`' for no hardware multiply, '`16bit`' for the original 16-bit-only multiply supported by early MCUs. '`32bit`' for the 16/32-bit multiply supported by later MCUs and '`f5series`' for the 16/32-bit multiply supported by F5-series MCUs. A value of '`auto`' can also be given. This tells GCC to deduce the hardware multiply support based upon the MCU name provided by the '`-mmcu`' option. If no '`-mmcu`' option is specified or if the MCU name is not

recognized then no hardware multiply support is assumed. `auto` is the default setting.

Hardware multiplies are normally performed by calling a library routine. This saves space in the generated code. When compiling at '`-O3`' or higher however the hardware multiplier is invoked inline. This makes for bigger, but faster code.

The hardware multiply routines disable interrupts whilst running and restore the previous interrupt state when they finish. This makes them safe to use inside interrupt handlers as well as in normal code.

`-minrt` Enable the use of a minimum runtime environment - no static initializers or constructors. This is intended for memory-constrained devices. The compiler includes special symbols in some objects that tell the linker and runtime which code fragments are required.

`-mcode-region=`
`-mdata-region=`
These options tell the compiler where to place functions and data that do not have one of the `lower`, `upper`, `either` or `section` attributes. Possible values are `lower`, `upper`, `either` or `any`. The first three behave like the corresponding attribute. The fourth possible value - `any` - is the default. It leaves placement entirely up to the linker script and how it assigns the standard sections (`.text`, `.data`, etc) to the memory regions.

`-msilicon-errata=`
This option passes on a request to assembler to enable the fixes for the named silicon errata.

`-msilicon-errata-warn=`
This option passes on a request to the assembler to enable warning messages when a silicon errata might need to be applied.

3.18.31 NDS32 Options

These options are defined for NDS32 implementations:

`-mbig-endian`
Generate code in big-endian mode.

`-mlittle-endian`
Generate code in little-endian mode.

`-mreduced-regs`
Use reduced-set registers for register allocation.

`-mfull-regs`
Use full-set registers for register allocation.

`-mcmov` Generate conditional move instructions.

`-mno-cmov`
Do not generate conditional move instructions.

`-mperf-ext`
: Generate performance extension instructions.

`-mno-perf-ext`
: Do not generate performance extension instructions.

`-mv3push`
: Generate v3 push25/pop25 instructions.

`-mno-v3push`
: Do not generate v3 push25/pop25 instructions.

`-m16-bit`
: Generate 16-bit instructions.

`-mno-16-bit`
: Do not generate 16-bit instructions.

`-misr-vector-size=`*num*
: Specify the size of each interrupt vector, which must be 4 or 16.

`-mcache-block-size=`*num*
: Specify the size of each cache block, which must be a power of 2 between 4 and 512.

`-march=`*arch*
: Specify the name of the target architecture.

`-mcmodel=`*code-model*
: Set the code model to one of

  '`small`' All the data and read-only data segments must be within 512KB addressing space. The text segment must be within 16MB addressing space.

  '`medium`' The data segment must be within 512KB while the read-only data segment can be within 4GB addressing space. The text segment should be still within 16MB addressing space.

  '`large`' All the text and data segments can be within 4GB addressing space.

`-mctor-dtor`
: Enable constructor/destructor feature.

`-mrelax`
: Guide linker to relax instructions.

3.18.32 Nios II Options

These are the options defined for the Altera Nios II processor.

`-G` *num*
: Put global and static objects less than or equal to *num* bytes into the small data or BSS sections instead of the normal data or BSS sections. The default value of *num* is 8.

`-mgpopt=`*option*
`-mgpopt`
`-mno-gpopt`
: Generate (do not generate) GP-relative accesses. The following *option* names are recognized:

'none' Do not generate GP-relative accesses.

'local' Generate GP-relative accesses for small data objects that are not external, weak, or uninitialized common symbols. Also use GP-relative addressing for objects that have been explicitly placed in a small data section via a `section` attribute.

'global' As for 'local', but also generate GP-relative accesses for small data objects that are external, weak, or common. If you use this option, you must ensure that all parts of your program (including libraries) are compiled with the same '-G' setting.

'data' Generate GP-relative accesses for all data objects in the program. If you use this option, the entire data and BSS segments of your program must fit in 64K of memory and you must use an appropriate linker script to allocate them within the addressable range of the global pointer.

'all' Generate GP-relative addresses for function pointers as well as data pointers. If you use this option, the entire text, data, and BSS segments of your program must fit in 64K of memory and you must use an appropriate linker script to allocate them within the addressable range of the global pointer.

'-mgpopt' is equivalent to '-mgpopt=local', and '-mno-gpopt' is equivalent to '-mgpopt=none'.

The default is '-mgpopt' except when '-fpic' or '-fPIC' is specified to generate position-independent code. Note that the Nios II ABI does not permit GP-relative accesses from shared libraries.

You may need to specify '-mno-gpopt' explicitly when building programs that include large amounts of small data, including large GOT data sections. In this case, the 16-bit offset for GP-relative addressing may not be large enough to allow access to the entire small data section.

`-mel`
`-meb` Generate little-endian (default) or big-endian (experimental) code, respectively.

`-march=`*`arch`*
This specifies the name of the target Nios II architecture. GCC uses this name to determine what kind of instructions it can emit when generating assembly code. Permissible names are: 'r1', 'r2'.

The preprocessor macro `__nios2_arch__` is available to programs, with value 1 or 2, indicating the targeted ISA level.

`-mbypass-cache`
`-mno-bypass-cache`
Force all load and store instructions to always bypass cache by using I/O variants of the instructions. The default is not to bypass the cache.

`-mno-cache-volatile`
`-mcache-volatile`
: Volatile memory access bypass the cache using the I/O variants of the load and store instructions. The default is not to bypass the cache.

`-mno-fast-sw-div`
`-mfast-sw-div`
: Do not use table-based fast divide for small numbers. The default is to use the fast divide at '`-O3`' and above.

`-mno-hw-mul`
`-mhw-mul`
`-mno-hw-mulx`
`-mhw-mulx`
`-mno-hw-div`
`-mhw-div`
: Enable or disable emitting `mul`, `mulx` and `div` family of instructions by the compiler. The default is to emit `mul` and not emit `div` and `mulx`.

`-mbmx`
`-mno-bmx`
`-mcdx`
`-mno-cdx`
: Enable or disable generation of Nios II R2 BMX (bit manipulation) and CDX (code density) instructions. Enabling these instructions also requires '`-march=r2`'. Since these instructions are optional extensions to the R2 architecture, the default is not to emit them.

`-mcustom-`*`insn`*`=`*`N`*
`-mno-custom-`*`insn`*
: Each '`-mcustom-`*`insn`*`=`*`N`*' option enables use of a custom instruction with encoding *N* when generating code that uses *insn*. For example, '`-mcustom-fadds=253`' generates custom instruction 253 for single-precision floating-point add operations instead of the default behavior of using a library call.

  The following values of *insn* are supported. Except as otherwise noted, floating-point operations are expected to be implemented with normal IEEE 754 semantics and correspond directly to the C operators or the equivalent GCC built-in functions (see Section 6.58 [Other Builtins], page 545).

  Single-precision floating point:

  '`fadds`', '`fsubs`', '`fdivs`', '`fmuls`'
  : Binary arithmetic operations.

  '`fnegs`'
  : Unary negation.

  '`fabss`'
  : Unary absolute value.

  '`fcmpeqs`', '`fcmpges`', '`fcmpgts`', '`fcmples`', '`fcmplts`', '`fcmpnes`'
  : Comparison operations.

  '`fmins`', '`fmaxs`'
  : Floating-point minimum and maximum. These instructions are only generated if '`-ffinite-math-only`' is specified.

'fsqrts' Unary square root operation.

'fcoss', 'fsins', 'ftans', 'fatans', 'fexps', 'flogs'
: Floating-point trigonometric and exponential functions. These instructions are only generated if '-funsafe-math-optimizations' is also specified.

Double-precision floating point:

'faddd', 'fsubd', 'fdivd', 'fmuld'
: Binary arithmetic operations.

'fnegd' Unary negation.

'fabsd' Unary absolute value.

'fcmpeqd', 'fcmpged', 'fcmpgtd', 'fcmpled', 'fcmpltd', 'fcmpned'
: Comparison operations.

'fmind', 'fmaxd'
: Double-precision minimum and maximum. These instructions are only generated if '-ffinite-math-only' is specified.

'fsqrtd' Unary square root operation.

'fcosd', 'fsind', 'ftand', 'fatand', 'fexpd', 'flogd'
: Double-precision trigonometric and exponential functions. These instructions are only generated if '-funsafe-math-optimizations' is also specified.

Conversions:

'fextsd' Conversion from single precision to double precision.

'ftruncds'
: Conversion from double precision to single precision.

'fixsi', 'fixsu', 'fixdi', 'fixdu'
: Conversion from floating point to signed or unsigned integer types, with truncation towards zero.

'round' Conversion from single-precision floating point to signed integer, rounding to the nearest integer and ties away from zero. This corresponds to the __builtin_lroundf function when '-fno-math-errno' is used.

'floatis', 'floatus', 'floatid', 'floatud'
: Conversion from signed or unsigned integer types to floating-point types.

In addition, all of the following transfer instructions for internal registers X and Y must be provided to use any of the double-precision floating-point instructions. Custom instructions taking two double-precision source operands expect the first operand in the 64-bit register X. The other operand (or only operand of a unary operation) is given to the custom arithmetic instruction with the least significant half in source register *src1* and the most significant half in *src2*.

A custom instruction that returns a double-precision result returns the most significant 32 bits in the destination register and the other half in 32-bit register Y. GCC automatically generates the necessary code sequences to write register X and/or read register Y when double-precision floating-point instructions are used.

'fwrx' Write *src1* into the least significant half of X and *src2* into the most significant half of X.

'fwry' Write *src1* into Y.

'frdxhi', 'frdxlo'
Read the most or least (respectively) significant half of X and store it in *dest*.

'frdy' Read the value of Y and store it into *dest*.

Note that you can gain more local control over generation of Nios II custom instructions by using the `target("custom-insn=N")` and `target("no-custom-insn")` function attributes (see Section 6.31 [Function Attributes], page 407) or pragmas (see Section 6.61.15 [Function Specific Option Pragmas], page 675).

`-mcustom-fpu-cfg=name`
This option enables a predefined, named set of custom instruction encodings (see '-mcustom-*insn*' above). Currently, the following sets are defined:

'-mcustom-fpu-cfg=60-1' is equivalent to:

```
-mcustom-fmuls=252
-mcustom-fadds=253
-mcustom-fsubs=254
-fsingle-precision-constant
```

'-mcustom-fpu-cfg=60-2' is equivalent to:

```
-mcustom-fmuls=252
-mcustom-fadds=253
-mcustom-fsubs=254
-mcustom-fdivs=255
-fsingle-precision-constant
```

'-mcustom-fpu-cfg=72-3' is equivalent to:

```
-mcustom-floatus=243
-mcustom-fixsi=244
-mcustom-floatis=245
-mcustom-fcmpgts=246
-mcustom-fcmples=249
-mcustom-fcmpeqs=250
-mcustom-fcmpnes=251
-mcustom-fmuls=252
-mcustom-fadds=253
-mcustom-fsubs=254
-mcustom-fdivs=255
-fsingle-precision-constant
```

Custom instruction assignments given by individual '-mcustom-*insn*=' options override those given by '-mcustom-fpu-cfg=', regardless of the order of the options on the command line.

Note that you can gain more local control over selection of a FPU configuration by using the `target("custom-fpu-cfg=name")` function attribute (see Section 6.31 [Function Attributes], page 407) or pragma (see Section 6.61.15 [Function Specific Option Pragmas], page 675).

These additional '`-m`' options are available for the Altera Nios II ELF (bare-metal) target:

`-mhal` Link with HAL BSP. This suppresses linking with the GCC-provided C runtime startup and termination code, and is typically used in conjunction with '`-msys-crt0=`' to specify the location of the alternate startup code provided by the HAL BSP.

`-msmallc` Link with a limited version of the C library, '`-lsmallc`', rather than Newlib.

`-msys-crt0=`*`startfile`*
startfile is the file name of the startfile (crt0) to use when linking. This option is only useful in conjunction with '`-mhal`'.

`-msys-lib=`*`systemlib`*
systemlib is the library name of the library that provides low-level system calls required by the C library, e.g. `read` and `write`. This option is typically used to link with a library provided by a HAL BSP.

3.18.33 Nvidia PTX Options

These options are defined for Nvidia PTX:

`-m32`
`-m64` Generate code for 32-bit or 64-bit ABI.

`-mmainkernel`
Link in code for a __main kernel. This is for stand-alone instead of offloading execution.

`-moptimize`
Apply partitioned execution optimizations. This is the default when any level of optimization is selected.

3.18.34 PDP-11 Options

These options are defined for the PDP-11:

`-mfpu` Use hardware FPP floating point. This is the default. (FIS floating point on the PDP-11/40 is not supported.)

`-msoft-float`
Do not use hardware floating point.

`-mac0` Return floating-point results in ac0 (fr0 in Unix assembler syntax).

`-mno-ac0` Return floating-point results in memory. This is the default.

`-m40` Generate code for a PDP-11/40.

`-m45` Generate code for a PDP-11/45. This is the default.

`-m10` Generate code for a PDP-11/10.

`-mbcopy-builtin`
: Use inline `movmemhi` patterns for copying memory. This is the default.

`-mbcopy`
: Do not use inline `movmemhi` patterns for copying memory.

`-mint16`
`-mno-int32`
: Use 16-bit `int`. This is the default.

`-mint32`
`-mno-int16`
: Use 32-bit `int`.

`-mfloat64`
`-mno-float32`
: Use 64-bit `float`. This is the default.

`-mfloat32`
`-mno-float64`
: Use 32-bit `float`.

`-mabshi`
: Use `abshi2` pattern. This is the default.

`-mno-abshi`
: Do not use `abshi2` pattern.

`-mbranch-expensive`
: Pretend that branches are expensive. This is for experimenting with code generation only.

`-mbranch-cheap`
: Do not pretend that branches are expensive. This is the default.

`-munix-asm`
: Use Unix assembler syntax. This is the default when configured for 'pdp11-*-bsd'.

`-mdec-asm`
: Use DEC assembler syntax. This is the default when configured for any PDP-11 target other than 'pdp11-*-bsd'.

3.18.35 picoChip Options

These '-m' options are defined for picoChip implementations:

`-mae=`*ae_type*
: Set the instruction set, register set, and instruction scheduling parameters for array element type *ae_type*. Supported values for *ae_type* are 'ANY', 'MUL', and 'MAC'.

'-mae=ANY' selects a completely generic AE type. Code generated with this option runs on any of the other AE types. The code is not as efficient as it would be if compiled for a specific AE type, and some types of operation (e.g., multiplication) do not work properly on all types of AE.

'-mae=MUL' selects a MUL AE type. This is the most useful AE type for compiled code, and is the default.

'-mae=MAC' selects a DSP-style MAC AE. Code compiled with this option may suffer from poor performance of byte (char) manipulation, since the DSP AE does not provide hardware support for byte load/stores.

-msymbol-as-address
: Enable the compiler to directly use a symbol name as an address in a load/store instruction, without first loading it into a register. Typically, the use of this option generates larger programs, which run faster than when the option isn't used. However, the results vary from program to program, so it is left as a user option, rather than being permanently enabled.

-mno-inefficient-warnings
: Disables warnings about the generation of inefficient code. These warnings can be generated, for example, when compiling code that performs byte-level memory operations on the MAC AE type. The MAC AE has no hardware support for byte-level memory operations, so all byte load/stores must be synthesized from word load/store operations. This is inefficient and a warning is generated to indicate that you should rewrite the code to avoid byte operations, or to target an AE type that has the necessary hardware support. This option disables these warnings.

3.18.36 PowerPC Options

These are listed under See Section 3.18.38 [RS/6000 and PowerPC Options], page 294.

3.18.37 RL78 Options

-msim
: Links in additional target libraries to support operation within a simulator.

-mmul=none
-mmul=g10
-mmul=g13
-mmul=g14
-mmul=rl78
: Specifies the type of hardware multiplication and division support to be used. The simplest is none, which uses software for both multiplication and division. This is the default. The g13 value is for the hardware multiply/divide peripheral found on the RL78/G13 (S2 core) targets. The g14 value selects the use of the multiplication and division instructions supported by the RL78/G14 (S3 core) parts. The value rl78 is an alias for g14 and the value mg10 is an alias for none.

  In addition a C preprocessor macro is defined, based upon the setting of this option. Possible values are: __RL78_MUL_NONE__, __RL78_MUL_G13__ or __RL78_MUL_G14__.

-mcpu=g10
-mcpu=g13
-mcpu=g14
-mcpu=rl78
: Specifies the RL78 core to target. The default is the G14 core, also known as an S3 core or just RL78. The G13 or S2 core does not have multiply or

divide instructions, instead it uses a hardware peripheral for these operations. The G10 or S1 core does not have register banks, so it uses a different calling convention.

If this option is set it also selects the type of hardware multiply support to use, unless this is overridden by an explicit '-mmul=none' option on the command line. Thus specifying '-mcpu=g13' enables the use of the G13 hardware multiply peripheral and specifying '-mcpu=g10' disables the use of hardware multiplications altogether.

Note, although the RL78/G14 core is the default target, specifying '-mcpu=g14' or '-mcpu=rl78' on the command line does change the behavior of the toolchain since it also enables G14 hardware multiply support. If these options are not specified on the command line then software multiplication routines will be used even though the code targets the RL78 core. This is for backwards compatibility with older toolchains which did not have hardware multiply and divide support.

In addition a C preprocessor macro is defined, based upon the setting of this option. Possible values are: `__RL78_G10__`, `__RL78_G13__` or `__RL78_G14__`.

`-mg10`
`-mg13`
`-mg14`
`-mrl78` These are aliases for the corresponding '-mcpu=' option. They are provided for backwards compatibility.

`-mallregs`
Allow the compiler to use all of the available registers. By default registers `r24..r31` are reserved for use in interrupt handlers. With this option enabled these registers can be used in ordinary functions as well.

`-m64bit-doubles`
`-m32bit-doubles`
Make the `double` data type be 64 bits ('-m64bit-doubles') or 32 bits ('-m32bit-doubles') in size. The default is '-m32bit-doubles'.

3.18.38 IBM RS/6000 and PowerPC Options

These '-m' options are defined for the IBM RS/6000 and PowerPC:

`-mpowerpc-gpopt`
`-mno-powerpc-gpopt`
`-mpowerpc-gfxopt`
`-mno-powerpc-gfxopt`

`-mpowerpc64`
`-mno-powerpc64`
`-mmfcrf`
`-mno-mfcrf`
`-mpopcntb`
`-mno-popcntb`
`-mpopcntd`
`-mno-popcntd`
`-mfprnd`
`-mno-fprnd`
`-mcmpb`
`-mno-cmpb`
`-mmfpgpr`
`-mno-mfpgpr`
`-mhard-dfp`
`-mno-hard-dfp`

You use these options to specify which instructions are available on the processor you are using. The default value of these options is determined when configuring GCC. Specifying the '`-mcpu=`*cpu_type*' overrides the specification of these options. We recommend you use the '`-mcpu=`*cpu_type*' option rather than the options listed above.

Specifying '`-mpowerpc-gpopt`' allows GCC to use the optional PowerPC architecture instructions in the General Purpose group, including floating-point square root. Specifying '`-mpowerpc-gfxopt`' allows GCC to use the optional PowerPC architecture instructions in the Graphics group, including floating-point select.

The '`-mmfcrf`' option allows GCC to generate the move from condition register field instruction implemented on the POWER4 processor and other processors that support the PowerPC V2.01 architecture. The '`-mpopcntb`' option allows GCC to generate the popcount and double-precision FP reciprocal estimate instruction implemented on the POWER5 processor and other processors that support the PowerPC V2.02 architecture. The '`-mpopcntd`' option allows GCC to generate the popcount instruction implemented on the POWER7 processor and other processors that support the PowerPC V2.06 architecture. The '`-mfprnd`' option allows GCC to generate the FP round to integer instructions implemented on the POWER5+ processor and other processors that support the PowerPC V2.03 architecture. The '`-mcmpb`' option allows GCC to generate the compare bytes instruction implemented on the POWER6 processor and other processors that support the PowerPC V2.05 architecture. The '`-mmfpgpr`' option allows GCC to generate the FP move to/from general-purpose register instructions implemented on the POWER6X processor and other processors that support the extended PowerPC V2.05 architecture. The '`-mhard-dfp`' option allows GCC to generate the decimal floating-point instructions implemented on some POWER processors.

The '-mpowerpc64' option allows GCC to generate the additional 64-bit instructions that are found in the full PowerPC64 architecture and to treat GPRs as 64-bit, doubleword quantities. GCC defaults to '-mno-powerpc64'.

-mcpu=*cpu_type*

Set architecture type, register usage, and instruction scheduling parameters for machine type *cpu_type*. Supported values for *cpu_type* are '401', '403', '405', '405fp', '440', '440fp', '464', '464fp', '476', '476fp', '505', '601', '602', '603', '603e', '604', '604e', '620', '630', '740', '7400', '7450', '750', '801', '821', '823', '860', '970', '8540', 'a2', 'e300c2', 'e300c3', 'e500mc', 'e500mc64', 'e5500', 'e6500', 'ec603e', 'G3', 'G4', 'G5', 'titan', 'power3', 'power4', 'power5', 'power5+', 'power6', 'power6x', 'power7', 'power8', 'power9', 'powerpc', 'powerpc64', 'powerpc64le', and 'rs64'.

'-mcpu=powerpc', '-mcpu=powerpc64', and '-mcpu=powerpc64le' specify pure 32-bit PowerPC (either endian), 64-bit big endian PowerPC and 64-bit little endian PowerPC architecture machine types, with an appropriate, generic processor model assumed for scheduling purposes.

The other options specify a specific processor. Code generated under those options runs best on that processor, and may not run at all on others.

The '-mcpu' options automatically enable or disable the following options:

```
-maltivec -mfprnd -mhard-float -mmfcrf -mmultiple
-mpopcntb -mpopcntd -mpowerpc64
-mpowerpc-gpopt -mpowerpc-gfxopt -msingle-float -mdouble-float
-msimple-fpu -mstring -mmulhw -mdlmzb -mmfpgpr -mvsx
-mcrypto -mdirect-move -mpower8-fusion -mpower8-vector
-mquad-memory -mquad-memory-atomic -mmodulo -mfloat128 -mfloat128-hardware
-mpower9-fusion -mpower9-vector
```

The particular options set for any particular CPU varies between compiler versions, depending on what setting seems to produce optimal code for that CPU; it doesn't necessarily reflect the actual hardware's capabilities. If you wish to set an individual option to a particular value, you may specify it after the '-mcpu' option, like '-mcpu=970 -mno-altivec'.

On AIX, the '-maltivec' and '-mpowerpc64' options are not enabled or disabled by the '-mcpu' option at present because AIX does not have full support for these options. You may still enable or disable them individually if you're sure it'll work in your environment.

-mtune=*cpu_type*

Set the instruction scheduling parameters for machine type *cpu_type*, but do not set the architecture type or register usage, as '-mcpu=*cpu_type*' does. The same values for *cpu_type* are used for '-mtune' as for '-mcpu'. If both are specified, the code generated uses the architecture and registers set by '-mcpu', but the scheduling parameters set by '-mtune'.

-mcmodel=small

Generate PowerPC64 code for the small model: The TOC is limited to 64k.

-mcmodel=medium

Generate PowerPC64 code for the medium model: The TOC and other static data may be up to a total of 4G in size.

`-mcmodel=large`
: Generate PowerPC64 code for the large model: The TOC may be up to 4G in size. Other data and code is only limited by the 64-bit address space.

`-maltivec`
`-mno-altivec`
: Generate code that uses (does not use) AltiVec instructions, and also enable the use of built-in functions that allow more direct access to the AltiVec instruction set. You may also need to set '`-mabi=altivec`' to adjust the current ABI with AltiVec ABI enhancements.

When '`-maltivec`' is used, rather than '`-maltivec=le`' or '`-maltivec=be`', the element order for AltiVec intrinsics such as `vec_splat`, `vec_extract`, and `vec_insert` match array element order corresponding to the endianness of the target. That is, element zero identifies the leftmost element in a vector register when targeting a big-endian platform, and identifies the rightmost element in a vector register when targeting a little-endian platform.

`-maltivec=be`
: Generate AltiVec instructions using big-endian element order, regardless of whether the target is big- or little-endian. This is the default when targeting a big-endian platform.

The element order is used to interpret element numbers in AltiVec intrinsics such as `vec_splat`, `vec_extract`, and `vec_insert`. By default, these match array element order corresponding to the endianness for the target.

`-maltivec=le`
: Generate AltiVec instructions using little-endian element order, regardless of whether the target is big- or little-endian. This is the default when targeting a little-endian platform. This option is currently ignored when targeting a big-endian platform.

The element order is used to interpret element numbers in AltiVec intrinsics such as `vec_splat`, `vec_extract`, and `vec_insert`. By default, these match array element order corresponding to the endianness for the target.

`-mvrsave`
`-mno-vrsave`
: Generate VRSAVE instructions when generating AltiVec code.

`-mgen-cell-microcode`
: Generate Cell microcode instructions.

`-mwarn-cell-microcode`
: Warn when a Cell microcode instruction is emitted. An example of a Cell microcode instruction is a variable shift.

`-msecure-plt`
: Generate code that allows `ld` and `ld.so` to build executables and shared libraries with non-executable `.plt` and `.got` sections. This is a PowerPC 32-bit SYSV ABI option.

`-mbss-plt`
: Generate code that uses a BSS `.plt` section that `ld.so` fills in, and requires `.plt` and `.got` sections that are both writable and executable. This is a PowerPC 32-bit SYSV ABI option.

`-misel`
`-mno-isel`
: This switch enables or disables the generation of ISEL instructions.

`-misel=`*yes/no*
: This switch has been deprecated. Use '`-misel`' and '`-mno-isel`' instead.

`-mspe`
`-mno-spe`
: This switch enables or disables the generation of SPE simd instructions.

`-mpaired`
`-mno-paired`
: This switch enables or disables the generation of PAIRED simd instructions.

`-mspe=`*yes/no*
: This option has been deprecated. Use '`-mspe`' and '`-mno-spe`' instead.

`-mvsx`
`-mno-vsx`
: Generate code that uses (does not use) vector/scalar (VSX) instructions, and also enable the use of built-in functions that allow more direct access to the VSX instruction set.

`-mcrypto`
`-mno-crypto`
: Enable the use (disable) of the built-in functions that allow direct access to the cryptographic instructions that were added in version 2.07 of the PowerPC ISA.

`-mdirect-move`
`-mno-direct-move`
: Generate code that uses (does not use) the instructions to move data between the general purpose registers and the vector/scalar (VSX) registers that were added in version 2.07 of the PowerPC ISA.

`-mpower8-fusion`
`-mno-power8-fusion`
: Generate code that keeps (does not keeps) some integer operations adjacent so that the instructions can be fused together on power8 and later processors.

`-mpower8-vector`
`-mno-power8-vector`
: Generate code that uses (does not use) the vector and scalar instructions that were added in version 2.07 of the PowerPC ISA. Also enable the use of built-in functions that allow more direct access to the vector instructions.

`-mquad-memory`
`-mno-quad-memory`
: Generate code that uses (does not use) the non-atomic quad word memory instructions. The '`-mquad-memory`' option requires use of 64-bit mode.

`-mquad-memory-atomic`
`-mno-quad-memory-atomic`
Generate code that uses (does not use) the atomic quad word memory instructions. The '-mquad-memory-atomic' option requires use of 64-bit mode.

`-mupper-regs-df`
`-mno-upper-regs-df`
Generate code that uses (does not use) the scalar double precision instructions that target all 64 registers in the vector/scalar floating point register set that were added in version 2.06 of the PowerPC ISA. '-mupper-regs-df' is turned on by default if you use any of the '-mcpu=power7', '-mcpu=power8', or '-mvsx' options.

`-mupper-regs-sf`
`-mno-upper-regs-sf`
Generate code that uses (does not use) the scalar single precision instructions that target all 64 registers in the vector/scalar floating point register set that were added in version 2.07 of the PowerPC ISA. '-mupper-regs-sf' is turned on by default if you use either of the '-mcpu=power8' or '-mpower8-vector' options.

`-mupper-regs`
`-mno-upper-regs`
Generate code that uses (does not use) the scalar instructions that target all 64 registers in the vector/scalar floating point register set, depending on the model of the machine.

If the '-mno-upper-regs' option is used, it turns off both '-mupper-regs-sf' and '-mupper-regs-df' options.

`-mfloat128`
`-mno-float128`
Enable/disable the *__float128* keyword for IEEE 128-bit floating point and use either software emulation for IEEE 128-bit floating point or hardware instructions.

The VSX instruction set ('-mvsx', '-mcpu=power7', or '-mcpu=power8') must be enabled to use the '-mfloat128' option. The `-mfloat128` option only works on PowerPC 64-bit Linux systems.

`-mfloat128-hardware`
`-mno-float128-hardware`
Enable/disable using ISA 3.0 hardware instructions to support the *__float128* data type.

`-mmodulo`
`-mno-modulo`
Generate code that uses (does not use) the ISA 3.0 integer modulo instructions. The '-mmodulo' option is enabled by default with the '-mcpu=power9' option.

`-mpower9-fusion`
`-mno-power9-fusion`
Generate code that keeps (does not keeps) some operations adjacent so that the instructions can be fused together on power9 and later processors.

`-mpower9-vector`
`-mno-power9-vector`
Generate code that uses (does not use) the vector and scalar instructions that were added in version 2.07 of the PowerPC ISA. Also enable the use of built-in functions that allow more direct access to the vector instructions.

`-mfloat-gprs=`*yes/single/double/no*
`-mfloat-gprs`
This switch enables or disables the generation of floating-point operations on the general-purpose registers for architectures that support it.

The argument '`yes`' or '`single`' enables the use of single-precision floating-point operations.

The argument '`double`' enables the use of single and double-precision floating-point operations.

The argument '`no`' disables floating-point operations on the general-purpose registers.

This option is currently only available on the MPC854x.

`-m32`
`-m64` Generate code for 32-bit or 64-bit environments of Darwin and SVR4 targets (including GNU/Linux). The 32-bit environment sets int, long and pointer to 32 bits and generates code that runs on any PowerPC variant. The 64-bit environment sets int to 32 bits and long and pointer to 64 bits, and generates code for PowerPC64, as for '`-mpowerpc64`'.

`-mfull-toc`
`-mno-fp-in-toc`
`-mno-sum-in-toc`
`-mminimal-toc`
Modify generation of the TOC (Table Of Contents), which is created for every executable file. The '`-mfull-toc`' option is selected by default. In that case, GCC allocates at least one TOC entry for each unique non-automatic variable reference in your program. GCC also places floating-point constants in the TOC. However, only 16,384 entries are available in the TOC.

If you receive a linker error message that saying you have overflowed the available TOC space, you can reduce the amount of TOC space used with the '`-mno-fp-in-toc`' and '`-mno-sum-in-toc`' options. '`-mno-fp-in-toc`' prevents GCC from putting floating-point constants in the TOC and '`-mno-sum-in-toc`' forces GCC to generate code to calculate the sum of an address and a constant at run time instead of putting that sum into the TOC. You may specify one or both of these options. Each causes GCC to produce very slightly slower and larger code at the expense of conserving TOC space.

If you still run out of space in the TOC even when you specify both of these options, specify '-mminimal-toc' instead. This option causes GCC to make only one TOC entry for every file. When you specify this option, GCC produces code that is slower and larger but which uses extremely little TOC space. You may wish to use this option only on files that contain less frequently-executed code.

-maix64
-maix32
: Enable 64-bit AIX ABI and calling convention: 64-bit pointers, 64-bit long type, and the infrastructure needed to support them. Specifying '-maix64' implies '-mpowerpc64', while '-maix32' disables the 64-bit ABI and implies '-mno-powerpc64'. GCC defaults to '-maix32'.

-mxl-compat
-mno-xl-compat
: Produce code that conforms more closely to IBM XL compiler semantics when using AIX-compatible ABI. Pass floating-point arguments to prototyped functions beyond the register save area (RSA) on the stack in addition to argument FPRs. Do not assume that most significant double in 128-bit long double value is properly rounded when comparing values and converting to double. Use XL symbol names for long double support routines.

The AIX calling convention was extended but not initially documented to handle an obscure K&R C case of calling a function that takes the address of its arguments with fewer arguments than declared. IBM XL compilers access floating-point arguments that do not fit in the RSA from the stack when a subroutine is compiled without optimization. Because always storing floating-point arguments on the stack is inefficient and rarely needed, this option is not enabled by default and only is necessary when calling subroutines compiled by IBM XL compilers without optimization.

-mpe
: Support *IBM RS/6000 SP Parallel Environment* (PE). Link an application written to use message passing with special startup code to enable the application to run. The system must have PE installed in the standard location ('/usr/lpp/ppe.poe/'), or the 'specs' file must be overridden with the '-specs=' option to specify the appropriate directory location. The Parallel Environment does not support threads, so the '-mpe' option and the '-pthread' option are incompatible.

-malign-natural
-malign-power
: On AIX, 32-bit Darwin, and 64-bit PowerPC GNU/Linux, the option '-malign-natural' overrides the ABI-defined alignment of larger types, such as floating-point doubles, on their natural size-based boundary. The option '-malign-power' instructs GCC to follow the ABI-specified alignment rules. GCC defaults to the standard alignment defined in the ABI.

On 64-bit Darwin, natural alignment is the default, and '-malign-power' is not supported.

`-msoft-float`
`-mhard-float`
: Generate code that does not use (uses) the floating-point register set. Software floating-point emulation is provided if you use the '-msoft-float' option, and pass the option to GCC when linking.

`-msingle-float`
`-mdouble-float`
: Generate code for single- or double-precision floating-point operations. '-mdouble-float' implies '-msingle-float'.

`-msimple-fpu`
: Do not generate `sqrt` and `div` instructions for hardware floating-point unit.

`-mfpu=`*name*
: Specify type of floating-point unit. Valid values for *name* are 'sp_lite' (equivalent to '-msingle-float -msimple-fpu'), 'dp_lite' (equivalent to '-mdouble-float -msimple-fpu'), 'sp_full' (equivalent to '-msingle-float'), and 'dp_full' (equivalent to '-mdouble-float').

`-mxilinx-fpu`
: Perform optimizations for the floating-point unit on Xilinx PPC 405/440.

`-mmultiple`
`-mno-multiple`
: Generate code that uses (does not use) the load multiple word instructions and the store multiple word instructions. These instructions are generated by default on POWER systems, and not generated on PowerPC systems. Do not use '-mmultiple' on little-endian PowerPC systems, since those instructions do not work when the processor is in little-endian mode. The exceptions are PPC740 and PPC750 which permit these instructions in little-endian mode.

`-mstring`
`-mno-string`
: Generate code that uses (does not use) the load string instructions and the store string word instructions to save multiple registers and do small block moves. These instructions are generated by default on POWER systems, and not generated on PowerPC systems. Do not use '-mstring' on little-endian PowerPC systems, since those instructions do not work when the processor is in little-endian mode. The exceptions are PPC740 and PPC750 which permit these instructions in little-endian mode.

`-mupdate`
`-mno-update`
: Generate code that uses (does not use) the load or store instructions that update the base register to the address of the calculated memory location. These instructions are generated by default. If you use '-mno-update', there is a small window between the time that the stack pointer is updated and the address of the previous frame is stored, which means code that walks the stack frame across interrupts or signals may get corrupted data.

`-mavoid-indexed-addresses`
`-mno-avoid-indexed-addresses`
: Generate code that tries to avoid (not avoid) the use of indexed load or store instructions. These instructions can incur a performance penalty on Power6 processors in certain situations, such as when stepping through large arrays that cross a 16M boundary. This option is enabled by default when targeting Power6 and disabled otherwise.

`-mfused-madd`
`-mno-fused-madd`
: Generate code that uses (does not use) the floating-point multiply and accumulate instructions. These instructions are generated by default if hardware floating point is used. The machine-dependent '`-mfused-madd`' option is now mapped to the machine-independent '`-ffp-contract=fast`' option, and '`-mno-fused-madd`' is mapped to '`-ffp-contract=off`'.

`-mmulhw`
`-mno-mulhw`
: Generate code that uses (does not use) the half-word multiply and multiply-accumulate instructions on the IBM 405, 440, 464 and 476 processors. These instructions are generated by default when targeting those processors.

`-mdlmzb`
`-mno-dlmzb`
: Generate code that uses (does not use) the string-search '`dlmzb`' instruction on the IBM 405, 440, 464 and 476 processors. This instruction is generated by default when targeting those processors.

`-mno-bit-align`
`-mbit-align`
: On System V.4 and embedded PowerPC systems do not (do) force structures and unions that contain bit-fields to be aligned to the base type of the bit-field.

  For example, by default a structure containing nothing but 8 `unsigned` bit-fields of length 1 is aligned to a 4-byte boundary and has a size of 4 bytes. By using '`-mno-bit-align`', the structure is aligned to a 1-byte boundary and is 1 byte in size.

`-mno-strict-align`
`-mstrict-align`
: On System V.4 and embedded PowerPC systems do not (do) assume that unaligned memory references are handled by the system.

`-mrelocatable`
`-mno-relocatable`
: Generate code that allows (does not allow) a static executable to be relocated to a different address at run time. A simple embedded PowerPC system loader should relocate the entire contents of `.got2` and 4-byte locations listed in the `.fixup` section, a table of 32-bit addresses generated by this option. For this to work, all objects linked together must be compiled with '`-mrelocatable`' or '`-mrelocatable-lib`'. '`-mrelocatable`' code aligns the stack to an 8-byte boundary.

`-mrelocatable-lib`
`-mno-relocatable-lib`
Like '`-mrelocatable`', '`-mrelocatable-lib`' generates a `.fixup` section to allow static executables to be relocated at run time, but '`-mrelocatable-lib`' does not use the smaller stack alignment of '`-mrelocatable`'. Objects compiled with '`-mrelocatable-lib`' may be linked with objects compiled with any combination of the '`-mrelocatable`' options.

`-mno-toc`
`-mtoc`
On System V.4 and embedded PowerPC systems do not (do) assume that register 2 contains a pointer to a global area pointing to the addresses used in the program.

`-mlittle`
`-mlittle-endian`
On System V.4 and embedded PowerPC systems compile code for the processor in little-endian mode. The '`-mlittle-endian`' option is the same as '`-mlittle`'.

`-mbig`
`-mbig-endian`
On System V.4 and embedded PowerPC systems compile code for the processor in big-endian mode. The '`-mbig-endian`' option is the same as '`-mbig`'.

`-mdynamic-no-pic`
On Darwin and Mac OS X systems, compile code so that it is not relocatable, but that its external references are relocatable. The resulting code is suitable for applications, but not shared libraries.

`-msingle-pic-base`
Treat the register used for PIC addressing as read-only, rather than loading it in the prologue for each function. The runtime system is responsible for initializing this register with an appropriate value before execution begins.

`-mprioritize-restricted-insns=`*`priority`*
This option controls the priority that is assigned to dispatch-slot restricted instructions during the second scheduling pass. The argument *priority* takes the value '`0`', '`1`', or '`2`' to assign no, highest, or second-highest (respectively) priority to dispatch-slot restricted instructions.

`-msched-costly-dep=`*`dependence_type`*
This option controls which dependences are considered costly by the target during instruction scheduling. The argument *dependence_type* takes one of the following values:

'`no`' No dependence is costly.

'`all`' All dependences are costly.

'`true_store_to_load`'
A true dependence from store to load is costly.

'`store_to_load`'
Any dependence from store to load is costly.

number Any dependence for which the latency is greater than or equal to *number* is costly.

`-minsert-sched-nops=`*scheme*

This option controls which NOP insertion scheme is used during the second scheduling pass. The argument *scheme* takes one of the following values:

'`no`' Don't insert NOPs.

'`pad`' Pad with NOPs any dispatch group that has vacant issue slots, according to the scheduler's grouping.

'`regroup_exact`'

Insert NOPs to force costly dependent insns into separate groups. Insert exactly as many NOPs as needed to force an insn to a new group, according to the estimated processor grouping.

number Insert NOPs to force costly dependent insns into separate groups. Insert *number* NOPs to force an insn to a new group.

`-mcall-sysv`

On System V.4 and embedded PowerPC systems compile code using calling conventions that adhere to the March 1995 draft of the System V Application Binary Interface, PowerPC processor supplement. This is the default unless you configured GCC using '`powerpc-*-eabiaix`'.

`-mcall-sysv-eabi`
`-mcall-eabi`

Specify both '`-mcall-sysv`' and '`-meabi`' options.

`-mcall-sysv-noeabi`

Specify both '`-mcall-sysv`' and '`-mno-eabi`' options.

`-mcall-aixdesc`

On System V.4 and embedded PowerPC systems compile code for the AIX operating system.

`-mcall-linux`

On System V.4 and embedded PowerPC systems compile code for the Linux-based GNU system.

`-mcall-freebsd`

On System V.4 and embedded PowerPC systems compile code for the FreeBSD operating system.

`-mcall-netbsd`

On System V.4 and embedded PowerPC systems compile code for the NetBSD operating system.

`-mcall-openbsd`

On System V.4 and embedded PowerPC systems compile code for the OpenBSD operating system.

`-maix-struct-return`

Return all structures in memory (as specified by the AIX ABI).

`-msvr4-struct-return`
: Return structures smaller than 8 bytes in registers (as specified by the SVR4 ABI).

`-mabi=abi-type`
: Extend the current ABI with a particular extension, or remove such extension. Valid values are 'altivec', 'no-altivec', 'spe', 'no-spe', 'ibmlongdouble', 'ieeelongdouble', 'elfv1', 'elfv2'.

`-mabi=spe`
: Extend the current ABI with SPE ABI extensions. This does not change the default ABI, instead it adds the SPE ABI extensions to the current ABI.

`-mabi=no-spe`
: Disable Book-E SPE ABI extensions for the current ABI.

`-mabi=ibmlongdouble`
: Change the current ABI to use IBM extended-precision long double. This is a PowerPC 32-bit SYSV ABI option.

`-mabi=ieeelongdouble`
: Change the current ABI to use IEEE extended-precision long double. This is a PowerPC 32-bit Linux ABI option.

`-mabi=elfv1`
: Change the current ABI to use the ELFv1 ABI. This is the default ABI for big-endian PowerPC 64-bit Linux. Overriding the default ABI requires special system support and is likely to fail in spectacular ways.

`-mabi=elfv2`
: Change the current ABI to use the ELFv2 ABI. This is the default ABI for little-endian PowerPC 64-bit Linux. Overriding the default ABI requires special system support and is likely to fail in spectacular ways.

`-mprototype`
`-mno-prototype`
: On System V.4 and embedded PowerPC systems assume that all calls to variable argument functions are properly prototyped. Otherwise, the compiler must insert an instruction before every non-prototyped call to set or clear bit 6 of the condition code register (CR) to indicate whether floating-point values are passed in the floating-point registers in case the function takes variable arguments. With '-mprototype', only calls to prototyped variable argument functions set or clear the bit.

`-msim`
: On embedded PowerPC systems, assume that the startup module is called 'sim-crt0.o' and that the standard C libraries are 'libsim.a' and 'libc.a'. This is the default for 'powerpc-*-eabisim' configurations.

`-mmvme`
: On embedded PowerPC systems, assume that the startup module is called 'crt0.o' and the standard C libraries are 'libmvme.a' and 'libc.a'.

`-mads`
: On embedded PowerPC systems, assume that the startup module is called 'crt0.o' and the standard C libraries are 'libads.a' and 'libc.a'.

`-myellowknife`
: On embedded PowerPC systems, assume that the startup module is called 'crt0.o' and the standard C libraries are 'libyk.a' and 'libc.a'.

`-mvxworks`
: On System V.4 and embedded PowerPC systems, specify that you are compiling for a VxWorks system.

`-memb`
: On embedded PowerPC systems, set the PPC_EMB bit in the ELF flags header to indicate that 'eabi' extended relocations are used.

`-meabi`
`-mno-eabi`
: On System V.4 and embedded PowerPC systems do (do not) adhere to the Embedded Applications Binary Interface (EABI), which is a set of modifications to the System V.4 specifications. Selecting '-meabi' means that the stack is aligned to an 8-byte boundary, a function __eabi is called from main to set up the EABI environment, and the '-msdata' option can use both r2 and r13 to point to two separate small data areas. Selecting '-mno-eabi' means that the stack is aligned to a 16-byte boundary, no EABI initialization function is called from main, and the '-msdata' option only uses r13 to point to a single small data area. The '-meabi' option is on by default if you configured GCC using one of the 'powerpc*-*-eabi*' options.

`-msdata=eabi`
: On System V.4 and embedded PowerPC systems, put small initialized const global and static data in the .sdata2 section, which is pointed to by register r2. Put small initialized non-const global and static data in the .sdata section, which is pointed to by register r13. Put small uninitialized global and static data in the .sbss section, which is adjacent to the .sdata section. The '-msdata=eabi' option is incompatible with the '-mrelocatable' option. The '-msdata=eabi' option also sets the '-memb' option.

`-msdata=sysv`
: On System V.4 and embedded PowerPC systems, put small global and static data in the .sdata section, which is pointed to by register r13. Put small uninitialized global and static data in the .sbss section, which is adjacent to the .sdata section. The '-msdata=sysv' option is incompatible with the '-mrelocatable' option.

`-msdata=default`
`-msdata`
: On System V.4 and embedded PowerPC systems, if '-meabi' is used, compile code the same as '-msdata=eabi', otherwise compile code the same as '-msdata=sysv'.

`-msdata=data`
: On System V.4 and embedded PowerPC systems, put small global data in the .sdata section. Put small uninitialized global data in the .sbss section. Do not use register r13 to address small data however. This is the default behavior unless other '-msdata' options are used.

`-msdata=none`
`-mno-sdata`
: On embedded PowerPC systems, put all initialized global and static data in the `.data` section, and all uninitialized data in the `.bss` section.

`-mblock-move-inline-limit=`*num*
: Inline all block moves (such as calls to `memcpy` or structure copies) less than or equal to *num* bytes. The minimum value for *num* is 32 bytes on 32-bit targets and 64 bytes on 64-bit targets. The default value is target-specific.

`-G` *num*
: On embedded PowerPC systems, put global and static items less than or equal to *num* bytes into the small data or BSS sections instead of the normal data or BSS section. By default, *num* is 8. The '`-G` *num*' switch is also passed to the linker. All modules should be compiled with the same '`-G` *num*' value.

`-mregnames`
`-mno-regnames`
: On System V.4 and embedded PowerPC systems do (do not) emit register names in the assembly language output using symbolic forms.

`-mlongcall`
`-mno-longcall`
: By default assume that all calls are far away so that a longer and more expensive calling sequence is required. This is required for calls farther than 32 megabytes (33,554,432 bytes) from the current location. A short call is generated if the compiler knows the call cannot be that far away. This setting can be overridden by the `shortcall` function attribute, or by `#pragma longcall(0)`.

Some linkers are capable of detecting out-of-range calls and generating glue code on the fly. On these systems, long calls are unnecessary and generate slower code. As of this writing, the AIX linker can do this, as can the GNU linker for PowerPC/64. It is planned to add this feature to the GNU linker for 32-bit PowerPC systems as well.

On Darwin/PPC systems, `#pragma longcall` generates `jbsr callee, L42`, plus a *branch island* (glue code). The two target addresses represent the callee and the branch island. The Darwin/PPC linker prefers the first address and generates a `bl callee` if the PPC `bl` instruction reaches the callee directly; otherwise, the linker generates `bl L42` to call the branch island. The branch island is appended to the body of the calling function; it computes the full 32-bit address of the callee and jumps to it.

On Mach-O (Darwin) systems, this option directs the compiler emit to the glue for every direct call, and the Darwin linker decides whether to use or discard it.

In the future, GCC may ignore all longcall specifications when the linker is known to generate glue.

`-mtls-markers`
`-mno-tls-markers`
: Mark (do not mark) calls to `__tls_get_addr` with a relocation specifying the function argument. The relocation allows the linker to reliably associate func-

tion call with argument setup instructions for TLS optimization, which in turn allows GCC to better schedule the sequence.

`-pthread` Adds support for multithreading with the *pthreads* library. This option sets flags for both the preprocessor and linker.

`-mrecip`
`-mno-recip`

This option enables use of the reciprocal estimate and reciprocal square root estimate instructions with additional Newton-Raphson steps to increase precision instead of doing a divide or square root and divide for floating-point arguments. You should use the '`-ffast-math`' option when using '`-mrecip`' (or at least '`-funsafe-math-optimizations`', '`-ffinite-math-only`', '`-freciprocal-math`' and '`-fno-trapping-math`'). Note that while the throughput of the sequence is generally higher than the throughput of the non-reciprocal instruction, the precision of the sequence can be decreased by up to 2 ulp (i.e. the inverse of 1.0 equals 0.99999994) for reciprocal square roots.

`-mrecip=`*opt*

This option controls which reciprocal estimate instructions may be used. *opt* is a comma-separated list of options, which may be preceded by a `!` to invert the option:

'`all`' Enable all estimate instructions.

'`default`' Enable the default instructions, equivalent to '`-mrecip`'.

'`none`' Disable all estimate instructions, equivalent to '`-mno-recip`'.

'`div`' Enable the reciprocal approximation instructions for both single and double precision.

'`divf`' Enable the single-precision reciprocal approximation instructions.

'`divd`' Enable the double-precision reciprocal approximation instructions.

'`rsqrt`' Enable the reciprocal square root approximation instructions for both single and double precision.

'`rsqrtf`' Enable the single-precision reciprocal square root approximation instructions.

'`rsqrtd`' Enable the double-precision reciprocal square root approximation instructions.

So, for example, '`-mrecip=all,!rsqrtd`' enables all of the reciprocal estimate instructions, except for the `FRSQRTE`, `XSRSQRTEDP`, and `XVRSQRTEDP` instructions which handle the double-precision reciprocal square root calculations.

`-mrecip-precision`
`-mno-recip-precision`

Assume (do not assume) that the reciprocal estimate instructions provide higher-precision estimates than is mandated by the PowerPC ABI. Selecting '`-mcpu=power6`', '`-mcpu=power7`' or '`-mcpu=power8`' automatically selects

'-mrecip-precision'. The double-precision square root estimate instructions are not generated by default on low-precision machines, since they do not provide an estimate that converges after three steps.

-mveclibabi=*type*
: Specifies the ABI type to use for vectorizing intrinsics using an external library. The only type supported at present is 'mass', which specifies to use IBM's Mathematical Acceleration Subsystem (MASS) libraries for vectorizing intrinsics using external libraries. GCC currently emits calls to acosd2, acosf4, acoshd2, acoshf4, asind2, asinf4, asinhd2, asinhf4, atan2d2, atan2f4, atand2, atanf4, atanhd2, atanhf4, cbrtd2, cbrtf4, cosd2, cosf4, coshd2, coshf4, erfcd2, erfcf4, erfd2, erff4, exp2d2, exp2f4, expd2, expf4, expm1d2, expm1f4, hypotd2, hypotf4, lgammad2, lgammaf4, log10d2, log10f4, log1pd2, log1pf4, log2d2, log2f4, logd2, logf4, powd2, powf4, sind2, sinf4, sinhd2, sinhf4, sqrtd2, sqrtf4, tand2, tanf4, tanhd2, and tanhf4 when generating code for power7. Both '-ftree-vectorize' and '-funsafe-math-optimizations' must also be enabled. The MASS libraries must be specified at link time.

-mfriz
-mno-friz
: Generate (do not generate) the friz instruction when the '-funsafe-math-optimizations' option is used to optimize rounding of floating-point values to 64-bit integer and back to floating point. The friz instruction does not return the same value if the floating-point number is too large to fit in an integer.

-mpointers-to-nested-functions
-mno-pointers-to-nested-functions
: Generate (do not generate) code to load up the static chain register (r11) when calling through a pointer on AIX and 64-bit Linux systems where a function pointer points to a 3-word descriptor giving the function address, TOC value to be loaded in register r2, and static chain value to be loaded in register r11. The '-mpointers-to-nested-functions' is on by default. You cannot call through pointers to nested functions or pointers to functions compiled in other languages that use the static chain if you use '-mno-pointers-to-nested-functions'.

-msave-toc-indirect
-mno-save-toc-indirect
: Generate (do not generate) code to save the TOC value in the reserved stack location in the function prologue if the function calls through a pointer on AIX and 64-bit Linux systems. If the TOC value is not saved in the prologue, it is saved just before the call through the pointer. The '-mno-save-toc-indirect' option is the default.

-mcompat-align-parm
-mno-compat-align-parm
: Generate (do not generate) code to pass structure parameters with a maximum alignment of 64 bits, for compatibility with older versions of GCC.

Older versions of GCC (prior to 4.9.0) incorrectly did not align a structure parameter on a 128-bit boundary when that structure contained a member requiring 128-bit alignment. This is corrected in more recent versions of GCC. This option may be used to generate code that is compatible with functions compiled with older versions of GCC.

The '-mno-compat-align-parm' option is the default.

3.18.39 RX Options

These command-line options are defined for RX targets:

-m64bit-doubles
-m32bit-doubles
: Make the double data type be 64 bits ('-m64bit-doubles') or 32 bits ('-m32bit-doubles') in size. The default is '-m32bit-doubles'. *Note* RX floating-point hardware only works on 32-bit values, which is why the default is '-m32bit-doubles'.

-fpu
-nofpu
: Enables ('-fpu') or disables ('-nofpu') the use of RX floating-point hardware. The default is enabled for the RX600 series and disabled for the RX200 series.

  Floating-point instructions are only generated for 32-bit floating-point values, however, so the FPU hardware is not used for doubles if the '-m64bit-doubles' option is used.

  Note If the '-fpu' option is enabled then '-funsafe-math-optimizations' is also enabled automatically. This is because the RX FPU instructions are themselves unsafe.

-mcpu=*name*
: Selects the type of RX CPU to be targeted. Currently three types are supported, the generic 'RX600' and 'RX200' series hardware and the specific 'RX610' CPU. The default is 'RX600'.

  The only difference between 'RX600' and 'RX610' is that the 'RX610' does not support the MVTIPL instruction.

  The 'RX200' series does not have a hardware floating-point unit and so '-nofpu' is enabled by default when this type is selected.

-mbig-endian-data
-mlittle-endian-data
: Store data (but not code) in the big-endian format. The default is '-mlittle-endian-data', i.e. to store data in the little-endian format.

-msmall-data-limit=*N*
: Specifies the maximum size in bytes of global and static variables which can be placed into the small data area. Using the small data area can lead to smaller and faster code, but the size of area is limited and it is up to the programmer to ensure that the area does not overflow. Also when the small data area is used one of the RX's registers (usually r13) is reserved for use pointing to this area, so it is no longer available for use by the compiler. This could result in slower

and/or larger code if variables are pushed onto the stack instead of being held in this register.

Note, common variables (variables that have not been initialized) and constants are not placed into the small data area as they are assigned to other sections in the output executable.

The default value is zero, which disables this feature. Note, this feature is not enabled by default with higher optimization levels ('-O2' etc) because of the potentially detrimental effects of reserving a register. It is up to the programmer to experiment and discover whether this feature is of benefit to their program. See the description of the '-mpid' option for a description of how the actual register to hold the small data area pointer is chosen.

`-msim`
`-mno-sim`
Use the simulator runtime. The default is to use the libgloss board-specific runtime.

`-mas100-syntax`
`-mno-as100-syntax`
When generating assembler output use a syntax that is compatible with Renesas's AS100 assembler. This syntax can also be handled by the GAS assembler, but it has some restrictions so it is not generated by default.

`-mmax-constant-size=N`
Specifies the maximum size, in bytes, of a constant that can be used as an operand in a RX instruction. Although the RX instruction set does allow constants of up to 4 bytes in length to be used in instructions, a longer value equates to a longer instruction. Thus in some circumstances it can be beneficial to restrict the size of constants that are used in instructions. Constants that are too big are instead placed into a constant pool and referenced via register indirection.

The value *N* can be between 0 and 4. A value of 0 (the default) or 4 means that constants of any size are allowed.

`-mrelax`
Enable linker relaxation. Linker relaxation is a process whereby the linker attempts to reduce the size of a program by finding shorter versions of various instructions. Disabled by default.

`-mint-register=N`
Specify the number of registers to reserve for fast interrupt handler functions. The value *N* can be between 0 and 4. A value of 1 means that register `r13` is reserved for the exclusive use of fast interrupt handlers. A value of 2 reserves `r13` and `r12`. A value of 3 reserves `r13`, `r12` and `r11`, and a value of 4 reserves `r13` through `r10`. A value of 0, the default, does not reserve any registers.

`-msave-acc-in-interrupts`
Specifies that interrupt handler functions should preserve the accumulator register. This is only necessary if normal code might use the accumulator register, for example because it performs 64-bit multiplications. The default is to ignore the accumulator as this makes the interrupt handlers faster.

-mpid
-mno-pid Enables the generation of position independent data. When enabled any access to constant data is done via an offset from a base address held in a register. This allows the location of constant data to be determined at run time without requiring the executable to be relocated, which is a benefit to embedded applications with tight memory constraints. Data that can be modified is not affected by this option.

Note, using this feature reserves a register, usually `r13`, for the constant data base address. This can result in slower and/or larger code, especially in complicated functions.

The actual register chosen to hold the constant data base address depends upon whether the '`-msmall-data-limit`' and/or the '`-mint-register`' command-line options are enabled. Starting with register `r13` and proceeding downwards, registers are allocated first to satisfy the requirements of '`-mint-register`', then '`-mpid`' and finally '`-msmall-data-limit`'. Thus it is possible for the small data area register to be `r8` if both '`-mint-register=4`' and '`-mpid`' are specified on the command line.

By default this feature is not enabled. The default can be restored via the '`-mno-pid`' command-line option.

-mno-warn-multiple-fast-interrupts
-mwarn-multiple-fast-interrupts
Prevents GCC from issuing a warning message if it finds more than one fast interrupt handler when it is compiling a file. The default is to issue a warning for each extra fast interrupt handler found, as the RX only supports one such interrupt.

-mallow-string-insns
-mno-allow-string-insns
Enables or disables the use of the string manipulation instructions `SMOVF`, `SCMPU`, `SMOVB`, `SMOVU`, `SUNTIL` `SWHILE` and also the `RMPA` instruction. These instructions may prefetch data, which is not safe to do if accessing an I/O register. (See section 12.2.7 of the RX62N Group User's Manual for more information).

The default is to allow these instructions, but it is not possible for GCC to reliably detect all circumstances where a string instruction might be used to access an I/O register, so their use cannot be disabled automatically. Instead it is reliant upon the programmer to use the '`-mno-allow-string-insns`' option if their program accesses I/O space.

When the instructions are enabled GCC defines the C preprocessor symbol `__RX_ALLOW_STRING_INSNS__`, otherwise it defines the symbol `__RX_DISALLOW_STRING_INSNS__`.

-mjsr
-mno-jsr Use only (or not only) `JSR` instructions to access functions. This option can be used when code size exceeds the range of `BSR` instructions. Note that '`-mno-jsr`' does not mean to not use `JSR` but instead means that any type of branch may be used.

Note: The generic GCC command-line option '-ffixed-*reg*' has special significance to the RX port when used with the interrupt function attribute. This attribute indicates a function intended to process fast interrupts. GCC ensures that it only uses the registers r10, r11, r12 and/or r13 and only provided that the normal use of the corresponding registers have been restricted via the '-ffixed-*reg*' or '-mint-register' command-line options.

3.18.40 S/390 and zSeries Options

These are the '-m' options defined for the S/390 and zSeries architecture.

-mhard-float
-msoft-float
: Use (do not use) the hardware floating-point instructions and registers for floating-point operations. When '-msoft-float' is specified, functions in 'libgcc.a' are used to perform floating-point operations. When '-mhard-float' is specified, the compiler generates IEEE floating-point instructions. This is the default.

-mhard-dfp
-mno-hard-dfp
: Use (do not use) the hardware decimal-floating-point instructions for decimal-floating-point operations. When '-mno-hard-dfp' is specified, functions in 'libgcc.a' are used to perform decimal-floating-point operations. When '-mhard-dfp' is specified, the compiler generates decimal-floating-point hardware instructions. This is the default for '-march=z9-ec' or higher.

-mlong-double-64
-mlong-double-128
: These switches control the size of long double type. A size of 64 bits makes the long double type equivalent to the double type. This is the default.

-mbackchain
-mno-backchain
: Store (do not store) the address of the caller's frame as backchain pointer into the callee's stack frame. A backchain may be needed to allow debugging using tools that do not understand DWARF call frame information. When '-mno-packed-stack' is in effect, the backchain pointer is stored at the bottom of the stack frame; when '-mpacked-stack' is in effect, the backchain is placed into the topmost word of the 96/160 byte register save area.

: In general, code compiled with '-mbackchain' is call-compatible with code compiled with '-mmo-backchain'; however, use of the backchain for debugging purposes usually requires that the whole binary is built with '-mbackchain'. Note that the combination of '-mbackchain', '-mpacked-stack' and '-mhard-float' is not supported. In order to build a linux kernel use '-msoft-float'.

: The default is to not maintain the backchain.

-mpacked-stack
-mno-packed-stack
: Use (do not use) the packed stack layout. When '-mno-packed-stack' is specified, the compiler uses the all fields of the 96/160 byte register save area

only for their default purpose; unused fields still take up stack space. When '`-mpacked-stack`' is specified, register save slots are densely packed at the top of the register save area; unused space is reused for other purposes, allowing for more efficient use of the available stack space. However, when '`-mbackchain`' is also in effect, the topmost word of the save area is always used to store the backchain, and the return address register is always saved two words below the backchain.

As long as the stack frame backchain is not used, code generated with '`-mpacked-stack`' is call-compatible with code generated with '`-mno-packed-stack`'. Note that some non-FSF releases of GCC 2.95 for S/390 or zSeries generated code that uses the stack frame backchain at run time, not just for debugging purposes. Such code is not call-compatible with code compiled with '`-mpacked-stack`'. Also, note that the combination of '`-mbackchain`', '`-mpacked-stack`' and '`-mhard-float`' is not supported. In order to build a linux kernel use '`-msoft-float`'.

The default is to not use the packed stack layout.

`-msmall-exec`
`-mno-small-exec`
: Generate (or do not generate) code using the `bras` instruction to do subroutine calls. This only works reliably if the total executable size does not exceed 64k. The default is to use the `basr` instruction instead, which does not have this limitation.

`-m64`
`-m31`
: When '`-m31`' is specified, generate code compliant to the GNU/Linux for S/390 ABI. When '`-m64`' is specified, generate code compliant to the GNU/Linux for zSeries ABI. This allows GCC in particular to generate 64-bit instructions. For the '`s390`' targets, the default is '`-m31`', while the '`s390x`' targets default to '`-m64`'.

`-mzarch`
`-mesa`
: When '`-mzarch`' is specified, generate code using the instructions available on z/Architecture. When '`-mesa`' is specified, generate code using the instructions available on ESA/390. Note that '`-mesa`' is not possible with '`-m64`'. When generating code compliant to the GNU/Linux for S/390 ABI, the default is '`-mesa`'. When generating code compliant to the GNU/Linux for zSeries ABI, the default is '`-mzarch`'.

`-mhtm`
`-mno-htm`
: The '`-mhtm`' option enables a set of builtins making use of instructions available with the transactional execution facility introduced with the IBM zEnterprise EC12 machine generation Section 6.59.23 [S/390 System z Built-in Functions], page 638. '`-mhtm`' is enabled by default when using '`-march=zEC12`'.

`-mvx`
`-mno-vx`
: When '`-mvx`' is specified, generate code using the instructions available with the vector extension facility introduced with the IBM z13 machine generation. This option changes the ABI for some vector type values with regard to alignment

and calling conventions. In case vector type values are being used in an ABI-relevant context a GAS '.gnu_attribute' command will be added to mark the resulting binary with the ABI used. '-mvx' is enabled by default when using '-march=z13'.

-mzvector
-mno-zvector
The '-mzvector' option enables vector language extensions and builtins using instructions available with the vector extension facility introduced with the IBM z13 machine generation. This option adds support for 'vector' to be used as a keyword to define vector type variables and arguments. 'vector' is only available when GNU extensions are enabled. It will not be expanded when requesting strict standard compliance e.g. with '-std=c99'. In addition to the GCC low-level builtins '-mzvector' enables a set of builtins added for compatibility with AltiVec-style implementations like Power and Cell. In order to make use of these builtins the header file 'vecintrin.h' needs to be included. '-mzvector' is disabled by default.

-mmvcle
-mno-mvcle
Generate (or do not generate) code using the mvcle instruction to perform block moves. When '-mno-mvcle' is specified, use a mvc loop instead. This is the default unless optimizing for size.

-mdebug
-mno-debug
Print (or do not print) additional debug information when compiling. The default is to not print debug information.

-march=*cpu-type*
Generate code that runs on *cpu-type*, which is the name of a system representing a certain processor type. Possible values for *cpu-type* are 'z900', 'z990', 'z9-109', 'z9-ec', 'z10', 'z196', 'zEC12', and 'z13'. The default is '-march=z900'. 'g5' and 'g6' are deprecated and will be removed with future releases.

-mtune=*cpu-type*
Tune to *cpu-type* everything applicable about the generated code, except for the ABI and the set of available instructions. The list of *cpu-type* values is the same as for '-march'. The default is the value used for '-march'.

-mtpf-trace
-mno-tpf-trace
Generate code that adds (does not add) in TPF OS specific branches to trace routines in the operating system. This option is off by default, even when compiling for the TPF OS.

`-mfused-madd`
`-mno-fused-madd`
Generate code that uses (does not use) the floating-point multiply and accumulate instructions. These instructions are generated by default if hardware floating point is used.

`-mwarn-framesize=`*`framesize`*
Emit a warning if the current function exceeds the given frame size. Because this is a compile-time check it doesn't need to be a real problem when the program runs. It is intended to identify functions that most probably cause a stack overflow. It is useful to be used in an environment with limited stack size e.g. the linux kernel.

`-mwarn-dynamicstack`
Emit a warning if the function calls `alloca` or uses dynamically-sized arrays. This is generally a bad idea with a limited stack size.

`-mstack-guard=`*`stack-guard`*
`-mstack-size=`*`stack-size`*
If these options are provided the S/390 back end emits additional instructions in the function prologue that trigger a trap if the stack size is *stack-guard* bytes above the *stack-size* (remember that the stack on S/390 grows downward). If the *stack-guard* option is omitted the smallest power of 2 larger than the frame size of the compiled function is chosen. These options are intended to be used to help debugging stack overflow problems. The additionally emitted code causes only little overhead and hence can also be used in production-like systems without greater performance degradation. The given values have to be exact powers of 2 and *stack-size* has to be greater than *stack-guard* without exceeding 64k. In order to be efficient the extra code makes the assumption that the stack starts at an address aligned to the value given by *stack-size*. The *stack-guard* option can only be used in conjunction with *stack-size*.

`-mhotpatch=`*`pre-halfwords,post-halfwords`*
If the hotpatch option is enabled, a "hot-patching" function prologue is generated for all functions in the compilation unit. The funtion label is prepended with the given number of two-byte NOP instructions (*pre-halfwords*, maximum 1000000). After the label, 2 * *post-halfwords* bytes are appended, using the largest NOP like instructions the architecture allows (maximum 1000000).

If both arguments are zero, hotpatching is disabled.

This option can be overridden for individual functions with the `hotpatch` attribute.

3.18.41 Score Options

These options are defined for Score implementations:

`-meb` Compile code for big-endian mode. This is the default.

`-mel` Compile code for little-endian mode.

`-mnhwloop`
Disable generation of `bcnz` instructions.

`-muls` Enable generation of unaligned load and store instructions.

`-mmac` Enable the use of multiply-accumulate instructions. Disabled by default.

`-mscore5` Specify the SCORE5 as the target architecture.

`-mscore5u`
Specify the SCORE5U of the target architecture.

`-mscore7` Specify the SCORE7 as the target architecture. This is the default.

`-mscore7d`
Specify the SCORE7D as the target architecture.

3.18.42 SH Options

These '`-m`' options are defined for the SH implementations:

`-m1` Generate code for the SH1.

`-m2` Generate code for the SH2.

`-m2e` Generate code for the SH2e.

`-m2a-nofpu`
Generate code for the SH2a without FPU, or for a SH2a-FPU in such a way that the floating-point unit is not used.

`-m2a-single-only`
Generate code for the SH2a-FPU, in such a way that no double-precision floating-point operations are used.

`-m2a-single`
Generate code for the SH2a-FPU assuming the floating-point unit is in single-precision mode by default.

`-m2a` Generate code for the SH2a-FPU assuming the floating-point unit is in double-precision mode by default.

`-m3` Generate code for the SH3.

`-m3e` Generate code for the SH3e.

`-m4-nofpu`
Generate code for the SH4 without a floating-point unit.

`-m4-single-only`
Generate code for the SH4 with a floating-point unit that only supports single-precision arithmetic.

`-m4-single`
Generate code for the SH4 assuming the floating-point unit is in single-precision mode by default.

`-m4` Generate code for the SH4.

`-m4-100` Generate code for SH4-100.

`-m4-100-nofpu`
: Generate code for SH4-100 in such a way that the floating-point unit is not used.

`-m4-100-single`
: Generate code for SH4-100 assuming the floating-point unit is in single-precision mode by default.

`-m4-100-single-only`
: Generate code for SH4-100 in such a way that no double-precision floating-point operations are used.

`-m4-200`
: Generate code for SH4-200.

`-m4-200-nofpu`
: Generate code for SH4-200 without in such a way that the floating-point unit is not used.

`-m4-200-single`
: Generate code for SH4-200 assuming the floating-point unit is in single-precision mode by default.

`-m4-200-single-only`
: Generate code for SH4-200 in such a way that no double-precision floating-point operations are used.

`-m4-300`
: Generate code for SH4-300.

`-m4-300-nofpu`
: Generate code for SH4-300 without in such a way that the floating-point unit is not used.

`-m4-300-single`
: Generate code for SH4-300 in such a way that no double-precision floating-point operations are used.

`-m4-300-single-only`
: Generate code for SH4-300 in such a way that no double-precision floating-point operations are used.

`-m4-340`
: Generate code for SH4-340 (no MMU, no FPU).

`-m4-500`
: Generate code for SH4-500 (no FPU). Passes '`-isa=sh4-nofpu`' to the assembler.

`-m4a-nofpu`
: Generate code for the SH4al-dsp, or for a SH4a in such a way that the floating-point unit is not used.

`-m4a-single-only`
: Generate code for the SH4a, in such a way that no double-precision floating-point operations are used.

`-m4a-single`
: Generate code for the SH4a assuming the floating-point unit is in single-precision mode by default.

`-m4a` Generate code for the SH4a.

`-m4al` Same as '`-m4a-nofpu`', except that it implicitly passes '`-dsp`' to the assembler. GCC doesn't generate any DSP instructions at the moment.

`-mb` Compile code for the processor in big-endian mode.

`-ml` Compile code for the processor in little-endian mode.

`-mdalign` Align doubles at 64-bit boundaries. Note that this changes the calling conventions, and thus some functions from the standard C library do not work unless you recompile it first with '`-mdalign`'.

`-mrelax` Shorten some address references at link time, when possible; uses the linker option '`-relax`'.

`-mbigtable`
Use 32-bit offsets in `switch` tables. The default is to use 16-bit offsets.

`-mbitops` Enable the use of bit manipulation instructions on SH2A.

`-mfmovd` Enable the use of the instruction `fmovd`. Check '`-mdalign`' for alignment constraints.

`-mrenesas`
Comply with the calling conventions defined by Renesas.

`-mno-renesas`
Comply with the calling conventions defined for GCC before the Renesas conventions were available. This option is the default for all targets of the SH toolchain.

`-mnomacsave`
Mark the `MAC` register as call-clobbered, even if '`-mrenesas`' is given.

`-mieee`
`-mno-ieee`
Control the IEEE compliance of floating-point comparisons, which affects the handling of cases where the result of a comparison is unordered. By default '`-mieee`' is implicitly enabled. If '`-ffinite-math-only`' is enabled '`-mno-ieee`' is implicitly set, which results in faster floating-point greater-equal and less-equal comparisons. The implicit settings can be overridden by specifying either '`-mieee`' or '`-mno-ieee`'.

`-minline-ic_invalidate`
Inline code to invalidate instruction cache entries after setting up nested function trampolines. This option has no effect if '`-musermode`' is in effect and the selected code generation option (e.g. '`-m4`') does not allow the use of the `icbi` instruction. If the selected code generation option does not allow the use of the `icbi` instruction, and '`-musermode`' is not in effect, the inlined code manipulates the instruction cache address array directly with an associative write. This not only requires privileged mode at run time, but it also fails if the cache line had been mapped via the TLB and has become unmapped.

`-misize` Dump instruction size and location in the assembly code.

`-mpadstruct`
: This option is deprecated. It pads structures to multiple of 4 bytes, which is incompatible with the SH ABI.

`-matomic-model=`*model*
: Sets the model of atomic operations and additional parameters as a comma separated list. For details on the atomic built-in functions see Section 6.52 [__atomic Builtins], page 534. The following models and parameters are supported:

  '`none`' Disable compiler generated atomic sequences and emit library calls for atomic operations. This is the default if the target is not `sh*-*-linux*`.

  '`soft-gusa`'
  : Generate GNU/Linux compatible gUSA software atomic sequences for the atomic built-in functions. The generated atomic sequences require additional support from the interrupt/exception handling code of the system and are only suitable for SH3* and SH4* single-core systems. This option is enabled by default when the target is `sh*-*-linux*` and SH3* or SH4*. When the target is SH4A, this option also partially utilizes the hardware atomic instructions `movli.l` and `movco.l` to create more efficient code, unless '`strict`' is specified.

  '`soft-tcb`'
  : Generate software atomic sequences that use a variable in the thread control block. This is a variation of the gUSA sequences which can also be used on SH1* and SH2* targets. The generated atomic sequences require additional support from the interrupt/exception handling code of the system and are only suitable for single-core systems. When using this model, the '`gbr-offset=`' parameter has to be specified as well.

  '`soft-imask`'
  : Generate software atomic sequences that temporarily disable interrupts by setting `SR.IMASK = 1111`. This model works only when the program runs in privileged mode and is only suitable for single-core systems. Additional support from the interrupt/exception handling code of the system is not required. This model is enabled by default when the target is `sh*-*-linux*` and SH1* or SH2*.

  '`hard-llcs`'
  : Generate hardware atomic sequences using the `movli.l` and `movco.l` instructions only. This is only available on SH4A and is suitable for multi-core systems. Since the hardware instructions support only 32 bit atomic variables access to 8 or 16 bit variables is emulated with 32 bit accesses. Code compiled with this option is also compatible with other software atomic model interrupt/exception handling systems if executed on an SH4A

system. Additional support from the interrupt/exception handling code of the system is not required for this model.

'gbr-offset='
: This parameter specifies the offset in bytes of the variable in the thread control block structure that should be used by the generated atomic sequences when the 'soft-tcb' model has been selected. For other models this parameter is ignored. The specified value must be an integer multiple of four and in the range 0-1020.

'strict'
: This parameter prevents mixed usage of multiple atomic models, even if they are compatible, and makes the compiler generate atomic sequences of the specified model only.

-mtas
: Generate the `tas.b` opcode for `__atomic_test_and_set`. Notice that depending on the particular hardware and software configuration this can degrade overall performance due to the operand cache line flushes that are implied by the `tas.b` instruction. On multi-core SH4A processors the `tas.b` instruction must be used with caution since it can result in data corruption for certain cache configurations.

-mprefergot
: When generating position-independent code, emit function calls using the Global Offset Table instead of the Procedure Linkage Table.

-musermode
-mno-usermode
: Don't allow (allow) the compiler generating privileged mode code. Specifying '-musermode' also implies '-mno-inline-ic_invalidate' if the inlined code would not work in user mode. '-musermode' is the default when the target is `sh*-*-linux*`. If the target is SH1* or SH2* '-musermode' has no effect, since there is no user mode.

-multcost=*number*
: Set the cost to assume for a multiply insn.

-mdiv=*strategy*
: Set the division strategy to be used for integer division operations. *strategy* can be one of:

'call-div1'
: Calls a library function that uses the single-step division instruction `div1` to perform the operation. Division by zero calculates an unspecified result and does not trap. This is the default except for SH4, SH2A and SHcompact.

'call-fp'
: Calls a library function that performs the operation in double precision floating point. Division by zero causes a floating-point exception. This is the default for SHcompact with FPU. Specifying this for targets that do not have a double precision FPU defaults to `call-div1`.

'call-table'
Calls a library function that uses a lookup table for small divisors and the div1 instruction with case distinction for larger divisors. Division by zero calculates an unspecified result and does not trap. This is the default for SH4. Specifying this for targets that do not have dynamic shift instructions defaults to call-div1.

When a division strategy has not been specified the default strategy is selected based on the current target. For SH2A the default strategy is to use the divs and divu instructions instead of library function calls.

-maccumulate-outgoing-args
Reserve space once for outgoing arguments in the function prologue rather than around each call. Generally beneficial for performance and size. Also needed for unwinding to avoid changing the stack frame around conditional code.

-mdivsi3_libfunc=*name*
Set the name of the library function used for 32-bit signed division to *name*. This only affects the name used in the 'call' division strategies, and the compiler still expects the same sets of input/output/clobbered registers as if this option were not present.

-mfixed-range=*register-range*
Generate code treating the given register range as fixed registers. A fixed register is one that the register allocator can not use. This is useful when compiling kernel code. A register range is specified as two registers separated by a dash. Multiple register ranges can be specified separated by a comma.

-mbranch-cost=*num*
Assume *num* to be the cost for a branch instruction. Higher numbers make the compiler try to generate more branch-free code if possible. If not specified the value is selected depending on the processor type that is being compiled for.

-mzdcbranch
-mno-zdcbranch
Assume (do not assume) that zero displacement conditional branch instructions bt and bf are fast. If '-mzdcbranch' is specified, the compiler prefers zero displacement branch code sequences. This is enabled by default when generating code for SH4 and SH4A. It can be explicitly disabled by specifying '-mno-zdcbranch'.

-mcbranch-force-delay-slot
Force the usage of delay slots for conditional branches, which stuffs the delay slot with a nop if a suitable instruction can't be found. By default this option is disabled. It can be enabled to work around hardware bugs as found in the original SH7055.

-mfused-madd
-mno-fused-madd
Generate code that uses (does not use) the floating-point multiply and accumulate instructions. These instructions are generated by default if hardware floating point is used. The machine-dependent '-mfused-madd' option is

now mapped to the machine-independent '-ffp-contract=fast' option, and '-mno-fused-madd' is mapped to '-ffp-contract=off'.

-mfsca
-mno-fsca
: Allow or disallow the compiler to emit the fsca instruction for sine and cosine approximations. The option '-mfsca' must be used in combination with '-funsafe-math-optimizations'. It is enabled by default when generating code for SH4A. Using '-mno-fsca' disables sine and cosine approximations even if '-funsafe-math-optimizations' is in effect.

-mfsrra
-mno-fsrra
: Allow or disallow the compiler to emit the fsrra instruction for reciprocal square root approximations. The option '-mfsrra' must be used in combination with '-funsafe-math-optimizations' and '-ffinite-math-only'. It is enabled by default when generating code for SH4A. Using '-mno-fsrra' disables reciprocal square root approximations even if '-funsafe-math-optimizations' and '-ffinite-math-only' are in effect.

-mpretend-cmove
: Prefer zero-displacement conditional branches for conditional move instruction patterns. This can result in faster code on the SH4 processor.

-mfdpic
: Generate code using the FDPIC ABI.

3.18.43 Solaris 2 Options

These '-m' options are supported on Solaris 2:

-mclear-hwcap
: '-mclear-hwcap' tells the compiler to remove the hardware capabilities generated by the Solaris assembler. This is only necessary when object files use ISA extensions not supported by the current machine, but check at runtime whether or not to use them.

-mimpure-text
: '-mimpure-text', used in addition to '-shared', tells the compiler to not pass '-z text' to the linker when linking a shared object. Using this option, you can link position-dependent code into a shared object.

'-mimpure-text' suppresses the "relocations remain against allocatable but non-writable sections" linker error message. However, the necessary relocations trigger copy-on-write, and the shared object is not actually shared across processes. Instead of using '-mimpure-text', you should compile all source code with '-fpic' or '-fPIC'.

These switches are supported in addition to the above on Solaris 2:

-pthreads
: Add support for multithreading using the POSIX threads library. This option sets flags for both the preprocessor and linker. This option does not affect the thread safety of object code produced by the compiler or that of libraries supplied with it.

`-pthread` This is a synonym for '`-pthreads`'.

3.18.44 SPARC Options

These '`-m`' options are supported on the SPARC:

`-mno-app-regs`
`-mapp-regs`
: Specify '`-mapp-regs`' to generate output using the global registers 2 through 4, which the SPARC SVR4 ABI reserves for applications. Like the global register 1, each global register 2 through 4 is then treated as an allocable register that is clobbered by function calls. This is the default.

  To be fully SVR4 ABI-compliant at the cost of some performance loss, specify '`-mno-app-regs`'. You should compile libraries and system software with this option.

`-mflat`
`-mno-flat`
: With '`-mflat`', the compiler does not generate save/restore instructions and uses a "flat" or single register window model. This model is compatible with the regular register window model. The local registers and the input registers (0–5) are still treated as "call-saved" registers and are saved on the stack as needed.

  With '`-mno-flat`' (the default), the compiler generates save/restore instructions (except for leaf functions). This is the normal operating mode.

`-mfpu`
`-mhard-float`
: Generate output containing floating-point instructions. This is the default.

`-mno-fpu`
`-msoft-float`
: Generate output containing library calls for floating point. **Warning:** the requisite libraries are not available for all SPARC targets. Normally the facilities of the machine's usual C compiler are used, but this cannot be done directly in cross-compilation. You must make your own arrangements to provide suitable library functions for cross-compilation. The embedded targets '`sparc-*-aout`' and '`sparclite-*-*`' do provide software floating-point support.

  '`-msoft-float`' changes the calling convention in the output file; therefore, it is only useful if you compile *all* of a program with this option. In particular, you need to compile '`libgcc.a`', the library that comes with GCC, with '`-msoft-float`' in order for this to work.

`-mhard-quad-float`
: Generate output containing quad-word (long double) floating-point instructions.

`-msoft-quad-float`
: Generate output containing library calls for quad-word (long double) floating-point instructions. The functions called are those specified in the SPARC ABI. This is the default.

As of this writing, there are no SPARC implementations that have hardware support for the quad-word floating-point instructions. They all invoke a trap handler for one of these instructions, and then the trap handler emulates the effect of the instruction. Because of the trap handler overhead, this is much slower than calling the ABI library routines. Thus the '`-msoft-quad-float`' option is the default.

`-mno-unaligned-doubles`
`-munaligned-doubles`

Assume that doubles have 8-byte alignment. This is the default.

With '`-munaligned-doubles`', GCC assumes that doubles have 8-byte alignment only if they are contained in another type, or if they have an absolute address. Otherwise, it assumes they have 4-byte alignment. Specifying this option avoids some rare compatibility problems with code generated by other compilers. It is not the default because it results in a performance loss, especially for floating-point code.

`-muser-mode`
`-mno-user-mode`

Do not generate code that can only run in supervisor mode. This is relevant only for the `casa` instruction emitted for the LEON3 processor. This is the default.

`-mfaster-structs`
`-mno-faster-structs`

With '`-mfaster-structs`', the compiler assumes that structures should have 8-byte alignment. This enables the use of pairs of `ldd` and `std` instructions for copies in structure assignment, in place of twice as many `ld` and `st` pairs. However, the use of this changed alignment directly violates the SPARC ABI. Thus, it's intended only for use on targets where the developer acknowledges that their resulting code is not directly in line with the rules of the ABI.

`-mstd-struct-return`
`-mno-std-struct-return`

With '`-mstd-struct-return`', the compiler generates checking code in functions returning structures or unions to detect size mismatches between the two sides of function calls, as per the 32-bit ABI.

The default is '`-mno-std-struct-return`'. This option has no effect in 64-bit mode.

`-mcpu=`*`cpu_type`*

Set the instruction set, register set, and instruction scheduling parameters for machine type *cpu_type*. Supported values for *cpu_type* are '`v7`', '`cypress`', '`v8`', '`supersparc`', '`hypersparc`', '`leon`', '`leon3`', '`leon3v7`', '`sparclite`', '`f930`', '`f934`', '`sparclite86x`', '`sparclet`', '`tsc701`', '`v9`', '`ultrasparc`', '`ultrasparc3`', '`niagara`', '`niagara2`', '`niagara3`' and '`niagara4`'.

Native Solaris and GNU/Linux toolchains also support the value '`native`', which selects the best architecture option for the host processor. '`-mcpu=native`' has no effect if GCC does not recognize the processor.

Default instruction scheduling parameters are used for values that select an architecture and not an implementation. These are '`v7`', '`v8`', '`sparclite`', '`sparclet`', '`v9`'.

Here is a list of each supported architecture and their supported implementations.

v7 cypress, leon3v7

v8 supersparc, hypersparc, leon, leon3

sparclite f930, f934, sparclite86x

sparclet tsc701

v9 ultrasparc, ultrasparc3, niagara, niagara2, niagara3, niagara4

By default (unless configured otherwise), GCC generates code for the V7 variant of the SPARC architecture. With '`-mcpu=cypress`', the compiler additionally optimizes it for the Cypress CY7C602 chip, as used in the SPARCStation/SPARCServer 3xx series. This is also appropriate for the older SPARCStation 1, 2, IPX etc.

With '`-mcpu=v8`', GCC generates code for the V8 variant of the SPARC architecture. The only difference from V7 code is that the compiler emits the integer multiply and integer divide instructions which exist in SPARC-V8 but not in SPARC-V7. With '`-mcpu=supersparc`', the compiler additionally optimizes it for the SuperSPARC chip, as used in the SPARCStation 10, 1000 and 2000 series.

With '`-mcpu=sparclite`', GCC generates code for the SPARClite variant of the SPARC architecture. This adds the integer multiply, integer divide step and scan (`ffs`) instructions which exist in SPARClite but not in SPARC-V7. With '`-mcpu=f930`', the compiler additionally optimizes it for the Fujitsu MB86930 chip, which is the original SPARClite, with no FPU. With '`-mcpu=f934`', the compiler additionally optimizes it for the Fujitsu MB86934 chip, which is the more recent SPARClite with FPU.

With '`-mcpu=sparclet`', GCC generates code for the SPARClet variant of the SPARC architecture. This adds the integer multiply, multiply/accumulate, integer divide step and scan (`ffs`) instructions which exist in SPARClet but not in SPARC-V7. With '`-mcpu=tsc701`', the compiler additionally optimizes it for the TEMIC SPARClet chip.

With '`-mcpu=v9`', GCC generates code for the V9 variant of the SPARC architecture. This adds 64-bit integer and floating-point move instructions, 3 additional floating-point condition code registers and conditional move instructions. With '`-mcpu=ultrasparc`', the compiler additionally optimizes it for the Sun UltraSPARC I/II/IIi chips. With '`-mcpu=ultrasparc3`', the compiler additionally optimizes it for the Sun UltraSPARC III/III+/IIIi/IIIi+/IV/IV+ chips. With '`-mcpu=niagara`', the compiler additionally optimizes it for Sun UltraSPARC T1 chips. With '`-mcpu=niagara2`', the compiler additionally optimizes it for Sun UltraSPARC T2 chips. With '`-mcpu=niagara3`', the compiler additionally optimizes it for Sun UltraSPARC T3 chips. With '`-mcpu=niagara4`', the compiler additionally optimizes it for Sun UltraSPARC T4 chips.

`-mtune=cpu_type`
: Set the instruction scheduling parameters for machine type *cpu_type*, but do not set the instruction set or register set that the option '`-mcpu=cpu_type`' does.

  The same values for '`-mcpu=cpu_type`' can be used for '`-mtune=cpu_type`', but the only useful values are those that select a particular CPU implementation. Those are '`cypress`', '`supersparc`', '`hypersparc`', '`leon`', '`leon3`', '`leon3v7`', '`f930`', '`f934`', '`sparclite86x`', '`tsc701`', '`ultrasparc`', '`ultrasparc3`', '`niagara`', '`niagara2`', '`niagara3`' and '`niagara4`'. With native Solaris and GNU/Linux toolchains, '`native`' can also be used.

`-mv8plus`
`-mno-v8plus`
: With '`-mv8plus`', GCC generates code for the SPARC-V8+ ABI. The difference from the V8 ABI is that the global and out registers are considered 64 bits wide. This is enabled by default on Solaris in 32-bit mode for all SPARC-V9 processors.

`-mvis`
`-mno-vis`
: With '`-mvis`', GCC generates code that takes advantage of the UltraSPARC Visual Instruction Set extensions. The default is '`-mno-vis`'.

`-mvis2`
`-mno-vis2`
: With '`-mvis2`', GCC generates code that takes advantage of version 2.0 of the UltraSPARC Visual Instruction Set extensions. The default is '`-mvis2`' when targeting a cpu that supports such instructions, such as UltraSPARC-III and later. Setting '`-mvis2`' also sets '`-mvis`'.

`-mvis3`
`-mno-vis3`
: With '`-mvis3`', GCC generates code that takes advantage of version 3.0 of the UltraSPARC Visual Instruction Set extensions. The default is '`-mvis3`' when targeting a cpu that supports such instructions, such as niagara-3 and later. Setting '`-mvis3`' also sets '`-mvis2`' and '`-mvis`'.

`-mcbcond`
`-mno-cbcond`
: With '`-mcbcond`', GCC generates code that takes advantage of compare-and-branch instructions, as defined in the Sparc Architecture 2011. The default is '`-mcbcond`' when targeting a cpu that supports such instructions, such as niagara-4 and later.

`-mpopc`
`-mno-popc`
: With '`-mpopc`', GCC generates code that takes advantage of the UltraSPARC population count instruction. The default is '`-mpopc`' when targeting a cpu that supports such instructions, such as Niagara-2 and later.

`-mfmaf`
`-mno-fmaf`
With '`-mfmaf`', GCC generates code that takes advantage of the UltraSPARC Fused Multiply-Add Floating-point extensions. The default is '`-mfmaf`' when targeting a cpu that supports such instructions, such as Niagara-3 and later.

`-mfix-at697f`
Enable the documented workaround for the single erratum of the Atmel AT697F processor (which corresponds to erratum #13 of the AT697E processor).

`-mfix-ut699`
Enable the documented workarounds for the floating-point errata and the data cache nullify errata of the UT699 processor.

These '`-m`' options are supported in addition to the above on SPARC-V9 processors in 64-bit environments:

`-m32`
`-m64` Generate code for a 32-bit or 64-bit environment. The 32-bit environment sets int, long and pointer to 32 bits. The 64-bit environment sets int to 32 bits and long and pointer to 64 bits.

`-mcmodel=`*`which`*
Set the code model to one of

'`medlow`' The Medium/Low code model: 64-bit addresses, programs must be linked in the low 32 bits of memory. Programs can be statically or dynamically linked.

'`medmid`' The Medium/Middle code model: 64-bit addresses, programs must be linked in the low 44 bits of memory, the text and data segments must be less than 2GB in size and the data segment must be located within 2GB of the text segment.

'`medany`' The Medium/Anywhere code model: 64-bit addresses, programs may be linked anywhere in memory, the text and data segments must be less than 2GB in size and the data segment must be located within 2GB of the text segment.

'`embmedany`'
The Medium/Anywhere code model for embedded systems: 64-bit addresses, the text and data segments must be less than 2GB in size, both starting anywhere in memory (determined at link time). The global register %g4 points to the base of the data segment. Programs are statically linked and PIC is not supported.

`-mmemory-model=`*`mem-model`*
Set the memory model in force on the processor to one of

'`default`' The default memory model for the processor and operating system.

'`rmo`' Relaxed Memory Order

'`pso`' Partial Store Order

'tso' Total Store Order

'sc' Sequential Consistency

These memory models are formally defined in Appendix D of the Sparc V9 architecture manual, as set in the processor's `PSTATE.MM` field.

`-mstack-bias`
`-mno-stack-bias`
With '`-mstack-bias`', GCC assumes that the stack pointer, and frame pointer if present, are offset by −2047 which must be added back when making stack frame references. This is the default in 64-bit mode. Otherwise, assume no such offset is present.

3.18.45 SPU Options

These '`-m`' options are supported on the SPU:

`-mwarn-reloc`
`-merror-reloc`
The loader for SPU does not handle dynamic relocations. By default, GCC gives an error when it generates code that requires a dynamic relocation. '`-mno-error-reloc`' disables the error, '`-mwarn-reloc`' generates a warning instead.

`-msafe-dma`
`-munsafe-dma`
Instructions that initiate or test completion of DMA must not be reordered with respect to loads and stores of the memory that is being accessed. With '`-munsafe-dma`' you must use the `volatile` keyword to protect memory accesses, but that can lead to inefficient code in places where the memory is known to not change. Rather than mark the memory as volatile, you can use '`-msafe-dma`' to tell the compiler to treat the DMA instructions as potentially affecting all memory.

`-mbranch-hints`
By default, GCC generates a branch hint instruction to avoid pipeline stalls for always-taken or probably-taken branches. A hint is not generated closer than 8 instructions away from its branch. There is little reason to disable them, except for debugging purposes, or to make an object a little bit smaller.

`-msmall-mem`
`-mlarge-mem`
By default, GCC generates code assuming that addresses are never larger than 18 bits. With '`-mlarge-mem`' code is generated that assumes a full 32-bit address.

`-mstdmain`
By default, GCC links against startup code that assumes the SPU-style main function interface (which has an unconventional parameter list). With '`-mstdmain`', GCC links your program against startup code that assumes a C99-style interface to `main`, including a local copy of `argv` strings.

`-mfixed-range=register-range`
: Generate code treating the given register range as fixed registers. A fixed register is one that the register allocator cannot use. This is useful when compiling kernel code. A register range is specified as two registers separated by a dash. Multiple register ranges can be specified separated by a comma.

`-mea32`
`-mea64`
: Compile code assuming that pointers to the PPU address space accessed via the `__ea` named address space qualifier are either 32 or 64 bits wide. The default is 32 bits. As this is an ABI-changing option, all object code in an executable must be compiled with the same setting.

`-maddress-space-conversion`
`-mno-address-space-conversion`
: Allow/disallow treating the `__ea` address space as superset of the generic address space. This enables explicit type casts between `__ea` and generic pointer as well as implicit conversions of generic pointers to `__ea` pointers. The default is to allow address space pointer conversions.

`-mcache-size=cache-size`
: This option controls the version of libgcc that the compiler links to an executable and selects a software-managed cache for accessing variables in the `__ea` address space with a particular cache size. Possible options for *cache-size* are '`8`', '`16`', '`32`', '`64`' and '`128`'. The default cache size is 64KB.

`-matomic-updates`
`-mno-atomic-updates`
: This option controls the version of libgcc that the compiler links to an executable and selects whether atomic updates to the software-managed cache of PPU-side variables are used. If you use atomic updates, changes to a PPU variable from SPU code using the `__ea` named address space qualifier do not interfere with changes to other PPU variables residing in the same cache line from PPU code. If you do not use atomic updates, such interference may occur; however, writing back cache lines is more efficient. The default behavior is to use atomic updates.

`-mdual-nops`
`-mdual-nops=n`
: By default, GCC inserts nops to increase dual issue when it expects it to increase performance. *n* can be a value from 0 to 10. A smaller *n* inserts fewer nops. 10 is the default, 0 is the same as '`-mno-dual-nops`'. Disabled with '`-Os`'.

`-mhint-max-nops=n`
: Maximum number of nops to insert for a branch hint. A branch hint must be at least 8 instructions away from the branch it is affecting. GCC inserts up to *n* nops to enforce this, otherwise it does not generate the branch hint.

`-mhint-max-distance=n`
: The encoding of the branch hint instruction limits the hint to be within 256 instructions of the branch it is affecting. By default, GCC makes sure it is within 125.

`-msafe-hints`
: Work around a hardware bug that causes the SPU to stall indefinitely. By default, GCC inserts the `hbrp` instruction to make sure this stall won't happen.

3.18.46 Options for System V

These additional options are available on System V Release 4 for compatibility with other compilers on those systems:

`-G` Create a shared object. It is recommended that '`-symbolic`' or '`-shared`' be used instead.

`-Qy` Identify the versions of each tool used by the compiler, in a `.ident` assembler directive in the output.

`-Qn` Refrain from adding `.ident` directives to the output file (this is the default).

`-YP,`*`dirs`* Search the directories *dirs*, and no others, for libraries specified with '`-l`'.

`-Ym,`*`dir`* Look in the directory *dir* to find the M4 preprocessor. The assembler uses this option.

3.18.47 TILE-Gx Options

These '`-m`' options are supported on the TILE-Gx:

`-mcmodel=small`
: Generate code for the small model. The distance for direct calls is limited to 500M in either direction. PC-relative addresses are 32 bits. Absolute addresses support the full address range.

`-mcmodel=large`
: Generate code for the large model. There is no limitation on call distance, pc-relative addresses, or absolute addresses.

`-mcpu=`*`name`*
: Selects the type of CPU to be targeted. Currently the only supported type is '`tilegx`'.

`-m32`
`-m64` Generate code for a 32-bit or 64-bit environment. The 32-bit environment sets int, long, and pointer to 32 bits. The 64-bit environment sets int to 32 bits and long and pointer to 64 bits.

`-mbig-endian`
`-mlittle-endian`
: Generate code in big/little endian mode, respectively.

3.18.48 TILEPro Options

These '`-m`' options are supported on the TILEPro:

`-mcpu=`*`name`*
: Selects the type of CPU to be targeted. Currently the only supported type is '`tilepro`'.

`-m32` Generate code for a 32-bit environment, which sets int, long, and pointer to 32 bits. This is the only supported behavior so the flag is essentially ignored.

3.18.49 V850 Options

These '-m' options are defined for V850 implementations:

-mlong-calls
-mno-long-calls
: Treat all calls as being far away (near). If calls are assumed to be far away, the compiler always loads the function's address into a register, and calls indirect through the pointer.

-mno-ep
-mep
: Do not optimize (do optimize) basic blocks that use the same index pointer 4 or more times to copy pointer into the ep register, and use the shorter sld and sst instructions. The '-mep' option is on by default if you optimize.

-mno-prolog-function
-mprolog-function
: Do not use (do use) external functions to save and restore registers at the prologue and epilogue of a function. The external functions are slower, but use less code space if more than one function saves the same number of registers. The '-mprolog-function' option is on by default if you optimize.

-mspace
: Try to make the code as small as possible. At present, this just turns on the '-mep' and '-mprolog-function' options.

-mtda=*n*
: Put static or global variables whose size is *n* bytes or less into the tiny data area that register ep points to. The tiny data area can hold up to 256 bytes in total (128 bytes for byte references).

-msda=*n*
: Put static or global variables whose size is *n* bytes or less into the small data area that register gp points to. The small data area can hold up to 64 kilobytes.

-mzda=*n*
: Put static or global variables whose size is *n* bytes or less into the first 32 kilobytes of memory.

-mv850
: Specify that the target processor is the V850.

-mv850e3v5
: Specify that the target processor is the V850E3V5. The preprocessor constant __v850e3v5__ is defined if this option is used.

-mv850e2v4
: Specify that the target processor is the V850E3V5. This is an alias for the '-mv850e3v5' option.

-mv850e2v3
: Specify that the target processor is the V850E2V3. The preprocessor constant __v850e2v3__ is defined if this option is used.

-mv850e2
: Specify that the target processor is the V850E2. The preprocessor constant __v850e2__ is defined if this option is used.

-mv850e1
: Specify that the target processor is the V850E1. The preprocessor constants __v850e1__ and __v850e__ are defined if this option is used.

`-mv850es` Specify that the target processor is the V850ES. This is an alias for the '`-mv850e1`' option.

`-mv850e` Specify that the target processor is the V850E. The preprocessor constant `__v850e__` is defined if this option is used.

If neither '`-mv850`' nor '`-mv850e`' nor '`-mv850e1`' nor '`-mv850e2`' nor '`-mv850e2v3`' nor '`-mv850e3v5`' are defined then a default target processor is chosen and the relevant '`__v850*__`' preprocessor constant is defined.

The preprocessor constants `__v850` and `__v851__` are always defined, regardless of which processor variant is the target.

`-mdisable-callt`
`-mno-disable-callt`

This option suppresses generation of the `CALLT` instruction for the v850e, v850e1, v850e2, v850e2v3 and v850e3v5 flavors of the v850 architecture.

This option is enabled by default when the RH850 ABI is in use (see '`-mrh850-abi`'), and disabled by default when the GCC ABI is in use. If `CALLT` instructions are being generated then the C preprocessor symbol `__V850_CALLT__` is defined.

`-mrelax`
`-mno-relax`

Pass on (or do not pass on) the '`-mrelax`' command-line option to the assembler.

`-mlong-jumps`
`-mno-long-jumps`

Disable (or re-enable) the generation of PC-relative jump instructions.

`-msoft-float`
`-mhard-float`

Disable (or re-enable) the generation of hardware floating point instructions. This option is only significant when the target architecture is '`V850E2V3`' or higher. If hardware floating point instructions are being generated then the C preprocessor symbol `__FPU_OK__` is defined, otherwise the symbol `__NO_FPU__` is defined.

`-mloop` Enables the use of the e3v5 LOOP instruction. The use of this instruction is not enabled by default when the e3v5 architecture is selected because its use is still experimental.

`-mrh850-abi`
`-mghs` Enables support for the RH850 version of the V850 ABI. This is the default. With this version of the ABI the following rules apply:

- Integer sized structures and unions are returned via a memory pointer rather than a register.
- Large structures and unions (more than 8 bytes in size) are passed by value.
- Functions are aligned to 16-bit boundaries.
- The '`-m8byte-align`' command-line option is supported.
- The '`-mdisable-callt`' command-line option is enabled by default. The '`-mno-disable-callt`' command-line option is not supported.

When this version of the ABI is enabled the C preprocessor symbol `__V850_RH850_ABI__` is defined.

`-mgcc-abi`
: Enables support for the old GCC version of the V850 ABI. With this version of the ABI the following rules apply:

- Integer sized structures and unions are returned in register `r10`.
- Large structures and unions (more than 8 bytes in size) are passed by reference.
- Functions are aligned to 32-bit boundaries, unless optimizing for size.
- The '`-m8byte-align`' command-line option is not supported.
- The '`-mdisable-callt`' command-line option is supported but not enabled by default.

When this version of the ABI is enabled the C preprocessor symbol `__V850_GCC_ABI__` is defined.

`-m8byte-align`
`-mno-8byte-align`
: Enables support for `double` and `long long` types to be aligned on 8-byte boundaries. The default is to restrict the alignment of all objects to at most 4-bytes. When '`-m8byte-align`' is in effect the C preprocessor symbol `__V850_8BYTE_ALIGN__` is defined.

`-mbig-switch`
: Generate code suitable for big switch tables. Use this option only if the assembler/linker complain about out of range branches within a switch table.

`-mapp-regs`
: This option causes r2 and r5 to be used in the code generated by the compiler. This setting is the default.

`-mno-app-regs`
: This option causes r2 and r5 to be treated as fixed registers.

3.18.50 VAX Options

These '`-m`' options are defined for the VAX:

`-munix`
: Do not output certain jump instructions (`aobleq` and so on) that the Unix assembler for the VAX cannot handle across long ranges.

`-mgnu`
: Do output those jump instructions, on the assumption that the GNU assembler is being used.

`-mg`
: Output code for G-format floating-point numbers instead of D-format.

3.18.51 Visium Options

`-mdebug`
: A program which performs file I/O and is destined to run on an MCM target should be linked with this option. It causes the libraries libc.a and libdebug.a to be linked. The program should be run on the target under the control of the GDB remote debugging stub.

`-msim` A program which performs file I/O and is destined to run on the simulator should be linked with option. This causes libraries libc.a and libsim.a to be linked.

`-mfpu`
`-mhard-float`
: Generate code containing floating-point instructions. This is the default.

`-mno-fpu`
`-msoft-float`
: Generate code containing library calls for floating-point.

  '`-msoft-float`' changes the calling convention in the output file; therefore, it is only useful if you compile *all* of a program with this option. In particular, you need to compile '`libgcc.a`', the library that comes with GCC, with '`-msoft-float`' in order for this to work.

`-mcpu=`*`cpu_type`*
: Set the instruction set, register set, and instruction scheduling parameters for machine type *cpu_type*. Supported values for *cpu_type* are '`mcm`', '`gr5`' and '`gr6`'.

  '`mcm`' is a synonym of '`gr5`' present for backward compatibility.

  By default (unless configured otherwise), GCC generates code for the GR5 variant of the Visium architecture.

  With '`-mcpu=gr6`', GCC generates code for the GR6 variant of the Visium architecture. The only difference from GR5 code is that the compiler will generate block move instructions.

`-mtune=`*`cpu_type`*
: Set the instruction scheduling parameters for machine type *cpu_type*, but do not set the instruction set or register set that the option '`-mcpu=`*`cpu_type`*' would.

`-msv-mode`
: Generate code for the supervisor mode, where there are no restrictions on the access to general registers. This is the default.

`-muser-mode`
: Generate code for the user mode, where the access to some general registers is forbidden: on the GR5, registers r24 to r31 cannot be accessed in this mode; on the GR6, only registers r29 to r31 are affected.

3.18.52 VMS Options

These '`-m`' options are defined for the VMS implementations:

`-mvms-return-codes`
: Return VMS condition codes from `main`. The default is to return POSIX-style condition (e.g. error) codes.

`-mdebug-main=`*`prefix`*
: Flag the first routine whose name starts with *prefix* as the main routine for the debugger.

`-mmalloc64`
: Default to 64-bit memory allocation routines.

`-mpointer-size=`*size*
: Set the default size of pointers. Possible options for *size* are '`32`' or '`short`' for 32 bit pointers, '`64`' or '`long`' for 64 bit pointers, and '`no`' for supporting only 32 bit pointers. The later option disables `pragma pointer_size`.

3.18.53 VxWorks Options

The options in this section are defined for all VxWorks targets. Options specific to the target hardware are listed with the other options for that target.

`-mrtp`
: GCC can generate code for both VxWorks kernels and real time processes (RTPs). This option switches from the former to the latter. It also defines the preprocessor macro `__RTP__`.

`-non-static`
: Link an RTP executable against shared libraries rather than static libraries. The options '`-static`' and '`-shared`' can also be used for RTPs (see Section 3.14 [Link Options], page 171); '`-static`' is the default.

`-Bstatic`
`-Bdynamic`
: These options are passed down to the linker. They are defined for compatibility with Diab.

`-Xbind-lazy`
: Enable lazy binding of function calls. This option is equivalent to '`-Wl,-z,now`' and is defined for compatibility with Diab.

`-Xbind-now`
: Disable lazy binding of function calls. This option is the default and is defined for compatibility with Diab.

3.18.54 x86 Options

These '`-m`' options are defined for the x86 family of computers.

`-march=`*cpu-type*
: Generate instructions for the machine type *cpu-type*. In contrast to '`-mtune=`*cpu-type*', which merely tunes the generated code for the specified *cpu-type*, '`-march=`*cpu-type*' allows GCC to generate code that may not run at all on processors other than the one indicated. Specifying '`-march=`*cpu-type*' implies '`-mtune=`*cpu-type*'.

  The choices for *cpu-type* are:

  '`native`'
  : This selects the CPU to generate code for at compilation time by determining the processor type of the compiling machine. Using '`-march=native`' enables all instruction subsets supported by the local machine (hence the result might not run on different machines). Using '`-mtune=native`' produces code optimized for the local machine under the constraints of the selected instruction set.

'i386' Original Intel i386 CPU.

'i486' Intel i486 CPU. (No scheduling is implemented for this chip.)

'i586'
'pentium' Intel Pentium CPU with no MMX support.

'lakemont'
Intel Lakemont MCU, based on Intel Pentium CPU.

'pentium-mmx'
Intel Pentium MMX CPU, based on Pentium core with MMX instruction set support.

'pentiumpro'
Intel Pentium Pro CPU.

'i686' When used with '-march', the Pentium Pro instruction set is used, so the code runs on all i686 family chips. When used with '-mtune', it has the same meaning as 'generic'.

'pentium2'
Intel Pentium II CPU, based on Pentium Pro core with MMX instruction set support.

'pentium3'
'pentium3m'
Intel Pentium III CPU, based on Pentium Pro core with MMX and SSE instruction set support.

'pentium-m'
Intel Pentium M; low-power version of Intel Pentium III CPU with MMX, SSE and SSE2 instruction set support. Used by Centrino notebooks.

'pentium4'
'pentium4m'
Intel Pentium 4 CPU with MMX, SSE and SSE2 instruction set support.

'prescott'
Improved version of Intel Pentium 4 CPU with MMX, SSE, SSE2 and SSE3 instruction set support.

'nocona' Improved version of Intel Pentium 4 CPU with 64-bit extensions, MMX, SSE, SSE2 and SSE3 instruction set support.

'core2' Intel Core 2 CPU with 64-bit extensions, MMX, SSE, SSE2, SSE3 and SSSE3 instruction set support.

'nehalem' Intel Nehalem CPU with 64-bit extensions, MMX, SSE, SSE2, SSE3, SSSE3, SSE4.1, SSE4.2 and POPCNT instruction set support.

'westmere'
: Intel Westmere CPU with 64-bit extensions, MMX, SSE, SSE2, SSE3, SSSE3, SSE4.1, SSE4.2, POPCNT, AES and PCLMUL instruction set support.

'sandybridge'
: Intel Sandy Bridge CPU with 64-bit extensions, MMX, SSE, SSE2, SSE3, SSSE3, SSE4.1, SSE4.2, POPCNT, AVX, AES and PCLMUL instruction set support.

'ivybridge'
: Intel Ivy Bridge CPU with 64-bit extensions, MMX, SSE, SSE2, SSE3, SSSE3, SSE4.1, SSE4.2, POPCNT, AVX, AES, PCLMUL, FSGSBASE, RDRND and F16C instruction set support.

'haswell'
: Intel Haswell CPU with 64-bit extensions, MOVBE, MMX, SSE, SSE2, SSE3, SSSE3, SSE4.1, SSE4.2, POPCNT, AVX, AVX2, AES, PCLMUL, FSGSBASE, RDRND, FMA, BMI, BMI2 and F16C instruction set support.

'broadwell'
: Intel Broadwell CPU with 64-bit extensions, MOVBE, MMX, SSE, SSE2, SSE3, SSSE3, SSE4.1, SSE4.2, POPCNT, AVX, AVX2, AES, PCLMUL, FSGSBASE, RDRND, FMA, BMI, BMI2, F16C, RDSEED, ADCX and PREFETCHW instruction set support.

'skylake'
: Intel Skylake CPU with 64-bit extensions, MOVBE, MMX, SSE, SSE2, SSE3, SSSE3, SSE4.1, SSE4.2, POPCNT, AVX, AVX2, AES, PCLMUL, FSGSBASE, RDRND, FMA, BMI, BMI2, F16C, RDSEED, ADCX, PREFETCHW, CLFLUSHOPT, XSAVEC and XSAVES instruction set support.

'bonnell'
: Intel Bonnell CPU with 64-bit extensions, MOVBE, MMX, SSE, SSE2, SSE3 and SSSE3 instruction set support.

'silvermont'
: Intel Silvermont CPU with 64-bit extensions, MOVBE, MMX, SSE, SSE2, SSE3, SSSE3, SSE4.1, SSE4.2, POPCNT, AES, PCLMUL and RDRND instruction set support.

'knl'
: Intel Knight's Landing CPU with 64-bit extensions, MOVBE, MMX, SSE, SSE2, SSE3, SSSE3, SSE4.1, SSE4.2, POPCNT, AVX, AVX2, AES, PCLMUL, FSGSBASE, RDRND, FMA, BMI, BMI2, F16C, RDSEED, ADCX, PREFETCHW, AVX512F, AVX512PF, AVX512ER and AVX512CD instruction set support.

'skylake-avx512'
: Intel Skylake Server CPU with 64-bit extensions, MOVBE, MMX, SSE, SSE2, SSE3, SSSE3, SSE4.1, SSE4.2, POPCNT, PKU, AVX, AVX2, AES, PCLMUL, FSGSBASE, RDRND, FMA, BMI, BMI2, F16C, RDSEED, ADCX, PREFETCHW, CLFLUSHOPT, XSAVEC, XSAVES, AVX512F, AVX512VL, AVX512BW, AVX512DQ and AVX512CD instruction set support.

'k6' AMD K6 CPU with MMX instruction set support.

'k6-2'
'k6-3' Improved versions of AMD K6 CPU with MMX and 3DNow! instruction set support.

'athlon'
'athlon-tbird'
AMD Athlon CPU with MMX, 3dNOW!, enhanced 3DNow! and SSE prefetch instructions support.

'athlon-4'
'athlon-xp'
'athlon-mp'
Improved AMD Athlon CPU with MMX, 3DNow!, enhanced 3DNow! and full SSE instruction set support.

'k8'
'opteron'
'athlon64'
'athlon-fx'
Processors based on the AMD K8 core with x86-64 instruction set support, including the AMD Opteron, Athlon 64, and Athlon 64 FX processors. (This supersets MMX, SSE, SSE2, 3DNow!, enhanced 3DNow! and 64-bit instruction set extensions.)

'k8-sse3'
'opteron-sse3'
'athlon64-sse3'
Improved versions of AMD K8 cores with SSE3 instruction set support.

'amdfam10'
'barcelona'
CPUs based on AMD Family 10h cores with x86-64 instruction set support. (This supersets MMX, SSE, SSE2, SSE3, SSE4A, 3DNow!, enhanced 3DNow!, ABM and 64-bit instruction set extensions.)

'bdver1' CPUs based on AMD Family 15h cores with x86-64 instruction set support. (This supersets FMA4, AVX, XOP, LWP, AES, PCL_MUL, CX16, MMX, SSE, SSE2, SSE3, SSE4A, SSSE3, SSE4.1, SSE4.2, ABM and 64-bit instruction set extensions.)

'bdver2' AMD Family 15h core based CPUs with x86-64 instruction set support. (This supersets BMI, TBM, F16C, FMA, FMA4, AVX, XOP, LWP, AES, PCL_MUL, CX16, MMX, SSE, SSE2, SSE3, SSE4A, SSSE3, SSE4.1, SSE4.2, ABM and 64-bit instruction set extensions.)

'bdver3' AMD Family 15h core based CPUs with x86-64 instruction set support. (This supersets BMI, TBM, F16C, FMA, FMA4, FSGSBASE, AVX, XOP, LWP, AES, PCL_MUL, CX16, MMX, SSE,

SSE2, SSE3, SSE4A, SSSE3, SSE4.1, SSE4.2, ABM and 64-bit instruction set extensions.

`bdver4'
: AMD Family 15h core based CPUs with x86-64 instruction set support. (This supersets BMI, BMI2, TBM, F16C, FMA, FMA4, FSGSBASE, AVX, AVX2, XOP, LWP, AES, PCL_MUL, CX16, MOVBE, MMX, SSE, SSE2, SSE3, SSE4A, SSSE3, SSE4.1, SSE4.2, ABM and 64-bit instruction set extensions.

`znver1'
: AMD Family 17h core based CPUs with x86-64 instruction set support. (This supersets BMI, BMI2, F16C, FMA, FSGSBASE, AVX, AVX2, ADCX, RDSEED, MWAITX, SHA, CLZERO, AES, PCL_MUL, CX16, MOVBE, MMX, SSE, SSE2, SSE3, SSE4A, SSSE3, SSE4.1, SSE4.2, ABM, XSAVEC, XSAVES, CLFLUSHOPT, POPCNT, and 64-bit instruction set extensions.

`btver1'
: CPUs based on AMD Family 14h cores with x86-64 instruction set support. (This supersets MMX, SSE, SSE2, SSE3, SSSE3, SSE4A, CX16, ABM and 64-bit instruction set extensions.)

`btver2'
: CPUs based on AMD Family 16h cores with x86-64 instruction set support. This includes MOVBE, F16C, BMI, AVX, PCL_MUL, AES, SSE4.2, SSE4.1, CX16, ABM, SSE4A, SSSE3, SSE3, SSE2, SSE, MMX and 64-bit instruction set extensions.

`winchip-c6'
: IDT WinChip C6 CPU, dealt in same way as i486 with additional MMX instruction set support.

`winchip2'
: IDT WinChip 2 CPU, dealt in same way as i486 with additional MMX and 3DNow! instruction set support.

`c3'
: VIA C3 CPU with MMX and 3DNow! instruction set support. (No scheduling is implemented for this chip.)

`c3-2'
: VIA C3-2 (Nehemiah/C5XL) CPU with MMX and SSE instruction set support. (No scheduling is implemented for this chip.)

`geode'
: AMD Geode embedded processor with MMX and 3DNow! instruction set support.

`-mtune=`*`cpu-type`*
: Tune to *cpu-type* everything applicable about the generated code, except for the ABI and the set of available instructions. While picking a specific *cpu-type* schedules things appropriately for that particular chip, the compiler does not generate any code that cannot run on the default machine type unless you use a `-march=`*`cpu-type`*' option. For example, if GCC is configured for i686-pc-linux-gnu then `-mtune=pentium4' generates code that is tuned for Pentium 4 but still runs on i686 machines.

  The choices for *cpu-type* are the same as for `-march'. In addition, `-mtune' supports 2 extra choices for *cpu-type*:

'generic' Produce code optimized for the most common IA32/AMD64/EM64T processors. If you know the CPU on which your code will run, then you should use the corresponding '-mtune' or '-march' option instead of '-mtune=generic'. But, if you do not know exactly what CPU users of your application will have, then you should use this option.

As new processors are deployed in the marketplace, the behavior of this option will change. Therefore, if you upgrade to a newer version of GCC, code generation controlled by this option will change to reflect the processors that are most common at the time that version of GCC is released.

There is no '-march=generic' option because '-march' indicates the instruction set the compiler can use, and there is no generic instruction set applicable to all processors. In contrast, '-mtune' indicates the processor (or, in this case, collection of processors) for which the code is optimized.

'intel' Produce code optimized for the most current Intel processors, which are Haswell and Silvermont for this version of GCC. If you know the CPU on which your code will run, then you should use the corresponding '-mtune' or '-march' option instead of '-mtune=intel'. But, if you want your application performs better on both Haswell and Silvermont, then you should use this option.

As new Intel processors are deployed in the marketplace, the behavior of this option will change. Therefore, if you upgrade to a newer version of GCC, code generation controlled by this option will change to reflect the most current Intel processors at the time that version of GCC is released.

There is no '-march=intel' option because '-march' indicates the instruction set the compiler can use, and there is no common instruction set applicable to all processors. In contrast, '-mtune' indicates the processor (or, in this case, collection of processors) for which the code is optimized.

-mcpu=*cpu-type*
A deprecated synonym for '-mtune'.

-mfpmath=*unit*
Generate floating-point arithmetic for selected unit *unit*. The choices for *unit* are:

'387' Use the standard 387 floating-point coprocessor present on the majority of chips and emulated otherwise. Code compiled with this option runs almost everywhere. The temporary results are computed in 80-bit precision instead of the precision specified by the type, resulting in slightly different results compared to most of other chips. See '-ffloat-store' for more detailed description.

This is the default choice for x86-32 targets.

'sse' Use scalar floating-point instructions present in the SSE instruction set. This instruction set is supported by Pentium III and newer chips, and in the AMD line by Athlon-4, Athlon XP and Athlon MP chips. The earlier version of the SSE instruction set supports only single-precision arithmetic, thus the double and extended-precision arithmetic are still done using 387. A later version, present only in Pentium 4 and AMD x86-64 chips, supports double-precision arithmetic too.

For the x86-32 compiler, you must use '-march=*cpu-type*', '-msse' or '-msse2' switches to enable SSE extensions and make this option effective. For the x86-64 compiler, these extensions are enabled by default.

The resulting code should be considerably faster in the majority of cases and avoid the numerical instability problems of 387 code, but may break some existing code that expects temporaries to be 80 bits.

This is the default choice for the x86-64 compiler.

'sse,387'
'sse+387'
'both' Attempt to utilize both instruction sets at once. This effectively doubles the amount of available registers, and on chips with separate execution units for 387 and SSE the execution resources too. Use this option with care, as it is still experimental, because the GCC register allocator does not model separate functional units well, resulting in unstable performance.

-masm=*dialect*

Output assembly instructions using selected *dialect*. Also affects which dialect is used for basic asm (see Section 6.44.1 [Basic Asm], page 475) and extended asm (see Section 6.44.2 [Extended Asm], page 477). Supported choices (in dialect order) are 'att' or 'intel'. The default is 'att'. Darwin does not support 'intel'.

-mieee-fp
-mno-ieee-fp

Control whether or not the compiler uses IEEE floating-point comparisons. These correctly handle the case where the result of a comparison is unordered.

-msoft-float

Generate output containing library calls for floating point.

Warning: the requisite libraries are not part of GCC. Normally the facilities of the machine's usual C compiler are used, but this can't be done directly in cross-compilation. You must make your own arrangements to provide suitable library functions for cross-compilation.

On machines where a function returns floating-point results in the 80387 register stack, some floating-point opcodes may be emitted even if '-msoft-float' is used.

`-mno-fp-ret-in-387`

Do not use the FPU registers for return values of functions.

The usual calling convention has functions return values of types `float` and `double` in an FPU register, even if there is no FPU. The idea is that the operating system should emulate an FPU.

The option '`-mno-fp-ret-in-387`' causes such values to be returned in ordinary CPU registers instead.

`-mno-fancy-math-387`

Some 387 emulators do not support the `sin`, `cos` and `sqrt` instructions for the 387. Specify this option to avoid generating those instructions. This option is the default on OpenBSD and NetBSD. This option is overridden when '`-march`' indicates that the target CPU always has an FPU and so the instruction does not need emulation. These instructions are not generated unless you also use the '`-funsafe-math-optimizations`' switch.

`-malign-double`
`-mno-align-double`

Control whether GCC aligns `double`, `long double`, and `long long` variables on a two-word boundary or a one-word boundary. Aligning `double` variables on a two-word boundary produces code that runs somewhat faster on a Pentium at the expense of more memory.

On x86-64, '`-malign-double`' is enabled by default.

Warning: if you use the '`-malign-double`' switch, structures containing the above types are aligned differently than the published application binary interface specifications for the x86-32 and are not binary compatible with structures in code compiled without that switch.

`-m96bit-long-double`
`-m128bit-long-double`

These switches control the size of `long double` type. The x86-32 application binary interface specifies the size to be 96 bits, so '`-m96bit-long-double`' is the default in 32-bit mode.

Modern architectures (Pentium and newer) prefer `long double` to be aligned to an 8- or 16-byte boundary. In arrays or structures conforming to the ABI, this is not possible. So specifying '`-m128bit-long-double`' aligns `long double` to a 16-byte boundary by padding the `long double` with an additional 32-bit zero.

In the x86-64 compiler, '`-m128bit-long-double`' is the default choice as its ABI specifies that `long double` is aligned on 16-byte boundary.

Notice that neither of these options enable any extra precision over the x87 standard of 80 bits for a `long double`.

Warning: if you override the default value for your target ABI, this changes the size of structures and arrays containing `long double` variables, as well as modifying the function calling convention for functions taking `long double`. Hence they are not binary-compatible with code compiled without that switch.

`-mlong-double-64`
`-mlong-double-80`
`-mlong-double-128`

These switches control the size of `long double` type. A size of 64 bits makes the `long double` type equivalent to the `double` type. This is the default for 32-bit Bionic C library. A size of 128 bits makes the `long double` type equivalent to the `__float128` type. This is the default for 64-bit Bionic C library.

Warning: if you override the default value for your target ABI, this changes the size of structures and arrays containing `long double` variables, as well as modifying the function calling convention for functions taking `long double`. Hence they are not binary-compatible with code compiled without that switch.

`-malign-data=`*`type`*

Control how GCC aligns variables. Supported values for *type* are '`compat`' uses increased alignment value compatible uses GCC 4.8 and earlier, '`abi`' uses alignment value as specified by the psABI, and '`cacheline`' uses increased alignment value to match the cache line size. '`compat`' is the default.

`-mlarge-data-threshold=`*`threshold`*

When '`-mcmodel=medium`' is specified, data objects larger than *threshold* are placed in the large data section. This value must be the same across all objects linked into the binary, and defaults to 65535.

`-mrtd` Use a different function-calling convention, in which functions that take a fixed number of arguments return with the `ret` *`num`* instruction, which pops their arguments while returning. This saves one instruction in the caller since there is no need to pop the arguments there.

You can specify that an individual function is called with this calling sequence with the function attribute `stdcall`. You can also override the '`-mrtd`' option by using the function attribute `cdecl`. See Section 6.31 [Function Attributes], page 407.

Warning: this calling convention is incompatible with the one normally used on Unix, so you cannot use it if you need to call libraries compiled with the Unix compiler.

Also, you must provide function prototypes for all functions that take variable numbers of arguments (including `printf`); otherwise incorrect code is generated for calls to those functions.

In addition, seriously incorrect code results if you call a function with too many arguments. (Normally, extra arguments are harmlessly ignored.)

`-mregparm=`*`num`*

Control how many registers are used to pass integer arguments. By default, no registers are used to pass arguments, and at most 3 registers can be used. You can control this behavior for a specific function by using the function attribute `regparm`. See Section 6.31 [Function Attributes], page 407.

Warning: if you use this switch, and *num* is nonzero, then you must build all modules with the same value, including any libraries. This includes the system libraries and startup modules.

`-msseregparm`
: Use SSE register passing conventions for float and double arguments and return values. You can control this behavior for a specific function by using the function attribute `sseregparm`. See Section 6.31 [Function Attributes], page 407.

  Warning: if you use this switch then you must build all modules with the same value, including any libraries. This includes the system libraries and startup modules.

`-mvect8-ret-in-mem`
: Return 8-byte vectors in memory instead of MMX registers. This is the default on Solaris 8 and 9 and VxWorks to match the ABI of the Sun Studio compilers until version 12. Later compiler versions (starting with Studio 12 Update 1) follow the ABI used by other x86 targets, which is the default on Solaris 10 and later. *Only* use this option if you need to remain compatible with existing code produced by those previous compiler versions or older versions of GCC.

`-mpc32`
`-mpc64`
`-mpc80`
: Set 80387 floating-point precision to 32, 64 or 80 bits. When '`-mpc32`' is specified, the significands of results of floating-point operations are rounded to 24 bits (single precision); '`-mpc64`' rounds the significands of results of floating-point operations to 53 bits (double precision) and '`-mpc80`' rounds the significands of results of floating-point operations to 64 bits (extended double precision), which is the default. When this option is used, floating-point operations in higher precisions are not available to the programmer without setting the FPU control word explicitly.

  Setting the rounding of floating-point operations to less than the default 80 bits can speed some programs by 2% or more. Note that some mathematical libraries assume that extended-precision (80-bit) floating-point operations are enabled by default; routines in such libraries could suffer significant loss of accuracy, typically through so-called "catastrophic cancellation", when this option is used to set the precision to less than extended precision.

`-mstackrealign`
: Realign the stack at entry. On the x86, the '`-mstackrealign`' option generates an alternate prologue and epilogue that realigns the run-time stack if necessary. This supports mixing legacy codes that keep 4-byte stack alignment with modern codes that keep 16-byte stack alignment for SSE compatibility. See also the attribute `force_align_arg_pointer`, applicable to individual functions.

`-mpreferred-stack-boundary=`*`num`*
: Attempt to keep the stack boundary aligned to a 2 raised to *num* byte boundary. If '`-mpreferred-stack-boundary`' is not specified, the default is 4 (16 bytes or 128 bits).

  Warning: When generating code for the x86-64 architecture with SSE extensions disabled, '`-mpreferred-stack-boundary=3`' can be used to keep the stack boundary aligned to 8 byte boundary. Since x86-64 ABI require 16 byte stack alignment, this is ABI incompatible and intended to be used in controlled environment where stack space is important limitation. This option leads to wrong code when functions compiled with 16 byte stack alignment (such as functions from a standard library) are called with misaligned stack. In this case, SSE instructions may lead to misaligned memory access traps. In addition, variable arguments are handled incorrectly for 16 byte aligned objects (including x87 long double and __int128), leading to wrong results. You must build all modules with '-mpreferred-stack-boundary=3', including any libraries. This includes the system libraries and startup modules.

`-mincoming-stack-boundary=`*`num`*

Assume the incoming stack is aligned to a 2 raised to *num* byte boundary. If '-mincoming-stack-boundary' is not specified, the one specified by '-mpreferred-stack-boundary' is used.

On Pentium and Pentium Pro, `double` and `long double` values should be aligned to an 8-byte boundary (see '-malign-double') or suffer significant run time performance penalties. On Pentium III, the Streaming SIMD Extension (SSE) data type `__m128` may not work properly if it is not 16-byte aligned.

To ensure proper alignment of this values on the stack, the stack boundary must be as aligned as that required by any value stored on the stack. Further, every function must be generated such that it keeps the stack aligned. Thus calling a function compiled with a higher preferred stack boundary from a function compiled with a lower preferred stack boundary most likely misaligns the stack. It is recommended that libraries that use callbacks always use the default setting.

This extra alignment does consume extra stack space, and generally increases code size. Code that is sensitive to stack space usage, such as embedded systems and operating system kernels, may want to reduce the preferred alignment to '-mpreferred-stack-boundary=2'.

`-mmmx`
`-msse`
`-msse2`
`-msse3`
`-mssse3`
`-msse4`
`-msse4a`
`-msse4.1`
`-msse4.2`
`-mavx`
`-mavx2`
`-mavx512f`
`-mavx512pf`
`-mavx512er`
`-mavx512cd`
`-mavx512vl`
`-mavx512bw`
`-mavx512dq`
`-mavx512ifma`

-mavx512vbmi
-msha
-maes
-mpclmul
-mclfushopt
-mfsgsbase
-mrdrnd
-mf16c
-mfma
-mfma4
-mprefetchwt1
-mxop
-mlwp
-m3dnow
-mpopcnt
-mabm
-mbmi
-mbmi2
-mlzcnt
-mfxsr
-mxsave
-mxsaveopt
-mxsavec
-mxsaves
-mrtm
-mtbm
-mmpx
-mmwaitx
-mclzero
-mpku

These switches enable the use of instructions in the MMX, SSE, SSE2, SSE3, SSSE3, SSE4.1, AVX, AVX2, AVX512F, AVX512PF, AVX512ER, AVX512CD, SHA, AES, PCLMUL, FSGSBASE, RDRND, F16C, FMA, SSE4A, FMA4, XOP, LWP, ABM, AVX512VL, AVX512BW, AVX512DQ, AVX512IFMA AVX512VBMI, BMI, BMI2, FXSR, XSAVE, XSAVEOPT, LZCNT, RTM, MPX, MWAITX, PKU or 3DNow! extended instruction sets. Each has a corresponding '-mno-' option to disable use of these instructions.

These extensions are also available as built-in functions: see Section 6.59.30 [x86 Built-in Functions], page 644, for details of the functions enabled and disabled by these switches.

To generate SSE/SSE2 instructions automatically from floating-point code (as opposed to 387 instructions), see '-mfpmath=sse'.

GCC depresses SSEx instructions when '-mavx' is used. Instead, it generates new AVX instructions or AVX equivalence for all SSEx instructions when needed.

These options enable GCC to use these extended instructions in generated code, even without '-mfpmath=sse'. Applications that perform run-time CPU detection must compile separate files for each supported architecture, using the appropriate flags. In particular, the file containing the CPU detection code should be compiled without these options.

`-mdump-tune-features`
This option instructs GCC to dump the names of the x86 performance tuning features and default settings. The names can be used in '`-mtune-ctrl=`*`feature-list`*'.

`-mtune-ctrl=`*`feature-list`*
This option is used to do fine grain control of x86 code generation features. *feature-list* is a comma separated list of *feature* names. See also '`-mdump-tune-features`'. When specified, the *feature* is turned on if it is not preceded with '`^`', otherwise, it is turned off. '`-mtune-ctrl=`*`feature-list`*' is intended to be used by GCC developers. Using it may lead to code paths not covered by testing and can potentially result in compiler ICEs or runtime errors.

`-mno-default`
This option instructs GCC to turn off all tunable features. See also '`-mtune-ctrl=`*`feature-list`*' and '`-mdump-tune-features`'.

`-mcld`
This option instructs GCC to emit a `cld` instruction in the prologue of functions that use string instructions. String instructions depend on the DF flag to select between autoincrement or autodecrement mode. While the ABI specifies the DF flag to be cleared on function entry, some operating systems violate this specification by not clearing the DF flag in their exception dispatchers. The exception handler can be invoked with the DF flag set, which leads to wrong direction mode when string instructions are used. This option can be enabled by default on 32-bit x86 targets by configuring GCC with the '`--enable-cld`' configure option. Generation of `cld` instructions can be suppressed with the '`-mno-cld`' compiler option in this case.

`-mvzeroupper`
This option instructs GCC to emit a `vzeroupper` instruction before a transfer of control flow out of the function to minimize the AVX to SSE transition penalty as well as remove unnecessary `zeroupper` intrinsics.

`-mprefer-avx128`
This option instructs GCC to use 128-bit AVX instructions instead of 256-bit AVX instructions in the auto-vectorizer.

`-mcx16`
This option enables GCC to generate `CMPXCHG16B` instructions. `CMPXCHG16B` allows for atomic operations on 128-bit double quadword (or oword) data types. This is useful for high-resolution counters that can be updated by multiple processors (or cores). This instruction is generated as part of atomic built-in functions: see Section 6.51 [__sync Builtins], page 532 or Section 6.52 [__atomic Builtins], page 534 for details.

`-msahf`
This option enables generation of `SAHF` instructions in 64-bit code. Early Intel Pentium 4 CPUs with Intel 64 support, prior to the introduction of Pentium 4 G1 step in December 2005, lacked the `LAHF` and `SAHF` instructions which are supported by AMD64. These are load and store instructions, respectively, for certain status flags. In 64-bit mode, the `SAHF` instruction is used to optimize

fmod, drem, and remainder built-in functions; see Section 6.58 [Other Builtins], page 545 for details.

-mmovbe
: This option enables use of the movbe instruction to implement __builtin_bswap32 and __builtin_bswap64.

-mcrc32
: This option enables built-in functions __builtin_ia32_crc32qi, __builtin_ia32_crc32hi, __builtin_ia32_crc32si and __builtin_ia32_crc32di to generate the crc32 machine instruction.

-mrecip
: This option enables use of RCPSS and RSQRTSS instructions (and their vectorized variants RCPPS and RSQRTPS) with an additional Newton-Raphson step to increase precision instead of DIVSS and SQRTSS (and their vectorized variants) for single-precision floating-point arguments. These instructions are generated only when '-funsafe-math-optimizations' is enabled together with '-ffinite-math-only' and '-fno-trapping-math'. Note that while the throughput of the sequence is higher than the throughput of the non-reciprocal instruction, the precision of the sequence can be decreased by up to 2 ulp (i.e. the inverse of 1.0 equals 0.99999994).

Note that GCC implements 1.0f/sqrtf(*x*) in terms of RSQRTSS (or RSQRTPS) already with '-ffast-math' (or the above option combination), and doesn't need '-mrecip'.

Also note that GCC emits the above sequence with additional Newton-Raphson step for vectorized single-float division and vectorized sqrtf(*x*) already with '-ffast-math' (or the above option combination), and doesn't need '-mrecip'.

-mrecip=*opt*
: This option controls which reciprocal estimate instructions may be used. *opt* is a comma-separated list of options, which may be preceded by a '!' to invert the option:

'all'
: Enable all estimate instructions.

'default'
: Enable the default instructions, equivalent to '-mrecip'.

'none'
: Disable all estimate instructions, equivalent to '-mno-recip'.

'div'
: Enable the approximation for scalar division.

'vec-div'
: Enable the approximation for vectorized division.

'sqrt'
: Enable the approximation for scalar square root.

'vec-sqrt'
: Enable the approximation for vectorized square root.

So, for example, '-mrecip=all,!sqrt' enables all of the reciprocal approximations, except for square root.

-mveclibabi=*type*
: Specifies the ABI type to use for vectorizing intrinsics using an external library. Supported values for *type* are 'svml' for the Intel short vector math library and 'acml' for the AMD math core library. To use this option, both

'-ftree-vectorize' and '-funsafe-math-optimizations' have to be enabled, and an SVML or ACML ABI-compatible library must be specified at link time.

GCC currently emits calls to vmldExp2, vmldLn2, vmldLog102, vmldLog102, vmldPow2, vmldTanh2, vmldTan2, vmldAtan2, vmldAtanh2, vmldCbrt2, vmldSinh2, vmldSin2, vmldAsinh2, vmldAsin2, vmldCosh2, vmldCos2, vmldAcosh2, vmldAcos2, vmlsExp4, vmlsLn4, vmlsLog104, vmlsLog104, vmlsPow4, vmlsTanh4, vmlsTan4, vmlsAtan4, vmlsAtanh4, vmlsCbrt4, vmlsSinh4, vmlsSin4, vmlsAsinh4, vmlsAsin4, vmlsCosh4, vmlsCos4, vmlsAcosh4 and vmlsAcos4 for corresponding function type when '-mveclibabi=svml' is used, and __vrd2_sin, __vrd2_cos, __vrd2_exp, __vrd2_log, __vrd2_log2, __vrd2_log10, __vrs4_sinf, __vrs4_cosf, __vrs4_expf, __vrs4_logf, __vrs4_log2f, __vrs4_log10f and __vrs4_powf for the corresponding function type when '-mveclibabi=acml' is used.

-mabi=*name*

Generate code for the specified calling convention. Permissible values are 'sysv' for the ABI used on GNU/Linux and other systems, and 'ms' for the Microsoft ABI. The default is to use the Microsoft ABI when targeting Microsoft Windows and the SysV ABI on all other systems. You can control this behavior for specific functions by using the function attributes ms_abi and sysv_abi. See Section 6.31 [Function Attributes], page 407.

-mtls-dialect=*type*

Generate code to access thread-local storage using the 'gnu' or 'gnu2' conventions. 'gnu' is the conservative default; 'gnu2' is more efficient, but it may add compile- and run-time requirements that cannot be satisfied on all systems.

-mpush-args
-mno-push-args

Use PUSH operations to store outgoing parameters. This method is shorter and usually equally fast as method using SUB/MOV operations and is enabled by default. In some cases disabling it may improve performance because of improved scheduling and reduced dependencies.

-maccumulate-outgoing-args

If enabled, the maximum amount of space required for outgoing arguments is computed in the function prologue. This is faster on most modern CPUs because of reduced dependencies, improved scheduling and reduced stack usage when the preferred stack boundary is not equal to 2. The drawback is a notable increase in code size. This switch implies '-mno-push-args'.

-mthreads

Support thread-safe exception handling on MinGW. Programs that rely on thread-safe exception handling must compile and link all code with the '-mthreads' option. When compiling, '-mthreads' defines '-D_MT'; when linking, it links in a special thread helper library '-lmingwthrd' which cleans up per-thread exception-handling data.

-mms-bitfields
-mno-ms-bitfields

Enable/disable bit-field layout compatible with the native Microsoft Windows compiler.

If `packed` is used on a structure, or if bit-fields are used, it may be that the Microsoft ABI lays out the structure differently than the way GCC normally does. Particularly when moving packed data between functions compiled with GCC and the native Microsoft compiler (either via function call or as data in a file), it may be necessary to access either format.

This option is enabled by default for Microsoft Windows targets. This behavior can also be controlled locally by use of variable or type attributes. For more information, see Section 6.32.14 [x86 Variable Attributes], page 459 and Section 6.33.6 [x86 Type Attributes], page 466.

The Microsoft structure layout algorithm is fairly simple with the exception of the bit-field packing. The padding and alignment of members of structures and whether a bit-field can straddle a storage-unit boundary are determine by these rules:

1. Structure members are stored sequentially in the order in which they are declared: the first member has the lowest memory address and the last member the highest.
2. Every data object has an alignment requirement. The alignment requirement for all data except structures, unions, and arrays is either the size of the object or the current packing size (specified with either the `aligned` attribute or the `pack` pragma), whichever is less. For structures, unions, and arrays, the alignment requirement is the largest alignment requirement of its members. Every object is allocated an offset so that:
   ```
   offset % alignment_requirement == 0
   ```
3. Adjacent bit-fields are packed into the same 1-, 2-, or 4-byte allocation unit if the integral types are the same size and if the next bit-field fits into the current allocation unit without crossing the boundary imposed by the common alignment requirements of the bit-fields.

MSVC interprets zero-length bit-fields in the following ways:

1. If a zero-length bit-field is inserted between two bit-fields that are normally coalesced, the bit-fields are not coalesced.

   For example:
   ```
   struct
    {
      unsigned long bf_1 : 12;
      unsigned long : 0;
      unsigned long bf_2 : 12;
    } t1;
   ```
   The size of `t1` is 8 bytes with the zero-length bit-field. If the zero-length bit-field were removed, `t1`'s size would be 4 bytes.
2. If a zero-length bit-field is inserted after a bit-field, `foo`, and the alignment of the zero-length bit-field is greater than the member that follows it, `bar`, `bar` is aligned as the type of the zero-length bit-field.

For example:

```
struct
 {
   char foo : 4;
   short : 0;
   char bar;
 } t2;

struct
 {
   char foo : 4;
   short : 0;
   double bar;
 } t3;
```

For `t2`, `bar` is placed at offset 2, rather than offset 1. Accordingly, the size of `t2` is 4. For `t3`, the zero-length bit-field does not affect the alignment of `bar` or, as a result, the size of the structure.

Taking this into account, it is important to note the following:

1. If a zero-length bit-field follows a normal bit-field, the type of the zero-length bit-field may affect the alignment of the structure as whole. For example, `t2` has a size of 4 bytes, since the zero-length bit-field follows a normal bit-field, and is of type short.
2. Even if a zero-length bit-field is not followed by a normal bit-field, it may still affect the alignment of the structure:

   ```
   struct
    {
      char foo : 6;
      long : 0;
    } t4;
   ```

   Here, `t4` takes up 4 bytes.
3. Zero-length bit-fields following non-bit-field members are ignored:

   ```
   struct
    {
      char foo;
      long : 0;
      char bar;
    } t5;
   ```

   Here, `t5` takes up 2 bytes.

`-mno-align-stringops`
: Do not align the destination of inlined string operations. This switch reduces code size and improves performance in case the destination is already aligned, but GCC doesn't know about it.

`-minline-all-stringops`
: By default GCC inlines string operations only when the destination is known to be aligned to least a 4-byte boundary. This enables more inlining and increases code size, but may improve performance of code that depends on fast `memcpy`, `strlen`, and `memset` for short lengths.

`-minline-stringops-dynamically`
: For string operations of unknown size, use run-time checks with inline code for small blocks and a library call for large blocks.

`-mstringop-strategy=`*alg*
: Override the internal decision heuristic for the particular algorithm to use for inlining string operations. The allowed values for *alg* are:

  '`rep_byte`'
  '`rep_4byte`'
  '`rep_8byte`'
  : Expand using i386 `rep` prefix of the specified size.

  '`byte_loop`'
  '`loop`'
  '`unrolled_loop`'
  : Expand into an inline loop.

  '`libcall`' Always use a library call.

`-mmemcpy-strategy=`*strategy*
: Override the internal decision heuristic to decide if `__builtin_memcpy` should be inlined and what inline algorithm to use when the expected size of the copy operation is known. *strategy* is a comma-separated list of *alg*:*max_size*:*dest_align* triplets. *alg* is specified in '`-mstringop-strategy`', *max_size* specifies the max byte size with which inline algorithm *alg* is allowed. For the last triplet, the *max_size* must be `-1`. The *max_size* of the triplets in the list must be specified in increasing order. The minimal byte size for *alg* is `0` for the first triplet and `max_size + 1` of the preceding range.

`-mmemset-strategy=`*strategy*
: The option is similar to '`-mmemcpy-strategy=`' except that it is to control `__builtin_memset` expansion.

`-momit-leaf-frame-pointer`
: Don't keep the frame pointer in a register for leaf functions. This avoids the instructions to save, set up, and restore frame pointers and makes an extra register available in leaf functions. The option '`-fomit-leaf-frame-pointer`' removes the frame pointer for leaf functions, which might make debugging harder.

`-mtls-direct-seg-refs`
`-mno-tls-direct-seg-refs`
: Controls whether TLS variables may be accessed with offsets from the TLS segment register (`%gs` for 32-bit, `%fs` for 64-bit), or whether the thread base pointer must be added. Whether or not this is valid depends on the operating system, and whether it maps the segment to cover the entire TLS area.

  For systems that use the GNU C Library, the default is on.

`-msse2avx`
`-mno-sse2avx`
: Specify that the assembler should encode SSE instructions with VEX prefix. The option '`-mavx`' turns this on by default.

`-mfentry`
`-mno-fentry`
If profiling is active ('-pg'), put the profiling counter call before the prologue. Note: On x86 architectures the attribute `ms_hook_prologue` isn't possible at the moment for '-mfentry' and '-pg'.

`-mrecord-mcount`
`-mno-record-mcount`
If profiling is active ('-pg'), generate a __mcount_loc section that contains pointers to each profiling call. This is useful for automatically patching and out calls.

`-mnop-mcount`
`-mno-nop-mcount`
If profiling is active ('-pg'), generate the calls to the profiling functions as nops. This is useful when they should be patched in later dynamically. This is likely only useful together with '-mrecord-mcount'.

`-mskip-rax-setup`
`-mno-skip-rax-setup`
When generating code for the x86-64 architecture with SSE extensions disabled, '-mskip-rax-setup' can be used to skip setting up RAX register when there are no variable arguments passed in vector registers.

Warning: Since RAX register is used to avoid unnecessarily saving vector registers on stack when passing variable arguments, the impacts of this option are callees may waste some stack space, misbehave or jump to a random location. GCC 4.4 or newer don't have those issues, regardless the RAX register value.

`-m8bit-idiv`
`-mno-8bit-idiv`
On some processors, like Intel Atom, 8-bit unsigned integer divide is much faster than 32-bit/64-bit integer divide. This option generates a run-time check. If both dividend and divisor are within range of 0 to 255, 8-bit unsigned integer divide is used instead of 32-bit/64-bit integer divide.

`-mavx256-split-unaligned-load`
`-mavx256-split-unaligned-store`
Split 32-byte AVX unaligned load and store.

`-mstack-protector-guard=`*`guard`*
Generate stack protection code using canary at *guard*. Supported locations are 'global' for global canary or 'tls' for per-thread canary in the TLS block (the default). This option has effect only when '-fstack-protector' or '-fstack-protector-all' is specified.

`-mmitigate-rop`
Try to avoid generating code sequences that contain unintended return opcodes, to mitigate against certain forms of attack. At the moment, this option is limited in what it can do and should not be relied on to provide serious protection.

These '-m' switches are supported in addition to the above on x86-64 processors in 64-bit environments.

-m32
-m64
-mx32
-m16
-miamcu Generate code for a 16-bit, 32-bit or 64-bit environment. The '-m32' option sets int, long, and pointer types to 32 bits, and generates code that runs on any i386 system.

The '-m64' option sets int to 32 bits and long and pointer types to 64 bits, and generates code for the x86-64 architecture. For Darwin only the '-m64' option also turns off the '-fno-pic' and '-mdynamic-no-pic' options.

The '-mx32' option sets int, long, and pointer types to 32 bits, and generates code for the x86-64 architecture.

The '-m16' option is the same as '-m32', except for that it outputs the .code16gcc assembly directive at the beginning of the assembly output so that the binary can run in 16-bit mode.

The '-miamcu' option generates code which conforms to Intel MCU psABI. It requires the '-m32' option to be turned on.

-mno-red-zone
Do not use a so-called "red zone" for x86-64 code. The red zone is mandated by the x86-64 ABI; it is a 128-byte area beyond the location of the stack pointer that is not modified by signal or interrupt handlers and therefore can be used for temporary data without adjusting the stack pointer. The flag '-mno-red-zone' disables this red zone.

-mcmodel=small
Generate code for the small code model: the program and its symbols must be linked in the lower 2 GB of the address space. Pointers are 64 bits. Programs can be statically or dynamically linked. This is the default code model.

-mcmodel=kernel
Generate code for the kernel code model. The kernel runs in the negative 2 GB of the address space. This model has to be used for Linux kernel code.

-mcmodel=medium
Generate code for the medium model: the program is linked in the lower 2 GB of the address space. Small symbols are also placed there. Symbols with sizes larger than '-mlarge-data-threshold' are put into large data or BSS sections and can be located above 2GB. Programs can be statically or dynamically linked.

-mcmodel=large
Generate code for the large model. This model makes no assumptions about addresses and sizes of sections.

-maddress-mode=long
Generate code for long address mode. This is only supported for 64-bit and x32 environments. It is the default address mode for 64-bit environments.

`-maddress-mode=short`
: Generate code for short address mode. This is only supported for 32-bit and x32 environments. It is the default address mode for 32-bit and x32 environments.

3.18.55 x86 Windows Options

These additional options are available for Microsoft Windows targets:

`-mconsole`
: This option specifies that a console application is to be generated, by instructing the linker to set the PE header subsystem type required for console applications. This option is available for Cygwin and MinGW targets and is enabled by default on those targets.

`-mdll`
: This option is available for Cygwin and MinGW targets. It specifies that a DLL—a dynamic link library—is to be generated, enabling the selection of the required runtime startup object and entry point.

`-mnop-fun-dllimport`
: This option is available for Cygwin and MinGW targets. It specifies that the `dllimport` attribute should be ignored.

`-mthread`
: This option is available for MinGW targets. It specifies that MinGW-specific thread support is to be used.

`-municode`
: This option is available for MinGW-w64 targets. It causes the `UNICODE` preprocessor macro to be predefined, and chooses Unicode-capable runtime startup code.

`-mwin32`
: This option is available for Cygwin and MinGW targets. It specifies that the typical Microsoft Windows predefined macros are to be set in the pre-processor, but does not influence the choice of runtime library/startup code.

`-mwindows`
: This option is available for Cygwin and MinGW targets. It specifies that a GUI application is to be generated by instructing the linker to set the PE header subsystem type appropriately.

`-fno-set-stack-executable`
: This option is available for MinGW targets. It specifies that the executable flag for the stack used by nested functions isn't set. This is necessary for binaries running in kernel mode of Microsoft Windows, as there the User32 API, which is used to set executable privileges, isn't available.

`-fwritable-relocated-rdata`
: This option is available for MinGW and Cygwin targets. It specifies that relocated-data in read-only section is put into the `.data` section. This is a necessary for older runtimes not supporting modification of `.rdata` sections for pseudo-relocation.

`-mpe-aligned-commons`
: This option is available for Cygwin and MinGW targets. It specifies that the GNU extension to the PE file format that permits the correct alignment of

COMMON variables should be used when generating code. It is enabled by default if GCC detects that the target assembler found during configuration supports the feature.

See also under Section 3.18.54 [x86 Options], page 337 for standard options.

3.18.56 Xstormy16 Options

These options are defined for Xstormy16:

`-msim` Choose startup files and linker script suitable for the simulator.

3.18.57 Xtensa Options

These options are supported for Xtensa targets:

`-mconst16`
`-mno-const16`
: Enable or disable use of `CONST16` instructions for loading constant values. The `CONST16` instruction is currently not a standard option from Tensilica. When enabled, `CONST16` instructions are always used in place of the standard `L32R` instructions. The use of `CONST16` is enabled by default only if the `L32R` instruction is not available.

`-mfused-madd`
`-mno-fused-madd`
: Enable or disable use of fused multiply/add and multiply/subtract instructions in the floating-point option. This has no effect if the floating-point option is not also enabled. Disabling fused multiply/add and multiply/subtract instructions forces the compiler to use separate instructions for the multiply and add/subtract operations. This may be desirable in some cases where strict IEEE 754-compliant results are required: the fused multiply add/subtract instructions do not round the intermediate result, thereby producing results with *more* bits of precision than specified by the IEEE standard. Disabling fused multiply add/subtract instructions also ensures that the program output is not sensitive to the compiler's ability to combine multiply and add/subtract operations.

`-mserialize-volatile`
`-mno-serialize-volatile`
: When this option is enabled, GCC inserts `MEMW` instructions before `volatile` memory references to guarantee sequential consistency. The default is '`-mserialize-volatile`'. Use '`-mno-serialize-volatile`' to omit the `MEMW` instructions.

`-mforce-no-pic`
: For targets, like GNU/Linux, where all user-mode Xtensa code must be position-independent code (PIC), this option disables PIC for compiling kernel code.

`-mtext-section-literals`
`-mno-text-section-literals`

These options control the treatment of literal pools. The default is '`-mno-text-section-literals`', which places literals in a separate section in the output file. This allows the literal pool to be placed in a data RAM/ROM, and it also allows the linker to combine literal pools from separate object files to remove redundant literals and improve code size. With '`-mtext-section-literals`', the literals are interspersed in the text section in order to keep them as close as possible to their references. This may be necessary for large assembly files. Literals for each function are placed right before that function.

`-mauto-litpools`
`-mno-auto-litpools`

These options control the treatment of literal pools. The default is '`-mno-auto-litpools`', which places literals in a separate section in the output file unless '`-mtext-section-literals`' is used. With '`-mauto-litpools`' the literals are interspersed in the text section by the assembler. Compiler does not produce explicit `.literal` directives and loads literals into registers with `MOVI` instructions instead of `L32R` to let the assembler do relaxation and place literals as necessary. This option allows assembler to create several literal pools per function and assemble very big functions, which may not be possible with '`-mtext-section-literals`'.

`-mtarget-align`
`-mno-target-align`

When this option is enabled, GCC instructs the assembler to automatically align instructions to reduce branch penalties at the expense of some code density. The assembler attempts to widen density instructions to align branch targets and the instructions following call instructions. If there are not enough preceding safe density instructions to align a target, no widening is performed. The default is '`-mtarget-align`'. These options do not affect the treatment of auto-aligned instructions like `LOOP`, which the assembler always aligns, either by widening density instructions or by inserting NOP instructions.

`-mlongcalls`
`-mno-longcalls`

When this option is enabled, GCC instructs the assembler to translate direct calls to indirect calls unless it can determine that the target of a direct call is in the range allowed by the call instruction. This translation typically occurs for calls to functions in other source files. Specifically, the assembler translates a direct `CALL` instruction into an `L32R` followed by a `CALLX` instruction. The default is '`-mno-longcalls`'. This option should be used in programs where the call target can potentially be out of range. This option is implemented in the assembler, not the compiler, so the assembly code generated by GCC still shows direct call instructions—look at the disassembled object code to see the actual instructions. Note that the assembler uses an indirect call for every cross-file call, not just those that really are out of range.

3.18.58 zSeries Options

These are listed under See Section 3.18.40 [S/390 and zSeries Options], page 314.

3.19 Specifying Subprocesses and the Switches to Pass to Them

gcc is a driver program. It performs its job by invoking a sequence of other programs to do the work of compiling, assembling and linking. GCC interprets its command-line parameters and uses these to deduce which programs it should invoke, and which command-line options it ought to place on their command lines. This behavior is controlled by *spec strings*. In most cases there is one spec string for each program that GCC can invoke, but a few programs have multiple spec strings to control their behavior. The spec strings built into GCC can be overridden by using the '-specs=' command-line switch to specify a spec file.

Spec files are plain-text files that are used to construct spec strings. They consist of a sequence of directives separated by blank lines. The type of directive is determined by the first non-whitespace character on the line, which can be one of the following:

%*command* Issues a *command* to the spec file processor. The commands that can appear here are:

> %include <*file*>
>
> Search for *file* and insert its text at the current point in the specs file.
>
> %include_noerr <*file*>
>
> Just like '%include', but do not generate an error message if the include file cannot be found.
>
> %rename *old_name new_name*
>
> Rename the spec string *old_name* to *new_name*.

*[*spec_name*]:

This tells the compiler to create, override or delete the named spec string. All lines after this directive up to the next directive or blank line are considered to be the text for the spec string. If this results in an empty string then the spec is deleted. (Or, if the spec did not exist, then nothing happens.) Otherwise, if the spec does not currently exist a new spec is created. If the spec does exist then its contents are overridden by the text of this directive, unless the first character of that text is the '+' character, in which case the text is appended to the spec.

[*suffix*]:

Creates a new '[*suffix*] spec' pair. All lines after this directive and up to the next directive or blank line are considered to make up the spec string for the indicated suffix. When the compiler encounters an input file with the named suffix, it processes the spec string in order to work out how to compile that file. For example:

```
.ZZ:
z-compile -input %i
```

This says that any input file whose name ends in '`.ZZ`' should be passed to the program '`z-compile`', which should be invoked with the command-line switch '`-input`' and with the result of performing the '`%i`' substitution. (See below.)

As an alternative to providing a spec string, the text following a suffix directive can be one of the following:

`@language`
: This says that the suffix is an alias for a known *language*. This is similar to using the '`-x`' command-line switch to GCC to specify a language explicitly. For example:

```
.ZZ:
@c++
```

Says that .ZZ files are, in fact, C++ source files.

`#name`
: This causes an error messages saying:

```
name compiler not installed on this system.
```

GCC already has an extensive list of suffixes built into it. This directive adds an entry to the end of the list of suffixes, but since the list is searched from the end backwards, it is effectively possible to override earlier entries using this technique.

GCC has the following spec strings built into it. Spec files can override these strings or create their own. Note that individual targets can also add their own spec strings to this list.

```
asm          Options to pass to the assembler
asm_final    Options to pass to the assembler post-processor
cpp          Options to pass to the C preprocessor
cc1          Options to pass to the C compiler
cc1plus      Options to pass to the C++ compiler
endfile      Object files to include at the end of the link
link         Options to pass to the linker
lib          Libraries to include on the command line to the linker
libgcc       Decides which GCC support library to pass to the linker
linker       Sets the name of the linker
predefines   Defines to be passed to the C preprocessor
signed_char  Defines to pass to CPP to say whether char is signed
             by default
startfile    Object files to include at the start of the link
```

Here is a small example of a spec file:

```
%rename lib                 old_lib

*lib:
--start-group -lgcc -lc -leval1 --end-group %(old_lib)
```

This example renames the spec called '`lib`' to '`old_lib`' and then overrides the previous definition of '`lib`' with a new one. The new definition adds in some extra command-line options before including the text of the old definition.

Spec strings are a list of command-line options to be passed to their corresponding program. In addition, the spec strings can contain '`%`'-prefixed sequences to substitute variable text or to conditionally insert text into the command line. Using these constructs it is possible to generate quite complex command lines.

Here is a table of all defined '%'-sequences for spec strings. Note that spaces are not generated automatically around the results of expanding these sequences. Therefore you can concatenate them together or combine them with constant text in a single argument.

`%%` Substitute one '%' into the program name or argument.

`%i` Substitute the name of the input file being processed.

`%b` Substitute the basename of the input file being processed. This is the substring up to (and not including) the last period and not including the directory.

`%B` This is the same as '`%b`', but include the file suffix (text after the last period).

`%d` Marks the argument containing or following the '`%d`' as a temporary file name, so that that file is deleted if GCC exits successfully. Unlike '`%g`', this contributes no text to the argument.

`%gsuffix` Substitute a file name that has suffix *suffix* and is chosen once per compilation, and mark the argument in the same way as '`%d`'. To reduce exposure to denial-of-service attacks, the file name is now chosen in a way that is hard to predict even when previously chosen file names are known. For example, '`%g.s ... %g.o ... %g.s`' might turn into '`ccUVUUAU.s ccXYAXZ12.o ccUVUUAU.s`'. *suffix* matches the regexp '`[.A-Za-z]*`' or the special string '`%O`', which is treated exactly as if '`%O`' had been preprocessed. Previously, '`%g`' was simply substituted with a file name chosen once per compilation, without regard to any appended suffix (which was therefore treated just like ordinary text), making such attacks more likely to succeed.

`%usuffix` Like '`%g`', but generates a new temporary file name each time it appears instead of once per compilation.

`%Usuffix` Substitutes the last file name generated with '`%usuffix`', generating a new one if there is no such last file name. In the absence of any '`%usuffix`', this is just like '`%gsuffix`', except they don't share the same suffix *space*, so '`%g.s ... %U.s ... %g.s ... %U.s`' involves the generation of two distinct file names, one for each '`%g.s`' and another for each '`%U.s`'. Previously, '`%U`' was simply substituted with a file name chosen for the previous '`%u`', without regard to any appended suffix.

`%jsuffix` Substitutes the name of the `HOST_BIT_BUCKET`, if any, and if it is writable, and if '`-save-temps`' is not used; otherwise, substitute the name of a temporary file, just like '`%u`'. This temporary file is not meant for communication between processes, but rather as a junk disposal mechanism.

`%|suffix`
`%msuffix` Like '`%g`', except if '`-pipe`' is in effect. In that case '`%|`' substitutes a single dash and '`%m`' substitutes nothing at all. These are the two most common ways to instruct a program that it should read from standard input or write to standard output. If you need something more elaborate you can use an '`%{pipe:X}`' construct: see for example '`f/lang-specs.h`'.

`%.SUFFIX` Substitutes *.SUFFIX* for the suffixes of a matched switch's args when it is subsequently output with '`%*`'. *SUFFIX* is terminated by the next space or %.

%w
: Marks the argument containing or following the '%w' as the designated output file of this compilation. This puts the argument into the sequence of arguments that '%o' substitutes.

%o
: Substitutes the names of all the output files, with spaces automatically placed around them. You should write spaces around the '%o' as well or the results are undefined. '%o' is for use in the specs for running the linker. Input files whose names have no recognized suffix are not compiled at all, but they are included among the output files, so they are linked.

%O
: Substitutes the suffix for object files. Note that this is handled specially when it immediately follows '%g, %u, or %U', because of the need for those to form complete file names. The handling is such that '%O' is treated exactly as if it had already been substituted, except that '%g, %u, and %U' do not currently support additional *suffix* characters following '%O' as they do following, for example, '.o'.

%p
: Substitutes the standard macro predefinitions for the current target machine. Use this when running cpp.

%P
: Like '%p', but puts '__' before and after the name of each predefined macro, except for macros that start with '__' or with '_*L*', where *L* is an uppercase letter. This is for ISO C.

%I
: Substitute any of '-iprefix' (made from GCC_EXEC_PREFIX), '-isysroot' (made from TARGET_SYSTEM_ROOT), '-isystem' (made from COMPILER_PATH and '-B' options) and '-imultilib' as necessary.

%s
: Current argument is the name of a library or startup file of some sort. Search for that file in a standard list of directories and substitute the full name found. The current working directory is included in the list of directories scanned.

%T
: Current argument is the name of a linker script. Search for that file in the current list of directories to scan for libraries. If the file is located insert a '--script' option into the command line followed by the full path name found. If the file is not found then generate an error message. Note: the current working directory is not searched.

%e*str*
: Print *str* as an error message. *str* is terminated by a newline. Use this when inconsistent options are detected.

%(*name*)
: Substitute the contents of spec string *name* at this point.

%x{*option*}
: Accumulate an option for '%X'.

%X
: Output the accumulated linker options specified by '-Wl' or a '%x' spec string.

%Y
: Output the accumulated assembler options specified by '-Wa'.

%Z
: Output the accumulated preprocessor options specified by '-Wp'.

%a
: Process the asm spec. This is used to compute the switches to be passed to the assembler.

`%A` Process the `asm_final` spec. This is a spec string for passing switches to an assembler post-processor, if such a program is needed.

`%l` Process the `link` spec. This is the spec for computing the command line passed to the linker. Typically it makes use of the '`%L %G %S %D and %E`' sequences.

`%D` Dump out a '`-L`' option for each directory that GCC believes might contain startup files. If the target supports multilibs then the current multilib directory is prepended to each of these paths.

`%L` Process the `lib` spec. This is a spec string for deciding which libraries are included on the command line to the linker.

`%G` Process the `libgcc` spec. This is a spec string for deciding which GCC support library is included on the command line to the linker.

`%S` Process the `startfile` spec. This is a spec for deciding which object files are the first ones passed to the linker. Typically this might be a file named '`crt0.o`'.

`%E` Process the `endfile` spec. This is a spec string that specifies the last object files that are passed to the linker.

`%C` Process the `cpp` spec. This is used to construct the arguments to be passed to the C preprocessor.

`%1` Process the `cc1` spec. This is used to construct the options to be passed to the actual C compiler (`cc1`).

`%2` Process the `cc1plus` spec. This is used to construct the options to be passed to the actual C++ compiler (`cc1plus`).

`%*` Substitute the variable part of a matched option. See below. Note that each comma in the substituted string is replaced by a single space.

`%<S` Remove all occurrences of `-S` from the command line. Note—this command is position dependent. '`%`' commands in the spec string before this one see `-S`, '`%`' commands in the spec string after this one do not.

`%:function(args)`

Call the named function *function*, passing it *args*. *args* is first processed as a nested spec string, then split into an argument vector in the usual fashion. The function returns a string which is processed as if it had appeared literally as part of the current spec.

The following built-in spec functions are provided:

`getenv` The `getenv` spec function takes two arguments: an environment variable name and a string. If the environment variable is not defined, a fatal error is issued. Otherwise, the return value is the value of the environment variable concatenated with the string. For example, if `TOPDIR` is defined as '`/path/to/top`', then:

```
%:getenv(TOPDIR /include)
```

expands to '`/path/to/top/include`'.

`if-exists`
: The `if-exists` spec function takes one argument, an absolute pathname to a file. If the file exists, `if-exists` returns the pathname. Here is a small example of its usage:

```
*startfile:
crt0%O%s %:if-exists(crti%O%s) crtbegin%O%s
```

`if-exists-else`
: The `if-exists-else` spec function is similar to the `if-exists` spec function, except that it takes two arguments. The first argument is an absolute pathname to a file. If the file exists, `if-exists-else` returns the pathname. If it does not exist, it returns the second argument. This way, `if-exists-else` can be used to select one file or another, based on the existence of the first. Here is a small example of its usage:

```
*startfile:
crt0%O%s %:if-exists(crti%O%s) \
%:if-exists-else(crtbeginT%O%s crtbegin%O%s)
```

`replace-outfile`
: The `replace-outfile` spec function takes two arguments. It looks for the first argument in the outfiles array and replaces it with the second argument. Here is a small example of its usage:

```
%{fgnu-runtime:%:replace-outfile(-lobjc -lobjc-gnu)}
```

`remove-outfile`
: The `remove-outfile` spec function takes one argument. It looks for the first argument in the outfiles array and removes it. Here is a small example its usage:

```
%:remove-outfile(-lm)
```

`pass-through-libs`
: The `pass-through-libs` spec function takes any number of arguments. It finds any '`-l`' options and any non-options ending in '`.a`' (which it assumes are the names of linker input library archive files) and returns a result containing all the found arguments each prepended by '`-plugin-opt=-pass-through=`' and joined by spaces. This list is intended to be passed to the LTO linker plugin.

```
%:pass-through-libs(%G %L %G)
```

`print-asm-header`
: The `print-asm-header` function takes no arguments and simply prints a banner like:

```
Assembler options
=================

Use "-Wa,OPTION" to pass "OPTION" to the assembler.
```

It is used to separate compiler options from assembler options in the '`--target-help`' output.

`%{S}`
: Substitutes the `-S` switch, if that switch is given to GCC. If that switch is not specified, this substitutes nothing. Note that the leading dash is omitted

when specifying this option, and it is automatically inserted if the substitution is performed. Thus the spec string '`%{foo}`' matches the command-line option '`-foo`' and outputs the command-line option '`-foo`'.

`%W{S}`
: Like %{S} but mark last argument supplied within as a file to be deleted on failure.

`%{S*}`
: Substitutes all the switches specified to GCC whose names start with `-S`, but which also take an argument. This is used for switches like '`-o`', '`-D`', '`-I`', etc. GCC considers '`-o foo`' as being one switch whose name starts with '`o`'. %{o*} substitutes this text, including the space. Thus two arguments are generated.

`%{S*&T*}`
: Like %{`S`*}, but preserve order of `S` and `T` options (the order of `S` and `T` in the spec is not significant). There can be any number of ampersand-separated variables; for each the wild card is optional. Useful for CPP as '`%{D*&U*&A*}`'.

`%{S:X}`
: Substitutes `X`, if the '`-S`' switch is given to GCC.

`%{!S:X}`
: Substitutes `X`, if the '`-S`' switch is *not* given to GCC.

`%{S*:X}`
: Substitutes `X` if one or more switches whose names start with `-S` are specified to GCC. Normally `X` is substituted only once, no matter how many such switches appeared. However, if `%*` appears somewhere in `X`, then `X` is substituted once for each matching switch, with the `%*` replaced by the part of that switch matching the `*`.

  If `%*` appears as the last part of a spec sequence then a space is added after the end of the last substitution. If there is more text in the sequence, however, then a space is not generated. This allows the `%*` substitution to be used as part of a larger string. For example, a spec string like this:

  ```
  %{mcu=*:--script=%*/memory.ld}
  ```

  when matching an option like '`-mcu=newchip`' produces:

  ```
  --script=newchip/memory.ld
  ```

`%{.S:X}`
: Substitutes `X`, if processing a file with suffix `S`.

`%{!.S:X}`
: Substitutes `X`, if *not* processing a file with suffix `S`.

`%{,S:X}`
: Substitutes `X`, if processing a file for language `S`.

`%{!,S:X}`
: Substitutes `X`, if not processing a file for language `S`.

`%{S|P:X}`
: Substitutes `X` if either `-S` or `-P` is given to GCC. This may be combined with '`!`', '`.`', '`,`', and `*` sequences as well, although they have a stronger binding than the '`|`'. If `%*` appears in `X`, all of the alternatives must be starred, and only the first matching alternative is substituted.

  For example, a spec string like this:

  ```
  %{.c:-foo} %{!.c:-bar} %{.c|d:-baz} %{!.c|d:-boggle}
  ```

  outputs the following command-line options from the following input command-line options:

  ```
  fred.c        -foo -baz
  jim.d         -bar -boggle
  -d fred.c     -foo -baz -boggle
  -d jim.d      -bar -baz -boggle
  ```

`%{S:X; T:Y; :D}`
: If `S` is given to GCC, substitutes `X`; else if `T` is given to GCC, substitutes `Y`; else substitutes `D`. There can be as many clauses as you need. This may be combined with `.`, `,`, `!`, `|`, and `*` as needed.

The conditional text `X` in a `%{S:X}` or similar construct may contain other nested '%' constructs or spaces, or even newlines. They are processed as usual, as described above. Trailing white space in `X` is ignored. White space may also appear anywhere on the left side of the colon in these constructs, except between `.` or `*` and the corresponding word.

The '`-O`', '`-f`', '`-m`', and '`-W`' switches are handled specifically in these constructs. If another value of '`-O`' or the negated form of a '`-f`', '`-m`', or '`-W`' switch is found later in the command line, the earlier switch value is ignored, except with {`S*`} where `S` is just one letter, which passes all matching options.

The character '`|`' at the beginning of the predicate text is used to indicate that a command should be piped to the following command, but only if '`-pipe`' is specified.

It is built into GCC which switches take arguments and which do not. (You might think it would be useful to generalize this to allow each compiler's spec to say which switches take arguments. But this cannot be done in a consistent fashion. GCC cannot even decide which input files have been specified without knowing which switches take arguments, and it must know which input files to compile in order to tell which compilers to run).

GCC also knows implicitly that arguments starting in '`-l`' are to be treated as compiler output files, and passed to the linker in their proper position among the other output files.

3.20 Environment Variables Affecting GCC

This section describes several environment variables that affect how GCC operates. Some of them work by specifying directories or prefixes to use when searching for various kinds of files. Some are used to specify other aspects of the compilation environment.

Note that you can also specify places to search using options such as '`-B`', '`-I`' and '`-L`' (see Section 3.15 [Directory Options], page 175). These take precedence over places specified using environment variables, which in turn take precedence over those specified by the configuration of GCC. See Section "Controlling the Compilation Driver '`gcc`'" in *GNU Compiler Collection (GCC) Internals*.

`LANG`
`LC_CTYPE`
`LC_MESSAGES`
`LC_ALL`
: These environment variables control the way that GCC uses localization information which allows GCC to work with different national conventions. GCC inspects the locale categories `LC_CTYPE` and `LC_MESSAGES` if it has been configured to do so. These locale categories can be set to any value supported by your installation. A typical value is '`en_GB.UTF-8`' for English in the United Kingdom encoded in UTF-8.

: The `LC_CTYPE` environment variable specifies character classification. GCC uses it to determine the character boundaries in a string; this is needed for some multibyte encodings that contain quote and escape characters that are otherwise interpreted as a string end or escape.

The `LC_MESSAGES` environment variable specifies the language to use in diagnostic messages.

If the `LC_ALL` environment variable is set, it overrides the value of `LC_CTYPE` and `LC_MESSAGES`; otherwise, `LC_CTYPE` and `LC_MESSAGES` default to the value of the `LANG` environment variable. If none of these variables are set, GCC defaults to traditional C English behavior.

`TMPDIR` If `TMPDIR` is set, it specifies the directory to use for temporary files. GCC uses temporary files to hold the output of one stage of compilation which is to be used as input to the next stage: for example, the output of the preprocessor, which is the input to the compiler proper.

`GCC_COMPARE_DEBUG`

Setting `GCC_COMPARE_DEBUG` is nearly equivalent to passing '`-fcompare-debug`' to the compiler driver. See the documentation of this option for more details.

`GCC_EXEC_PREFIX`

If `GCC_EXEC_PREFIX` is set, it specifies a prefix to use in the names of the subprograms executed by the compiler. No slash is added when this prefix is combined with the name of a subprogram, but you can specify a prefix that ends with a slash if you wish.

If `GCC_EXEC_PREFIX` is not set, GCC attempts to figure out an appropriate prefix to use based on the pathname it is invoked with.

If GCC cannot find the subprogram using the specified prefix, it tries looking in the usual places for the subprogram.

The default value of `GCC_EXEC_PREFIX` is '*prefix*`/lib/gcc/`' where *prefix* is the prefix to the installed compiler. In many cases *prefix* is the value of `prefix` when you ran the '`configure`' script.

Other prefixes specified with '`-B`' take precedence over this prefix.

This prefix is also used for finding files such as '`crt0.o`' that are used for linking.

In addition, the prefix is used in an unusual way in finding the directories to search for header files. For each of the standard directories whose name normally begins with '`/usr/local/lib/gcc`' (more precisely, with the value of `GCC_INCLUDE_DIR`), GCC tries replacing that beginning with the specified prefix to produce an alternate directory name. Thus, with '`-Bfoo/`', GCC searches '`foo/bar`' just before it searches the standard directory '`/usr/local/lib/bar`'. If a standard directory begins with the configured *prefix* then the value of *prefix* is replaced by `GCC_EXEC_PREFIX` when looking for header files.

`COMPILER_PATH`

The value of `COMPILER_PATH` is a colon-separated list of directories, much like `PATH`. GCC tries the directories thus specified when searching for subprograms, if it can't find the subprograms using `GCC_EXEC_PREFIX`.

`LIBRARY_PATH`

The value of `LIBRARY_PATH` is a colon-separated list of directories, much like `PATH`. When configured as a native compiler, GCC tries the directories thus specified when searching for special linker files, if it can't find them using `GCC_EXEC_PREFIX`. Linking using GCC also uses these directories when searching for ordinary libraries for the '-l' option (but directories specified with '-L' come first).

LANG
This variable is used to pass locale information to the compiler. One way in which this information is used is to determine the character set to be used when character literals, string literals and comments are parsed in C and C++. When the compiler is configured to allow multibyte characters, the following values for LANG are recognized:

'C-JIS' Recognize JIS characters.

'C-SJIS' Recognize SJIS characters.

'C-EUCJP' Recognize EUCJP characters.

If LANG is not defined, or if it has some other value, then the compiler uses mblen and mbtowc as defined by the default locale to recognize and translate multibyte characters.

Some additional environment variables affect the behavior of the preprocessor.

CPATH
C_INCLUDE_PATH
CPLUS_INCLUDE_PATH
OBJC_INCLUDE_PATH
Each variable's value is a list of directories separated by a special character, much like PATH, in which to look for header files. The special character, PATH_SEPARATOR, is target-dependent and determined at GCC build time. For Microsoft Windows-based targets it is a semicolon, and for almost all other targets it is a colon.

CPATH specifies a list of directories to be searched as if specified with '-I', but after any paths given with '-I' options on the command line. This environment variable is used regardless of which language is being preprocessed.

The remaining environment variables apply only when preprocessing the particular language indicated. Each specifies a list of directories to be searched as if specified with '-isystem', but after any paths given with '-isystem' options on the command line.

In all these variables, an empty element instructs the compiler to search its current working directory. Empty elements can appear at the beginning or end of a path. For instance, if the value of CPATH is :/special/include, that has the same effect as '-I. -I/special/include'.

DEPENDENCIES_OUTPUT
If this variable is set, its value specifies how to output dependencies for Make based on the non-system header files processed by the compiler. System header files are ignored in the dependency output.

The value of DEPENDENCIES_OUTPUT can be just a file name, in which case the Make rules are written to that file, guessing the target name from the source file name. Or the value can have the form '*file target*', in which case the rules are written to file *file* using *target* as the target name.

In other words, this environment variable is equivalent to combining the options '-MM' and '-MF' (see Section 3.12 [Preprocessor Options], page 159), with an optional '-MT' switch too.

`SUNPRO_DEPENDENCIES`
: This variable is the same as `DEPENDENCIES_OUTPUT` (see above), except that system header files are not ignored, so it implies '-M' rather than '-MM'. However, the dependence on the main input file is omitted. See Section 3.12 [Preprocessor Options], page 159.

3.21 Using Precompiled Headers

Often large projects have many header files that are included in every source file. The time the compiler takes to process these header files over and over again can account for nearly all of the time required to build the project. To make builds faster, GCC allows you to *precompile* a header file.

To create a precompiled header file, simply compile it as you would any other file, if necessary using the '-x' option to make the driver treat it as a C or C++ header file. You may want to use a tool like `make` to keep the precompiled header up-to-date when the headers it contains change.

A precompiled header file is searched for when `#include` is seen in the compilation. As it searches for the included file (see Section "Search Path" in *The C Preprocessor*) the compiler looks for a precompiled header in each directory just before it looks for the include file in that directory. The name searched for is the name specified in the `#include` with '.gch' appended. If the precompiled header file can't be used, it is ignored.

For instance, if you have `#include "all.h"`, and you have 'all.h.gch' in the same directory as 'all.h', then the precompiled header file is used if possible, and the original header is used otherwise.

Alternatively, you might decide to put the precompiled header file in a directory and use '-I' to ensure that directory is searched before (or instead of) the directory containing the original header. Then, if you want to check that the precompiled header file is always used, you can put a file of the same name as the original header in this directory containing an `#error` command.

This also works with '-include'. So yet another way to use precompiled headers, good for projects not designed with precompiled header files in mind, is to simply take most of the header files used by a project, include them from another header file, precompile that header file, and '-include' the precompiled header. If the header files have guards against multiple inclusion, they are skipped because they've already been included (in the precompiled header).

If you need to precompile the same header file for different languages, targets, or compiler options, you can instead make a *directory* named like 'all.h.gch', and put each precompiled header in the directory, perhaps using '-o'. It doesn't matter what you call the files in the directory; every precompiled header in the directory is considered. The first precompiled header encountered in the directory that is valid for this compilation is used; they're searched in no particular order.

There are many other possibilities, limited only by your imagination, good sense, and the constraints of your build system.

A precompiled header file can be used only when these conditions apply:

- Only one precompiled header can be used in a particular compilation.
- A precompiled header can't be used once the first C token is seen. You can have preprocessor directives before a precompiled header; you cannot include a precompiled header from inside another header.
- The precompiled header file must be produced for the same language as the current compilation. You can't use a C precompiled header for a C++ compilation.
- The precompiled header file must have been produced by the same compiler binary as the current compilation is using.
- Any macros defined before the precompiled header is included must either be defined in the same way as when the precompiled header was generated, or must not affect the precompiled header, which usually means that they don't appear in the precompiled header at all.

  The '`-D`' option is one way to define a macro before a precompiled header is included; using a `#define` can also do it. There are also some options that define macros implicitly, like '`-O`' and '`-Wdeprecated`'; the same rule applies to macros defined this way.
- If debugging information is output when using the precompiled header, using '`-g`' or similar, the same kind of debugging information must have been output when building the precompiled header. However, a precompiled header built using '`-g`' can be used in a compilation when no debugging information is being output.
- The same '`-m`' options must generally be used when building and using the precompiled header. See Section 3.18 [Submodel Options], page 202, for any cases where this rule is relaxed.
- Each of the following options must be the same when building and using the precompiled header:

  ```
  -fexceptions
  ```
- Some other command-line options starting with '`-f`', '`-p`', or '`-O`' must be defined in the same way as when the precompiled header was generated. At present, it's not clear which options are safe to change and which are not; the safest choice is to use exactly the same options when generating and using the precompiled header. The following are known to be safe:

  ```
  -fmessage-length= -fpreprocessed -fsched-interblock
  -fsched-spec -fsched-spec-load -fsched-spec-load-dangerous
  -fsched-verbose=number -fschedule-insns -fvisibility=
  -pedantic-errors
  ```

For all of these except the last, the compiler automatically ignores the precompiled header if the conditions aren't met. If you find an option combination that doesn't work and doesn't cause the precompiled header to be ignored, please consider filing a bug report, see Chapter 13 [Bugs], page 747.

If you do use differing options when generating and using the precompiled header, the actual behavior is a mixture of the behavior for the options. For instance, if you use '`-g`' to generate the precompiled header but not when using it, you may or may not get debugging information for routines in the precompiled header.

4 C Implementation-Defined Behavior

A conforming implementation of ISO C is required to document its choice of behavior in each of the areas that are designated "implementation defined". The following lists all such areas, along with the section numbers from the ISO/IEC 9899:1990, ISO/IEC 9899:1999 and ISO/IEC 9899:2011 standards. Some areas are only implementation-defined in one version of the standard.

Some choices depend on the externally determined ABI for the platform (including standard character encodings) which GCC follows; these are listed as "determined by ABI" below. See Chapter 9 [Binary Compatibility], page 713, and `http://gcc.gnu.org/readings.html`. Some choices are documented in the preprocessor manual. See Section "Implementation-defined behavior" in *The C Preprocessor*. Some choices are made by the library and operating system (or other environment when compiling for a freestanding environment); refer to their documentation for details.

4.1 Translation

- *How a diagnostic is identified (C90 3.7, C99 and C11 3.10, C90, C99 and C11 5.1.1.3).*

  Diagnostics consist of all the output sent to stderr by GCC.
- *Whether each nonempty sequence of white-space characters other than new-line is retained or replaced by one space character in translation phase 3 (C90, C99 and C11 5.1.1.2).*

  See Section "Implementation-defined behavior" in *The C Preprocessor*.

4.2 Environment

The behavior of most of these points are dependent on the implementation of the C library, and are not defined by GCC itself.

- *The mapping between physical source file multibyte characters and the source character set in translation phase 1 (C90, C99 and C11 5.1.1.2).*

  See Section "Implementation-defined behavior" in *The C Preprocessor*.

4.3 Identifiers

- *Which additional multibyte characters may appear in identifiers and their correspondence to universal character names (C99 and C11 6.4.2).*

  See Section "Implementation-defined behavior" in *The C Preprocessor*.
- *The number of significant initial characters in an identifier (C90 6.1.2, C90, C99 and C11 5.2.4.1, C99 and C11 6.4.2).*

  For internal names, all characters are significant. For external names, the number of significant characters are defined by the linker; for almost all targets, all characters are significant.
- *Whether case distinctions are significant in an identifier with external linkage (C90 6.1.2).*

  This is a property of the linker. C99 and C11 require that case distinctions are always significant in identifiers with external linkage and systems without this property are not supported by GCC.

4.4 Characters

- *The number of bits in a byte (C90 3.4, C99 and C11 3.6).*

  Determined by ABI.
- *The values of the members of the execution character set (C90, C99 and C11 5.2.1).*

  Determined by ABI.
- *The unique value of the member of the execution character set produced for each of the standard alphabetic escape sequences (C90, C99 and C11 5.2.2).*

  Determined by ABI.
- *The value of a* `char` *object into which has been stored any character other than a member of the basic execution character set (C90 6.1.2.5, C99 and C11 6.2.5).*

  Determined by ABI.
- *Which of* `signed char` *or* `unsigned char` *has the same range, representation, and behavior as "plain"* `char` *(C90 6.1.2.5, C90 6.2.1.1, C99 and C11 6.2.5, C99 and C11 6.3.1.1).*

  Determined by ABI. The options '`-funsigned-char`' and '`-fsigned-char`' change the default. See Section 3.4 [Options Controlling C Dialect], page 33.
- *The mapping of members of the source character set (in character constants and string literals) to members of the execution character set (C90 6.1.3.4, C99 and C11 6.4.4.4, C90, C99 and C11 5.1.1.2).*

  Determined by ABI.
- *The value of an integer character constant containing more than one character or containing a character or escape sequence that does not map to a single-byte execution character (C90 6.1.3.4, C99 and C11 6.4.4.4).*

  See Section "Implementation-defined behavior" in *The C Preprocessor*.
- *The value of a wide character constant containing more than one multibyte character or a single multibyte character that maps to multiple members of the extended execution character set, or containing a multibyte character or escape sequence not represented in the extended execution character set (C90 6.1.3.4, C99 and C11 6.4.4.4).*

  See Section "Implementation-defined behavior" in *The C Preprocessor*.
- *The current locale used to convert a wide character constant consisting of a single multibyte character that maps to a member of the extended execution character set into a corresponding wide character code (C90 6.1.3.4, C99 and C11 6.4.4.4).*

  See Section "Implementation-defined behavior" in *The C Preprocessor*.
- *Whether differently-prefixed wide string literal tokens can be concatenated and, if so, the treatment of the resulting multibyte character sequence (C11 6.4.5).*

  Such tokens may not be concatenated.
- *The current locale used to convert a wide string literal into corresponding wide character codes (C90 6.1.4, C99 and C11 6.4.5).*

  See Section "Implementation-defined behavior" in *The C Preprocessor*.
- *The value of a string literal containing a multibyte character or escape sequence not represented in the execution character set (C90 6.1.4, C99 and C11 6.4.5).*

  See Section "Implementation-defined behavior" in *The C Preprocessor*.

- *The encoding of any of* `wchar_t`, `char16_t`, *and* `char32_t` *where the corresponding standard encoding macro (*`__STDC_ISO_10646__`, `__STDC_UTF_16__`, *or* `__STDC_UTF_32__`*) is not defined (C11 6.10.8.2).*

  See Section "Implementation-defined behavior" in *The C Preprocessor*. `char16_t` and `char32_t` literals are always encoded in UTF-16 and UTF-32 respectively.

4.5 Integers

- *Any extended integer types that exist in the implementation (C99 and C11 6.2.5).*

  GCC does not support any extended integer types.

- *Whether signed integer types are represented using sign and magnitude, two's complement, or one's complement, and whether the extraordinary value is a trap representation or an ordinary value (C99 and C11 6.2.6.2).*

  GCC supports only two's complement integer types, and all bit patterns are ordinary values.

- *The rank of any extended integer type relative to another extended integer type with the same precision (C99 and C11 6.3.1.1).*

  GCC does not support any extended integer types.

- *The result of, or the signal raised by, converting an integer to a signed integer type when the value cannot be represented in an object of that type (C90 6.2.1.2, C99 and C11 6.3.1.3).*

  For conversion to a type of width N, the value is reduced modulo 2^N to be within range of the type; no signal is raised.

- *The results of some bitwise operations on signed integers (C90 6.3, C99 and C11 6.5).*

  Bitwise operators act on the representation of the value including both the sign and value bits, where the sign bit is considered immediately above the highest-value value bit. Signed '`>>`' acts on negative numbers by sign extension.

  As an extension to the C language, GCC does not use the latitude given in C99 and C11 only to treat certain aspects of signed '`<<`' as undefined. However, '`-fsanitize=shift`' (and '`-fsanitize=undefined`') will diagnose such cases. They are also diagnosed where constant expressions are required.

- *The sign of the remainder on integer division (C90 6.3.5).*

  GCC always follows the C99 and C11 requirement that the result of division is truncated towards zero.

4.6 Floating Point

- *The accuracy of the floating-point operations and of the library functions in* `<math.h>` *and* `<complex.h>` *that return floating-point results (C90, C99 and C11 5.2.4.2.2).*

  The accuracy is unknown.

- *The rounding behaviors characterized by non-standard values of* `FLT_ROUNDS` *(C90, C99 and C11 5.2.4.2.2).*

  GCC does not use such values.

- *The evaluation methods characterized by non-standard negative values of* `FLT_EVAL_METHOD` *(C99 and C11 5.2.4.2.2).*

  GCC does not use such values.
- *The direction of rounding when an integer is converted to a floating-point number that cannot exactly represent the original value (C90 6.2.1.3, C99 and C11 6.3.1.4).*

  C99 Annex F is followed.
- *The direction of rounding when a floating-point number is converted to a narrower floating-point number (C90 6.2.1.4, C99 and C11 6.3.1.5).*

  C99 Annex F is followed.
- *How the nearest representable value or the larger or smaller representable value immediately adjacent to the nearest representable value is chosen for certain floating constants (C90 6.1.3.1, C99 and C11 6.4.4.2).*

  C99 Annex F is followed.
- *Whether and how floating expressions are contracted when not disallowed by the* `FP_CONTRACT` *pragma (C99 and C11 6.5).*

  Expressions are currently only contracted if '`-ffp-contract=fast`', '`-funsafe-math-optimizations`' or '`-ffast-math`' are used. This is subject to change.
- *The default state for the* `FENV_ACCESS` *pragma (C99 and C11 7.6.1).*

  This pragma is not implemented, but the default is to "off" unless '`-frounding-math`' is used in which case it is "on".
- *Additional floating-point exceptions, rounding modes, environments, and classifications, and their macro names (C99 and C11 7.6, C99 and C11 7.12).*

  This is dependent on the implementation of the C library, and is not defined by GCC itself.
- *The default state for the* `FP_CONTRACT` *pragma (C99 and C11 7.12.2).*

  This pragma is not implemented. Expressions are currently only contracted if '`-ffp-contract=fast`', '`-funsafe-math-optimizations`' or '`-ffast-math`' are used. This is subject to change.
- *Whether the "inexact" floating-point exception can be raised when the rounded result actually does equal the mathematical result in an IEC 60559 conformant implementation (C99 F.9).*

  This is dependent on the implementation of the C library, and is not defined by GCC itself.
- *Whether the "underflow" (and "inexact") floating-point exception can be raised when a result is tiny but not inexact in an IEC 60559 conformant implementation (C99 F.9).*

  This is dependent on the implementation of the C library, and is not defined by GCC itself.

4.7 Arrays and Pointers

- *The result of converting a pointer to an integer or vice versa (C90 6.3.4, C99 and C11 6.3.2.3).*

A cast from pointer to integer discards most-significant bits if the pointer representation is larger than the integer type, sign-extends[1] if the pointer representation is smaller than the integer type, otherwise the bits are unchanged.

A cast from integer to pointer discards most-significant bits if the pointer representation is smaller than the integer type, extends according to the signedness of the integer type if the pointer representation is larger than the integer type, otherwise the bits are unchanged.

When casting from pointer to integer and back again, the resulting pointer must reference the same object as the original pointer, otherwise the behavior is undefined. That is, one may not use integer arithmetic to avoid the undefined behavior of pointer arithmetic as proscribed in C99 and C11 6.5.6/8.

- *The size of the result of subtracting two pointers to elements of the same array (C90 6.3.6, C99 and C11 6.5.6).*

  The value is as specified in the standard and the type is determined by the ABI.

4.8 Hints

- *The extent to which suggestions made by using the* `register` *storage-class specifier are effective (C90 6.5.1, C99 and C11 6.7.1).*

  The `register` specifier affects code generation only in these ways:

  - When used as part of the register variable extension, see Section 6.44.5 [Explicit Register Variables], page 524.
  - When '`-O0`' is in use, the compiler allocates distinct stack memory for all variables that do not have the `register` storage-class specifier; if `register` is specified, the variable may have a shorter lifespan than the code would indicate and may never be placed in memory.
  - On some rare x86 targets, `setjmp` doesn't save the registers in all circumstances. In those cases, GCC doesn't allocate any variables in registers unless they are marked `register`.

- *The extent to which suggestions made by using the inline function specifier are effective (C99 and C11 6.7.4).*

  GCC will not inline any functions if the '`-fno-inline`' option is used or if '`-O0`' is used. Otherwise, GCC may still be unable to inline a function for many reasons; the '`-Winline`' option may be used to determine if a function has not been inlined and why not.

4.9 Structures, Unions, Enumerations, and Bit-Fields

- *A member of a union object is accessed using a member of a different type (C90 6.3.2.3).*

  The relevant bytes of the representation of the object are treated as an object of the type used for the access. See [Type-punning], page 116. This may be a trap representation.

- *Whether a "plain"* `int` *bit-field is treated as a* `signed int` *bit-field or as an* `unsigned int` *bit-field (C90 6.5.2, C90 6.5.2.1, C99 and C11 6.7.2, C99 and C11 6.7.2.1).*

---

[1] Future versions of GCC may zero-extend, or use a target-defined `ptr_extend` pattern. Do not rely on sign extension.

By default it is treated as `signed int` but this may be changed by the '`-funsigned-bitfields`' option.

- *Allowable bit-field types other than* `_Bool`, `signed int`, *and* `unsigned int` *(C99 and C11 6.7.2.1).*

  Other integer types, such as `long int`, and enumerated types are permitted even in strictly conforming mode.

- *Whether atomic types are permitted for bit-fields (C11 6.7.2.1).*

  Atomic types are not permitted for bit-fields.

- *Whether a bit-field can straddle a storage-unit boundary (C90 6.5.2.1, C99 and C11 6.7.2.1).*

  Determined by ABI.

- *The order of allocation of bit-fields within a unit (C90 6.5.2.1, C99 and C11 6.7.2.1).*

  Determined by ABI.

- *The alignment of non-bit-field members of structures (C90 6.5.2.1, C99 and C11 6.7.2.1).*

  Determined by ABI.

- *The integer type compatible with each enumerated type (C90 6.5.2.2, C99 and C11 6.7.2.2).*

  Normally, the type is `unsigned int` if there are no negative values in the enumeration, otherwise `int`. If '`-fshort-enums`' is specified, then if there are negative values it is the first of `signed char`, `short` and `int` that can represent all the values, otherwise it is the first of `unsigned char`, `unsigned short` and `unsigned int` that can represent all the values.

  On some targets, '`-fshort-enums`' is the default; this is determined by the ABI.

4.10 Qualifiers

- *What constitutes an access to an object that has volatile-qualified type (C90 6.5.3, C99 and C11 6.7.3).*

  Such an object is normally accessed by pointers and used for accessing hardware. In most expressions, it is intuitively obvious what is a read and what is a write. For example

  ```
  volatile int *dst = somevalue;
  volatile int *src = someothervalue;
  *dst = *src;
  ```

  will cause a read of the volatile object pointed to by *src* and store the value into the volatile object pointed to by *dst*. There is no guarantee that these reads and writes are atomic, especially for objects larger than `int`.

  However, if the volatile storage is not being modified, and the value of the volatile storage is not used, then the situation is less obvious. For example

  ```
  volatile int *src = somevalue;
  *src;
  ```

  According to the C standard, such an expression is an rvalue whose type is the unqualified version of its original type, i.e. `int`. Whether GCC interprets this as a read of the volatile object being pointed to or only as a request to evaluate the expression for its side-effects depends on this type.

If it is a scalar type, or on most targets an aggregate type whose only member object is of a scalar type, or a union type whose member objects are of scalar types, the expression is interpreted by GCC as a read of the volatile object; in the other cases, the expression is only evaluated for its side-effects.

4.11 Declarators

- *The maximum number of declarators that may modify an arithmetic, structure or union type (C90 6.5.4).*

  GCC is only limited by available memory.

4.12 Statements

- *The maximum number of* `case` *values in a* `switch` *statement (C90 6.6.4.2).*

  GCC is only limited by available memory.

4.13 Preprocessing Directives

See Section "Implementation-defined behavior" in *The C Preprocessor*, for details of these aspects of implementation-defined behavior.

- *The locations within* `#pragma` *directives where header name preprocessing tokens are recognized (C11 6.4, C11 6.4.7).*
- *How sequences in both forms of header names are mapped to headers or external source file names (C90 6.1.7, C99 and C11 6.4.7).*
- *Whether the value of a character constant in a constant expression that controls conditional inclusion matches the value of the same character constant in the execution character set (C90 6.8.1, C99 and C11 6.10.1).*
- *Whether the value of a single-character character constant in a constant expression that controls conditional inclusion may have a negative value (C90 6.8.1, C99 and C11 6.10.1).*
- *The places that are searched for an included '*`<>`*' delimited header, and how the places are specified or the header is identified (C90 6.8.2, C99 and C11 6.10.2).*
- *How the named source file is searched for in an included '*`""`*' delimited header (C90 6.8.2, C99 and C11 6.10.2).*
- *The method by which preprocessing tokens (possibly resulting from macro expansion) in a* `#include` *directive are combined into a header name (C90 6.8.2, C99 and C11 6.10.2).*
- *The nesting limit for* `#include` *processing (C90 6.8.2, C99 and C11 6.10.2).*
- *Whether the '*`#`*' operator inserts a '*`\`*' character before the '*`\`*' character that begins a universal character name in a character constant or string literal (C99 and C11 6.10.3.2).*
- *The behavior on each recognized non-*`STDC` `#pragma` *directive (C90 6.8.6, C99 and C11 6.10.6).*

See Section "Pragmas" in *The C Preprocessor*, for details of pragmas accepted by GCC on all targets. See Section 6.61 [Pragmas Accepted by GCC], page 668, for details of target-specific pragmas.

- *The definitions for* __DATE__ *and* __TIME__ *when respectively, the date and time of translation are not available (C90 6.8.8, C99 6.10.8, C11 6.10.8.1).*

4.14 Library Functions

The behavior of most of these points are dependent on the implementation of the C library, and are not defined by GCC itself.

- *The null pointer constant to which the macro* NULL *expands (C90 7.1.6, C99 7.17, C11 7.19).*

  In <stddef.h>, NULL expands to ((void *)0). GCC does not provide the other headers which define NULL and some library implementations may use other definitions in those headers.

4.15 Architecture

- *The values or expressions assigned to the macros specified in the headers* <float.h>, <limits.h>, *and* <stdint.h> *(C90, C99 and C11 5.2.4.2, C99 7.18.2, C99 7.18.3, C11 7.20.2, C11 7.20.3).*

  Determined by ABI.
- *The result of attempting to indirectly access an object with automatic or thread storage duration from a thread other than the one with which it is associated (C11 6.2.4).*

  Such accesses are supported, subject to the same requirements for synchronization for concurrent accesses as for concurrent accesses to any object.
- *The number, order, and encoding of bytes in any object (when not explicitly specified in this International Standard) (C99 and C11 6.2.6.1).*

  Determined by ABI.
- *Whether any extended alignments are supported and the contexts in which they are supported (C11 6.2.8).*

  Extended alignments up to 2^{28} (bytes) are supported for objects of automatic storage duration. Alignments supported for objects of static and thread storage duration are determined by the ABI.
- *Valid alignment values other than those returned by an _Alignof expression for fundamental types, if any (C11 6.2.8).*

  Valid alignments are powers of 2 up to and including 2^{28}.
- *The value of the result of the* sizeof *and* _Alignof *operators (C90 6.3.3.4, C99 and C11 6.5.3.4).*

  Determined by ABI.

4.16 Locale-Specific Behavior

The behavior of these points are dependent on the implementation of the C library, and are not defined by GCC itself.

5 C++ Implementation-Defined Behavior

A conforming implementation of ISO C++ is required to document its choice of behavior in each of the areas that are designated "implementation defined". The following lists all such areas, along with the section numbers from the ISO/IEC 14882:1998 and ISO/IEC 14882:2003 standards. Some areas are only implementation-defined in one version of the standard.

Some choices depend on the externally determined ABI for the platform (including standard character encodings) which GCC follows; these are listed as "determined by ABI" below. See Chapter 9 [Binary Compatibility], page 713, and `http://gcc.gnu.org/readings.html`. Some choices are documented in the preprocessor manual. See Section "Implementation-defined behavior" in *The C Preprocessor*. Some choices are documented in the corresponding document for the C language. See Chapter 4 [C Implementation], page 373. Some choices are made by the library and operating system (or other environment when compiling for a freestanding environment); refer to their documentation for details.

5.1 Conditionally-Supported Behavior

Each implementation shall include documentation that identifies all conditionally-supported constructs that it does not support (C++0x 1.4).

- *Whether an argument of class type with a non-trivial copy constructor or destructor can be passed to ... (C++0x 5.2.2).*

  Such argument passing is supported, using the same pass-by-invisible-reference approach used for normal function arguments of such types.

5.2 Exception Handling

- *In the situation where no matching handler is found, it is implementation-defined whether or not the stack is unwound before std::terminate() is called (C++98 15.5.1).*

  The stack is not unwound before std::terminate is called.

GNU General Public License

Version 3, 29 June 2007

Copyright © 2007 Free Software Foundation, Inc. `http://fsf.org/`

Everyone is permitted to copy and distribute verbatim copies of this license document, but changing it is not allowed.

Preamble

The GNU General Public License is a free, copyleft license for software and other kinds of works.

The licenses for most software and other practical works are designed to take away your freedom to share and change the works. By contrast, the GNU General Public License is intended to guarantee your freedom to share and change all versions of a program–to make sure it remains free software for all its users. We, the Free Software Foundation, use the GNU General Public License for most of our software; it applies also to any other work released this way by its authors. You can apply it to your programs, too.

When we speak of free software, we are referring to freedom, not price. Our General Public Licenses are designed to make sure that you have the freedom to distribute copies of free software (and charge for them if you wish), that you receive source code or can get it if you want it, that you can change the software or use pieces of it in new free programs, and that you know you can do these things.

To protect your rights, we need to prevent others from denying you these rights or asking you to surrender the rights. Therefore, you have certain responsibilities if you distribute copies of the software, or if you modify it: responsibilities to respect the freedom of others.

For example, if you distribute copies of such a program, whether gratis or for a fee, you must pass on to the recipients the same freedoms that you received. You must make sure that they, too, receive or can get the source code. And you must show them these terms so they know their rights.

Developers that use the GNU GPL protect your rights with two steps: (1) assert copyright on the software, and (2) offer you this License giving you legal permission to copy, distribute and/or modify it.

For the developers' and authors' protection, the GPL clearly explains that there is no warranty for this free software. For both users' and authors' sake, the GPL requires that modified versions be marked as changed, so that their problems will not be attributed erroneously to authors of previous versions.

Some devices are designed to deny users access to install or run modified versions of the software inside them, although the manufacturer can do so. This is fundamentally incompatible with the aim of protecting users' freedom to change the software. The systematic pattern of such abuse occurs in the area of products for individuals to use, which is precisely where it is most unacceptable. Therefore, we have designed this version of the GPL to prohibit the practice for those products. If such problems arise substantially in other domains, we stand ready to extend this provision to those domains in future versions of the GPL, as needed to protect the freedom of users.

Finally, every program is threatened constantly by software patents. States should not allow patents to restrict development and use of software on general-purpose computers, but in those that do, we wish to avoid the special danger that patents applied to a free program could make it effectively proprietary. To prevent this, the GPL assures that patents cannot be used to render the program non-free.

The precise terms and conditions for copying, distribution and modification follow.

TERMS AND CONDITIONS

0. Definitions.

   "This License" refers to version 3 of the GNU General Public License.

   "Copyright" also means copyright-like laws that apply to other kinds of works, such as semiconductor masks.

   "The Program" refers to any copyrightable work licensed under this License. Each licensee is addressed as "you". "Licensees" and "recipients" may be individuals or organizations.

   To "modify" a work means to copy from or adapt all or part of the work in a fashion requiring copyright permission, other than the making of an exact copy. The resulting work is called a "modified version" of the earlier work or a work "based on" the earlier work.

   A "covered work" means either the unmodified Program or a work based on the Program.

   To "propagate" a work means to do anything with it that, without permission, would make you directly or secondarily liable for infringement under applicable copyright law, except executing it on a computer or modifying a private copy. Propagation includes copying, distribution (with or without modification), making available to the public, and in some countries other activities as well.

   To "convey" a work means any kind of propagation that enables other parties to make or receive copies. Mere interaction with a user through a computer network, with no transfer of a copy, is not conveying.

   An interactive user interface displays "Appropriate Legal Notices" to the extent that it includes a convenient and prominently visible feature that (1) displays an appropriate copyright notice, and (2) tells the user that there is no warranty for the work (except to the extent that warranties are provided), that licensees may convey the work under this License, and how to view a copy of this License. If the interface presents a list of user commands or options, such as a menu, a prominent item in the list meets this criterion.

1. Source Code.

   The "source code" for a work means the preferred form of the work for making modifications to it. "Object code" means any non-source form of a work.

   A "Standard Interface" means an interface that either is an official standard defined by a recognized standards body, or, in the case of interfaces specified for a particular programming language, one that is widely used among developers working in that language.

The "System Libraries" of an executable work include anything, other than the work as a whole, that (a) is included in the normal form of packaging a Major Component, but which is not part of that Major Component, and (b) serves only to enable use of the work with that Major Component, or to implement a Standard Interface for which an implementation is available to the public in source code form. A "Major Component", in this context, means a major essential component (kernel, window system, and so on) of the specific operating system (if any) on which the executable work runs, or a compiler used to produce the work, or an object code interpreter used to run it.

The "Corresponding Source" for a work in object code form means all the source code needed to generate, install, and (for an executable work) run the object code and to modify the work, including scripts to control those activities. However, it does not include the work's System Libraries, or general-purpose tools or generally available free programs which are used unmodified in performing those activities but which are not part of the work. For example, Corresponding Source includes interface definition files associated with source files for the work, and the source code for shared libraries and dynamically linked subprograms that the work is specifically designed to require, such as by intimate data communication or control flow between those subprograms and other parts of the work.

The Corresponding Source need not include anything that users can regenerate automatically from other parts of the Corresponding Source.

The Corresponding Source for a work in source code form is that same work.

2. Basic Permissions.

   All rights granted under this License are granted for the term of copyright on the Program, and are irrevocable provided the stated conditions are met. This License explicitly affirms your unlimited permission to run the unmodified Program. The output from running a covered work is covered by this License only if the output, given its content, constitutes a covered work. This License acknowledges your rights of fair use or other equivalent, as provided by copyright law.

   You may make, run and propagate covered works that you do not convey, without conditions so long as your license otherwise remains in force. You may convey covered works to others for the sole purpose of having them make modifications exclusively for you, or provide you with facilities for running those works, provided that you comply with the terms of this License in conveying all material for which you do not control copyright. Those thus making or running the covered works for you must do so exclusively on your behalf, under your direction and control, on terms that prohibit them from making any copies of your copyrighted material outside their relationship with you.

   Conveying under any other circumstances is permitted solely under the conditions stated below. Sublicensing is not allowed; section 10 makes it unnecessary.

3. Protecting Users' Legal Rights From Anti-Circumvention Law.

   No covered work shall be deemed part of an effective technological measure under any applicable law fulfilling obligations under article 11 of the WIPO copyright treaty adopted on 20 December 1996, or similar laws prohibiting or restricting circumvention of such measures.

When you convey a covered work, you waive any legal power to forbid circumvention of technological measures to the extent such circumvention is effected by exercising rights under this License with respect to the covered work, and you disclaim any intention to limit operation or modification of the work as a means of enforcing, against the work's users, your or third parties' legal rights to forbid circumvention of technological measures.

4. Conveying Verbatim Copies.

   You may convey verbatim copies of the Program's source code as you receive it, in any medium, provided that you conspicuously and appropriately publish on each copy an appropriate copyright notice; keep intact all notices stating that this License and any non-permissive terms added in accord with section 7 apply to the code; keep intact all notices of the absence of any warranty; and give all recipients a copy of this License along with the Program.

   You may charge any price or no price for each copy that you convey, and you may offer support or warranty protection for a fee.

5. Conveying Modified Source Versions.

   You may convey a work based on the Program, or the modifications to produce it from the Program, in the form of source code under the terms of section 4, provided that you also meet all of these conditions:

   a. The work must carry prominent notices stating that you modified it, and giving a relevant date.
   b. The work must carry prominent notices stating that it is released under this License and any conditions added under section 7. This requirement modifies the requirement in section 4 to "keep intact all notices".
   c. You must license the entire work, as a whole, under this License to anyone who comes into possession of a copy. This License will therefore apply, along with any applicable section 7 additional terms, to the whole of the work, and all its parts, regardless of how they are packaged. This License gives no permission to license the work in any other way, but it does not invalidate such permission if you have separately received it.
   d. If the work has interactive user interfaces, each must display Appropriate Legal Notices; however, if the Program has interactive interfaces that do not display Appropriate Legal Notices, your work need not make them do so.

   A compilation of a covered work with other separate and independent works, which are not by their nature extensions of the covered work, and which are not combined with it such as to form a larger program, in or on a volume of a storage or distribution medium, is called an "aggregate" if the compilation and its resulting copyright are not used to limit the access or legal rights of the compilation's users beyond what the individual works permit. Inclusion of a covered work in an aggregate does not cause this License to apply to the other parts of the aggregate.

6. Conveying Non-Source Forms.

   You may convey a covered work in object code form under the terms of sections 4 and 5, provided that you also convey the machine-readable Corresponding Source under the terms of this License, in one of these ways:

a. Convey the object code in, or embodied in, a physical product (including a physical distribution medium), accompanied by the Corresponding Source fixed on a durable physical medium customarily used for software interchange.
b. Convey the object code in, or embodied in, a physical product (including a physical distribution medium), accompanied by a written offer, valid for at least three years and valid for as long as you offer spare parts or customer support for that product model, to give anyone who possesses the object code either (1) a copy of the Corresponding Source for all the software in the product that is covered by this License, on a durable physical medium customarily used for software interchange, for a price no more than your reasonable cost of physically performing this conveying of source, or (2) access to copy the Corresponding Source from a network server at no charge.
c. Convey individual copies of the object code with a copy of the written offer to provide the Corresponding Source. This alternative is allowed only occasionally and noncommercially, and only if you received the object code with such an offer, in accord with subsection 6b.
d. Convey the object code by offering access from a designated place (gratis or for a charge), and offer equivalent access to the Corresponding Source in the same way through the same place at no further charge. You need not require recipients to copy the Corresponding Source along with the object code. If the place to copy the object code is a network server, the Corresponding Source may be on a different server (operated by you or a third party) that supports equivalent copying facilities, provided you maintain clear directions next to the object code saying where to find the Corresponding Source. Regardless of what server hosts the Corresponding Source, you remain obligated to ensure that it is available for as long as needed to satisfy these requirements.
e. Convey the object code using peer-to-peer transmission, provided you inform other peers where the object code and Corresponding Source of the work are being offered to the general public at no charge under subsection 6d.

A separable portion of the object code, whose source code is excluded from the Corresponding Source as a System Library, need not be included in conveying the object code work.

A "User Product" is either (1) a "consumer product", which means any tangible personal property which is normally used for personal, family, or household purposes, or (2) anything designed or sold for incorporation into a dwelling. In determining whether a product is a consumer product, doubtful cases shall be resolved in favor of coverage. For a particular product received by a particular user, "normally used" refers to a typical or common use of that class of product, regardless of the status of the particular user or of the way in which the particular user actually uses, or expects or is expected to use, the product. A product is a consumer product regardless of whether the product has substantial commercial, industrial or non-consumer uses, unless such uses represent the only significant mode of use of the product.

"Installation Information" for a User Product means any methods, procedures, authorization keys, or other information required to install and execute modified versions of a covered work in that User Product from a modified version of its Corresponding Source.

The information must suffice to ensure that the continued functioning of the modified object code is in no case prevented or interfered with solely because modification has been made.

If you convey an object code work under this section in, or with, or specifically for use in, a User Product, and the conveying occurs as part of a transaction in which the right of possession and use of the User Product is transferred to the recipient in perpetuity or for a fixed term (regardless of how the transaction is characterized), the Corresponding Source conveyed under this section must be accompanied by the Installation Information. But this requirement does not apply if neither you nor any third party retains the ability to install modified object code on the User Product (for example, the work has been installed in ROM).

The requirement to provide Installation Information does not include a requirement to continue to provide support service, warranty, or updates for a work that has been modified or installed by the recipient, or for the User Product in which it has been modified or installed. Access to a network may be denied when the modification itself materially and adversely affects the operation of the network or violates the rules and protocols for communication across the network.

Corresponding Source conveyed, and Installation Information provided, in accord with this section must be in a format that is publicly documented (and with an implementation available to the public in source code form), and must require no special password or key for unpacking, reading or copying.

7. Additional Terms.

   "Additional permissions" are terms that supplement the terms of this License by making exceptions from one or more of its conditions. Additional permissions that are applicable to the entire Program shall be treated as though they were included in this License, to the extent that they are valid under applicable law. If additional permissions apply only to part of the Program, that part may be used separately under those permissions, but the entire Program remains governed by this License without regard to the additional permissions.

   When you convey a copy of a covered work, you may at your option remove any additional permissions from that copy, or from any part of it. (Additional permissions may be written to require their own removal in certain cases when you modify the work.) You may place additional permissions on material, added by you to a covered work, for which you have or can give appropriate copyright permission.

   Notwithstanding any other provision of this License, for material you add to a covered work, you may (if authorized by the copyright holders of that material) supplement the terms of this License with terms:

   a. Disclaiming warranty or limiting liability differently from the terms of sections 15 and 16 of this License; or
   b. Requiring preservation of specified reasonable legal notices or author attributions in that material or in the Appropriate Legal Notices displayed by works containing it; or
   c. Prohibiting misrepresentation of the origin of that material, or requiring that modified versions of such material be marked in reasonable ways as different from the original version; or

d. Limiting the use for publicity purposes of names of licensors or authors of the material; or
e. Declining to grant rights under trademark law for use of some trade names, trademarks, or service marks; or
f. Requiring indemnification of licensors and authors of that material by anyone who conveys the material (or modified versions of it) with contractual assumptions of liability to the recipient, for any liability that these contractual assumptions directly impose on those licensors and authors.

All other non-permissive additional terms are considered "further restrictions" within the meaning of section 10. If the Program as you received it, or any part of it, contains a notice stating that it is governed by this License along with a term that is a further restriction, you may remove that term. If a license document contains a further restriction but permits relicensing or conveying under this License, you may add to a covered work material governed by the terms of that license document, provided that the further restriction does not survive such relicensing or conveying.

If you add terms to a covered work in accord with this section, you must place, in the relevant source files, a statement of the additional terms that apply to those files, or a notice indicating where to find the applicable terms.

Additional terms, permissive or non-permissive, may be stated in the form of a separately written license, or stated as exceptions; the above requirements apply either way.

8. Termination.

You may not propagate or modify a covered work except as expressly provided under this License. Any attempt otherwise to propagate or modify it is void, and will automatically terminate your rights under this License (including any patent licenses granted under the third paragraph of section 11).

However, if you cease all violation of this License, then your license from a particular copyright holder is reinstated (a) provisionally, unless and until the copyright holder explicitly and finally terminates your license, and (b) permanently, if the copyright holder fails to notify you of the violation by some reasonable means prior to 60 days after the cessation.

Moreover, your license from a particular copyright holder is reinstated permanently if the copyright holder notifies you of the violation by some reasonable means, this is the first time you have received notice of violation of this License (for any work) from that copyright holder, and you cure the violation prior to 30 days after your receipt of the notice.

Termination of your rights under this section does not terminate the licenses of parties who have received copies or rights from you under this License. If your rights have been terminated and not permanently reinstated, you do not qualify to receive new licenses for the same material under section 10.

9. Acceptance Not Required for Having Copies.

You are not required to accept this License in order to receive or run a copy of the Program. Ancillary propagation of a covered work occurring solely as a consequence of using peer-to-peer transmission to receive a copy likewise does not require acceptance.

However, nothing other than this License grants you permission to propagate or modify any covered work. These actions infringe copyright if you do not accept this License. Therefore, by modifying or propagating a covered work, you indicate your acceptance of this License to do so.

10. Automatic Licensing of Downstream Recipients.

    Each time you convey a covered work, the recipient automatically receives a license from the original licensors, to run, modify and propagate that work, subject to this License. You are not responsible for enforcing compliance by third parties with this License.

    An "entity transaction" is a transaction transferring control of an organization, or substantially all assets of one, or subdividing an organization, or merging organizations. If propagation of a covered work results from an entity transaction, each party to that transaction who receives a copy of the work also receives whatever licenses to the work the party's predecessor in interest had or could give under the previous paragraph, plus a right to possession of the Corresponding Source of the work from the predecessor in interest, if the predecessor has it or can get it with reasonable efforts.

    You may not impose any further restrictions on the exercise of the rights granted or affirmed under this License. For example, you may not impose a license fee, royalty, or other charge for exercise of rights granted under this License, and you may not initiate litigation (including a cross-claim or counterclaim in a lawsuit) alleging that any patent claim is infringed by making, using, selling, offering for sale, or importing the Program or any portion of it.

11. Patents.

    A "contributor" is a copyright holder who authorizes use under this License of the Program or a work on which the Program is based. The work thus licensed is called the contributor's "contributor version".

    A contributor's "essential patent claims" are all patent claims owned or controlled by the contributor, whether already acquired or hereafter acquired, that would be infringed by some manner, permitted by this License, of making, using, or selling its contributor version, but do not include claims that would be infringed only as a consequence of further modification of the contributor version. For purposes of this definition, "control" includes the right to grant patent sublicenses in a manner consistent with the requirements of this License.

    Each contributor grants you a non-exclusive, worldwide, royalty-free patent license under the contributor's essential patent claims, to make, use, sell, offer for sale, import and otherwise run, modify and propagate the contents of its contributor version.

    In the following three paragraphs, a "patent license" is any express agreement or commitment, however denominated, not to enforce a patent (such as an express permission to practice a patent or covenant not to sue for patent infringement). To "grant" such a patent license to a party means to make such an agreement or commitment not to enforce a patent against the party.

    If you convey a covered work, knowingly relying on a patent license, and the Corresponding Source of the work is not available for anyone to copy, free of charge and under the terms of this License, through a publicly available network server or other readily accessible means, then you must either (1) cause the Corresponding Source to be so available, or (2) arrange to deprive yourself of the benefit of the patent license for this particular work, or (3) arrange, in a manner consistent with the requirements of this License, to extend the patent license to downstream recipients. "Knowingly relying" means you have actual knowledge that, but for the patent license, your conveying the covered work in a country, or your recipient's use of the covered work in a country, would infringe one or more identifiable patents in that country that you have reason to believe are valid.

If, pursuant to or in connection with a single transaction or arrangement, you convey, or propagate by procuring conveyance of, a covered work, and grant a patent license to some of the parties receiving the covered work authorizing them to use, propagate, modify or convey a specific copy of the covered work, then the patent license you grant is automatically extended to all recipients of the covered work and works based on it.

A patent license is "discriminatory" if it does not include within the scope of its coverage, prohibits the exercise of, or is conditioned on the non-exercise of one or more of the rights that are specifically granted under this License. You may not convey a covered work if you are a party to an arrangement with a third party that is in the business of distributing software, under which you make payment to the third party based on the extent of your activity of conveying the work, and under which the third party grants, to any of the parties who would receive the covered work from you, a discriminatory patent license (a) in connection with copies of the covered work conveyed by you (or copies made from those copies), or (b) primarily for and in connection with specific products or compilations that contain the covered work, unless you entered into that arrangement, or that patent license was granted, prior to 28 March 2007.

Nothing in this License shall be construed as excluding or limiting any implied license or other defenses to infringement that may otherwise be available to you under applicable patent law.

12. No Surrender of Others' Freedom.

    If conditions are imposed on you (whether by court order, agreement or otherwise) that contradict the conditions of this License, they do not excuse you from the conditions of this License. If you cannot convey a covered work so as to satisfy simultaneously your obligations under this License and any other pertinent obligations, then as a consequence you may not convey it at all. For example, if you agree to terms that obligate you to collect a royalty for further conveying from those to whom you convey the Program, the only way you could satisfy both those terms and this License would be to refrain entirely from conveying the Program.

13. Use with the GNU Affero General Public License.

    Notwithstanding any other provision of this License, you have permission to link or combine any covered work with a work licensed under version 3 of the GNU Affero General Public License into a single combined work, and to convey the resulting work. The terms of this License will continue to apply to the part which is the covered work, but the special requirements of the GNU Affero General Public License, section 13, concerning interaction through a network will apply to the combination as such.

14. Revised Versions of this License.

The Free Software Foundation may publish revised and/or new versions of the GNU General Public License from time to time. Such new versions will be similar in spirit to the present version, but may differ in detail to address new problems or concerns.

Each version is given a distinguishing version number. If the Program specifies that a certain numbered version of the GNU General Public License "or any later version" applies to it, you have the option of following the terms and conditions either of that numbered version or of any later version published by the Free Software Foundation. If the Program does not specify a version number of the GNU General Public License, you may choose any version ever published by the Free Software Foundation.

If the Program specifies that a proxy can decide which future versions of the GNU General Public License can be used, that proxy's public statement of acceptance of a version permanently authorizes you to choose that version for the Program.

Later license versions may give you additional or different permissions. However, no additional obligations are imposed on any author or copyright holder as a result of your choosing to follow a later version.

15. Disclaimer of Warranty.

    THERE IS NO WARRANTY FOR THE PROGRAM, TO THE EXTENT PERMITTED BY APPLICABLE LAW. EXCEPT WHEN OTHERWISE STATED IN WRITING THE COPYRIGHT HOLDERS AND/OR OTHER PARTIES PROVIDE THE PROGRAM "AS IS" WITHOUT WARRANTY OF ANY KIND, EITHER EXPRESSED OR IMPLIED, INCLUDING, BUT NOT LIMITED TO, THE IMPLIED WARRANTIES OF MERCHANTABILITY AND FITNESS FOR A PARTICULAR PURPOSE. THE ENTIRE RISK AS TO THE QUALITY AND PERFORMANCE OF THE PROGRAM IS WITH YOU. SHOULD THE PROGRAM PROVE DEFECTIVE, YOU ASSUME THE COST OF ALL NECESSARY SERVICING, REPAIR OR CORRECTION.

16. Limitation of Liability.

    IN NO EVENT UNLESS REQUIRED BY APPLICABLE LAW OR AGREED TO IN WRITING WILL ANY COPYRIGHT HOLDER, OR ANY OTHER PARTY WHO MODIFIES AND/OR CONVEYS THE PROGRAM AS PERMITTED ABOVE, BE LIABLE TO YOU FOR DAMAGES, INCLUDING ANY GENERAL, SPECIAL, INCIDENTAL OR CONSEQUENTIAL DAMAGES ARISING OUT OF THE USE OR INABILITY TO USE THE PROGRAM (INCLUDING BUT NOT LIMITED TO LOSS OF DATA OR DATA BEING RENDERED INACCURATE OR LOSSES SUSTAINED BY YOU OR THIRD PARTIES OR A FAILURE OF THE PROGRAM TO OPERATE WITH ANY OTHER PROGRAMS), EVEN IF SUCH HOLDER OR OTHER PARTY HAS BEEN ADVISED OF THE POSSIBILITY OF SUCH DAMAGES.

17. Interpretation of Sections 15 and 16.

    If the disclaimer of warranty and limitation of liability provided above cannot be given local legal effect according to their terms, reviewing courts shall apply local law that most closely approximates an absolute waiver of all civil liability in connection with the Program, unless a warranty or assumption of liability accompanies a copy of the Program in return for a fee.

END OF TERMS AND CONDITIONS

How to Apply These Terms to Your New Programs

If you develop a new program, and you want it to be of the greatest possible use to the public, the best way to achieve this is to make it free software which everyone can redistribute and change under these terms.

To do so, attach the following notices to the program. It is safest to attach them to the start of each source file to most effectively state the exclusion of warranty; and each file should have at least the "copyright" line and a pointer to where the full notice is found.

```
one line to give the program's name and a brief idea of what it does.
Copyright (C) year name of author

This program is free software: you can redistribute it and/or modify
it under the terms of the GNU General Public License as published by
the Free Software Foundation, either version 3 of the License, or (at
your option) any later version.

This program is distributed in the hope that it will be useful, but
WITHOUT ANY WARRANTY; without even the implied warranty of
MERCHANTABILITY or FITNESS FOR A PARTICULAR PURPOSE.  See the GNU
General Public License for more details.

You should have received a copy of the GNU General Public License
along with this program.  If not, see http://www.gnu.org/licenses/.
```

Also add information on how to contact you by electronic and paper mail.

If the program does terminal interaction, make it output a short notice like this when it starts in an interactive mode:

```
program Copyright (C) year name of author
This program comes with ABSOLUTELY NO WARRANTY; for details type 'show w'.
This is free software, and you are welcome to redistribute it
under certain conditions; type 'show c' for details.
```

The hypothetical commands 'show w' and 'show c' should show the appropriate parts of the General Public License. Of course, your program's commands might be different; for a GUI interface, you would use an "about box".

You should also get your employer (if you work as a programmer) or school, if any, to sign a "copyright disclaimer" for the program, if necessary. For more information on this, and how to apply and follow the GNU GPL, see http://www.gnu.org/licenses/.

The GNU General Public License does not permit incorporating your program into proprietary programs. If your program is a subroutine library, you may consider it more useful to permit linking proprietary applications with the library. If this is what you want to do, use the GNU Lesser General Public License instead of this License. But first, please read http://www.gnu.org/philosophy/why-not-lgpl.html.

www.ingramcontent.com/pod-product-compliance
Lightning Source LLC
LaVergne TN
LVHW060133070326
832902LV00018B/2782